THE CULT PLACES OF THE AEGEAN

THE CULT PLACES
OF THE AEGEAN

Bogdan Rutkowski

YALE UNIVERSITY PRESS
NEW HAVEN AND LONDON
1986

Designed by Mary Carruthers.
Typeset in VIP Bembo by
Clavier Phototypesetting Ltd, Southend-on-Sea, Essex.
Printed and bound in Great Britain at The Bath Press, Avon.

Library of Congress Cataloging in Publication Data

Rutkowski, Bogdan.
    The Cult places in the Aegean.

    Rev. ed. of: The Cult places in the Aegean world. 1972.
    Bibliography: p.
    Includes index.
    1. Shrines — Aegean Sea Region. 2. Aegean Sea Region — Religion. 3. Aegean Sea Region — Antiquities.
4. Excavations (Archaeology) — Aegean Sea Region.
I. Rutkowski, Bogdan. The Cult places in the Aegean world.
II. Title.
BL785.R88   1985   292.35   85-40469
ISBN 0-300-02962-4

Preface

THIS BOOK represents the fruit of over twenty years' study of the cult places and various aspects of early Aegean religion. Although it covers the same field as my *Cult Places in the Aegean World* (1972), which is long out of print, this volume is much enlarged and revised, due to my detailed studies of many sites and objects in the museums. First of all I should mention the elaboration of the plans of many peak sanctuaries, which were excavated by my friends Professor S. Alexiou and Dr. C. Davaras, detailed studies of many important shrines, e.g. the temples at Gournia and Karphi, some of the caves, and sacred enclosures. Important results of excavations at peak sanctuaries and sacred caves are being prepared in the form of a final publication, e.g. the British School Excavations at Petsophas and the finds from the caves at Amnissos, Avdou and Patsos. Of course, all the studies are too detailed to be discussed extensively in this book but I have made general use of the material available. My studies in the field and in the museums will soon appear as separate monographs.

B.R.

Acknowledgements

I am particularly indebted to many friends and colleagues for permission to use the material derived from unpublished sites. First of all my heartfelt thanks are due to Professor S. Alexiou and Dr. C. Davaras for allowing me the study of the topography of many peak sanctuaries, primarily Philiorimos at Gonies, Pyrgos at Tylissos, Vigla, Prinias, Karphi, Vrysinas, among others. I am also obliged to Professor N. Platon for his kind permission to make a topographical study of Kophinas. Dr. Y. Tsedakis kindly allowed me to study the site of Drapanon, and others in West Crete. To the ephors of Antiquities in Crete I owe the opportunity of studies in the field to Dr. C. Davaras, Professor Y. Sakellarakis and Dr. Y. Tsedakis. Professor C. Doumas discussed with me the unpublished frescoes from Thera and Professor N. Lambrinoudakis the new finds at the sanctuary of Apollon Maleatas in Epidauros. Professor N. Platon kindly allowed me to study the finds from Piskokephalo, Russes and Sphakia, and Professor V. Lambrinoudakis the finds from the sanctuary of Apollon Maleatas. I wish to thank the directors and curators of many museums for allowing me to study the material used in this book: Professor S. Alexiou, Dr. M. Bourboudakis, Mrs. A. Karetsou, Dr. A. Lembesi, Professor Y. Sakellarakis (Archaeological Museum, Iraklion), Dr. C. Davaras (Museum, Ayios Nikolaos), Dr. Y. Tsedakis (Museums, Chania and Rethymnon), Professor C. Doumas, Dr. P. Calligas, and Professor Y. Sakellarakis (National Museum, Athens), Dr. J. Bailey (Department of Greek and Roman Antiquities, British Museum, London), Mrs. A. Brown and Dr. M. Vickers (Ashmolean Museum, Oxford), Dr. R. Nicholls (Fitzwilliam Museum, Cambridge) and others.

I am very obliged to the following colleagues for sending me photographs: A. Karetsou, K. Kilian, C. Renfrew, W. Taylour and Y. Tsedakis. Nearly all the other photographs were made by the present writer. Most of the drawings have been re-drawn by Mrs. G. Nowakowska, but a few of them were supplied by Mr. K. Nowicki. For the translation of my book and for useful suggestions I am indebted to Mrs. C. Douglas Kozlowska and for the index to Piotr Taracha. My sincere thanks are due also to Mr. J. Nicoll and Ms. Mary Carruthers for useful suggestions and for seeing the book through the press.

Contents

Abbreviations

1. Periodicals and series

AA	*Archäologischer Anzeiger*, Berlin.
AAA	*Archeologika Analekta eks Athinon*, Athens.
AD	*Archeologikon Deltion*, Athens.
AE	*Archeologiki Ephemeris*, Athens.
AM	*Mitteilungen des Deutschen Archäologischen Instituts. Athenische Abteilung*, Berlin.
Ann	*Annuario della Scuola Archeologica di Atene*, Bergamo.
AnzAlt	*Anzeiger für die Altertumswissenschaft*, Vienna.
AR	*Archaeological Reports*, London.
ArchHom	*Archaeologia Homerica*, ed. by F. Matz and H. G. Buchholz, vols. I-III, Göttingen, 1967. ff.
ARW	*Archiv für die Religionswissenschaft*, Berlin.
AS	*Anatolian Studies*, London.
BA	*Bolletino d'Arte*, Rome.
BABesch	*Bulletin van de Vereeniging tot Bevordering der Kennis van de Antieke Beschaving te'S Grovenhagen*.
BCH	*Bulletin de Correspondance Hellénique*, Paris.
BICS	*Bulletin of the Institute of Classical Studies*, London.
BMFAB	*Bulletin, Museum of Fine Arts*, Boston.
BMMA	*Bulletin, The Metropolitan Museum of Art*, New York.
BSA	*Annual of the British School at Athens*, London.
BullBudé	*Bulletin de l'Association de Guillaume Budé*, Paris.
BullLund	*Kungl. humanistiska vetenskapsamfundet i Lund. Arsberättelse*, Lund.
CMS	*Corpus des Minoischen und Mykenischen Siegel*, ed. by F. Matz and I. Pini, vol. I ff, Berlin, 1964 ff.
DESE	*Deltion Elleniki Spileologiki Eterias*, Athens.
EEEPA	*Epeteris Epistimonikon Erevnon. Panepistemiou Athinon*, Athens.
EEKS	*Epeteris Eterias Kritikon Spoudon*, Athens.
EEPhSPA	*Epistimoniki Epeteris Philosophikis Scholis tou Panepistemiou Athinon*, Athens.
Ergon	*To Ergon tis Archeologikis Eterias kata to . . .*, Athens.
Etcret	*Études crétoises*, Paris.
FA	*Fasti Archaeologici*, Florence.
GRBS	*Greek, Roman, and Byzantine Studies*, San Antonio.
ILN	*Illustrated London News*, London.
JdI	*Jahrbuch des Deutschen Archäologischen Instituts*, Berlin.
JHS	*The Journal of Hellenic Studies*, London.
JOAI	*Jahreshefte des Österreichischen Archäologischen Instituts in Wien*, Vienna.
KCh	*Kritika Chronika*, Iraklion.
MA	*Monumenti Antichi pubblicati per Cura della Accademia Nazionale dei Lincei*, Milan.
MI	*Museo Italiano di Antichità Classica*, Naples.

OpArch	*Opuscula Archaeologica*, Lund.
OpAth	*Opuscula Atheniensia*, Lund.
PAE	*Praktika tis en Athinas Archailogikis Eterias*, Athens.
PP	*La Parola del Passato*, Naples.
PPS	*Proceedings of the Prehistoric Society*, Cambridge.
PZ	*Prähistorische Zeitschrift*, Berlin.
RA	*Revue Archéologique*, Paris.
RE	*Paulys Realencyclopädie der classischen Altertumswissenschaft*, Stuttgart.
REA	*Revue des Études Anciennes*, Bordeaux.
REG	*Revue des Études Grecques*, Paris.
RendLinc	*Atti della Accademia Nazionale dei Lincei. Rendiconti*, Rome.
RHR	*Revue de l'Histoire des Religions*, Paris.
SMEA	*Studi Micenei ed Egeo-Anatolici*, Rome.

2. Books and articles

Alin, MFund	P. Alin, *Das Ende des mykenischen Fundstätten* (Lund, 1962).
AttiCongMic	*Atti e Memorie del I Congresso Internazionale di Micenologia, Rome 1967, testi definitivi* (Rome, 1968).
Banti, CulM	L. Banti, 'I Culti Minoici e Greci di Haghia Triada', Ann, 3/4 (1941/3), 10-74.
Asine	O. Frödin, A. Persson, *Asine* (Stockholm 1938).
Biesantz, KSG	H. Biesantz, *Kretisch-mykenische Siegelbilder* (Marburg, 1954).
Boardman, CC	J. Boardman, *The Cretan Collection in Oxford* (Oxford, 1961).
Brandt, GG	E. Brandt, *Gruss und Gebet. Eine Studie zu Gebärden in der minoisch-mykenischen und frühgriechischen Kunst* (Wiesbaden, 1965).
BSA Suppl I	Supplementary Papers to BSA, I (London, 1923).
Buchholz, Herk	H.-G. Buchholz, *Zur Herkunft der kretischen Doppelaxt* (Munich, 1959).
Cook	A. B. Cook, *Zeus. A Study in Ancient Religion*, I (1914), II (1925), III (1940) Cambridge.
CPl	B. Rutkowski, *Cult Places in the Aegean World* (Warsaw, 1972).
Desborough, LM	V.R d'A. Desborough, *The Last Mycenaeans and their Successors* (Oxford, 1964).
Dussaud, CivPr	R. Dussaud, *Les Civilisations préhelléniques dans le basin de la mer Égée* (Paris, 1914).
Europa	*Europa. Studien zur Geschichte und Epigraphik der frühen Aegaeis. Festschrift für Ernst Grumach* (Berlin, 1967).
Evans, PofM	A. Evans, *The Palace of Minos at Knossos*, I-IV (London, 1921-35).
Evans, PrT	A. Evans, 'The Prehistoric Tombs of Knossos', *Archaeologia*, 59 (1904), 391-562.
Evans, ScM	A. Evans, *Scripta Minoa*, I (London, 1909).
Evans, TDA	A. Evans, 'The Tomb of the Double Axes and Associated Groups and the Pillar Room and Ritual Vessels of the "Little Palace" at Knossos', *Archaeologia*, 65 (1914), 1-94.
Evans, TPC	A. Evans, 'The Mycenaean Tree and Pillar Cult', JHS, 21 (1901), 91ff.
Faure, Cav	P. Faure, 'Cavernes et sites aus deux extremités de la Crète', BCH, 86 (1962), 36-52.
Faure, CPC	P. Faure, 'Cultes populaires dans la Crète antique', BCH, 96 (1972), 389ff.
Faure, CulS	P. Faure, 'Cultes de sommets et cultes de cavernes en Crète', BCH, 87 (1963), 493ff.
Faure, GRCr	P. Faure, 'Grottes crétoises', BCH, 80 (1956), 95ff.
Faure, Fonct	P. Faure, *Fonctions des cavernes crétoises* (Paris, 1964).

Faure, Lab   P. Faure, 'A le recherche du vrai labyrinthe de Crète', KCh, 17 (1963), 315ff.

Faure, NR   P. Faure, 'Nouvelles recherches de spéleologie et de topographie crétoises', BCH, 84 (1960), 189ff.

Faure, NRT   P. Faure, 'Nouvelles recherches sur les trois sortes de sanctuaires crétois', BCH, 91 (1967), 114ff.

Faure, SPT   P. Faure, 'Spéleologie et topographie crétoises', BCH, 82 (1958), 495ff.

Faure, STSS   P. Faure, 'Sur trois sortes de sanctuaires crétois', BCH, 93 (1969), 174ff.

Festòs   L. Pernier, *Il Palazzo Minoico di Festòs*, I (Rome, 1935); L. Pernier and L. Banti, *Il Palazzo Minoico di Festòs*, II (Rome, 1950).

FGK   B. Rutkowski, 'Frühgriechische Kultdarstellungen', AM, Beihefte No. 8 (Berlin, 1981).

Furtwängler, AG   A. Furtwängler, *Antike Gemmen* (Leipzig-Berlin, 1900).

Furumark, MP   A. Furumark, *The Mycenaean Pottery. Analysis and Classification* (Stockholm, 1941).

Gansiniec, AegRel   R. Gansiniec, 'Religia egejska' ('Aegean Religion') in *Zarys Dziejów Religii* (*An Outline of the History of Religion*) (Warsaw, 1964), 380ff.

Gesell   G. C. Gesell, 'The Archaeological Evidence for the Minoan House Cult and its Survival in Iron Age Crete' (diss.) (Ann Arbor, 1972).

Glotz, CivEg   G. Glotz, *La civilisation égéenne* (Paris, 1952).

Gournia   H. Boyd Hawes, B. E. Williams, R. B. Seager and E. H. Hall, *Gournia, Vasiliki and other Prehistoric Sites on the Isthmus of Hierapetra, Crete* (Philadelphia, 1908).

Graham, Palaces   J. W. Graham, *The Palaces of Crete* (Princeton, 1962).

Hägg, MKult   R. Hägg, 'Mykenische Kultstätten im archäologischen Material', OpAth, 8 (1968), 39ff.

Hall, Sphoung   E. H. Hall, 'Excavations in Eastern Crete', Sphoungaras, University of Pennsylvania, *The Museum. Anthropological Publications*, III.2 (Philadelphia, 1912).

Hazzidakis Tyl   J. Hazzidakis, 'Les villas minoennes de Tylissos', Etcret, 3 (Paris, 1934).

Hiller   S. Hiller, *Das minoische Kreta nach den Ausgrabungen des letzten Jahrzehnts* (Vienna, 1977).

Hood, Arts   S. Hood, *The Arts in Prehistoric Greece* (Harmondsworth, 1978).

Hood, TS   S. Hood, 'Minoan Town-Shrines' in *Greece and the Eastern Mediterranean in Ancient History and Prehistory*, Studies Presented to Fritz Schachermeyr (Berlin-New York, 1977), 158ff.

Hope Simpson, Gaz   R. Hope Simpson, *A Gazetteer of Mycenaean Sites* (London, 1965).

Hope Simp-Dick   R. Hope Simpson and O. T. P. K. Dickinson, *A Gazetteer of Aegean Civilisation in the Bronze Age*, I: 'The Mainland and Islands' (Göteborg, 1979).

IC   *Inscriptiones Creticae*, by M. Guarducci, Rome.

Kenna, CrS   V. Kenna, *Cretan Seals* (London, 1960).

Levi, Studies   'Antichità Cretesi', Studi in onore di Doro Levi, I (Catania, 1978).

Levi, Fest I   D. Levi, *Festòs e la civiltà minoica* (Rome, 1976).

Marinatos-Hirmer, Kr   S. Marinatos, M. Hirmer, *Kreta und das mykenische Hellas* (Munich, 1959).

Marinatos-Hirmer, KrT   S. Marinatos, M. Hirmer, *Kreta, Thera und das mykenische Hellas* (Munich, 1973).

Matz, FS   F. Matz, *Die frühkretische Siegel* (Berlin-Leipzig, 1928).

Matz, Gött   F. Matz, *Göttererscheinung und Kultbild im minoischen Kreta* (Mainz, 1958).

Minoica   Minoica. Festschrift F. J. Sundwall, ed. by E. Grumach (Berlin, 1958).

Mirie   S. Mirié, 'Das Thronraumareal des Palastes von Knossos' in *Saarbrücker Beiträge zur Altertumskunde*, 26 (Bonn, 1979).

Mylonas, CCent	G. Mylonas, 'To thryskeutikon Kendron ton Mikinon' ('The Cult Centre of Mycenae'), *Pragmateiai tis Akademias Athinon*, 33, 1972.
Mylonas, MycMA	G. Mylonas, *Mycenae and the Mycenaean Age* (Princeton, 1966).
Mylonas, MycRel	G. Mylonas, 'Mykinaiki threskeia. Naoi, vomoi, kai temene' ('Mycenaean Religion. Temples, altars and temenae'), *Pragmateiai tis Akademias Athinon*, 39, 1977.
Nilsson, MMR	M. P. Nilsson, *The Minoan-Mycenean Religion and its Survival in the Greek Religion* (Lund, 1927).
Nilsson, MMR²	M. P. Nilsson, ibid., 2nd ed. (Lund, 1950).
Pashley	R. Pashley, Travels in Crete (London and Cambridge, 1837).
Pendlebury, AC	J. Pendlebury, *The Archaeology of Crete* (London, 1939).
Pepragmena	*Pepragmena tou B Diethnous Kritologikou Synedriou* (Athens, 1968).
Persson, RelGr	A. Persson, *The Religion of Greece in Prehistoric Times* (Berkeley, 1942).
Picard, RelPreh	C. Picard, *Les religions préhelléniques* (Paris, 1948).
Platon, IK	N. Platon, 'To Ieron Maza(Kalou Choriou Pediados) kai ta minoika Iera koriphis', KCh, 5 (1951), 96ff.
Platon, MOI	N. Platon, 'Ta minoika oikiaka iera', KCr, 8 (1954), 428ff.
Robinson, Stud	Studies Presented to D. M. Robinson (St. Louis, 1950).
Rodenwaldt, Fr	G. Rodenwaldt, *Der Fries des Megarons von Mykenai* (Halle, 1921).
SanctSymp	'Sanctuaries and Cults in the Aegean Bronze Age', International Seminar at the Swedish Institute of Athens, 12-13 May 1980 (Athens, 1981).
Seager, Ps	R. Seager, 'Excavations on the Island of Pseira', *Anthropological Publications of the University of Pennsylvania*, 3, part 1 (Philadelphia, 1901).
Seager, Moch	R. Seager, *Explorations in the Island of Mochlos* (Boston-New York, 1912).
Spratt	T. B. A. Spratt, Travels and Researches in Crete (London, 1865).
Tiryns	Tiryns, *Die Ergebnisse der Ausgrabungen des Instituts*, I (1912).
Tyree	E. Tyree, 'Cretan Sacred Caves: Archaeological Evidence' (diss.) (Ann Arbor, 1974).
Valmin, SME	N. Valmin, *Swedish Messenia Expedition* (Lund, 1938).
ValSymp	Valcamonica Symposium 72, 'Actes du Symposium International sur les religions de la préhistoire' (Capo di Ponte, 1975).
Ventris-Chadwick	M. Ventris, J. Chadwick, *Documents in Mycenaean Greek* (Cambridge, 1956).
Vermeule, GBA	E. Vermeule, *Greece in the Bronze Age* (Chicago and London, 1964).
Vermeule, Götterkult	E. Townsend Vermeule, 'Götterkult', ArchHom III, Chapter V (Göttingen, 1974).
Xanthoudides, VTM	S. Xanthoudides, *The Vaulted Tombs of Mesarà* (London, 1924).
Yavis, Alt	C. Yavis, *Greek Altars* (St. Louis, 1949).
Zervos, Crète	Chr. Zervos, *L'art de la Crète néolithique et minoenne* (Paris, 1956).

3. Museums

AM	Ashmolean Museum, Oxford.
BM	British Museum, London.
HM	Archaeological Museum, Herakleion.
NM	National Museum, Athens.

Introduction

PLACES of worship constitute one of the most important elements in every civilisation, whether ancient or modern. Whereas the function of such places is fairly easy to describe in more modern times, the distant past presents a difficult problem to the student of religion who has nothing, or practically nothing, to go on but the archaeological remains. Therefore investigation of the cult places is a matter of vital urgency and importance if we wish to achieve a break-through in studies of Bronze Age Greece. The last hundred years have seen not only exciting archaeological discoveries, but also bold attempts to collect the knowledge obtained from them. G. Karo[1] and M. P. Nilsson[2] were pioneers in this field. Anyone studying the sanctuaries and the objects found in them[3] finds himself confronted with the problem of how the discoveries should be treated. Should all the material, including finds from the Minoan and Mycenaean civilisations alike, be treated as a whole, as was still done by Nilsson?[4] Or should Crete and the Greek mainland be taken separately?[5] This is not an easy question to answer. On the one hand are the disparities as regards external forms — e.g. differences of pottery styles, or types of burial in the Middle Bronze Age, etc. — which rule out the possibility of direct comparisons or of treating certain problems jointly for the two civilisations. Even in the particular field which interests us — the cult places — there are also certain categories, such as the lustral basins, which as far as we know are all but one confined to Crete. Yet on the other hand the question of the temples has become one of general Aegean relevance. Still more complicated is the question of the religious iconography of these two civilisations, within the limits studied in this book. Some problems — the temple façades seen in the iconography, for instance[6] — simply cannot be treated in separate areas, but must be viewed within the context of the Aegean as a whole. Yet even so the choice of source should always be subordinated to the end purpose of the research. In endeavouring to reconstruct the Mycenaean sanctuaries, for instance, one should above all study source material belonging to the Mycenaean culture area, even if Minoan sources seem to be of equal worth. In this connection we should recall the different opinions as to the origin of the gold rings found on the Greek mainland. For it is not at all certain whether they were made there, or perhaps in Crete. Yet, as far as the subject of this book is concerned, surely the question of whether they were made in Crete, or on the Greek mainland under strong Cretan influence, is of little practical significance. For the decorative elements on the gold rings were so simple and so standardised (e.g. the façade of a building, a column, etc.), that both their literal and their symbolic meaning were immediately clear to everyone. What is more, there is a distinct similarity between some of the buildings depicted on rings, and Mycenaean buildings that have survived. One may take as an illustration of this a gold ring from Dendra. Unique among other scenes, it shows a building with a portico, which may be compared with an LH II temple with a portico at Eleusis. Further, it can be claimed that the façades of the sanctuaries were, generally speaking, like those of the citadels or of imposing tombs. Hence the use of the façade and the column as symbols which could, among other things, denote a sacred building, was not confined to Crete alone.

Still another question dealt with in this book is the range of source material which the archaeologist should try to collect. The author's views[7] on this matter were first expressed in 1972. His approach may be described as that of a historian who draws on all the available sources of information that can help him to study a problem and reach conclusions on it. It is wrong to think that the archaeologist is restricted to the evidence provided by the archaeological remains in the field, or to finds in museums. He can also, with profit, extend the range of his explorations to all sorts of spheres that may have a bearing on his chosen subject.

He can, for instance, get help from speleology. A particular debt of gratitude is due to P. Faure and E. Platakis, and to members of the Greek Speleological Society,[8] for developing this line of approach to archaeology. Geology, zoology and botany likewise have a big contribution to make to our subject and should be consulted, although unfortunately this postulate, despite its urgency, is not at present easy to fulfil. In the present state of research little is to be expected from the written texts dating from the Aegean period. They cannot as yet be exploited to the full, but can only serve as auxiliary material.

The main problem, however, is not just greater range and variety of types of source material, or improved interpretation. Another difficulty, of equal importance, is that many doubts can be expressed about the way in which the archaeological finds have been published, and about the conclusions arrived at from studies of them. Ideally, the finds should be discussed without bias and as scrupulously as possible. Proper use of the finds is hampered still further by the fact that nineteenth-century archaeology, encumbered by tradition, permitted much speculation that has been passed down to the archaeology of our own day as residue. Now is the time to re-examine the criteria on the basis of which certain places have been accepted as sanctuaries. Following this line of thought, and coming to the question of determining whether a given building was sacred or not, it should be noted that the Aegean world produced no sacred structures whose functions could, from their ground plan, clearly be described as sacred. This remark holds good, too, of the underground rooms with pillars or crypts.

Some authors seem to suggest that the empty chambers in Bronze Age houses, that is, those in which no objects were found, could have been either sanctuaries or crypts. In inclining to this interpretation, they were influenced by their use of analogies with later times.[9] But those sanctuaries dating from historical times, in which no objects were discovered, represented a specific architectural form. Their ground-plan was quite distinct. In the case of the Bronze Age sanctuaries, the adoption of a criterion such as the possession of a certain type of ground-plan is not possible. Hence reliance on a negative criterion — that is, here, the argument that lack of objects in a room proves it was a sanctuary — is very risky, for in the place of scientific argument it introduces the subjective intuition of the archaeologist. Thus we come to the conclusion that neither the building's ground-plan, nor the entire absence of finds, nor even the discovery in it of sacred objects, can be taken as decisive proof that the room in question was a sanctuary. All in all, the only reliable criterion for interpreting a room or part of a building, or a place as a sanctuary is the presence of sacred objects, that is objects used solely for cult purposes or of objects many of which were equivalent to those found in places which quite definitely have been recognised as sanctuaries. Of course no criteria are comprehensive enough to cover all the cases which the archaeologist encounters. Hence in some special cases particular caution is called for. Nevertheless for the basic group of material evidence, that is, the buildings containing finds, analysis of these finds is the only safe criterion for interpreting the given building or room as a sanctuary. It may be remarked here that we cannot approve of the tendency to regard every object whose ordinary, everyday purpose is not clear, as an object with a sacred function. For it may be that in highly developed civilisations the unusual form of some objects may have stemmed from a variety of needs — not only religious but perhaps aesthetic as well. Two scholars have put this point succinctly. As far back as 1925 R. Gansiniec,[10] after a visit to Knossos, wrote that the archaeologists seemed to have a mania for interpreting every find in terms of religion and symbolism — as if an object were of value only if it was a cult object. In 1950 the Biblical scholar C. C. McCown[11] declared that scholars studying the Hebrew cult relics should refrain from *a priori* assumptions, and base their conclusions solely on actual discoveries. He argued that if archaeology and history were to succeed in being to some extent scientific, they must be empirical. These authors succeeded in pinpointing the main difficulty of research in the domain of religion. This does not mean that we should desist from bold attempts to interpret the finds, but we do need to re-examine the function of every building that so far has been accepted as a place of worship, and in particular we should decide which finds actually indicate that an area, building or room was used for religious purposes.

Of course this book is not confined to discussion of the material evidence. The author's chief aim is to arrive at a synthesis, to indicate elements that are common to all sanctuaries throughout their history. The search for a synthesis is not an easy one. Many obstacles stand in the way, one of them being the often insuperable hurdle of interpreting the archaeological and

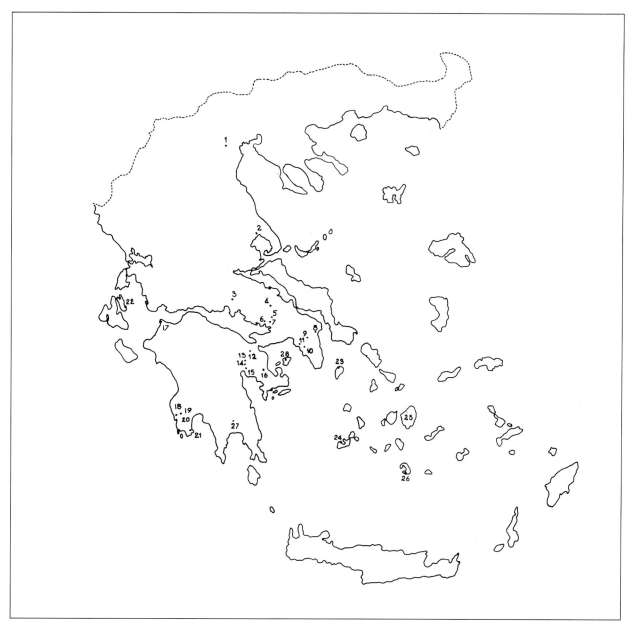

Map 1. Greek Mainland and the Islands (except Crete).

1. Nea Nikomedea
2. Volos
3. Delphi
4. Gla
5. Thebes
6. Litanes
7. Eutresis

8. Ninoi
9. Lichnospilia
10. Athens
11. Eleusis
12. A. Triada
13. Mycenae
14. Berbati

15. Tiryns
16. Epidaurus
17. Araxos
18. Pylos
19. Routsi Myrsinochori
20. Mouriatada
21. Asine

22. Ithaca
23. A. Irini
24. Phylakopi
25. Aplamata
26. Akrotiri
27. Vaphio
28. Aegina

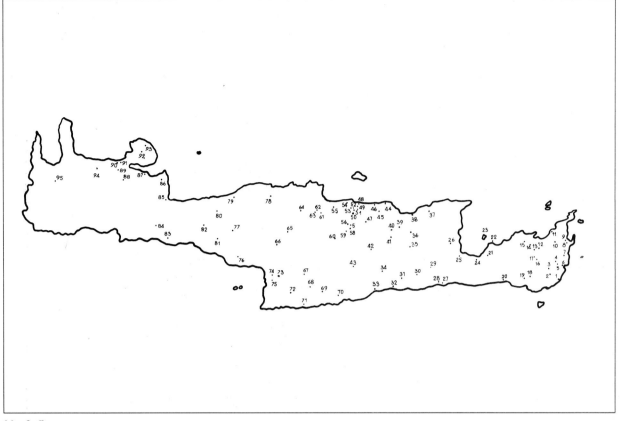

Map 2. Crete.

1. Ambelos
2. Plagia
3. Xykephalo
4. Vigla
5. Epano Zakro
6. Kato Zakro
7. Traostalos
8. Petsophas
9. Palaikastro
10. Modvi
11. Kalamaki
12. Prinias
13. Sphakia
14. Piskokephalo
15. Skopi
16. Vaveli
17. Skales
18. Etiami Kephala
19. Pervolakia
20. Makrygialos
21. Pachlitsani Agriada
22. Mochlos
23. Pseira
24. Gournia

25. Kalo Chorio
26. Thylakas
27. Myrtos Fournou
28. Myrtos Pirgos
29. Klisidi
30. Kato Symi
31. Arkokephalo
32. Vigla n. Keratokambos
33. Tsoutsouros
34. Skinias
35. Psychro
36. Karphi
37. Milatos
38. Mallia
39. A. Phaneromeni
40. Aski
41. Aphendis Christos
42. Arkalochori
43. Ligortino
44. Metochi
45. Skotino
46. Nirou Chani
47. Kephala n. Episkopi
48. Amnissos

49. Cave of Eileithyia
50. Knossos
51. Prasa
52. Mavro Spilio
53. Isopata
54. Katsaba
55. Keramoutsi
56. Anemospilia
57. Archanes Fourni
58. Jouktas
59. Staromyti
60. Vitsiles
61. Tylissos
62. Trapeza Tylissou
63. Pyrgos
64. Gonies
65. Idaean Cave
66. Kamares
67. Kania
68. Apesokari
69. Koumasa
70. Kophinas
71. Lebene
72. Kouroupas

73. Phaistos
74. A. Triada
75. Kamilari
76. Sachtouria
77. Patsos
78. Melidoni
79. Pankalochori
80. Vrisinas
81. Kostili n. Miksorouma
82. Ankouseliana
83. Agiasmatsi
84. Skordolakia
85. Korakies Trypa
86. Drapanon
87. Kalami
88. Skourochlada
89. Mameloukou Trypa
90. Kato Sarakina
91. Chania
92. Koumaro
93. Cave of Leras
94. Kera Spiliotissa
95. A. Sophia

iconographic material. Another is the frequent paucity of available, well documented sources. So it is not always possible for the author to fulfil all his intentions. He is sometimes, as in this book, compelled, when discussing very important finds, to accompany them with an interpretation that seems likely, although not altogether certain.

But although the author's desire to reach a synthesis is an important aim of this book, is not the only one. Another aim is an attempt to give an account of the history of the sanctuaries, and link it to the history of the society they served.[12] This is perhaps the most knotty of the problems which the author has attempted to address, for historical interpretation is one of the most neglected fields in the study of the civilisations of the Aegean world. Other obstacles encountered in such research arise for different reasons. Namely, as has been remarked above, the archaeologist who adopts the historical approach must not only draw on the traditionally humanistic disciplines, such as archaeology and the study of religion, but also on non-humanistic disciplines such as speleology, geology, or biology.

The terminology used in connection with the sanctuaries is not always uniform. Even the most common term, such as 'cult place' (used interchangably with 'sanctuary') is not at all easy to define. The term 'cult place', to put the matter in the most general terms, involves three aspects: places, rituals, and belief. As for the first of these aspects, it will be noted that there must be a clear boundary cutting off the secular area from the sacred,[13] with its furnishings, such as altars, cult idols, a temple, paraphernalia, votive offerings, etc. The second aspect expresses the active side of religion — the actions which take place in the cult place, such as the activities of the priests, the processions, the dances, mysteries, and making of sacrifices. Finally we come to the third aspect — religious belief, which made people come to the sanctuary because a divinity, or a being with superhuman powers appeared to these faithful people to live there.

'Cult place' is an umbrella term which covers diverse categories of places where worship took place. The various types of cult place can be divided into two groups: 1. Those outside the built-up areas; that is, caves, peak sanctuaries, sacred enclosures, spring sanctuaries and others, and 2. those inside the settlements; that is, temples, domestic and palace sanctuaries, altars, lustral basins, spring sanctuaries and temenae in the towns squares and in courtyards. This is, of course, a very schematic classification. It does not exhaust the whole range of cult places. But we should like to draw attention to the existence of certain basic features of them. In the natural cult places everything untouched and unformed by man — the sacred area itself, the rocks, the roof of the grotto, etc. — constituted this basic feature. Of course the elements contributed by man — for instance, the walls and the structures erected by him — could also sometimes be of great significance. In the cult places that were situated inside the settlements, on the other hand, the main feature of the cult place was the presence of a construction erected by man, although this construction was always linked with an open space, a town square, or a courtyard. In addition, it should be borne in mind that some of the cult places in the settlements (e.g. sacred places in front of altars out in the open air) were of a natural character which they retained throughout the whole of their existence. This was no doubt an aftermath from distant times, when the basic type of cult place was a natural and unaltered.

Let us look again at some of the individual terms used here. The term 'Peak sanctuary'[14] — sometimes used interchangably with 'temenos' — has a specific meaning. It denotes cult places situated on mountain tops, and sometimes surrounded by walls. There was always an altar, and occasionally a sacred building, in the peak sanctuaries. Another category of cult place consists of sacred enclosures, which are really a sub-type of the mountain temenae. The sacred enclosures differ from the peak sanctuaries in their location and in the kind of ceremonies practised there (although indeed a similarity of cult can occasionally be observed between the peak sanctuaries and the sacred enclosures). Sacred enclosures can be identified both in the iconography and in the archaeological remains. The word 'sanctuary' is also used in this book in the narrower sense of meaning a building, used for a wide range of cult purposes, and situated in a mountain temenos or in a sacred enclosure, or a room forming part of a dwelling-house. Public buildings open to the whole population of a given village or town are referred to here as 'temples'.[15]

I
History of research

IN ORDER to understand the point that has now been reached in research on cult places in the Aegean world it will repay us to review what has been done in the past.[1] If we look back at the early days of interest in this subject we find that the hypotheses propounded then have remained valid for a long number of years, but have often been enriched through the application of new methods and the discovery of new finds. In essence, then, there has been a working-out of problems formulated earlier. Interest has been shown in the Aegean world for a very long time, and certain changes have inevitably taken place, which provide us with grounds for dividing the the history of research into six periods. During the first period, that is, during Greco-Roman times, we can discern a budding of interest in cult places connected with the 'Heroic' Age. The next period, which lasted from the fifteenth to the eighteenth century, was characterised by attempts to rationalise the myths and legends that had come down from ancient times, and to locate their setting in a definite place and time. The third period, which took up nearly the whole of the nineteenth century, was spent in perfecting the techniques of field surveys, and, following the discovery of Mycenaean civilisation, in determining, mistakenly, as it happened, the principal elements of Mycenaean religion. The fourth period, lasting for the first quarter of the twentieth century, began with an attempt, in 1901, to elucidate the main characteristics of religion. During the twenty-five years that followed, a great deal of valuable archaeological material was excavated. The following period, again lasting for a quarter of a century, was devoted to attempts to arrive at a synthesis, based on the archaeological finds, that would embrace all the various elements of religion within a single whole. Finally, the typical features of the sixth period, starting in 1950 were an increased study of existing finds, and the use of new material, such as data from the natural and biological sciences (e.g. speleology), or the Linear B inscriptions, in the interpretation of religion.

The scientific investigation of cult places in the Aegean world began towards the end of the nineteenth century, together with the emergence of a new field of studies: 'Mycenaean civilisation'. But the first burgeoning of interest in the pre-Greek cult places can be traced much farther back, indeed to ancient times. This interest stemmed from a variety of reasons but especially from the fact that the people of classical Greece felt an affinity with the people who had lived in the period preceding the Dorian invasion. In fact one might go so far as to say that the inhabitants of ancient Hellas were even more firmly convinced than present-day scholars of the uninterrupted continuation between the 'Heroic' Age and later times.[2] A number of examples can be cited, but we shall quote only one of them here. During the time of Kimon the accidental discovery of the Carian tomb provided the Athenians with an excellent opportunity for recalling their illustrious past. The common people were convinced that the human remains taken from the tomb at Delos were those of the Athenian hero, Theseus,[3] and bore them to Athens in triumph. Here, then, we have an illustration of the interest shown in the 'Heroic' times by the people of a later date.

Some of the ancient sanctuaries on the mountain peaks and in the caves were places of worship both in pre-Greek and in later times. According to Greek legends, the grottoes were very often the birth-place of the gods and such versions are encountered in many different parts of Greece. A story repeated over and over again in the old tales has it that Zeus was born in Crete, and lived and died there. The writers of ancient times repeatedly referred to Zeus's grave as being situated at Knossos,[4] or on Mount Ida,[5] or on the top of Mount Dikte.[6] As time went on these places began to be visited not only by local inhabitants but also by pilgrims from far and wide. The supposed site of Zeus's tomb in a grotto on Mount Ida was already a celebrated cult place in Archaic and in Classical times. In their devoutness the pilgrims who visited this grotto believed the sacred objects there dated back to the time of Zeus. They believed that the altar, the god's throne, the great stone marking the site of the tomb, and the inscription referring to the tomb of Zeus, were relics dating from the time when the Thunderer had already departed this world.[7] In the attempts of these people of ancient times to locate this grotto, and to describe it, we can trace the beginnings of the scientific approach. This was not at all surprising in the Hellenic or Roman period, when science was developing and when the breath of euhemerism was forcing a confrontation between myth and reality.[8] Out of the soil of superstition, science put forth its shoots, but one cannot expect scientific scepticism to extend beyond the mental horizons of the period in question.

Judging from the fact that there are forty references to the tomb of Zeus, interest in his grave in Antiquity must have been widespread. But only two authors state specifically that certain travellers they describe visited Zeus's tomb.[9] This tradition of Antiquity persisted in later times as well: in the eleventh century Kedrenos spoke of Zeus's tomb on the mountain peak.[10] Psellos, a Byzantine scholar,[11] also wrote that in Crete he had been shown the mountain where Zeus was buried but had not located the spot with any greater precision. As a matter of fact it seems more likely that Psellos did not climb the peak himself at all but merely contented himself with repeating the tale handed down from Antiquity.[12]

The humanists of the Renaissance believed in the reality of the ancient myths and legends; they frequently quoted and even classified the ancient sources.[13] It is significant that the criticism of the Renaissance and the Enlightenment avoided certain domains of classical philology; their views on the pre-Greek cult places still bore the stamp of the writers of Greek and Roman times. But if the scholars of the Renaissance contributed nothing that was new to our interpretation of the texts where the cult places are mentioned, we still owe them a debt of gratitude in another field — for logically following up the message of the ancient texts and for trying to identify the tomb of Zeus with a definite grotto. For it was these fifteenth-century quests, such as that by Buondelmonti, which were the signpost to the discovery of the Minoan peak sanctuaries in our own day. These early quests started off with a classical text, and endeavoured to identify a passage in the text with a real, existing place. Naturally it would be too much to expect no errors to have been made. The Buondelmonti referred to above wrote in 1415 that Zeus was buried on a mountain which other travellers, too, called Monte Giove,[14] and which we call Jouktas. He said the tomb of Zeus was situated near a small Greek monastery. He seems to have thought Zeus's tomb was on the southern, higher peak of Mount Jouktas.[15] Not until the nineteenth century was it suggested that it was on the northern, lower peak, that is, on the spot where a Minoan sanctuary was identified towards the end of the nineteenth century. Buondelmonti's views were accepted by many scholars and travellers, and in Venetian times it was considered practically compulsory for travellers and pilgrims, eg. Radziwill[16] in 1584, visited Mount Jouktas on their way to the Holy Land, and Savary,[17] and others.[18] During the Renaissance it became fashionable to try to locate places mentioned in the myths. For instance, attempts were made to find the true site of the labyrinth from which Theseus escaped. It was generally believed to have been situated in the vicinity of Gortyn,[19] in the caves not far from Ampelouzos. Right up to the nineteenth century many travellers believed this version. But as early as the sixteenth century certain travellers, such as Belon and Radziwill,[20] had suggested the labyrinth was simply a quarry, and in the nineteenth century this view was fully confirmed.[21] This is another example of the active interest shown in this kind of subject by people of the Renaissance.[22]

The classical tradition was a powerful stimulus to studies that later led to the discovery of Mycenaean civilisation. When archaeology was in its infancy, the endeavour to identify localities mentioned in the classical texts with ancient ruins and sites was of prime importance, as we can see, for instance, from the interest shown in the Cretan labyrinth, or in the work of Schliemann.

During the Renaissance the analysis of classical texts in which the cult places were mentioned was not very remarkable when one considers the trends perceptible in other spheres at that time. As has been remarked above, the scholars of the Renaissance aimed at rationalising the myths, and adopted the ideas of euhemerism in this search for the origin of the gods. A typical example of this new approach to the study of the classical texts can be found in the comments made on the well-known passage in the Odyssey where Minos meets his divine father. From the sixteenth century onwards the humanists, such as Bartolomeo Zamberto da li Sonetti (in a work written in 1485 and published in 1532), Servet (1535) and others, thought Minos had been confirmed in his powers as the ruler of Crete in a grotto. This version no doubt reflected an idea formulated in Antiquity.[23]

Among the many reasons that hampered progress in this branch of knowledge at the beginning of modern times from the fifteenth century onwards, the negligible advance of archaeological studies was the most prominent. This, in turn, was due to political reasons.[24] Although several travellers — such as Pashley and Spratt in the nineteenth century — made journeys to the cradle of Greek civilisation during which they made astounding discoveries, these were exceptions. Particularly between the seventeenth and the nineteenth centuries archaeological research was at a standstill for the simple reason that political events made field research impossible.

A point worth recalling is that it was mainly the scholars of the nineteenth century who were specially interested in pre-Greek times. There was a continuation of philological interest in the 'Heroic' period, supplemented by topographic studies by travellers. To these travellers we owe a great debt. In a book published in 1837, for instance, Pashley[25] was the first person to give the correct location of the sanctuary on Jouktas. He also gave a precise description of the massive walls encircling the peak and mentioned the ruins of a building. He even attention to the many fragments of pottery found in the temenos area. These discoveries, then, bring us to the threshold of modern archaeology. Rarely was the confrontation of the literary texts with the topography so fruitful as in the case of the search for the cult places. In the nineteenth century, scholars were mainly concerned with analysis of the classical texts. But even here some of the comments made were interesting, and left their mark on the trend taken by future research. It was suggested, for example, by Baumlein[26] and Lenorment[27] that the cult places on the mountain peaks were of pre-Greek or 'Pelasgian' origin. Another suggestion that was pregnant with meaning for later research was the assertion that the cult of Demeter dated back to pre-Greek times[28] — later on this was the focal point of interest in the excavations at Eleusis. The nineteenth century also saw the emergence of an interest in the cult of the baetyl (starting from the study of the Lion Gate),[29] whereas the significance of the double axe (labrys) had been a matter of interest to scholars from the Renaissance onwards.[30] But the greatest step forward was made when the first excavations began. On the Greek mainland, the advance was more rapid than elsewhere owing to the explorations by Schliemann, from 1879 onwards. It was at this time that the term 'Mycenaean civilisation' was first heard, and it was at this time that we have the first awakening, however weak, of archaeological interest in Crete. In the nineteenth century, too, the 'Kamares' period first began to be studied.

Attempts have been made in the above passages to demonstrate the links between the various periods of scholarly research. For instance, the study of the literary texts, and attempts to interpret them anew, marked the way to explorations in the field. Material evidence was then needed to settle the question of the site of Zeus's tomb, and so an interest developed in the grottoes, especially those in the Mount Ida or Dikte area. In fact, the origin of archaeological studies on the Mount Ida cave provide us with the best-known example of the influence that classical philology exerted on archaeology.[31] The excavations which were started in 1886 brought an exceptionally rich harvest of Greek objects, but produced few finds from the Minoan period; the cave was only partially explored. This year also marked the discovery of Hermes' grotto at Patsos,[32] and of the first finds at Psychro,[33] during an attempt to find the site of the Dikteian grotto. Hogarth, however, in 1900, carried out larger excavations. In this case, another cult cave was discovered through following up a literary tradition. In the Odyssey XIX, 188, we find a reference to the cave of Eileithyia, which lay on the stormy bay of Amnissos. This intrigued scholars even in the first half of the nineteenth century.[34] Pashley made a vain attempt to discover the cave of Eileithyia in 1833, but later on, in 1886, Hazzidakis found a cave which was believed to have been the cave of Eileithyia.[35] He made an important statement, that the sherds found here covered all the periods — even the earliest. In 1894 Taramelli explored the Kamares grotto.[36] Although these were modest beginnings, up till 1900 research on the peak sanctuaries and sacred enclosures was even more meagre. The quest into this sphere, as has been remarked above, also began with studies of the literary texts. The endeavours to locate the tomb of Zeus led not only to the discovery of the Minoan cult grottoes, but also to the discovery of the Minoan sanctuaries on the mountain peaks. But up to

1900 these discoveries were only in their first, embryonic stages. In 1899 Taramelli gave a detailed description of the walls and the site occupied by the peak sanctuary on Jouktas. Evans opened a new chapter in this field, being the first to carry out archaeological investigations of the peak sanctuaries. In 1894 he surveyed one of the peaks near Epano Zakro,[37] and two years later others at the Stous Athropolitous site, which also is not far from Epano Zakro.[38] About this time (1894 and 1896) the first discoveries were made at Piskokephalo,[39] but no excavations were carried out then. Until 1900 all information came from surface investigations. At this time, too, nothing was known of the Minoan domestic sanctuaries, while the idea of sacred crypts was first mooted by Evans when he tried to prove, following the discoveries at Knossos and Phylakopi in 1899 and 1900,[40] that in the Mycenaean civilisation there was a cult of pillars and columns.

This was also the time when scholars were propounding many new concepts, and trying to synthesise the total body of knowledge. The many Mycenaean seals provided food for thought, for it was at once obvious that many of the scenes were connected with religion. The attempts to explain them were not always very fortunate. In 1897 Reichel[41] published a book in which he put forward the idea that the cult of the empty thrones, the places of the epiphany of the gods, was the most important feature of Mycenaean worship. He arrived at this mistaken idea through the erroneous interpretation of Mycenaean iconographic art — e.g. a gold ring from Mycenae. Apart from an unsound theoretical base, Reichel also placed too much reliance on analogies with Greek times.[42] Furtwängler[43] wrote of Reichel's book as follows: 'what is correct in this book was known long ago, while what is new is miscomprehension of the scenes, and exaggeration'.

As far as study of the cult place is concerned, then, the results of the nineteenth century were as follows: field observations, belief in the pre-Greek origin of the mountain sanctuaries, reflections on the cult of baetyls and columns, and a continued interest in the problem of the labrys. Many detailed observations were made, and many new ideas promulgated which, like those in Reichel's book, were universally discredited later. Yet it is true to say that the last quarter of the nineteenth century produced archaeological sources which were of such great value that they opened up prospects for new, more reliable interpretations.

When one considers the speculative theories being advanced at that time by many scholars, one can appreciate more readily the importance of the role played by Evans. Towards the end of the nineteenth century Evans, by this time already a hardened traveller and mature scholar with a wealth of philological and ethnological knowledge behind him, began his explorations in Crete. His excavation at Knossos in 1900 had been preceded by numerous travels around the island. Subsequently the early part of the twentieth century was taken up with systematic excavations by the Italians at Phaistos, the Americans at Gournia, and the British at Zakro and Palaikastro. At that time many objects dating from antiquity found their way into the hands of traders and thence into private collections. Evans himself was able to buy a considerable collection of Minoan and Mycenaean glyptic art. Although work on the newly discovered 'Mycenaean' civilisation was still more or less in its infancy, Evans realised how far Reichel's ideas were from the truth. In this of course he was not the only critic, being joined by others such as Furtwängler and von Fritze.[44] In 1901 Evans published his famous pamphlet[45] in which, influenced by the comparative ethnology school, he propounded the view that the principal feature of Mycenaean religion was the cult of trees and boughs, as well as columns and baetyls. Evans based his arguments not only on his studies of Aegean art (mainly glyptic), but also on evidence beyond the Aegean world. For instance, he drew comparisons with Mohammendan folk customs and rituals — in Macedonia and other Turkish provinces — and with Asia Minor. Initially, Evans's ideas were met, for the most part, with scorn and derision,[46] and even later they were not always accepted. Nevertheless, after some amendments were introduced, Evans's ideas were generally accepted, and have found a lasting place in the literature. The year 1901 thus marks the birth of a new trend in research on the religions of the peoples living in the Aegean.

In the early period of research on the cult places it was thought that the principal sanctuaries were situated out in the country, away from the towns and villages. This idea stemmed from the work of the ethnologists, particularly from their assertion that there has been a widespread cult of trees and boughs in diverse regions throughout the world. It also stemmed from the belief as to the preponderance of natural cult places over other ones. These views arose because of the flimsiness of our knowledge of the cult places in the Aegean world — for instance, at the beginning of the twentieth century practically no domestic sanctuaries were known at all. This view as to the rural situation of the cult places was first propounded by Karo in 1904.[47] To begin with it met with wide acceptance, but later on, in the 1930s, it was completely rejected, for instance by Karo[48] and Nilsson,[49] as being quite out-of-date.

Many of Evans's theories, and those of other scholars as well, still had their roots in the traditions of the nineteenth century. The best example of this, which has already been quoted above, is the work that was done on the tomb of Zeus. Although right from ancient times up to the end of the nineteenth century scholars were fascinated by the story of Zeus, it was not until near the end of last century that Taramelli[50] described in detail the site (cf. above) and asserted that there had been a Mycenaean sanctuary on the peak. Evans's excavations in 1909 carried the investigations further. They brought to light votive offerings, cult objects, and the remains of walls that were thought as a holy building dating from Minoan times. It was not yet possible to say definitely what role the peak sanctuaries played, since too few sites of this kind had been discovered. Nevertheless, Evans asserted that the peak sanctuaries represented one of the chief types of Minoan cult place. This is an assertion which has been fully documented by recent studies. In this case, too, we are struck by the fact that Evans's idea stemmed from the traditions of nineteenth-century research. It is interesting to note that his hypothesis was ahead of the available archaeological evidence, which even in 1921 was insufficient to provide grounds for such an assumption.[51] The majority of scholars who wrote about the cult places, e.g. Dussaud[52] and others, did not pay any attention to the peak sanctuaries at all.

Another less important detail bears out what has been said about the continuous growth of knowledge of the cult places on mountain peaks. Evans said he thought that Mount Jouktas had been a place of refuge to which the local population took recourse in times of danger. In this idea he was preceded by Pashley (1837) and Taramelli (1899). The first of these wrote as follows.[53] 'On the eastern side of the mountain and about a hundred paces from its summit, I found considerable remains of ancient walls . . . Above this wall, I observed, scattered over the ground many pieces of ancient pottery, which, as well as the wall, would rather serve to indicate an abode of the living than a resting-place of the dead' (that is, the tomb of Zeus). Taramelli[54] writes quite clearly that in his view Jouktas was used as a place of refuge. Interest in the myth that Zeus was born in Crete also led to archaeological explorations in the caves. Whereas in the nineteenth century the caves were explored because it was hoped that a connection could be found between them and the ancient texts, in the twentieth century there was a gradual shift of focus, and the caves began to be regarded with interest chiefly because they were thought to be one of the principal kinds of Minoan cult places.

Of course our aim here has not just been to show that many scholars, including Evans and others, drew upon the knowledge of preceding generations, nor have we tried to minimise the great importance of the archaeologists of the twentieth century. Our sole aim is to oppose the division that is often made between the age in which our knowledge of the past was based mainly on philological concepts, and the age of archaeological excavation, since the two are inseparably connected. The gist of our remarks has been to prove that despite the great changes that took place in archaeology in the last quarter of the nineteenth century — including the discovery of Mycenaean civilisation — the views of the philologists and travellers still remained the basis of many conceptions which were developed only in the twentieth century, in the light of the new finds, and — what is more important — in the light of other categories of finds. To begin with, even in the twentieth century there was a close dependence on philological methods of work. What we have drawn attention to, then, is that the very subject matter of research gradually altered and developed slowly, and that there was a gradual but steady enrichment of ideas. The excavations that were carried out in the twentieth century did not sever this new discipline — Minoan-Mycenaean archaeology — from the research of the previous period.

The excavations that were carried out between 1901 and 1925 were of importance to research on the cult places. It is true that there were not many new discoveries that shed light on the cult places, but the small scale trial excavations at previously known sites were of real importance. In 1901 Evans made diggings in the cave at Skotino,[55] and then in 1912 Hazzidakis carried out similar investigations in one at Arkalochori,[56] although it had previously been looted by the local population. In 1912 the British School of Archaeology at Athens conducted excavations at Kamares, which were crowned with considerable success.[57] All these enterprises were of importance to the history of the cult places in Crete although neither the way in which the excavations were carried out, nor the publications that ensued were usually up to the standard of those times. Apart from preliminary reports, the excavations were never published in detail.

During the same quarter century, there was a vast increase in our knowledge about the peak sanctuaries. Only the excavations carried out by Myres at Petsophas, which were immediately followed by an extensive report, provide the foundations of our knowledge about this type of cult place, and have remained so till the present day.[58] Conversely the excavations carried out by Xanthoudides in 1906 were reported very briefly,[59] his death prevented the full publication of the finds. Digging on Mount Jouktas in 1909, Evans revealed some interesting objects which with a few exceptions, were never published; it was not until 1921 that the plan of the sanctuary was published.[60] Explorations were also made at other sites which were later termed peak sanctuaries.

At the beginning of this century it became almost certain that we could not expect to find in the Aegean world temples similar to the later Greek monuments or to those of Egypt or Asia Minor in the Bronze Age. But the excavations have given us a wealth of information about the various types of domestic sanctuaries. The diggings in 1901-5 revealed palace sanctuaries (at Knossos and at Phaistos)[61] and also domestic sanctuaries in various parts of the island (such as at Chamaizi, Palaikastro, and Gournia).[62] The finds at Knossos, especially those in the Sacred Repository, had an important effect on many concepts.[63] But although these discoveries were of great importance the reports of the excavations were not exhaustive and, in any case, were not very careful. It looks as if little importance was attached to the final publication of archaeological finds in those days, and even the field techniques were far from being satisfactory.

Altogether 29 different rooms were classified as sacred crypts. This was the term used by Evans, who identified 18 of them. These came to light mainly in the period up to 1909, during the excavation at Knossos, Gournia, A. Triada, Kato Zakro, and Palaikastro.[64]

The next great period of research, from 1926 to 1950, was chiefly characterised by the comprehensive approach to the Minoan and Mycenaean civilisations.[65] This approach was also used with regard to the sphere of religion.[66] Some scholars brought up questions which hitherto had been ignored altogether — especially the function of religion in society. The studies of this type on the Aegean world were characteristic of a later period.[67] It should not be forgotten either that the Pettazzoni school contributed much to this field, although their approach was not followed by the scholars who worked on pre-Greek religions.[68]

At the end of the nineteenth century, the new discoveries in the Aegean tempted scholars to hazard a general outline of the whole civilisation. Several works dealing with the Aegean civilisation as a whole already appeared towards the end of the nineteenth century, and many more appeared between 1901 and 1925. The great turning-point in this field, however, was brought about by Nilsson, whose book on Aegean religion appeared in 1927. The contribution made to archaeology by Nilsson has already been acknowledged above. But it should be stressed that besides describing Aegean religion, he also discussed the traces of it that survived to later times. However, although he studied all the fundamental elements of the cult, Nilsson paid comparatively little attention to the cult places (to which he devoted only two chapters) although he describes the work done on the function of the crypts and makes some pungent remarks on the sacred enclosures in other chapters where he discusses the sacred pillars and trees as well as the horns of consecration.[69]

In later times books giving a synopsis of the work that had been done on Aegean religion were by no means rare. A concise account of the subject was proffered by Pendlebury[70] in a handbook on the archaeology of Crete published in 1939. Then in 1942 Persson[71] published a study of religion. In 1948 this was followed by a succinct exposé by Picard,[72] which is especially notable for its extensive bibliography. The year 1950 saw a second edition of Nilsson's book referred to above.

But not all the publications were handbooks or reviews of past research. Many articles appeared which, although in some cases gave only marginal attention to the cult places, nevertheless set out the guide-lines for research in the future. For example, both Marinatos[73] in 1928 and Platon[74] made remarks on the religious significance of the stalagmites and stalactites in the Cretan caves, which were followed up by other scholars only thirty or forty years later. To quote another example, the new archaeological exploration at Eleusis[75] gave rise to the idea that there must have been temples in the Mycenaean civilisation.

But the matter did not end there. For other explorations brought equally important discoveries. On the Greek mainland the first clear instance of a Mycenaean sanctuary — at Asine — was discovered.[76] There were fruitful results of archaeological studies in Crete. Important caves were studied,[77] as well as peak sanctuaries,[78] but only preliminary reports or notes were made public. At that period a considerable amount of evidence about the domestic and palace sanctuaries was published.[79] On the other hand only modest additions were made to the information on sacred crypts.[80]

Preceded by the publication of a number of books in 1948-50, a new period really began in 1951. The features which characterised it are as follows: a considerable increase in the number of sites and finds, the undertaking of a large-scale surface-survey, the application of new research methods in the study of pre-Greek religion, and endeavours to use the Linear B script to throw more light on the Aegean civilisation.

It is only relatively recently that archaeologists have become fully aware of the difficulties involved in studying the sanctuaries. In our opinion, these difficulties stem from the fact that little serious work has been done regarding examinations of the sources. In a previous book (1972), we pointed out that the most urgent step towards real progress in the study of the sanctuaries would be to prepare the final publication of excavations already stored in the museums.[81] Work has already started on this task.[82] And finally, a realisation of the magnitude of the work waiting to be done on the sanctuaries must be combined with a constant improvement of theoretical approach. The elaboration of methodological problems is still in its infancy.[83]

In Nilsson's work there was already an attempt to clear out the dead wood from our information about Minoan and Mycenaean religion, and to get rid of the speculations which only cluttered up the literature. As the body of knowledge or nearly all spheres of the Aegean civilisation increased, careful, methodical study and review of the sources became the general custom. In Evans's time, it will be recalled, publication of the finds was so haphazard that diverse interpretations were possible. There was no proper archaeological documentation, for instance, for many finds. To be properly scientific, archeological work must include a meticulous analysis of the finds. A study by Banti[84] was a pioneer work on the domestic sanctuaries. Other works of this kind followed, the most important, perhaps, being studies by Platon. One of these, in which he discussed the peak sanctuaries (1951),[85] marked a turning-point in this field. Platon collected data about eleven sites which he regarded as peak sanctuaries, whereas Nilsson (1950) had described only four sites. Platon's research[86] on the crypts, published in 1954, was also a landmark. It contained a catalogue of all the then-known rooms regarded as sacred crypts, and gave a concise, systematic review of all the more important elements of the cult that took place in the crypts. Platon's review of the more important finds in the crypts led him to conclude that they were cult places. An important point to note is that he attached the least amount of weight to the religious function of the pillars; most weight was attached to the other objects found in the crypts. The work of other authors deserves mention, too: Yavis, for instance (1949), thought the religious scenes on several gems, where trees were depicted surrounded by a wall, were really meant to represent rural roadside shrines.[87]

Recently there has been a growth of interest in the sanctuaries. Dissertations have been written on archaeological finds which throw light on the grottoes in Crete, the domestic sanctuaries in mainland Greece and in Crete, and on interpretation of the Throne Room complex at Knossos.[88] There have also been some studies of the problem of the iconography of the sanctuaries.[89]

Archaeological discoveries of great significance were also made after 1951. Prominent among these were the great advances made in our knowledge of the Cretan caves, owing to the questionnaires sent out by the Greek Speleological Society, and to the explorations of caves by several scholars, Faure in particular. Apart from verifying past findings, Faure also discovered new grottoes of great consequence to the history of the cult places. As well as writing many articles reporting on his work, in 1964 Faure also published a book on the sacred caves,[90] analysing the rich collection of facts he had accumulated. One of the most fascinating aspects of his work was his attempt to use speleology to find out what purpose the caves were used for. Very important excavations on the grottoes were carried out by Greek archaeologists too, especially S. Marinatos, C. Davaras, and Y. Tsedakis.[91] Thanks to these investigations and excavations, many gaps were filled in as regards the material concerning Crete, especially the west part of the island. Faure's work was largely responsible for the new wave of systematic field work, especially in the mountain areas. After 1951 a large number of new sites were added to the peak sanctuaries that were already known.[92]

While Faure's work was of particular importance in that it increased the number of investigated sites, the excavations carried out by C. Davaras — e.g. at Petsophas, Traostalos, Modi, Vrysinas, etc. — and by A. Karetsou at Jouktas, were systematised studies of the peak sanctuaries.[93] The excavations by A. Lembesi at Kato Symi,[94] also produced very important results.

During the last few years there have been digs at many sanctuaries and temples in the Aegean. Among the most important (with the exception of that mentioned above) are the excavations by C. Poursat at Mallia, D. Levi at Kannia, N. Platon at Rousses, J. Caskey on Keos, Lord W. Taylour and G. Mylonas at Mycenae, K. Kilian at Tiryns, C. Renfrew at Philakopi, P. Warren at Knossos and Y. Sakellarakis at Archanes, among a number of others. They have inaugurated a new era in the history of research on the temples and sanctuaries in the Bronze Age.[95]

II
Sources

IN THE present chapter we shall deal only with those finds that throw light directly on the sanctuaries. First of all, a few words must be said about the classification of the evidence. The writers on the subject, with four exceptions, have been content to follow the traditional usage (based on practice) of dividing the discoveries into domestic and palace sanctuaries, peak sanctuaries, sacred crypts, and caves. Occasionally relics of a different type are mentioned, such as lustral basins, spring sanctuaries, and sanctuaries with a sacred tree, that is, sacred enclosures. Even in Nilsson's book on Aegean religion, where the aim was to put before the reader a general survey of the work that had been done in this field, there was on the whole no attempt at detailed classification. The very first attempts to classify the material concerning the cult places were undertaken by Platon, Faure and the author.[1] The classification we propose, which in essence is a developed form of that propounded in 1972, is given in the Introduction, on p. xix.

Crete. The archaeological evidence

When we discuss the various kinds of cult places, the problems that arise vary between one category and another; for instance, those emerging from a study of the sacred caves are rather different from those concerned with the domestic sanctuaries. For this reason, the remains of these places (the archaeological finds) have been divided into the following groups: caves, peak sanctuaries, sacred enclosures, temples, domestic and palace sanctuaries, lustral basins, house entrance sanctuaries, spring sanctuaries, and sacred areas in the courtyards. They will be discussed in that order.

Caves

From the explorations of the speleologists, especially Platakis and Faure, one can safely conjecture that on Crete alone there are about 2,000 grottoes, caverns, and cavities in the rocks. Recently a list of these was drawn up on the basis of a questionnaire distributed to the local inhabitants and on the information accumulated from individual observations in the field. But the number of caves and rock shelters which had some significance in the history of religion is very much smaller — indeed, only 34 or 36 such places can have been used for religious purposes. In this number we find grottoes which were undoubtedly holy places, as well as grottoes which very probably had a religious function, and also several caves which are occasionally included among the cult places, although it is not altogether certain whether they rank as cult places or not. The grottoes which quite definitely were cult places are no more than 16 in number.[2] Another 20 were most probably cult places (see p. 47).[3]

Until a short time ago our knowledge about the Cretan caves was very unsatisfactory, but this has improved a great deal since the aforesaid inventory was drawn up. Most likely none of the grottoes has been explored thoroughly, with the exception of one at Arklochori.[4] Fifteen caves might be said to belong to the best investigated group of caves,[5] although in some of them the exploration was no more than preliminary, and in others even a surface investigation was very far from complete.

Not only has no cave been explored thoroughly, but, more than that, not one grotto has complete, modern archaeological documentation on it. The published descriptions leave much to be desired, for as a rule the objects found in the caves have been only cursorily studied, and in some cases are no more than mentioned. The finds in the Ashmolean Museum in Oxford are the only ones which have been fully studied and documented.[6]

The majority of cult grottoes are fairly well preserved. At Arkalochori, however, a cave collapsed during explorations; while at Psychro, Hogarth blew up the entrance to the cave with dynamite, being anxious to gain easy access to the upper grotto (see p. 48). Sometimes damaged stalagmites and stalactites are encountered in the caves. Some of them would seem to have been destroyed in recent times. At Skales, for instance, stalagmites were removed in order to effect an entry into the cave.

Although speleology was in a position to supply information about the natural features that could have thrown considerable light on the cult grottoes, the historians of religion were rather late in turning to this source. Back in the nineteenth century, Raulin[7] recorded his observations of the temperature in certain caves, but more than half a century expired before this information was passed on in a published study on the grottoes. Similarly, in 1928 and 1930, observations were made on the role the stalactites played in the cults practised in the grottoes,[8] but it was not until after 1951 that we began to hear about systematic speleological investigations, a detailed description of the caves, or informations regarding the temperature of the interior of the caves, or the temperature and chemical composition of the water that collected in the grottoes.[9]

Architectural finds excavated in the grottoes and their immediate vicinity, which could shed a good deal of light on the kind of constructions that were erected there, are extremely sparse. The structures made in the grottoes must always have been of only minor significance, since the grotto interiors themselves were sufficiently mysterious to provide the right atmosphere. Hence there are few remains of constructions either in front of, or inside, the grottoes, although both kinds are sometimes encountered together (see p. 50). Walls built to encircle a sacred place are exceptionally rare, but are occasionally found (see p. 46).[10] Unfortunately the excavation and documentation of the finds *in situ* were very far from being perfect, since in those days not much attention was paid to relics of that kind.

Obviously the moveable objects — the cult objects and votive offerings, the simulacra and all the relics *in corpore* — provide us with the main clues as to the character and function of the cult places. With the exception of the objects already referred to in the Ashmolean Museum at Oxford, and in some other museums, we have no complete publications of finds.[11] The cult emblems and cult objects such as the gold double axes, sacrificial tables, etc., constitute the chief class of material evidence, although the smallest in number. The votive offerings, which were sometimes also used as cult objects, can be divided into those that were specially made for the cult, such as cult emblems, figurines, etc., and those that were ordinary everyday objects, such as farmers' and craftsmen's tools — hoes, axes, weapons such as daggers, and toilet requisites and ornaments. Pottery objects, especially vessels in which the sacrificial offerings were brought, or vases used for pouring the libations, were frequent discoveries.

It often happens that the information about the exact spot where the discoveries were made is rather vague, and this makes interpretation of the finds difficult. For example, the information supplied by the first explorers who found the votive double axes thrust into the stalactites and stalagmites of the grotto at Psychro has been an invaluable aid to us in understanding what function the grotto was used for. Likewise the objects found in the inner pool in this grotto tell us that in Minoan times lakes, pools, etc. had special significance. But in many other instances (e.g. at Amnissos), the exact place of the finds is not given, and so interpretation is difficult.

The only evidence about the function of the grottoes that can be treated as reliable comes from the cult objects, or sacred emblems, or votive offerings, or, at any rate, from those finds which are attested and which can be trusted to give us a true picture of the use that was made of the grotto. Nevertheless we are left with the question as to whether those grottoes which, according to trustworthy evidence, were used as holy places in MM and LM, were used as cult places in earlier times as well. This is a question which is very difficult to answer, since the finds dated to a period earlier than MM consist almost exclusively of pottery vessels. Of course, some of the natural elements of the grotto, such as its humidity, its temperature, or its accessibility, tell us at once that the grotto — such as the one at Kamares — could not have been used as a permanent dwelling-place. But it is always hard to tell which of the finds indicate that the cave was used as a seasonal dwelling, and which finds suggest it was used as a cult place.

Sometimes the extent to which a cave has been explored is the factor which determines j how much can be said about the use to which it was put in the various periods. In the cas grottoes such as the one at Tsoutsouros, which has been explored only by means of trial- or the one at Tylissos, where there has been only a surface examination, their functi earliest times must remain uncertain. In other grottoes, the basic obstacle is the inadequ the archaeological documentation. The investigation of the upper grotto at Psychro, Hogarth in 1900,[12] was a very professional job for those times. Observations were made oι ι stratigraphy, and a number of layers were distinguished. Unfortunately, however, these excavations were not published, and so the first (deepest) layer must remain an enigma. Its dating and significance cannot be known for certain. The explorers of some grottoes even stated specifically that they had seen no sign of stratification during their excavations; but unfortunately this statement was not made in the form of archaeological documentation. Thus the basic chronology of the grottoes must rest on analysis of the material evidence which, with the exception of some characteristic finds such as certain types of pottery, is not always easy to date (e.g. the bronze figurines).

Peak sanctuaries

Within a short time there was a tremendous increase in the amount of evidence on the peak sanctuaries,[13] but detailed study of this evidence has been confined to recent years. If we reject the doubtful or insufficiently explored places of this kind, we are left with about twenty places which can reliably be regarded as peak sanctuaries.

Field surveys of recent years have provided us with plentiful and valuable observations on the altitude of these places, their position, and the topography of the site.[14] But, as in the case of the sacred grottoes, the exploration and documentation of the peak sanctuaries is still far from satisfactory. There is a group which has been explored more thoroughly than the others, and whose relics have been adequately studied, but it consists of only a few cult places. There are six sites which, because of the extent of the excavations or the amount of material found there, are of key importance to our knowledge of the peak sanctuaries.[15] But the only publications that have appeared about these sites deal with part of the archaeological material from Petsophas and the plans of the sanctuaries on Jouktas (see p. 77) and Petsophas (see p. 80). The excavations at other sites were usually described only in preliminary reports. But now the situation has improved greatly. Excavations are continuing on Mt. Jouktas, aimed at full exploration of the site (see p. 96). On Mount Vrysinas, Petsophas, Modi, too, the sites are being fully explored.[16] Until the publication of these findings, there is very little documentation available on the peak sanctuaries. Many other peak sanctuaries have been inadequately investigated. Recent excavations on Mount Jouktas prove that the conclusions reached from previous excavations (especially excavations that were carried out over a short period) should be treated with great caution. The architectural remains on Mount Jouktas, which Evans defined as a sanctuary, are nowadays described with certainty as being an unroofed terrace — hence an open-air cult place partly protected by a sacred wall (see p. 77). Not all the sites have survived. For instance what seemed to have been an interesting site on the summit of Mount Plagia was destroyed during the building of a road,[17] and it is probable that valuable evidence was lost for ever.

Some aspects of the material have never been studied at all, and indeed never even mentioned. One important subject that has been neglected is the surface area and size of the peak sanctuaries. The size of the cult place can be ascertained if the wall surrounding the temenos has survived (as at Jouktas). In other cases, such as at Pyrgos (see p. 82), we can gain some idea from an examination of the surface at the site. Apart from the walls round the site, other constructions have survived, too. Chief among these are the sanctuary buildings. Another problem now slowly unfolds — the complicated question of what kind of buildings and other structures stood in the peak sanctuaries. Naturally the answer to this question can be derived from a study of the topography of the unexcavated temenae. The explored sanctuaries may have consisted of two or three rooms, as at Philiorimos (Gonies).[18] The situation on Mount Jouktas is even more complex,[19] for not only did the sanctuary contain a terrace and other rooms, but perhaps even a much bigger area was added (see p. 76). An altar, too, generally stood in the sacred area, as we can see on Mount Jouktas (see p. 77) and at Gonies.

A very large number of objects have been found at the peak sanctuaries. But except for

Jouktas (see p. 84), no cult statues have been published. Cult objects or cult paraphernalia *in corpore* or simulacra are frequent finds. Clay votive offerings, which were found in great numbers, have been the most characteristic finds. But our main information about various types of these figurines comes mainly from the work of Myres (1903) and Platon (1951),[20] which supplements our information on the unpublished material exhibited at the museums in Iraklion and Ayios Nikolaos. Other types of votive offerings are also known, e.g. bronze double axes (see p. 79), bronze figurines (see p. 78) and other objects of bronze and gold from Kophinas, Jouktas and Traostalos.

It is on the finds — mainly figurines, but sometimes pottery objects as well — that the chronology of the peak sanctuaries has been based. The pottery has mostly been dated to MM, but to later periods as well; the clay figurines come mostly from MM. But the criteria applied in dating them, especially the very primitive works, are not totally reliable. In certain cases it looks as if the earliest clay figurines were really produced in EM III.[21]

Sacred enclosures

As yet the evidence about this group is meagre. In this group we have included the archaeological remains of sanctuaries found in the country, away from the towns and villages. Altogether more than ten sites of this kind have been placed here.[22] Studying these places enables us to determine details of the topography which are not revealed in the pictorial art. They provide us with evidence, for instance, about the situation of the sacred enclosure, its height, and the distance between it and the nearest settlement. They corroborate evidence culled from the iconographic sources — for instance concerning the way the cult places were walled round.[23] The main body of information gained from this source concerns the lay-out of the sacred buildings, but also, although to a lesser degree, the cult objects and the votive offerings brought to the sacred enclosures. In addition to the principal sites that have given us the bulk of our information (e.g. at Kato Symi, see p. 103) there are some other sites which have not been closely investigated or which are of doubtful significance.[24]

Temples

Despite the author's conviction, expressed as early as 1972,[25] that temples were a universal feature of the towns and settlements, it was difficult at that time to cite more than two certain, and a few uncertain, examples. But later investigations and excavations in Crete and Keos, as well as in mainland Greece, greatly expanded the source material available (see Chapters VIII and IX). We now have evidence that throws light on this question from the period EM II onwards (Myrtos). Temples at Mallia dating from MM II, at Gournia (probably LM IB), Ayia Triada from LM, and at Karphi from late LM, enable us to understand some aspects of the public cult places in the towns and settlements. Elements which in particular are worth studying are: variations of the architectural forms, the cult statues and the sacred paraphernalia. Yet one of the main problems regarding the value of the sources is how to provide adequate reasons for defining a given sanctuary as a temple. For example, in the previous edition of this book (1972) the author expressed doubts about whether a villa at Kannia was a temple.[26]

Domestic and palace sanctuaries

At the present moment we know of more than 50 domestic sanctuaries, including those in palaces. The majority come from a late period, that is, LM, while a fewer number date from early times, that is, from the Neolithic to the end of MM IIIA. Very often the evidence about the domestic sanctuaries is incomplete. The existence of a domestic sanctuary is proved when a room is found with cult objects, or when sacred objects alone are discovered; the latter of these, which may have formed the furnishings of a sanctuary on the first floor and had fallen later to the room below, cannot be associated with any architectural remains. Excavations have revealed not only cult rooms proper (or their remains), but also annexes as well, e.g. the sacred repositories (see p. 127).

The architectural finds, consisting of the remains of walls, tell us about the construction and lay-out of the rooms, but provide very little information about the elevation of the buildings. The moveable objects, on the other hand, that is, the remains of the cult objects and votive

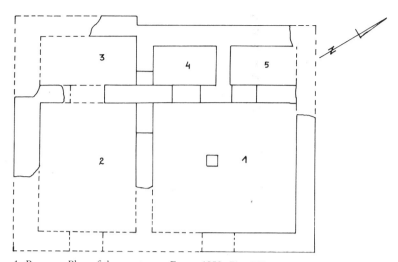

1. Rousses. Plan of the sanctuary. Ergon 1959, Fig. 152

2. Rousses, sanctuary. South-east wall of Rooms 1-2. Probably only part of the wall of Room 1 is original.

offerings, provide us with information about the furnishing of the sanctuaries and about the part they played in the lives of the inhabitants.

At Rousses (Chondrou Viannou) a MM III-LM I building measuring 10 × 8 m was excavated. It consists of two fairly big rooms, and three smaller ones (Fig. 1). The outer walls which are of considerable width (Fig. 2) would seem to indicate the possibility of the existence of an upper storey, maybe only over a part of the building, as in modern Cretan houses. Some of the rooms were found to contain relics that can be interpreted as the remains of offerings or sacred objects, e.g. stone offering tables. Many pithoi were discovered. In Room 1, a fragment of stone horns of consecration was found.[28] In a layer of black ash in the Room 2, fragments of many cups (probably upturned) were discovered. These are thought to have been left from sacrifices.[29] Various interpretations have been given as to the function of this building. It may have been a shrine in a house (a farmhouse, in fact), a sacred enclosure, or a temple.[30] It seems unlikely that it was a temple, because of its setting. It is situated close to a seasonal stream, a little higher than the surrounding area, but far away from the LM I settlement on Mount Tourkissa. From the character of the building[31] and its setting one would be much more likely to judge it to be a sacred enclosure.

We also know of a whole number of finds whose function is uncertain. We do not know whether they were cult finds or not, because either further corroboration is needed, or no final report of the excavations was published. Several cases of this kind were cited in 1972.[32] After further excavations to check the matter, C. Davaras (see p. 142) is convinced that at Chamaizi (MM IA) there was an almost oval house, with a sanctuary in only one of the rooms.

At Knossos, there is a building called the High Priest's House[33] about 500 m south of the palace. Only part of it has been excavated. A portico and a hall have survived, and have been interpreted as a sanctuary. But the objects found here, such as an altar and the stone base of a double axe, which possibly indicate that this building was put to a special use, were not found in situ. One cannot rule out the possibility, then, that this part of the building was not a sanctuary at all, but an imposing entrance (Figs 3 and 4).

We have another example of doubtful interpretation in the case of the long hall XXXVIII in house E at Mallia (Fig. 5).[34] This hall measures approximately 13.00 × 4.50 m. In the western section, which more or less forms a separate room, there was a hearth (dimensions 1.20 × 0.90 × 0.30 m), which was rectangular in shape, with slanting walls made of stone slabs covered with plaster. At the bottom of the hearth were charred wood remains, parts of a bone object, and broken bones. Dessenne, who excavated this house, thought the pit had been used in cult rites. Certainly the things found nearby — a libation table, two pedestalled plates, and vases ornamented with double axes — would seem to confirm his opinion. The possibility of the hall having been used simply for domestic purposes, however, cannot be excluded.

Sanctuaries were also said to have been discovered in a house excavated at Vathypetro.[35] In

1952, when the central, dwelling part of this house was being cleaned, a small room was revealed. During earlier excavations, the foundations of walls were uncovered here, but they did not form a whole room. Later on, during the clearing of the building, extensions of these walls were discovered. This room is rectangular, with a nearly square little room leading off it (see p. 34). This has never been found anywhere else. No objects were found in this room yet Marinatos, comparing it with the buildings on wall frescoes, asserted it was a sanctuary. Unfortunately, apart from this doubtful analogy, there is no other evidence to show the room was a sanctuary.

The House of Sacrificed Oxen at Knossos,[35a] dated to MM IIIB, is small (8.60 × 5.70). It was uncovered and briefly mentioned by Evans, but it has never been fully studied. The house lies close to the street. The basement or the floor level contained five rooms, one of which (Fig. 6, No. 5) has a high ledge (0.15 m), running around the walls. At two opposite corners of the ledge, the sculls of two large oxen had been set. In front of these stood terracotta tripod altars (0.56 and 0.90 m in diameter) (Fig. 7). A number of pottery pieces have been found by Evans on the level of the first story.

The discussion on this house was subordinate to two of Evans's assumptions: that the expiatic offering took place in the house, and therefore that the pottery belonging to the first story level is, in fact, a filling. It is not certain, however, whether the offering took place in this house. The presence of a bull's skull, as well as tripods often called altars, does not prove that Room 5 was of sacred character. Considering these doubts, is not our intention to resolve the questions involving this house. More can be known once the pottery found there has been studied thoroughly.

It is not certain either whether a room dug up at Vitsiles[36] had a function in the cult rites. The objects discovered here were as follows: tiny vases, an object which is thought to have been part of a kernos, a clay figurine 0.08 m high, part of a clay figurine representing some kind of animal, and a small black stone axe. This room was in use in the period MM IIIB.

Another group of finds must still be mentioned, of which no architectural traces have remained. In 1906 Mosso[37] unearthed a small group (No. 17) of Neolithic objects under Magazine 26 at Phaistos. They were lying on virgin rock at a depth of 4.00 m. These finds consisted of fragments of a large number of miniature vessels, a female figurine, a piece of magnetic iron, a number of sea shells, animal bones (ox and pig), awls and bone spoons. Pendlebury[38] thought these were the remains of a sanctuary, but they may equally well have been the remains of a dwelling-house.[39]

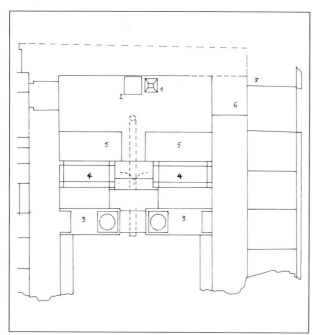

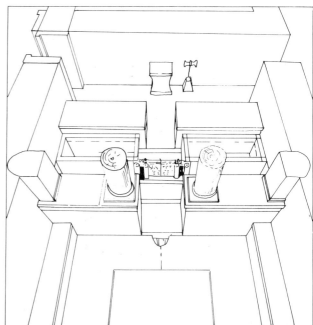

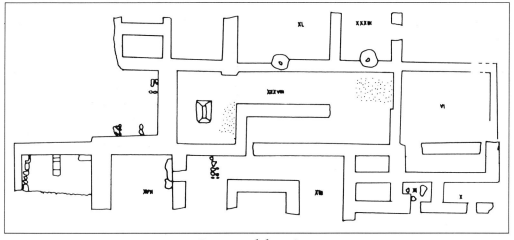

Lustral basins

The lustral basins constitute a group of finds that are characteristic of Crete, although one has also been found on Thera (see p. 137). Despite their similarity to bathrooms, they form a separate class[40] distinguished by their lower floor level (see p. 136). The group of 27 lustral basins now known to us (see Table III) supplies us with material for study dating mostly from the period MM III–LM I. There are very few specimens from MM II and LM II–IIIA. The evidence available at present gives us more information about the architecture of these places, and less about their furnishings. Only in the case of a few lustral basins do we know for certain that they were used as cult places, for sacred objects were found in them.

Sanctuaries at the entrance to houses

This is a new category of sanctuary, distinguished from the others because of certain specific characteristics. Two places, in our opinion, come into this category. One is a sanctuary in Room XVI in the palace at Mallia,[41] while the other is a cult place in an MM II house, also at Mallia (see p. 122). The main — or rather the only — reason for interpreting them as cult places is the presence in them of an altar or kernos (see p. 143).

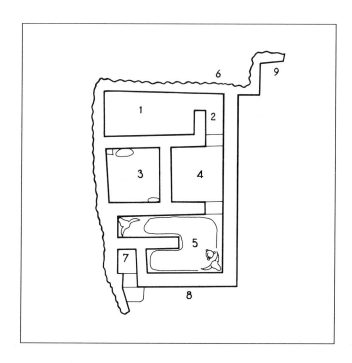

3. *(facing page, far left)* Knossos. House of the High Priest. Plan by Piet de Jong. Evans PofM IV Fig. 159.

4. *(left)* Knossos. House of the High Priest. Restored drawing by Piet de Jong. Evans PofM IV Fig. 157.

5. *above* Mallia. House E. Plan. Etcret 11, plan 7 (fragment).

6. *(left)* Knossos. House of the Sacrificial Oxen. Plan adapted from Evans PofM II Fig. 172.

Spring sanctuaries

The sacred significance of water is quite obvious to the historian of ancient religions, but there is little evidence for it in the archaeological sources dating from the Minoan period. Cult rites connected with water were performed in places such as grottoes and lustral basins where water played an important role. But other types of sanctuaries where water was of fundamental significance, such as rivers, are practically impossible to trace. The most interesting site dating from this period is the Caravanserai, south of the palace at Knossos.[42] The house excavated there was presumably a farmhouse, part of which was used as a dwelling (it included the remains of a bathroom), and part as farm premises. A room known as the 'Footbath' also belonged to the domestic part. Near the main complex of buildings was a room known as the 'Underground Spring Chamber' (see p. 125). Here was a spring, along with a water intake, which was used from LM I up to about 1,000 B.C. In our opinion this basin, like other water intakes may have had a practical function, which is obvious if only from its proximity to the farm premises, but at the same time it had a sacred function as well, which is evident from the votive offerimgs, especially the model of a sanctuary, the handleless bowls with food remains, and the fumigators found there. It is quite possible that the water intake in the palace at Zakro was also a cult place (see p. 122).[43]

Sacred areas in the courtyards

When the palace buildings and some villas were excavated, some relics of altar constructions were found inside. No doubt these were the material traces left from the sacred areas in the settlements and palaces. Several examples have survived (see p. 121). In this group we find constructions which are interpreted as altars because of their position in the courtyard (see p. 127) or because of the cult objects found in the vicinity — as at Nirou Chani. Probably in the courtyard at Gournia there was an altar crowned with horns of consecration.[44] Not all scholars are agreed as to the function of the stepped construction in the palace courtyard at Phaistos, but it was very likely used as an altar.[45] All the aforesaid constructions, which may have been used as altars, prove indirectly that there were holy areas or temenae situated in the courtyards, and that sacred rites were held there.

The theatrical areas must not be forgotten. Of course we have no definite proof that they were used as cult places. But it is possible that the theatre at Knossos and at Phaistos, and also some large courtyards such as that at Gournia (see p. 120), were used not only for secular gatherings, but sometimes for religious ones too.[46]

The iconographic evidence

The iconography froms a very important part of the material remains which tell us about the history of the cult places. Scores of scenes were executed by means of diverse techniques and made from different materials. Hence we have scenes depicted on gold rings (and one of bronze) and on clay impressions. In another group we have pictorial scenes on steatite vessels (and one of ivory) on clay vessels, models of cult buildings and, finally, scenes on the sarcophagus from Ayia Triada. The very length of this list shows that the diversity of techniques and raw materials used in the making of these objects, and the size of the space in which the scenes had to be depicted compelled the artists to use various symbols and simplifications which must have been fully comprehensible to the Minoans but are often not quite clear to us.

The question arises as to why some scenes are regarded as more reliable evidence than others.[47] The following factors had an effect on the precision with which the details were rendered in Aegean art: 1. the main trends followed by art in the given period — whether towards naturalism or towards schematism, 2. the kind of object on which the scene was portrayed. The latter factor was the more important of the two. It is only natural that the secular and religious scenes depicted on the wall paintings or on the rhyta (from MM II to LM I) are richer in detail and more reliable as historical sources (see p. 83), than the scenes on the tiny works of glyptic art, which because of their dimensions, shape, raw material and purpose were more or less compelled to resort to simplification and symbolism (see p. 100). Especially in the case of the glyptic art is it true to say that the artists' desire to depict a cult scene in symbolic form forced them to treat the details perfunctorily, and merely to note them summarily, for they were superfluous to an understanding of the meaning of the scene. Thus to a large extent the value of a work of art depends on which of these categories the work belongs to.

Since the religious scenes, and particularly the architecture, depicted in the iconography have been the subject of recently published wide discussion, information about them will not be repeated here.[48]

We should like only to stress that the iconographic finds generally supply incidental information that is useful in studies of architecture and of the cult places. The façade of a building, especially in the glyptic art, is usually a subordinate feature, for as a rule the main subject of the scene shows the cult rites taking place. Of course there are some exceptions to this rule e.g. on the ring from Mycenae (see p. 204). It is only in the scenes depicted on a rhyton from Zakro (see p. 83) and on frescoes from Knossos (see p. 000) that sacred architecture takes up the centre of the scene. The scenes on the Ayia Triada sarcophagus (see p. 102), and the models of sacred buildings (see p. 103) provide valuable information about the character of the sacred buildings.

Not all the scenes depicted on seals that have been used as sources for studying the sanctuaries are completely reliable for this purpose. In particular, talismanic sealstones bearing forms which look like buildings, which have been interpreted as rural sanctuaries, arouse doubt. It is more probable that the forms referred to here represent cult vessels. This is why they often occur in conjunction with boughs and diverse other shapes which look like snakes or horns of consecration.[49]

The written sources

The decipherment of Linear B proposed by Ventris in 1953 gave a tremendous impetus to studies of the script used by the Aegean peoples. Linear A inscriptions were found on objects from the sacred caves, the peak sanctuaries, and the domestic sanctuaries. Some scholars have tried to decipher the names of gods (e.g. Demeter or Asasara) in the texts.[50] But we are not at all sure as to whether the decipherment of the tablets can make any real contribution to the body of our knowledge until the experts have a clear idea as to the structure of the language in which the Linear A texts were written. It is for this reason that the Linear A texts have not been used in this book as sources that throw light on our subject.

In the Linear B texts we learn that gifts were brought to the Cretan sanctuaries, and were offered to Eileithyia or Zeus. Stella[51] undertook the interpretation of this information. As yet very little of the data obtained from the literary texts can be used with complete confidence to reconstruct the facts of the Minoan period. But the information that can be gleaned from Homer is particularly valuable, since it gives us an idea of the early form of the cult in the Eileithyia grotto at Amnissos.[52] Another useful source is Homer's account of the contacts between Minos and Zeus, for there we learn that the king's power was derived from the god.[53] Other texts tell us about the burial-place of Zeus.[54] Other literary passages mention the names of the gods, too, or cult mysteries.[55]

The Greek mainland and nearby islands. The archaeological evidence

Caves

We have not very much information about caves on the Greek mainland or nearby islands. So far, seven or eight are known at Attica, Peloponesos, Ithaca, and Amorgos. None of the finds referred to here has been published.[56] They have merely been subjected to preliminary analysis. A considerable number of points are still doubtful. Hence in a later section of this book these caves will simply be noted. One can justifiably believe, however, that further excavations in the caves will throw more light on this important subject.

High places

In mainland Greece some of the open-air sanctuaries are situated in high places — near the summits of mountains, or on hills. Although there is little topographical similarity to most of the peak sanctuaries in Crete, it is quite right to place them in the category: 'high places'[57] or peak sanctuaries. The latest excavations at the Apollo Maleatas sanctuary at Epidauros (see p. 202) have revealed traces of a construction interpreted as an altar, as well as objects of a cult nature. Some other places, too, may have been 'high places', although we usually know too little about the architecture and finds there to say so for certain.

Sacred enclosures

The sacred enclosures differ from the high places in their situation — that is, they are found at places that are lower, although it is sometimes hard to say whether a given cult place should be placed in the category of a high place, or in that of a sacred enclosure. Nor does there seem to be any basic difference in the cult furnishings. It may be noted, for instance, that votive double axes have come to light not only in the high places at Epidauros but also in other open-air sanctuaries.[58] Analysis of the sites in this group has not got very far. Research on all the sites is still at a preliminary stage.

Temples

The Mycenaean temples constitute a new problem in the study of Aegean culture.[59] The discoveries on Keos, at Mycenae, at Tiryns, and at Philakopi in Melos (see Chapter ix) not only have enlarged our knowledge about the cult places, but given us a chance to obtain a much deeper understanding of the Late Bronze Age. With the help of the finds we can now study not only the architecture of single temples, but also the character of temple complexes (e.g. at Mycenae) their position in the settlement, the equipment of the temples and other temenos buildings, the connections between the buildings and the open areas. New excavations have brought to light evidence not only on the religious function of the temple complexes, but also on their economic importance.

Domestic sanctuaries

So far only very few domestic sanctuaries have been discovered in mainland Greece. With the exception of Asine,[60] there are no detailed publications of finds. As regards the sources, one of the important problems is to establish which places classed as sanctuaries really did have that function (see Chapter XI, p. 213).

A review of the domestic shrines on the Greek mainland does not produce any considerable results. From all of the presumable sanctuaries only one, that at Asine, is an object which can be classified as definitely belonging to this group. Remainders are questionable; very little indicates their sacral purpose. Of course in Chapter IX we presented a discussion of the Mycenaean sacred areas and temples at Mycenae, Tiryns, on Keos and Philakopi on Melos, at Eleusis, on Delos and at Pylos. It is clear that we possess more information about public cults than we do about those of a private character.

Mycenaean relics in the Greek cult places

In many places where there are traces of Bronze Age settlement,[61] remains of later cult places have also been discovered. It is natural that the ruins of Bronze Age settlements, or other relics of that civilisation, are scattered about in many different places. It is possible that some of the Iron Age cult places were built on the site of the Bronze Age sacred enclosures, although evidence for this is poor.[62]

Hearths and altars

Hearths have been found in many houses. There is nothing about them to show, however, that cult rites were held round them. On the other hand it seems rather likely that the great hearths in the royal megarons, such as Pylos, Mycenae and Tiryns, were not used for secular purposes only. It is probable that sacrifices were occasionally made at the hearths.

The altar constructions that have been preserved in some places — e.g. at Tiryns, Pylos — and Nisakouli[63] proved that there were shrines in some public places, such as the courtyards inside the palace, in the houses near the palace, or in the open-air. It may be that the large open squares, too, such as in the citadel at Arne,[64] were put to uses that were not always secular, although on the other hand no evidence at all has survived that would seem to indicate that public places on the Greek mainland were used in the cult.

Lustral basins and spring sanctuaries

The lustral basins, which are so characteristic of some of the Cretan buildings, are not represented on the Greek mainland and the Cycladic islands, except the one found on Thera (see p. 137). There are remains of bathrooms, however, e.g. at Pylos,[65] which have no traces at all of cult rites having been performed there. Neither do we find any convincing trace, on the Greek mainland, of the shrines which must have been built at the springs, streams, and water intakes.

The iconographic evidence

We have spoken elsewhere[66] about the importance of the iconographic scenes on objects, in particular rings and sealings found on the Greek mainland, and expressed the view that they constitute a fully reliable form of evidence on the Mycenaean sanctuaries. The principal categories of scenes depicting sacred places and sacred architecture — mainly the façades of buildings, and altars — can be seen on rings and sealings, frescoes, gold and glass plaques, and clay vessels (see p. 204).

Written sources

As far as we can judge at present, the Linear B tablets supply us with information about sending offerings to the gods. The information they contain about gifts being sent to Poseidon in a cult place situated neither in a town nor in a palace but somewhere out in the country, is important to us here.[67] For it means that our thesis, based on analysis of the archaeological evidence, that some of the main cult places were situated out in the country, away from the towns and villages, is corroborated by the written sources.

7. Knossos. House of the Sacrificial Oxen. Two offering tables and an oxen horn (the tables were found separately). PZ 45 (1970) 163 Fig. 7.

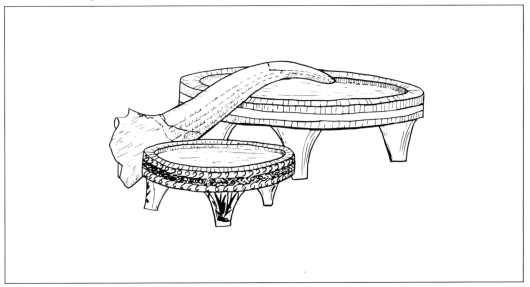

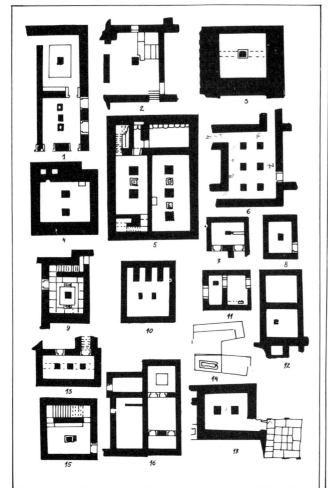

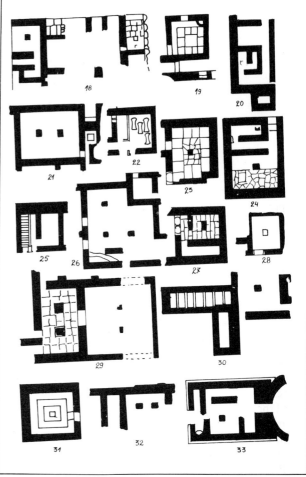

8. Crypts
   1. Knossos, palace. Central Crypt Complex.
   2. Knossos, palace. Room of the Lotus Lamp.
   3. Knossos, palace. South-west crypt.
   4. Knossos, Little Palace. South-west Crypt.
   5. Knossos, Little Palace. Basement Pillar Crypt Complex.
   6. Knossos, North Pillar Basement.
   7. Knossos, South-east House. Crypt C 1.
   8. Knossos, House of the Chancel Screen.
   9. Knossos, Royal Villa.
   10. Knossos, Monothlic Pillar Basement.
   11. Knossos, South-east House. Crypt L 1.
   12. Knossos, North-west House.
   13. Knossos, South House Monolithic Pillar Basement.
   14. Isopata, Tomb of the Double Axes.
   15. Knossos, South House. Pillar Crypt.
   16. Knossos, House of the Frescoes.
   17. Knossos, Temple Tomb.
       Platon MOI Pl. 9.

9. Crypts
   18. Knossos-Gypsades. Crypt of House B.
   19. Amnissos.
   20. Prasa.
   21. Vathypetro.
   22. Nirou Chani.
   23. Tylissos. House A.
   24. Tylissos. House Gamma.
   25. Sklavokambos. Room 8.
   26. Sklavokambos. Room 15-16.
   27. Phaistos, palace. Central Crypts XLV-22.
   28. Phaistos, House. Room XLI-102.
   29. Mallia, palace. Rooms VII-3-4.
   30. Mallia, palace, North Crypt.
   31. Ayia Triada. Royal Villa.
   32. Ayia Triada. Crypt of the House near the Tholos.
   33. Apesokari.
       Platon MOI Pl. 10.

III
Crypts

NOT ALL scholars are agreed that sacred crypts were known in Minoan and Mycenaean times. This is still a matter of controversy. In 1901 Evans was the first to make some observations on crypts.[1] His whole attention was taken up with the religious function of the pillar, and at all with the interiors in which the columns and pillars were situated. Not till we come to the time of Nilsson, who took a special interest in the cult of pillars and columns, do we find lengthy descriptions of the rooms known as crypts, of which he discussed more than a dozen examples — from Knossos, Phaistos, Ayia Triada, and Zakro.[2] After close study of the archaeological remains, Nilsson was unable to say definitely whether the crypts had a religious function or not.[3] In 1954 Platon published a paper dealing with this type of room in greater detail.[4] As he points out, the crypt had to be a dark place (usually a cellar) which the light of day did not penetrate; generally the ceiling was held up by a pillar which often supported a columnar chamber, that was likewise used for religious purposes, above the crypt. Nearly everything we know about the columnar sanctuaries comes from the iconographic finds and from the sparse remains of walls still in existence above the crypts.[5] Obviously the pillar must have been part of the construction. Platon did several important things: in the first place, he studied 45 crypts, and columnar shrines above them, and described them as far as this was possible (Figs. 8-10). In the second place, he introduced an important change of method. Before his day, discussion had centred mainly round the religious function of the pillar always found in these chambers. But Platon now shifted the centre of interest to the function of these chambers as a whole, and approached the problem in the light of all the available finds, not just the pillars — which on the whole were not cult objects. He tried to discover the function of these rooms from the character of the finds, such as emblems, cult objects, and offerings. When no cult objects were found in the crypt, he extended his attention to the finds in the neighbouring rooms. In the third place, he described all the crypts in turn. His method was to compare and classify the finds, arrange his material in certain groups, and discuss the most important features of the construction and the finds.[6] Despite all these undoubted advances, however, much still remains unexplained. Hence it is hoped that the re-opening of this question and a re-examination of the evidence, but especially of the finds which could have been used solely for religious purposes, will shed more light on the problem. First of all we shall see what the finds tell us about the crypts, and then we shall try to determine whether or not most of the elements constituting the furnishings and construction — particularly the pillar, the signs carved on it and on the walls, in a word, those elements that are thought to have had a definite religious significance — help us to establish whether or not the crypts had a religious function.

Among the crypts there is one group in which the most important finds have a specially close link with cult places. These are the altars or offering stands, and the cult idols. The word 'altar' may of course have a range of meanings. It may signify not only a structure made of stone, but also a natural rock or a moveable stone, or an object made of clay. Beginning our discussion of the crypts, we may cite a tholos tomb excavated at Apesokari.[7] The principal chamber — measuring 4.85 m in diameter — built of rough stones (Figs. 9:33;11), was found to contain only stoneware and pottery vessels, including lamps, and also skeletons in the contracted position. A narrow corridor (Passage B) connected this chamber with Rooms C, D and G. Two skeletons were found in Room E, which was separated from Room G by a wall 0.90 m thick. Room G, which was an irregular rectangle, measured approximately 3.75 × 4.00 m. In the middle there was a square pillar made of a few large rough stones. The pillar in Room G may have been solely a structural element, since it was rather too high to have been used as an

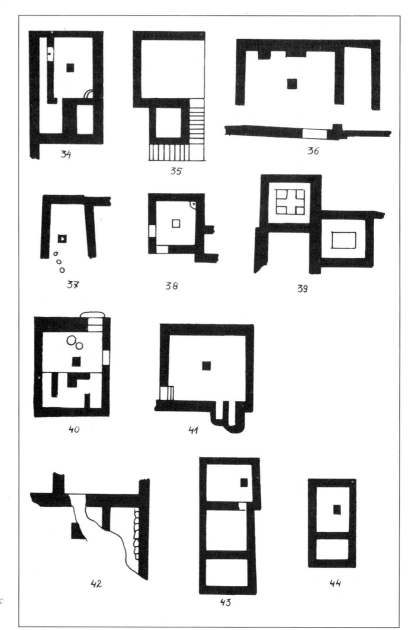

10. Crypts
34. Gournia, House Ee.
35. Pseira. House B.
36. Pseira. House D.
37. Palaikastro, Quarter delta.
38. Palaikastro, Quarter pi.
39. Palaikastro, Quarter chi.
40. Zakro, House A.
41. Zakro, House Delta.
42. Mycenae, Palace Crypt.
43. Philakopi, House of the Frescoes.
44. Philakopi. House of the Monolithic Pillar.
   Platon MOI Pl. 11.

11. Apesokari. Plan of the Tholos Tomb. S. Hood, The Minoans (1967) Fig. 127.

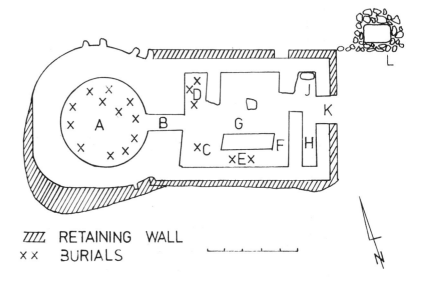

⧅⧅ RETAINING WALL
×× BURIALS

altar.[8] No human bones were found in this chamber. Although Room G had been plundered, several stone bird's-nest vases, fragments of two pottery vessels, and potsherds of an ordinary thick-walled pithos were discovered. A passage 1.60 m wide led out of this room to a small neighbouring chamber, Room J, which was intended for religious use. Room J was no more than 0.90 m wide. On the floor there was a flat hectagonal stone slab measuring 0.65 m in length and 0.35 m in breadth, probably an altar. In front of this lay a concretion, a natural stone in the shape of a human being with body and legs, on which the navel was the only distinct feature, having been drilled with a sharp instrument.[9] Room H next door was also used for a religious purpose. Outside the tomb there was a small construction L measuring approximately 0.20 to 0.25 m high and from 0.88 to 0.90 m long. Presumably this was an open-air altar made of rough stones. A great amount of pottery, such as cups and jugs, was found around the altar. Generally these vases were thin-walled, and frequently badly broken. Stone vessels, too, were found — especially bird's nest vessels. This tomb was used in MM IA.[10]

At Koumasa (see also Chapter V, p. 97) a room with a plaster floor and a stone base for a wooden column was discovered.[11] A conical object was probably a baetyl. There was also a rectangular terracotta offering table, dated to MM II. An offering bowl and pottery belong also to the same period. From a later time, LM IIIB, came four[12] snake tubes.

At Sklavokambos (Fig. 9:26;12) there were probably two crypts and an upper sanctuary (see below p. 29). In the south part of the villa an entrance led from the east. Two doors connected a long corridor (14) with a big rectangular space (15-16), about 8.20 by 11.30 m,[13] containing four pillars, 0.70 by 0.70 m, and 0.70 by 0.80 m. This was an atrium. To the south there was a wall, and behind, to the south-west, a rock with many cracks in it protruded above the surface of the room. This rock was covered with a layer of black, unburnt earth from 0.04 to 0.05 m thick — its colour was derived from the rotting of vegetation. There are also traces of fire — e.g. small pieces of charcoal, and incinerated animal bones. The cracks in the rock contained a large amount of black earth, many sherds, and two intact inverted conical cups. According to Marinatos this room was used as a kitchen, but later on was regarded as a crypt.[14] The rock with cracks was compared to a peak sanctuary, and the south-west corner was taken as a temenos. The two neolithic stone axes found not far from one of the pillars may also testify to the sacred function of the room.[15]

In the South-east House at Knossos, too, Room C 1 is a pillared crypt. It was in use from MM IIIA to LM IA (Fig. 8:7;13).[16] In the middle of the chamber (3.15 by 3.65 m) a pillar 2 m high has survived almost entirely. Three double axe signs have been found on three of its blocks.[17] Slightly north of the pillar was a stone base on which a double axe had once stood. In the west wall was a niche (Fig. 14) 0.35 m deep, 1.00 high, and at a height of about 0.25 m above the floor. Probably there were no windows in the rather dark room. A splendid purple gypsum lamp was discovered here.[18] In the south-west corner there was a pit or artificial cave in which sherds from the Neolithic and from LM III were discovered. It was blocked during the period when the room was in use. It has been suggested that the anteroom (B.1) and the

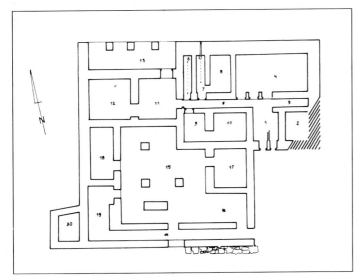

12. Sklavokambos. Plan of the villa. AE 1939/40, Fig. 4.

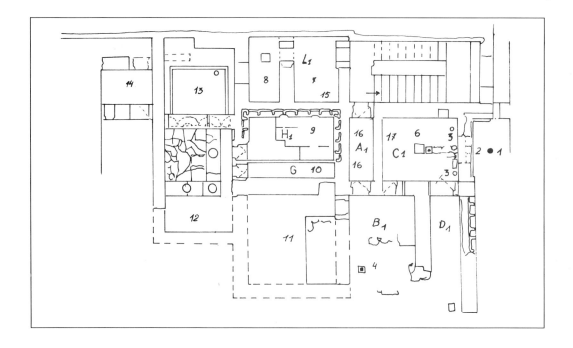

magewine (D.1) were used to store the sacred objects. In Room B.1 an offering stand with six feet, which was painted with rosettes and had an oval opening with no bottom, was unearthed. A stone slab with circular hollows in it was reported found in D.1. But it is probable that these objects came from an upper room — the columned shrine — together with an ivory sacred knot (about 0.10 m high) that most likely came from a chest found to the north of Room C.1, and fragmentary frescoes from Room A.1. How Room C.1 was entered from inside the house is not clear. One possibility is that it was reached from K.1 through crypt L.1 and A.1 and B.1, or from above. The east part of Rooms B.1 and D.1 no longer survives.

Another building at Knossos — the South House — was one of the most important private residences in the period from MM IIIB to LM IA or LM IB.[19] The crypt here measured 5.30 × 3.70 m, and in the centre of it a square gypsum pillar 1.80 m high still stood (Figs. 8:15;15). On the one side of the pillar, and quite near to it, a small pyramidal socket or base for a double axe

13. Knossos, South-east House. Plan. BSA 9, 1902/03, Pl. I.

14. Knossos, South-east House. Northern part of Crypt C 1, niche further in.

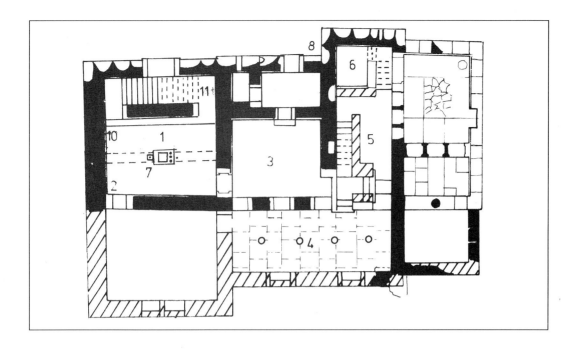

was found (7). On the other side there was a base with three holes which were rather too small for libation vessels, and which therefore, it was suggested, may have been intended for the horns of consecration or for a double axe (Fig. 16) (see the Shrine of the Double Axes, below). It has been suggested that a bench near the entrance, which was lower than usual, may have been intended for offerings.[20] According to Evans, a fragmentary amphora was a ritual vessel. Next to the crypt was a storeroom (see below, p. 36), and farther on a pillar crypt (see p. 36). Nearby, stairs led up to a room on a higher floor, known as the 'Upper Columnar Sanctuary' (Fig. 15). A gypsum bench of the usual height stood against the wall. It is thought that another pyramidal gypsum stand for a double axe came from the Columnar Sanctuary on the upper floor. It is likely, too, that a hoard of five silver vessels — including three bowls and a jug — that were found here (in Room 1) came from the upper floor.

Another group of crypts consists of those in which the most important finds are horns of

15. Knossos, South House. Plan. Evans PofM II Fig. 208.

16. Knossos, South House. Pillar Crypt (1) with base with three holes and a double axe base (7).

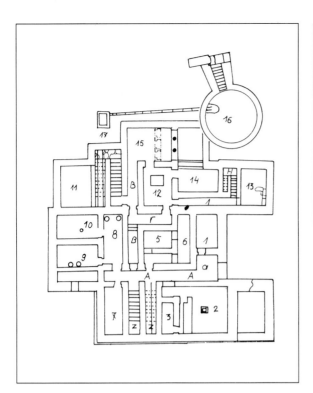

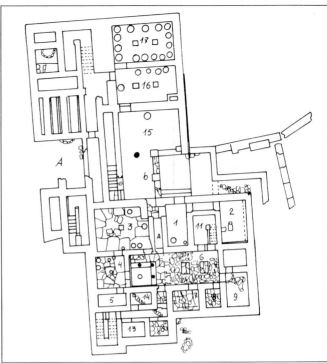

consecration, and double axes or bases for double axes. Two such crypts have already been described above. In a large house Gamma at Tylissos,[21] Room 2 (5.30 by 4.70 m) is taken as a crypt (Figs. 9:24;17). Staircase Z led down to corridor A and then to Room 2 which was divided into two parts, a lower one with a paved floor, and a second, higher one with a painted stone floor, only part of which has survived. In the south part of the room, two stones have been interpreted as the remains of a throne.[22] A square pillar stands in the middle of the room. It has been suggested that the western part of Room 2 was used as a storeroom in MM IIIA, and it was not until MM IIIB-MM IA that the entire cellar came to be used as a crypt. An annex (3) was possibly used for cult purposes, since stuccoed horns of consecration were found in it. On the plan (Fig. 9:24), the place where the horns were found is marked in the north-west corner of the room. But it is not clear if they constituted furnishings of Room 3, or if they had fallen down from an upper sanctuary. The last possibility is that they may have fallen from the roof of the building.

On the slopes of Gypsades Hill at Knossos, excavations have brought to light a Temple Tomb, dated to MM IIIB-LM IIIA, containing several chambers.[23] From the entrance one passes into a paved courtyard. Further in is an inner hall, and next to it is the almost square Outer Pillar Crypt (5.00 by 4.50 m), with two rectangular pillars (Fig. 8:17) both probably covered with red plaster. During LM IA the south-west corner embracing the pillars was walled off. Rubble debris was found, including the bones of about twenty people, and various sherds were uncovered. It is likely that the large plaster horns of consecration discovered here crowned the sanctuary on the upper floor. There was a gypsum pillar in the centre of the Inner Pillar Crypt. The vaulting consisted of the natural rock, painted blue, probably to represent the heavens. Near the entrance, the bones of a man and a child were discovered. But a LM IIIA deposit was uncovered in a pit inside the door. A sacrificial table or kernos with five holes, as well as offering vessels, were found here.[24]

House A at Tylissos, which has been dated to MM IIIB-LM IA,[25] has a room (Figs. 9:23;18 No. 3) that is regarded a crypt. Rectangular in shape (5.60 by 4.50 m), and probably windowless, it is situated near the main room (6). Part of the room was floored with slabs to begin with, and later on the whole of it was covered. On one of the slabs there is a star sign. A square pillar here, consisting of seven blocks, is 1.75 m high and was probably plastered. Traces of plaster were visible at the time of the excavation.[26] A pyramidal, stone, double axe base, as well as the bones of sheep, pigs and bulls were found. Many jugs, a pitcher and an odd vessel, pottery loom-weights,[27] and a steatite bowl were discovered, as well. A bronze male

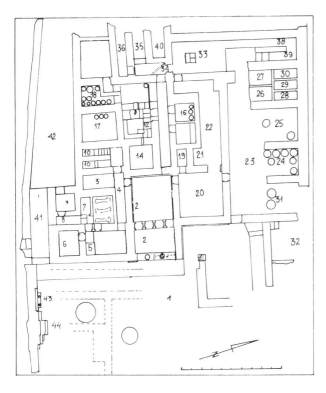

17. *(far left)* Tylissos, House Gamma. Plan. J. Hazzidakis, Etcret 3, Pl. 33.

18. *(left)* Tylissos. Plan of House A. J. Hazzidakis, Etcret 3, Pl. 33.

19. Nirou Chani. Plan of the villa. AE 1922, Fig. 1.

votary may have fallen from the upper floor. In the next room (4) vessels with vestiges of pigment — red, yellow, white — as well as bronze ingots were discovered. The next room (5) contained three bronze caldrons and several Linear A tablets.

A large house or villa at Nirou Chani (Figs. 9:22;19)[28] contained a courtyard, store rooms, and number of living- and work-rooms, etc. Rooms 17 and 18 held clay altars.[29] Near the Cretan megaron (2, 2a) corridor 4 ran as far as an anteroom (5) and led to two small chambers. One of them (7), whose size was about 2.00 × 2.70 m and which was probably windowless, contained four large double axes. This chamber is sometimes referred to as a sanctuary or crypt.[30] Tiny chamber 7a (approximately 1.00 × 1.60 m) had no windows, and for light had to depend on the door or a slit. A large amount of charcoal was found in this cell as well as vessels blackened with soot from the fire. Xanthoudides thought it was a kitchen.[31] Later on it was regarded, together with room 7, as a sacred crypt, since there were no windows, and since the vessels found there had not — it was believed — been affected by fire, although a large quantity of ash was found. Steatite floral vessels were also unearthed. Small room 6 — which is entered from anteroom 5 — has a bench. Nearby were small rooms 9 and 3, which would probably be better discussed together with rooms 7 and 7a. Room 7 may have been a store-room or a workshop. Yet another possible explanation is that the big double axes fell from the upper floor, where there may have been a sanctuary in MM IIIB-LM IA.

The Tomb of the Double Axes at Isopata[32] has a well-preserved chamber (2.25 × 4.50 m) hewn out of the soft limestone (Figs. 8:14;20). The entrance was blocked with hewn blocks of stone. This wall must have been demolished previously, for a tool — a bronze double axe — was found among the stones blocking the stomion (ante-room) at a height of about 1.20 m. No doubt it was left here when the tomb was opened. This tomb was irregular in shape, with two niches, separated by a wall projecting between them. This wall or buttress may originally have been erected because the builders of the tomb wanted to make a pillar in the centre, and then gave up this idea, being afraid the ceiling would collapse. This pillar is carved in low relief[33] on the side facing the entrance. The carving, it is thought, represents a column[34] or a double axe shaft.[35] The ceiling of the tomb has not survived. Along the left side of the tomb there is a stone bench 0.60 m high and from 0.92 to 1.20 m wide. On the right side there was a platform. Its most protruding part was a sort of shelf no more than 0.20 wide, also 0.60 m high. The next part of this platform was 0.15 m higher, and had a pit in it shaped like an axe (2.14-2.27 m long, 0.87-0.88 m wide, and 1.26 m deep). At one time this pit was covered with stones. Further in, on the right-hand side, there was a still higher platform. This tomb contained a group of

20. Isopata. Tomb of the Double Axes. Evans TDA Fig. 52.

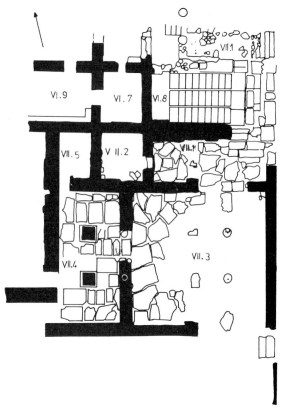

21. Mallia, palace. Plan of Rooms VII 3-4. Etcret IV, Plan 1 (fragment).

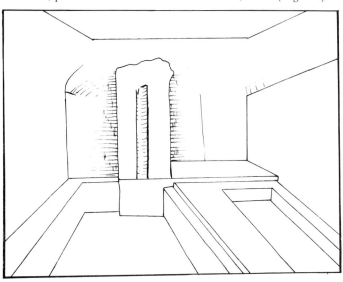

objects that had once belonged to a warrior. There were fragments of a steatite rhyton in the form of a bull's head, cylindrical clay vessels, two cult bronze double axes, in addition to weapons, such as the remains of a gold studded sword, a bronze knife, bronze arrowheads, personal belongings — such as a bronze razor, and gold, wooden, and amber beads — pieces of a silver vessel, richly decorated clay vases — jugs, amphorae, an alabastron, and a pedestalled goblet — a fumigator or a lamp, and a sealstone decorated with animals carved on it.

The majority of these objects, which date from LM III A1 were discovered on the floor of the tomb. The only other objects not found on the floor were a part of a silver cup and fragments of a pottery jug discovered on the bench (further in, on the left side), and a fumigator or lamp on the platform on the right side. Gold and wooden beads were discovered in the deep pit. It may be that the double axes, and some vessels, near the rocky projection were the personal belongings of the dead or the remains of a sacrifice.

Still another group of crypt consists of those where vessels used sometimes or often for cult purposes — rhyta, inverted cups or inscribed vessels — were discovered. The finds from the Tomb of the Double Axes at Isopata (Knossos) have already been mentioned above.

East of the courtyard of the palace at Mycenae there is a rectangular crypt built in LH IIIA. A square pillar still stands in it (Fig. 10:42). It was thought[36] that the crypt was a cult room, for it held a large number of conical vessels and a fragment of a stone rhyton dated to LH I,[37] kitchen pottery and loom weights were also found in this room.

In the palace at Phaistos, several rooms have been excavated on the north-east slope.[38] In one of them Room XLI-102, measuring 4.25 × 4.25 m (Fig. 9:28), there is a square pillar, with an incised double axe sign, of which two blocks still exist. Along one of the walls, a large number of domestic utensils have been found — in particular tripod vessels with soot on the bottom. A bull's head rhyton (approximately 0.25 m long) was excavated in the north-west corner. Pernier[39] was inclined to think that this room was the kitchen because it contained sooty vessels. Platon,[40] on the other hand, considered that this room was too dark to be a kitchen.[41] It was more likely to have been used in MM III than earlier.

An interesting discovery was also made at Gypsadhes, Knossis.[42] The South part of House B in question (or perhaps even a separate house?) has a crypt measuring 3.30 × 2.80 m (Fig. 9:18) with a pillar (measuring 0.55 × 0.55 m) in the centre. It is built of eight gypsum slabs of varying height. In this room there were about two hundred inverted cups, each of which covered a small heap of charred plant remains. They were carefully arranged in rows. The crypt also had two small annexes. More or less in the middle of the centre chamber was a pillar of which a single block has survived, fixed to the rocky floor. In a room facing south the floor is made of gypsum slabs, and in the middle was a pillar of which a single block 0.28 m high, was discovered. The north room (3.90 × 2.30 m) also has a pillar and a bench along the western wall. The only discoveries in the house consisted of pottery dated to MM IIIB–LM IA.

The house at Sklavokambos[43] seems to consist of two distinct parts, a north and a south one (Figs. 9:25;12). The objects found in Rooms 1 and 4, a stone hammer, a terracotta foot, sealings, cylindrical vessels, a terracotta bull's head and a stone rhyton or filler seem to have come from an upper sanctuary. The entrance to Room 8, which seems to have been completely dark, was under the stairs. The objects found in this room — inverted conical cups, miniature kotyloi and incense burners — suggested it may have been a shrine or crypt.[44]

Near the light-well of the Double Axe Hall of the Palace at Knossos in the House of the Monolithic Pillars a deep cellar, measuring 5.00 × 5.60 m, was excavated. It was formed from two monolithic limestone pillars[45] which stood on broad bases also of limestone (Fig. 8:10). In the north wall there are three spur walls forming four bays. An oval pit 0.50 m deep and 1.30 m in diameter was revealed between the pillars, near the south wall. No traces of a door were found. Pottery was discovered in the deepest layer, while at a depth of 4 m the excavations brought to light a vessel whose edge was ornamented with a dove, as well as a hieroglyphic seal, and pottery dating from MM II. In another layer, the discoveries included a pithos from LM II, in addition to two cups with inscriptions made in ink,[46] dating from MM III.

Evans, judging from the pillars, the bays and the pit as well as from the cups with inscriptions, supposed this place was a sanctuary. He thought it had been used as such from MM I to LM II, that is, from the very earliest time the room had been used. Later it was suggested,[47] that this room was a sacred crypt, but only in MM I–III, for, apart from the architectural elements and the pit in the floor, the dove-vessel and the inscribed cups date from that period.

It should be noted, however, that the religious nature of the dove-vessel is not certain. It is possible that some strange looking vases could have been used in everyday life. On the other hand it is also possible that cups with magic inscriptions were kept in ordinary houses, and not just in sanctuaries.

The next group of crypts consists of those in which the signs incised on the pillars or on the walls were an important element. The best known crypts of this kind are two situated in the west wing of the palace at Knossos, near the Sacred Repository and the Throne Room (Fig. 8:1).[48] They were in use from MM IA to LM II. Both were well built, the thickness of walls being not less than 1 m.[49] The East Pillar Crypt is a rectangular chamber (5.3 × 3.5 m) with a pillar on which many incised double axes were observed. Such signs were also found on the gypsum jambs and on the stone quoin. This chamber contained thirteen incised double axes. The floor is paved and two basins near the pillar are 0.25 m deep, their other dimensions being 0.80 × 0.47 m, and 0.80 × 0.53 m. When Hutchinson and Platon were repairing and clearing the palace in 1946, a pit lined with stone slabs — a presumably sacrificial deposit under the later floor — was found, containing a thick layer of ash along with animal bones, MM IA sherds, small conical cups and fragments of a stone lamp.[50] Ten pithoi were excavated in the room next to the crypt.

The West Pillar Crypt is nearly of the same size as the East one (5.5 × 3.8 m). It has a pillar with 17 incised double axes. The floor of this room, too, is paved. It has a depressed rectangle around the pillar. A stone bench was noted. But no finds were published. A doorway connects this room with the East Pillar Crypt and with the store-rooms. In the area of the Pillar Crypts there are many rooms, some of which have clearly sacred deposits, e.g. The Vat Room, the Temple Repositories, the Throne Room, and the so-called probable Tripartite Shrine (see below p. 127).

The west wing of the palace at Mallia has a room (VII 4) which is thought to have been a sacred crypt (Figs. 9:29;21).[51] It is situated next to room VII 3, the biggest in the west wing (9.13 × 8.77 m), which was partly floored with slabs. The east part of Room VII 3 was an open court divided from the central courtyard by a low parapet. At the south wall there was a bench. Crypt VII 4 measured 4.00 × 8.20 m, and was paved with stone slabs. The walls, made of large

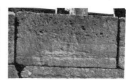

22. Knossos, North Pillar Basement. a–f. signs on blocks.

blocks of ammouda, were covered with red plaster, some of which has remained. The pillars were square, and on the northern one two signs were incised, a trident and a star. On the southern one were three double axes and a star. In the doorway to VII 3 there are two round column bases. At a later period the entrance was narrower, and the columns were incorporated in the wall. One of the rooms (VII 8) had a pit where some bones were found. There was also a stuccoed bench. The excavators believed this room was a 'piece d'habitation avec le foyer', but Gesell believes it was a preparation room (see also Chapter VII, p. 121). A cupole offering table was found in VII 13.

No detailed report of the finds was published and only one sherd from VII 4 was mentioned. The excavators[52] were not sure what purpose VII 4 was used for. Evans[53] thought it was a sacred crypt, because of its general affinity to other crypts. Later on it was stressed that VII 4 could not have been a store-room, for it was in the western, ceremonial part of the palace, and the walls were covered with red plaster, which could have been of religious significance.[54] The pillars and the walls had been very carefully made, so it is most unlikely this was an ordinary room. But in our opinion the arguments traditionally propounded are not really sufficient for us to recognise Room VII 4 as a sacred crypt. Sometimes store-rooms made of beautiful stone blocks do exist.[55] Room VII 4 lies on the axis of the altar, but it faces the store-rooms on the east side of the courtyard as well. It should be remembered that most of the royal chambers in the west wing of the palace were situated on the first floor.

The western part of the palace at Phaistos[56] contains Room XLV-22 (Fig. 9:27) which, according to some scholars, was a sanctuary.[57] It is said to have consisted of two parts — a pillar crypt, and a small store-room at one side. Double doors lead into this room, in which there are two limestone pillars, one in the doorway, and the other in the middle of the room. The sign of a trident has been incised on one of the pillars. The floor, dating from the time of the First Palace, was painted red. The only objects found on the stone floor of this room were pieces of pottery dating from MM III.

Not far from the palace at Phaistos, and lying south of it, is a house (MM I-IIIA) in which one of the rooms has an ante-chamber (Fig. 9:28).[58] Nearly in the centre of this room, which measures 3.80 × 4.60 m, stands a limestone pillar.[59] An ear of corn is carved on it. According to Pernier,[60] this pillar did not stand parallel to the walls of the house. Moreover, it stood not on the floor, but on a layer of earth, from which it may be concluded that it was not *in situ*; it must have been shifted during reconstruction work in the LM period.

We do not know what kind of objects were found in the crypt. Fragments of wall paintings, with geometric and flower motifs, which were discovered in 1900 and 1907, came from this house. The exact place where these fragments belong is not known for certain, but it was suggested that the paintings decorated the walls of the Columnar Sanctuary were situated over the crypt.[61] It is not certain whether a chapel was built on this spot in the next period, LM, but at any rate a temple was erected here to Rhea in Greek times.

The remains of a house were found about 20 m from the North Hall of the Palace of Knossos.[62] Fairly well preserved basements were brought to light. One of them measured 7.80 × 5.81 m. Inside it were found the limestone bases of four pillars; two of them had gypsum pillars still standing, one to a height of 2.10 m, and the other to a height of 1.70 m. The plan[63] published by Evans marks the position of six pillars, of which only four still remained on the site (Fig. 8:6). The walls were built of exceptionally large stone blocks [64] meticulously finished on the outside. Beside this basement, and to the west of it, a smaller room was discovered, built of smaller and less carefully worked, or even quite rough, stones. The room on the east was completely filled in again when the excavations were over. We have no information as to what kind of objects were found in it.

Many signs,[65] such as tridents and stars (Fig. 22a-f), were incised on the stone blocks. In this basement, such signs can be seen only on the bigger and more carefully worked blocks. On the blocks of the west wall were two signs — a star and a trident, while on those of the east wall there were four signs — two of them (tridents) on the southern stone, one on the next stone (a star), and one (a trident) on the third stone. All these signs were incised at a height of approximately 1-1.50 m above the present day level of the floor of the basement. The only sign found outside the pillar basement was incised on a stone in the north-west corridor (Fig. 22b). The two gypsum pillars had no signs on them.

Evans[66] defined this room as a sacred crypt because of the presence of these pillars. Later, too, it was suggested that the signs on the pillars had a sacred significance.[67] But, as will be explained below, if we accept that these pillars were no more than constructional elements, and that the signs on the stones did not necessarily mean the room was used for cult rituals,[68] then one can argue that the room with pillars was a cellar. It will be recalled that many cellars were built of beautifully hewn stones.[69] The signs in the crypts in the South-east House at Knossos, in the Pillar Basement at Knossos, and the Royal Tomb at Knossos and in House A at Tylissos have already been discussed above.

There are two crypts in which the emblems painted on vases were probably the most important element of the finds. In a large house at Prasa[70] one of the rooms (Fig. 9:20) had an unusual annex (B) leading off it. The latter measured 2.00 × 2.10 m, and its interior was further divided into two parts. Room B may have been a cellar, while the annex[71] was probably used as a sacred crypt, for it contained vessels dating from MM IIIB-LM IA, which are said to have been used in the making of sacrifices. The most important of these were one-handled cups, two stirrup vessels decorated with double axes and sacred knots (see below), and tableware and other pottery. It is thought that neighbouring Room A was also a cult place.[72]

In house B at Pseira, it is thought that one of the rooms, where a pithos decorated with a bucranion and double axes was discovered, may have been a crypt (Fig. 10:35).[73] Remains of stairs show that there must have been a room up above. (See also, below, the finds at the House of the Frescoes at Knossos.)

Quite a lot of rooms are said to have been sacred crypts because they had niches, pits, exceptionally fine floors, or places where presumably there was a throne. In the villa at Amnissos, which was in use from MM III to LM IA, one of the rooms (Fig. 9:19) contained fragments of wall frescoes. In the middle of the house there was an almost square room (No.

6)[74] whose function was not defined by the discoverer. Later on it was thought that this room may have been a crypt,[75] which the light penetrated if the doors situated north and west were opened. Because the floor was paved with stone slabs, it was presumed that the room was too fine to be used for domestic purposes. There is an empty space beside the wall, where there may have been wooden benches of which, however, no trace has remained. From the thickness of the walls and the presence of four steps of a staircase it may be concluded that the house consisted of a ground floor and a first floor.

It is not certain, however, if the room was dark or not, for only the lower part of the walls has survived, so we do not know if there were windows in Room 6 or not. Even tiny windows, or slits in the wall, would have provided enough light to illuminate the room.[76] The presence of windows, even if they were small, seems all the more likely in that on the west this room is adjacent to a small paved courtyard. There may also have been casements above the doors; as we can see was sometimes the case from a model of a building or sanctuary from Chaniale Teke.[77] The floor consisted of beautifully laid stone slabs, and there may also have been benches of the kind which are often found in private rooms.[78] Nothing is known about the finds in Room 6.

At Ayia Triada, Room 17, which is a small one (Fig. 9:31), is practically square (5.00 × 5.20 m).[79] The west wall was destroyed when the LM III building was being constructed. The north and west walls, made of large blocks of gesso, are in a better state of preservation. In the middle of the room there is a piece of grey limestone measuring 0.49 × 0.60 m; this was undoubtedly part of a pillar — the top was rough, and so it is logical to think that it was covered by another block. Half-way between the walls and the pillar there is a narrow strip of stone pavement. Otherwise the floor is an earthen one. In the anteroom there was a stone bench. In the next room five bronze figurines were discovered, one of which depicts a young male votary and another a female one, both in saluting pose, while another female worshipper holds both hands to her head.[80] The other two figurines are of sitting goats. Judging by the excellent quality of the construction and presence of the pillar in the middle of the room, Halbherr, followed by Evans, thought Room 17 had been used as a sanctuary.[81] Yet this is not at all certain. For in the first place not only sanctuaries, but houses were often made of beautifully chiselled blocks — e.g. in the Little Palace at Knossos. Banti has collected many instances of store-rooms, too, built of fine worked blocks.[82] She believes that Room 17 was a store-room[83] yet various arguments have been propounded against this theory. For instance, it was argued that Room 17 could not have been a store-room because no large pithoi were found in it. The bronze figurines and the bronze ingots found in the next room suggest that Room 17 (and probably the neighbouring one as well) was a sacred crypt.[84] It was remarked that in two little rooms leading out of the crypt there were a large number of bowls, with protuberances in the inside, which suggests that these rooms were used as a sacristy.

Yet it is not at all sure. For, as Banti has pointed out, the discovery of bronze figurines in a room does not necessarily mean it was used for a religious purpose. It may be added that the figurines are indicative of a general attitude of piety, rather than of the existence of a sanctuary. Moreover, bronze ingots were often kept in wealthy houses and palaces, as reserves of raw material. There is no evidence to show that the ingots or the bowls with protuberances inside were kept solely in the store-rooms of sanctuaries.

In the north-west insula of the Palace of Knossos is the Room of the Lotus Lamp (5.20 × 5.20 m).[85] It is entered from the central courtyard. Underneath it was a room called the 'Prison',[86] and directly on top of that were gypsum slabs that once formed a floor — about 1.10 m below the level of the courtyard. These slabs pass under the east wall of the Room of the Lotus Lamp (Fig. 8:2) and were also discovered in the room on the right, on the same level as the Room of the Lotus Lamp. It may therefore be concluded that in MM II the east wall was not yet erected, and that the Room of the Lotus Lamp was 2.70 m longer than it was later. The division into two rooms was made later, in MM II, when the east wall was erected and when slabs were laid to form a new floor 0.25 m above the previous one. At the same time, the ceiling was strengthened by the erection of a pillar, of which a gypsum slab which formed the base) is extant. In MM IIIB other changes were made in the crypt. For instance, a new floor was made, and a wall, dividing the room into two parts, was built along as far as the pillar. Fragments of frescoes, a lotus lamp, and a large alabaster basin all come from this period. The Temple Fresco, showing a crowd before the façade of a temple, probably came from the upper room. In the immediate vicinity there are also two small rooms, in one of which a large clay barrel

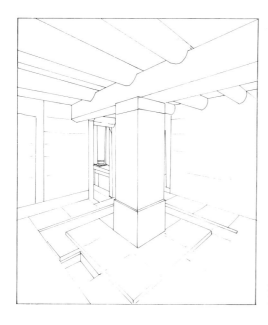

23. Knossos, Royal Villa. Reconstruction. Evans PofM II, Fig. 235.

was found. In the room facing north, the Saffron Gatherer Fresco, as well as steatite vases and two stone lamps, were found.

The following arguments have been put forward, suggesting that the Room of the Lotus Lamp was used for sacred purposes. It has been asserted, on the basis of the discovery here of a lamp of exceptional beauty, that the room was dark. The alabaster basin found in the east room was similar to one discovered in the room next to the Throne Room. The fragments of fine, hard plaster horns of consecration with a clay core — found in the courtyard near the Room of the Lotus Lamp — have also been said to suggest that the room's function was a sacred one.[87] It is argued that on the first floor there must have been a columnar sanctuary, for here excavations yielded fragments of religious paintings — e.g. the Temple Fresco, the Sacred Grove Fresco and the Saffron Gatherer[88] — as well as a ceiling ornamented with spirals on a blue background representing the dome of heaven.

But again we are entitled to some doubts. The pillar was very likely built for a constructional purpose since the wall holding up the ceiling was built along that far in MM IIIB. Moreover, it may be asked whether any of the objects found in the crypt were of an exclusively religious character? Could the large alabaster basin (0.80 m in diameter) not have been an object of everyday use? Then again richly decorated lamps are common enough in palaces, although it is no doubt true that some were used in sanctuaries as well. The purpose of the wall paintings is likewise a matter of dispute, although it must be pointed out only that frescoes are a fairly good indication of the sanctity of a place. On the other hand, the subjects of these frescoes are descriptive rather than ritual. They are probably parts of larger, descriptive decoration.

In the southern part of the Little Palace at Knossos, a Basement Pillar Crypt Complex (Fig. 8:5)[89] was excavated. Stairs led down to the South-west Crypt (5.50 by 3.75 m). This crypt consisted of two separate cellars divided by a wall with doors. The South-east Crypt was bigger (7.70 by 4.30 m), and had three pillars. There were two square basins in the floor each with a square depression. An object that may have been a bench stood at the west wall. The South-west Crypt had two pillars, and a basin sunk into the floor. There was a flight of stairs to the Upper Columnar Room, and a connection with the Entrance Hall and the Cretan Megaron.

One of the rooms in the Little Palace at Knossos, known as the South-west Crypt (6.23 × 4.75 m)[90] has two square pillars. (Fig. 8:4). There was also a low stone bench along the northern wall. The crypt could only be entered by a small antechamber. On the west stair and in a shaft near the crypt were found: a steatite stepped base for a double axe (0.15 m high),[91] a rhyton of inlaid steatite in the form of a bull's head (0.20 m high), and on the staircase — another bull's head rhyton of painted ware, and two clay alabastra. A lead female statuette with upraised hands found in the crypt has been dated to LM IIIB. The presumption is that these objects fell from the columnar room situated over the crypt.

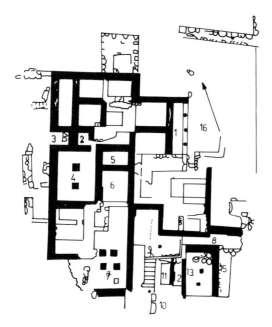

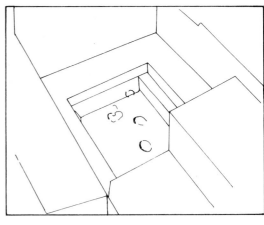

24. Vathypetro. Plan of the villa. PAE 1951, Fig. on p. 259.

25. Vathypetro. Villa. Pit. PAE 1951, 261, Fig. 2.

In the Royal Villa at Knossos[92] a passage leads from the main room — Megaron (C) — to a well preserved pillar crypt (D), dated to LM I-LM IIIA, whose interior measured 4.00×4.15 m (Figs. 8:9; 23). The walls were made of regularly arranged gypsum slabs, while the ceiling was held up by three great beams, one of which was supported by the middle pillar. The floor was of gypsum slabs. A drainage channel had been made in the floor, and two basins lined with stones were cut into it. On this evidence alone (for no sacred objects were reported here) it is supposed that the crypt was used for religious purposes.[93]

A number of rooms were excavated in the House of the Frescoes at Knossos. One of them may have been used as a crypt (Fig. 8:16) from MM IIIB to LM IA.[94] The room had no light, but the stone slabs forming the floor testify to its exceptional importance. Only the centre part of the room was paved with slabs. Three vessels decorated with double axes were found in this room. Nothing is known of other finds. Unfortunately vases with sacred symbols were not only used in sanctuaries.

It is supposed that a fresco — depicting monkeys and birds in a garden — excavated in one of the neighbouring rooms had fallen from the sanctuary above the crypt. Other pieces of the small fresco still bore the remains of inscriptions which were probably parts of a holy verse written on the wall. But in fact it is not certain whether these paintings really did adorn the sanctuary, and the meaning of the inscription is still not clear.[95] In one of the rooms a ladle of the Troullos type was found, as well as a marble sacrificial table with a Linear A inscription.[96]

Another house (Chi) dating from LM I, at Palaikastro has two rooms (66 and 74)[97] which interest us. One of them (66) had a floor laid out in the form of a Greek cross. In the next room (64) there was a large square stone slab on the floor (Fig. 10:39). No information is available about any objects found in these rooms. But thirty-five stone vessels, including a liparite rhyton, were discovered in the neighbouring rooms (61, 62, and further on 46). It has been suggested that Rooms 66 and 64 were sacred crypts because we know this spot was a sacred one, for in later times a temple dedicated to Diktaian Zeus was built on top of part of the buildings of insula Chi.

In a Minoan villa at Vathypetro (Fig. 24), one of the rooms (4) is likewise regarded as a sacred crypt (Fig. 9:21).[98] This was a room with two pillars. It has been supposed that the room was used to begin with as a store for pithoi, and later on as a sacred crypt. But no objects that could have had a cult function were discovered. Attention has been drawn to the adjacent room (2), which is also said to have been a small crypt (1.70×1.80 m).[99] There was an oblong pit in the floor ($1.40 \times 1.50 \times 0.30$ m) and round about the pit the floor was paved, thus forming a bench. Sherds of handleless cups were discovered in the layer at a depth of 0 to 0.15 m, while a thin layer of whitish material consisting of lime and gypsum was found between 0.15 and 0.17 or 0.18 m. The layer below consisted of earth with ordinary little inverted cups, which may have been placed here on purpose. Ritual filling-in of the pit has been suggested. (Fig. 25).

26. Knossos. South-east House. Interior of the annex to Crypt L 1 (No. 8).

House A at Zakro,[100] dating from LM I, was entered straight from the paved street. Its brick walls were erected on stone foundations. The walls of rooms were plastered, and part of the floor was laid with cemented stones — tarazza work. The main room, III-VI, measuring about 4.70 × 5.80 m, which was entered straight from the street (Fig. 10:40), was partitioned by a number of walls into several separate little rooms. In the front part of the room, but a little to one side, a low rectangular pillar stood on a stone base fixed to the cemented floor. All four sides of the pillar were covered with blue plaster.[101] The upper part of this pillar was not plastered, but merely polished. In view of the fact that remains of wood and plaster were discovered nearby, Hogarth thought that at one time this stone had been the base of a wooden pillar. Behind it was the brick wall. The interior was divided by two more partitions. Just beside the entrance there were three basins. One big one — with a diameter of 0.60 m — lay above a smaller one. A funnel had been made at the edge of the bigger basin, which was so placed that the funnel was directed into the smaller one. The third basin, which was smaller still, stood nearby, but it had no direct connection with the others. Hogarth was inclined to think these basins were used for making wine,[102] whereas Platon[103] took the view that they had some function in the ablution ritual, and that the entire room was a sacred crypt.

Rooms III, V and VI contained only sherds. Rooms, I, II, and VIII may have been store-rooms; nine small pithoi, five jugs, and thirteen inverted decorated cups were found in Room VIII. In Room VII part of the floor was laid with stone slabs, and part with bricks. A large number of finds, consisting of agricultural implements such as two hoes and a large knife, and of pottery dating from LM I, were found altogether in one heap. There were also about 500 seal impressions, that had no doubt been used to safeguard various objects stored in safe keeping here. Two fragments of Linear A tablets were also found.[104]

At Pseira, Room 2 of house D (Fig. 10:36)[105] had two buttresses which may have been built to support the ceiling. There is a square pillar in the middle of the room. The floor, like that of the annex nearby, is laid with stone slabs. It has been suggested that this was a sacred crypt, since both rooms had richly decorated pithoi, which must have been used for a special function. The house was used in LM IA (see pp. 166).

Finally, we come to a group of rooms which are thought to have been cult rooms mainly because of the kind of objects found in the neighbouring, connected rooms. In the South-east House[106] situated near the Palace of Knossos, there is an annex to L1 (measuring approximately 1.40 by 3.32 m), which in the MM II-LM I period was the vestibule to a small megaron, K.1 (Fig. 13;26). Possibly a stone bench, one block of which has survived, stood here in that period. In LM IIIB a pillar was erected at one side of the room. Limestone horns of consecration (0.20 by 0.19 m), which stood on a small platform or bench made of water-worn pebbles in Room L.1, date from the period LM IIIB. Room L. was bigger (2.20 × 3.20 m). The pottery found in this room places it in the LM IIIB period. Therefore it seems possible that there was an early crypt here, which later on had furnishings typical of the LM IIIB domestic sanctuaries.

Not very much can be said about the function of most of the rooms at Gournia, as the reports of the excavations are not very detailed. In the north-west part of the room, just beside the main street (Fig. 10:34), a small room (3.70 × 3.00 m), that is, Room E.30 in house Ee,[107] which has a pillar in the centre, has been regarded as a crypt. No doubt this room was entered not from the front of the house but through a vestibule. It is quite possible that the tiny rooms adjacent to Room Ee do not belong to this house at all. We have no information as to what Room Ec contained, but certainly in the room 29, which is nearby, a three-handled LM IA jar was found, decorated with double axes, sacred knots, and rich floral ornamentation. A small pithos dated from LM IA a second jar and a cup are also reported.

In the south-west part of the Palace of Knossos, there is a small crypt,[108] measuring approximately 4 × 5 m, between the Processional Corridor and the Great Propyleum. Access to the cellar was by a ladder or wooden staircase. The place where a pillar is thought to have been is marked on the plan of the room (Fig. 8:3). Gesell[109] observed that the 'incised block with a double axe and a star built into the reconstructed wall is the proper size of a pillar block'. It is thought that there was an Upper Columnar Room; both rooms were intended for cult purposes. In an annex a pit 4 m deep was discovered, believed to have held a votive deposit. It contained pottery dating from LM IA, including sherds of the kind of little cups that were generally used in the cult rituals — but which sometimes served ordinary everyday purposes, too. Some of them were painted a bright red. A small figurine of an ox was likewise found.

In the large and wealthy South House, which is one of the most important buildings at Knossos apart from the palace, a number of rooms were excavated. Apart from a cellar with a single pillar, and a crypt with three pillars other places that were excavated have been interpreted as a lustral basins, a lavatory, a vestibule, and cellars, etc. One of the rooms had a fresco representing a bird. A stairway led down to the cellar (6.50 × 2.80 m),[110] which had three rectangular pillars (Fig. 8:13) and a paved floor. Evans makes no reference at all to any objects discovered here. It is possible that the cellar could be locked. It led to an annex, where part of a pithos with relief decoration was discovered, as well as a hoard of bronze tools that included three large saws, an adze, two knives and two double axes. It has been asserted that not only the pillars, but also the annex with the hoard of bronze tools, was probably connected with the crypt, and was actually its treasury in MM IIIA-LM IB.[111]

A set of basements approached only by means of wooden stairs or ladders (Fig. 8:12) was excavated in the North-west Treasure House at Knossos.[112] In one of the rooms a pair of miniature bronze horns of consecration dated to MM III and an intaglio showing a double axe above the head of a bull were discovered. Fragments of large LM II amphorae with double axes incised on them, and an LM IIIB triple circular base decorated with double axes on leafy shafts rising from horns of consecration were found as well. According to Evans, this base pointed to the existence of a sanctuary here. In the northern part of the house two rooms have been interpreted as crypts. One measures about 3.00 × 3.70 m, while the other, to the north, a little bigger, is about 3.10 by 3.70 m.[113] In the southern room a gypsum column base stood on an ordinary floor of beaten clay. But one cannot exclude the possibility that it had fallen from the floor above. If that is so, a wooden pillar may have supported the ceiling. In Room C, which is very small (2.00 × 1.50 m), just south of the crypt, a hoard of bronze vessels, including fragments of five large basins and a ewer, was found. No finds were reported from the room with the column base or from the room to the north of it.

A number of rectangular rooms thought by some authors to have been shrines[114] were excavated in the 'House of the Frescoes' in the town of Phylakopi, on Melos, and have been dated to the second period of the town. One of these rooms had a rectangular pillar (Fig. 10:43) which had evidently been covered with red plaster.[115] Many fragments of frescoes were discovered here. In the centre of the room blue fragments of frescoes with flying fish, which had probably belonged to the room above, were discovered. A store-room with small plain cups, stone pestles, loom weights and a steatite lamp were also unearthed. Near the crypt described above, another one was excavated[116] and was found to have a monolithic rectangular pillar. The next room contained a column base which had probably fallen from the room above. Five painted pedestalled vases (fumigators?), which are thought to have had a cult connection, perhaps also came from the upper room (Fig. 10:44).

Near the Tholos at Ayia Triada[117] there is a building (4.90 × 3.50 m), which must have been part of a tomb or a house. Its north wall was missing (Fig. 9:32). There were two pillars in the western part of the room. Nothing was reported from the middle room. There are female figurines, one of them wearing a dress with knobs on it, and holding her hands on her hips, and also other statuettes with cylindrical skirts, with their arms extended forwards. A swinging figure was also found. Fragments of a bronze bull (?) and a clay bull, a steatite sphinx and an alabaster monkey are worth mentioning. An amulet bore the following symbols: a hand, a disc, a coiled snake, a beetle, a crawling snake and a scorpion. A Queen Thy scarab is also noteworthy. A stone bowl, a stone hammer and bronze daggers were found as well. The earliest objects are dated to EM II, but most of the objects come from MM IIIB-LM IA, while the figurines with cylindrical skirts have been dated to LM III.[118]

We now come to the group of crypts which, chiefly on the evidence of one or two pillars in them, are said to have been sanctuaries. On the Gypsades Hill at Knossos, house A, also called the West House[119] was discovered to contain more than a dozen rooms. But there is no information about the objects found in it. In Room 10 there was a single pillar.

In the South-west House at Knossos[120] one room believed to be a crypt was rectangular in shape, and contained two pillars. Pottery from MM II and sherds from LM III were found just beyond the thick eastern wall. At Knossos the House of the Chancel Screen was used from MM III to LM IA.[121] Room 10 (3.00 × 3.50 m), had a pillar in the middle (Fig. 8:8). A column base, which no doubt had fallen from the first floor, was likewise found in this room. The presence of a stairway provides additional proof that there had been a room above the crypt. No information is available about the objects discovered in the crypt here. Neither is it known for certain whether any light penetrated it. Next to it is a chamber known as the Room of the Sacred Rostrum.

In house Delta at Palaikastro[122] a room with a rectangular pillar in the middle was found near the megaron (Fig. 10:37). Nothing is known about any objects found in this room. The room next to this one contained column bases, which could have been part of the structure of a sanctuary situated over the crypt.

The excavation of house Pi at Palaikastro[123] revealed the presence of a polygonal room (Room 27, Fig. 10:38), with a pillar in the middle. This house was used from LM IA, and it is from this period that Room 27 dates.

Several conclusions can be drawn from the above discussion of the finds. But before doing so we must first have a look at the most important arguments used to prove that the crypts were sanctuaries. Tables I and II throw light on this question, but other arguments are needed to strengthen the hypothesis that all the crypts were sanctuaries. If cult images were found in the crypts it would be vital proof. But not a single anthropomorphic cult image has been found in any of the crypts, and indeed the aniconic idols discovered (a concretion and a baetyl) were found in places which probably were not crypts at all — the concretion being discovered in the tholos tomb at Apesokari, and the baetyl in the peak sanctuary at Koumasa. But of all the objects found in the crypts, pillars were the commonest; they were found in nearly all the crypts. In every crypt, as in many other places such as magazines and grain-stores, the pillar was part of the construction, and served to support the ceiling. True, in domestic premises the pillars had usually no signs carved on them (with a few exceptions, see below). But the question is whether the pillars, apart from this structural function, had a sacred function as well.

The concept of a pillar cult put forward by Evans can be traced back to some of the ideas propounded in the nineteenth century in connection with the interpretation of the Lion Gate at Mycenae. Evans declared that the indoor pillars were connected with the cult. As evidence in favour of this view he cited the pictorial art, certain analogies found in Mediterranean civilisations, and — most important — the sacred signs carved on the pillars. It will be worthwhile to consider briefly whether these arguments still hold today. Unfortunately the pictorial art in the Aegean provides no evidence that the structural pillars inside the houses had any religious significance. It is true, of course, that scenes exist where libations are being poured out over low pillars or altars (see below p. 212), and in the vicinity of columns. Yet it was proved long ago that the column cult cannot be equated with a cult of indoor pillars.[124] Of course there is another problem more important still. In the Aegean iconography a frequent motif is that of a column which is an object of worship. But one is free to ask whether in such

Table I

Crypts

No.	locality	pillar	altar (a), basin (b), pit (c)	niche (a), paved floor (b), bench (c)	cult image (a) cult objects and emblems (b)	symbols on pillars (a) blocks	emblems vases	rhyton (a), cup (b), tube stand (c), offering bowl (d)	other
1.	Amnissos	none		b; c?					
2.	Apesokari	1?		plaster floor	a				
3.	Ayia Triada	1		earth floor, gypsum footpath rock floor					
4.	Ayia Triada, near Tholos	2							
5.	Gournia, House Ee Room 30	1							
6.	Knossos, Palace, Central Crypts,								sacred deposit, cups, lamp, ash, bones
	a. East Crypt	1	2b	b		a: 13 DA			
	b. West Crypt	1		b; c; depression		a: 17 DA			
7.	Knossos Room of the Lotus Lamp	1		b					
8.	Knossos, Palace, Southwest Pillar Crypt (Great Propylon)	1							
9.	Knossos, North Pillar Basement	6				b			
10.	Knossos, Little Palace, Southwest Crypt	2	low c?						
11.	Knossos, Little Palace, Basement Crypts								
	a. Southeast	3	2b	c?					
	b. Southwest	2	1b	c?					
12.	Knossos, Royal Villa, Crypt D	1	2b	b					
13.	Knossos, House of the Chancel Screen, Room 10	1							
14.	Knossos, House of the Monolithic Pillars	2	c	4 bays			2 cups with inscription		dove vase
15.	Knossos, South House Pillar Crypt	1	bench for offerings?	b	holes for HC?				
16.	Knossos, South House, Pillar Basement	3		b					
17.	Knossos, Southeast House, Room C1	1	offering stand	artificial cave, b; c?	b: DA base	a: 3DA			stone lamp
18.	Knossos, Southeast House, Room L1	1		c					
19.	Knossos, House of the Frescoes						DA		
20.	Knossos, Northwest Treasure House								
21.	Knossos, Southwest House								
22.	Knossos, Gypsades, House A	1							
23.	Knossos, Gypsades, House B								
	a. South	1		cement floor				b: 200	
	b. Central	1		b; throne base?					
	c. North	1		b; c					
24.	Knossos, Temple Tomb a. Outer Pillar Crypt	2				b: DA			red painted pillars
	b. Sepulchral Crypt	1	depression	b; painted ceiling					
25.	Knossos, Tomb of the Double Axes	half column incised	b: DA shaped	c: 3	b: 2 DA		FE (handles)	a: 1	incense burners
26.	Koumasa	stone base	a: offering table	b: plaster	a: baetyl			c: 4 or 2; d: 1	

No.	locality	pillar	altar (a), basin (b), pit (c)	niche (a), paved floor (b), bench (c)	cult image (a) cult objects and emblems (b)	symbols on pillars (a) blocks	emblems vases	rhyton (a), cup (b), tube stand (c), offering bowl (d)	other
27.	Mallia, Pallace, Room VII 4	2		b; red plaster		a			
28.	Mycenae	1						a; b	
29.	Nirou Chani Room 7	none		plaster floor	b: 4 DA				
30.	Palaikastro, Block Delta	1							
31.	Palaikastro, Block Pi	1							
32.	Palaikastro, Block Chi	none		b					
33.	Phaistos, Palace, Central Crypt XLV-22	2		b		a			
34.	Phaistos, Palace, Room XLI	1		c: natural rock		a		a: bull shaped	coarseware tripod vessels
35.	Phaistos, South House	1		b		a			frescoes
36.	Phylakopi, House of the Frescoes	1 (painted red)							
37.	Phylakopi, House of the Monolithic Pillar	1							
38.	Prasa, House A	none					DA, SK		
39.	Pseira, House B	none					DA; bukranion		
40.	Pseira, House D	1		b					
41.	Sklavokambos, Room 8	none						b; inverted miniature kotyloi and incense burners	
42.	Sklavokambos, Room 15	4	rock; traces of fire						stone axes
43.	Tylissos, House A, Room 3	1		b	b: DA base	Star on flagstone			bronze figurine from upper room, animal bones
44.	Tylissos, House Gamma	1		b; throne?					
45.	Vathypetro	2							
46.	Vathypetro	none		c; pit					
47.	Zakro, House A	1							
48.	Zakro, House Delta	1							

DA — double axe
FE — figure of eight
HC — horns of consecrations
SN — sacral knot

Neighbouring rooms or rooms above the crypts

No.	column (Room above)	altar	niche (a)	cult object emblem (b)	frescoe	rhyton (a), inverted cup (b)	ingot	stone lamp	other
2.		x		(idol) natural					
3.			bench						5 figurines the fill: many figurines
4.									amulet, bird vase
5.				b: DA, SK on vase					
6a.	2								
6b.			basin						Temple Repository
7.				a: HC	Temple Frescoe		1		
9.	1								pit: many small cups, 1 figurine
10.				a? (female figurine)		a: conical cups			
11.	x								
13.	1								
15.	x			b: DA base					silver bowls and jug
16.	x								bronze tools

1 No.	2 column (Room above)	3 altar	4 niche (a)	5 cult object emblem (b)	6 frescoe	7 rhyton (a), inverted cup (b)	8 ingot	9 stone lamp	10 other
17.		stone slab with hollows		b: SK					
18.			pottery bench	b: HC					
24.	column base			b: HC					deposit: gold ring, knife, razor, comb, alabastron, pottery incense burner
27.			bench						
29.			bench						
32.						a			
36.					x				stone lamp, conical vessels
37.									
38.	1?					conical cups			
40.									decorated pithoi
43.							x		bronze cauldrons, clay tablet
44.				a: HC in Room 3					
45.			paved floor			b			
47.									bronze tools, over 500 clay sealings

Table II

Crypts

Chronological Table

No.	used in	total	remarks
5, 14, 21	MM II	3	
5-13, 15-20, 22, 23, 25-28	MM III	21	
1-3, 5, 7-13, 15-20, 22-28	LM I	24	
4, 5	LM II	2	+ probably No. 20
4, 5	LM IIIA	2	+ probably No. 20

scenes a column alone is meant, or whether, perhaps, this single column is supposed to represent the whole building. If we could accept this last hypothesis, then we would have to deal not with a column cult, but with rituals taking place before the façade of a building, the façade being represented symbolically by this one column.

The pictorial art by no means bears out the hypothesis that the structural pillars had a cult function. In these circumstances, Evans sought other arguments to support his hypothesis, partly by making reference to comparative material from the Bronze and Iron Ages in the Mediterranean, and to contemporary present-day Islamic folk culture. Evans believed that structural pillars inside the rooms were worshipped in ancient Israel. But the evidence we have does not bear out the view that the Israelite sacred columns and pillars were situated inside the rooms supporting the ceiling. As has been pointed out below,[25] it was customary for high pillars to be erected in front of the temples. Another objection to Evans's view is that analogies taken from folk culture in the eastern Mediterranean are too remote to be used as the main basis of the idea that in the Aegean there was a cult of the structural pillars in the crypts.

It follows that the hypothesis as to the existence of a pillar cult rests mainly on the sacred signs carved on them. But not many pillars have signs on them and indeed such pillars have been found in only seven crypts. Most of these signs were discovered not in crypts but in solidly built underground and ground floor premises such as store-rooms, corridors and entrance halls, etc.[126] Tylissos may be quoted as an example here. On one of the blocks of the exterior wall of house Gamma, we find a carving of a star.[127] Yet on its north side, the house faces the farmyard area, and right beside it is a trough which holds water led into it from a cistern through a stone channel, so it is not likely that the building with the star on it was a sanctuary.

An interesting example corroborating the view that signs on stones may have had a religious, or, more precisely, a symbolic meaning, may be cited here. This is the incurved altar (see below p. 131) from Sanctuary XVIII at Mallia,[128] on which two signs — a star and a cross — were carved. Yet these two signs were also noticed on a pillar in the circular cistern or silos at the south-west corner of the Palace at Mallia.[129] This would seem to give further support to the view that signs on pillars were indications of the piety of the Minoans, rather than the idea that they were denoting the existence of a sanctuary.

Another question worth going into is whether or not the rooms were the stone blocks had signs carved on them contained other sacred objects as well. The answer is that with the exception of three crypts, no sacred objects were found. In the East Crypt at the Central Crypts Complex of the Palace at Knossos there is a deposit which may have been the foundation deposit. At the Temple Tomb at Knossos horns of consecration were discovered which had fallen from the room above, which was a sanctuary. Even in the strongest case at Crypt C, South-east House, the stone base of a double axe and the stone sacrificial table which were found there were not discovered *in situ*, but probably fell from an upper storey. All in all, then, from the finds in the crypts it is difficult to say whether the pillars and crypts themselves had a religious significance.

The signs found on the pillars and stone blocks in the crypts generally numbered one or two to one block, although in exceptional cases a slightly higher number occurred. For instance, the pillars in the Central Crypts Complex at Knossos were incised with as many as thirty signs. The most common sign was undoubtedly that of the double axe, which almost invariably took the same stylised form on a shaft. Stars (Fig. 22b), tridents (Fig. 22f), ears of corn, etc., were less common. These signs were carved on stone ashlars, and always on the outer, worked surface (Fig. 22d). They were nearly always in places that could easily be seen. They appeared frequently on stone blocks, about 1.50 m above the level of the floor (Fig. 22c), or, less frequently, at a great height from the floor, on the stone pillars and on the ceiling. This is probably due to the fact that not many of the excavated buildings reach above the level of the basement or ground floor. The fact that such signs are to be found mostly on large stone blocks suggests that the place to look for is the well-constructed, more imposing buildings, such as the palaces — e.g. those at Knossos, Mallia, Phaistos, and Zakro — and, to a somewhat lesser extent, in some of the houses in the provinces — e.g. at Tylissos and Amnissos.

Certain conclusions can already be reached from the above review of the material. It should be remembered that the signs are fixed in type. The double axes carved on the diverse stone blocks differ little from each other. The same can be said about the stars and the tridents. At Knossos practically no other signs at all are found, except for the three mentioned above — the double axe, the star and the trident. Since these are so few in type, they can hardly be said to have been masons' marks.[130] Another point to note is that the presence of signs on the ashlars is insufficient proof that the crypts were used for sacred purposes. For, as we have already shown, the least number of signs were found in the crypts, and the most in the store-rooms and corridors.

It cannot be denied, however, that the signs found on the ashlars were symbols of divinity. The arguments for this view are as follows: the small number of such signs (that is, there were three basic types) in the crypts at Knossos, the repetition of one sign in particular (the double axe), and the almost invariable form of the sign. The sign, then, was a symbol[131] indicating that there was a deity looking after the building — perhaps guarding the magazines that were an important part of the palace. Ground floor and upper floor rooms were erected above the cellars and magazines. The purpose of these symbols of the deities, then, was to give strength to the construction. But they likewise had an apotropaic function, that is they were meant to ward off the destructive powers of evil forces and bad spirits that might bring disaster on the inhabitants. After all, one reason why emphasis was put on the solidity of construction was to prevent the buildings being destroyed by the frequent earthquakes.

In elucidating the function of the pillars in the crypts, we must also consider the question of the shallow basins generally found near the pillars. The bottom and sides of these basins, which were rarely more than half a metre in depth, were lined with stone slabs. There are only two crypts in each of which there were two basins not far from the pillar carved with sacred symbols. In another four of the pillared crypts there was one basin each, but a room with no pillar still had a single basin.

We must come back to the question of the kind of objects — apart from a pillar sometimes incised with sacred symbols — that were found in the crypts. As was mentioned above, Room C.1 in the South-east House at Knossos is the only one that had both a pillar with sacred signs and also sacred furnishings but it is an LM III domestic sanctuary. Our information about the other crypts in this group is more fragmentary still. At the beginning of the present century reports of excavations were generally not very precise, and so we have no published information regarding the contents of these basins. Consequently it is not certain whether they were intended for a sacred purpose.[132] Vathypetro is the only place with a pit which is known to have contained pottery, especially inverted cups. Apart from the floor which was laid with stone slabs, the only other evidence testifying to the sacred character of this crypt was based on the pit found there, and the presence of these cups. Elsewhere in this book, however, it is suggested that these cups could have been used not just in connection with the cult, but for a secular purpose as well. If this is so, it is not at all certain that the pit in the crypt at Vathypetro played a part in sacred ceremonies. Generally speaking, nothing definite can be said about the purpose of the basins and pits in the crypts at all. To go still further, if we presume that the crypts, despite their excellent construction, were mostly used as magazines, then the basins in question could have been used for some domestic purpose — for example, as a handy place to store food in. In the palace store-rooms there were even deeper pits, likewise lined with stone slabs, used for storing things. It should also be borne in mind that three crypts contained only a pillar and no sacred objects. In one crypt there was a layer of ash, and in another there were small tables which may sometimes have been used in the cult.

The presence of niches in the walls of some rooms has sometimes been used as an argument to prove that the crypts were places used for religious purposes. But these niches in the walls were very infrequent. As a matter of fact, only two have been found — one in Crypt C1 (in the South-east House), and another in the Double Axes Tomb. The use to which Crypt C1 was put has already been discussed above. Nothing was reported in this monolithic crypt except pillars, a pit, and a niche. As for the niche in the Double Axe Tomb, it cannot tell us anything about the function of niches in ordinary dwelling houses. It should be remembered that niches are quite common in stone dwelling houses, and are used for domestic purposes. They are frequently found in present-day stone-built cottages in Crete. For instance, old, half-ruined houses at Ayion Deka in Crete have niches in the rooms and also in the stables, that is, wherever they were needed. After all, it is cheaper to make a niche in the wall than it is to buy or make a wooden cupboard. In present-day Poland, too, we find that in rural areas abounding in stone, such as the Kielce region, the stone outbuildings very often have niches that are practically identical to the niches in the stone buildings on Crete. This underlines the idea that niches must be very common in stone buildings everywhere. No doubt the niches in the walls of the sanctuaries, too, must at one time have been used for keeping the cult objects. We have some evidence in favour of the sacred use of them (see p. 220) and the niche from Tiryns p. 220). Nevertheless, the presence of a niche alone provides us with inconclusive evidence as to the function of the room in which it was situated.

Benches were another structural element, but were rarely found in the crypts. Benches were excavated in the Tomb of the Double Axe. It was even suggested that a low bench at the crypt in the South House at Knossos served for offerings, because it was lower than usual. It is known that while these stone benches were an important element in the sanctuaries, they were also an ordinary, commonplace element of the Cretan houses. Consequently the presence of a bench can tell us nothing conclusive about the function of the room containing it.

Many crypts had paved floors. These mostly consisted of large, carefully fitted stone slabs. As a matter of fact, four of these crypts had nothing remarkable about them at all except for their beautifully laid stone floors. In another four the only characteristic element apart from the floor was a pillar in the crypt. One crypt had a floor of fitted stone slabs and at one time the ceiling had been supported by a pillar on which a sacred symbol is still visible. A crypt in House A at Tylissos was exceptional in that the base of a double axe was discovered there. It is questionable, however, if the base was *in situ*. It seems more probable that it fell from the first floor. Carefully laid floors are to be found in crypts where no cult objects have been discovered. The discovery of such a floor is insufficient evidence in itself to tell us what the crypt was used for, since beautifully laid floors have also come to light in many rooms and even magazines of the palaces. Neither can the fact that the walls are made of ideally fitting and carefully smoothed stone block be used as proof that the crypt was used for some special purpose.

Coming now to the moveable finds, we shall begin our review with the question of the sacred emblems. Of these, the most important seem to be the horns of consecration, which — as research by the writer has shown — probably indicate that the place where they stood was a sacred one.[133] *In corpore*, they either symbolise the presence of a divinity, or they indicate that the place where they stand is under the protection of a divinity. This is the symbolic importance especially of the horns of consecration standing on the roof of a building, or surmounting an altar (see below p. 100). The presence of large horns of consecration, or of miniature models of them, found in rooms, are a convincing argument as to the holy function of the premises. But none has ever been found in the principal chamber of any crypt. The horns of consecration discovered in the Temple Tomb at Knossos, which belonged to the furnishings of the sanctuary above the crypt, probably show the closest connection with the function of the place where they were found. We have another example in the South-east House at Knossos, in Room L.1. Here, too, however, we have a find which came from a neighbouring chamber, which in LM IIIB was a sanctuary, but of the domestic kind. Finally, in House Gamma at Tylissos, we have another interesting example of horns of consecration, likewise discovered in a room which was a side one, although it undoubtedly belonged to the crypt. On the other hand, it is likely that these horns of consecration originally belonged to the sanctuary on the first floor.

Passing now to another group of sacred objects we come to the cult double axes, and the bases used for holding wooden shafts surmounted by double axes. In helping us to identify cult places, their role was different. Like the horns of consecration, they, too, symbolise the presence of a divinity but did not always have to be in the sanctuaries or the stores of sacred objects. Their significance and their function seem to have been of a more complex nature in view of the fact that between MM and LM a change in their use took place. Nevertheless cult double axes are frequent features of cult places. With regard to the bases for double axes, the position is different. They have been discovered not only in cult places, such as Sanctuary N at Palaikastro, but also in rooms which were used for official occasions, or which were closely connected with the king. It has been suggested,[134] and rightly, that at Knossos the double axes may have become a symbol of secular authority. This is all the more likely in that the king, as the High Priest, no doubt was the god's deputy on earth. Thus the double axe base found in the Queen's Hall does not prove that this chamber was a sanctuary. Double axes and their bases are, however, rarely found in crypts.

The horns of consecration and the double axes depicted on vases had a different purpose. Generally speaking, the presence of such signs on vases does not prove that the vases were of sacred significance. True, they could have had such a significance, but to prove this, one would have to carry out rather complicated studies of the ornamentation of the vase, and the circumstances in which the vase was found, which is not always feasible. In other words, some of the vessels ornamented with sacred symbols could have been used exclusively or almost exclusively for cult practices, whereas others may have been used for this purpose only occasionally — this being a matter of chance. For it was the use to which the vessel was to be put, rather than its shape, which determined whether it would bear one of these sacred signs or not. This is especially true if the vessel was meant for water, or for a sacred fluid.

It is very important to note that apart from these vessels with sacred symbols, no other objects of a religious character were found in these two crypts. It has already been remarked that clay vessels such as these were found not only in cult places, but in secular ones as well.[135] Even if a vessel used for carrying or storing water had a sacred symbol on it, this did not necessarily mean that the vessel was used for a cult purpose alone. Some vessels were decorated with marine motifs intertwined with cult symbols, the significance of this being that it was believed a deity then looked after and blessed the contents, such as the drinking water or wine in the amphora, jug or pithos. Here a useful analogy comes to mind. It will be recalled that in early Byzantine times the mark of the Cross was stamped on the extremely popular plates which in those days were produced in enormous quantities, but this did not at all mean that a vessel stamped with this sign was a cult object used in a sanctuary, although food (e.g. bread) eaten at home off such a vessel did have a symbolical association. Yet double axes on vases have been found in only three crypts: the House of the Frescoes at Knossos, House A at Prasa, and House B at Pseira.

Particular importance has been attached to the basins found in the crypts, which were thought to have served in the cult rites. Such basins, however, have been found in only two crypts. The basin discovered at Zakro has already been discussed above, while that discovered in a crypt in the Room of the Lotus Lamp at Knossos bears no direct indication that it was used for a sacred purpose.

The inverted small clay cups covering little heaps of plant remains are intriguing. The discovery of 200 of these little handleless cups, arranged in even rows, in House B at Gypsades must have been very exciting for the excavators who came across them, especially as they were discovered in 1900 at the very beginning of Minoan archaeology. At that time the only possible explanation seemed to be that these had some religious significance. But apart from the cups, there were no other finds that could have suggested at least a hope as to the sanctity of this room, or even of the whole house. Our doubts as to the cult purpose of this crypt are strengthened still further by the fact that upturned cups were also found in House A at Zakro, but in this case they lay near pithoi stored in a magazine. The whole of House A, or at least that part of it which has survived, was a domestic building only. On this evidence, then, we are led to believe that the inverted cups were connected with some practical, everyday purpose.[136]

The inverted cups, however, may possibly have been used for sacred purposes in certain circumstance. As votive cups they have been found in certain grottoes (e.g. at Psychro). See also the finds that came to light near an altar at Heraion on Samos (see p. 210). At Archanes,[137] excavations yielded a rectangular house on the edge of the cemetery there. It was used not only as a dwelling, but for sacred rites as well. It had a wine-press,[138] while in one of the other rooms there were many small cups which according to J. Sakellarakis[139] were left over from cult rituals. On the other hand, it cannot be said that cups (or inverted cups) were used solely for religious practices. For at Akrotiri, on Thera,[140] handleless cups were discovered in a number of different rooms which were certainly used for domestic purposes. The position seems to be that these cups were so simple in form, as vessels for drinking out of and other purposes, that it is most likely they were used also for liquid offerings and for magic rites.

It has been argued that the ashes and other traces of fire discovered in several crypts were of special, that is, religious significance. But the evidence is far from conclusive. The traces of a burnt layer that were discovered at Nirou Chani, for example, may have been left from cooking.

Finally, a discovery of exceptional importance is that of the Neolithic stone axes made in a crypt at Sklavokambos. But surely it is possible that these ancient objects were used simply as ordinary tools?

In determining whether or not a crypt had been used for a sacred purpose, one of the factors taken into consideration was the nature of the objects found in the neighbouring rooms which may, along with the crypt, have formed a single entity. It is known for certain that several basement rooms could be entered only through the crypt. But the objects dug up in these innermost chambers next to the crypts provide only few indications of sacred function.

The bronze figurines thought to have been votive offerings were similar to those discovered in ordinary living quarters. In any case, the only places where these figurines were found is the room next to Crypt 17 at A. Triada, and the Crypt at Tylissos — the figurine from the upper room. Neither the bronze tools nor the Linear A tablets found in such rooms can be cited as conclusive evidence that the crypts were holy places, since both types of find are particularly characteristic of secular buildings.

A study of the crypts and their contents leads, then, to a number of conclusions. Some of the rooms which, everything suggests, were sacred ones, may have been discussed together with the domestic sanctuaries. Others which have been termed sacred seem rather to have been store-rooms or dwelling rooms. Many of them still remain enigmatic. Definition of the function of the crypts of the Central Palace Complex at Knossos, for instance, depends on which general concept we accept as regards the character of the west part of the palace. While stating our doubts as to previous interpretations of the crypts, we should like at the same time to point out the weakness of the material evidence that formed the basis of one of the most important conceptions that have affected our views on the history of Minoan civilisation.

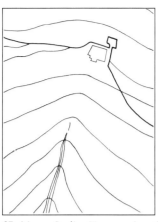

27. Mavro Spelio. Topography of the cave. BSA 28, 1926/7, 244 Fig. 1.

28. Mavro Spelio. Plan of the cave. BSA 28, 1926/7, 249 Fig. 3.

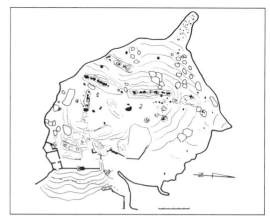

29. Ayia Sophia. Plan of the cave. E. Platakis, in: Tyree, Pl. 38.

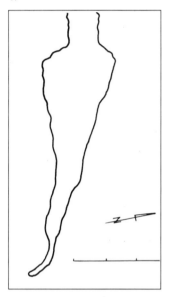

30. Arkalochori. Plan of the cave. BSA 19, 1912/3, Fig. 1.

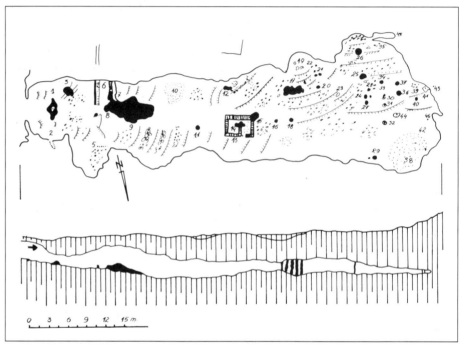

31. Amnissos. The Cave of Eileithyia. Plan and section of the cave. Kretika Protochronia 5, 1965, Fig. 1.

32. Amnissos. Entrance to the Cave of Eileithyia.

33. Arkalochori. Cave. What remains of the cave.

IV
The Caves in Crete

FOR VARIOUS reasons only a small number of the caves were regarded by the pilgrims as cult places. The most important reasons which made people look upon the caves as holy places may be mentioned here. First, the Minoans were awed by the mysterious appearance of the interior, by the fantastic shapes of the stalagmites and stalactites, and by the miraculous properties of the pure water which collected in the hollows in the rock. The effect made on people's minds by this suggestive atmosphere was made more potent still by the almost complete darkness that prevailed in most of the caves, for very few of the cult grottoes were lit partly or totally by daylight coming in from the entrance. The impression created by the damp walls, the dropping of water, and the unusual shapes of the stalactites and stalagmites, all in the flickering light of a lamp or a torch, must have been powerful. By the very nature of things the cave interiors do not lend themselves to strict classification. Nevertheless it may be said that there are three basic groups of grottoes. In one we have the rock shelters, another consists of grottoes with uncomplicated interiors that all look very much the same; and the third is comprised of great caves with many chambers and with side passages that are sometimes as complicated as labyrinths.

To illustrate the first group, we may mention the Hermes Grotto at Patsos,[1] which is 9.3 m deep, with a high entrance 18.00 m wide. Another shelter may be found at Mavro Spilio near Knossos.[2] Originally it was the outlet of a spring that here flowed out from the depths of the limestone rocks (Figs. 27,28). In its present shape, the cave consists of two parts: one is a stone structure on the outside, while the other, natural formation, is a small niche, about 2 m deep, with a long depression alongside the channel formed in the rock by the water. The A. Sophia Grotto,[3] near Topolia in western Crete, is a very large rock shelter (Fig. 29). Its dimensions are imposing: 80 m × 80 m, and it consists of two parts. The lower part further in is screened from the rest of the cave by five rows of imposing stalagmites.

There are numerous caves whose interiors are relatively uncomplicated. Some of them may be mentioned here. The front part of the cave of Eileithyia at Amnissos is lit by daylight (Figs. 31,32.[4] This low-ceilinged cave slopes almost imperceptibly towards the west; the floor is uneven, with the exception of the end part of the grotto. There is a pair of stalagmites in the middle of the main chamber, and to the west of this, a passage leads to three inner cavities, one of which consists of a lower and an upper storey. Through a very narrow passage one can enter a low, long chamber. To take another example, in the case of the cave at Arkalochori there was a low entrance 1.50 m wide and only 0.60 m high. Further in, the ceiling of the cave rose to a height of 1 m. Hazzidakis[5] excavated part of the cave and found that it narrowed steadily, in the end being reduced to no more than 2 m in width. The next part of the cave, which was explored next by Marinatos,[6] was also low-ceilinged. In Graeco-Roman times the rock collapsed and divided the cave into three parts. It is thought, however, that in Minoan times, too, the cave was very low, and that it then formed a single whole measuring about 30 × 10 m (Figs. 30,33). Inside this cave stalactites were formed. An elongated shape, and the absence of any important branches, is characteristic of the A. Paraskevis Cave at Skotino.[7] This is one of the most significant cult caves in Crete. Its length, at its maximum, is approximately 160 m. Four chambers may be distinguished in this cave: a narrow entrance passage leads into the first chamber, which is a large one 94 m long, 36 m wide, and about 50 m high. This chamber has good daylight lighting. In the centre of the chamber there are massive calcareous formations. Lower down there is a smaller chamber, 24.00 m long and 2.50 m high, which a weak light still penetrates. From there one enters a small chamber with many straight branches leading off it

34. Skotino. Entrance to the cave.

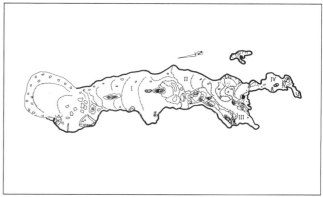

35. Skotino. Plan of the cave. DESE 1970, Fig. on p. 62.

(Figs. 34,35), and 4 m lower still is the fourth chamber, which is almost perfectly round (12.00 m × 12.50m). There are interesting stalagmites and concretions in the first and second chambers, and draperies in the third and fourth. The second chamber was probably the most important of the four, for the remains of sacrifices and votive offerings, including three Minoan figurines,[8] were discovered near a natural altar, at a depth of 20 cm. The entrance to the Kamares cave (Figs. 36,37)[9] is 33 m wide and 18-20 m high. It consists of two chambers, the main one, and an inner, smaller extension. The bottom of the cave slopes gently down towards the back and side. Daylight penetrates even the furthest reaches of the grotto. Great blocks of stone lie against the wall on the left. Through a narrow passage it is possible to squeeze one's way into an inner cave which is like a long chimney. The floor of this inner cave is strewn with tiny stones brought from outside. No stalagmites or stalactites were formed in the large chamber, solely in the smaller one. The A. Phaneromeni Cave[10] near Avdou also belongs to this group. It is 70 m long, and at its widest point measures 10 m (Fig. 38). The cave consists of two parts: a vestibule, and a damp inner chamber. Inside the cave, the stalagmites look like a forest of needles. One can squeeze past them into the further part of the cave.

In western Crete, on Akrotiri Promontory, there is another grotto called 'Arkoudia' or the Cave of Panagia.[11] It has two chambers (Fig. 40). Daylight penetrates the main one, which is 30 m long. In the middle of this chamber is the most interesting feature — a large stalagmite resembling a bear or a dog. The other chamber is much smaller.

The grottoes in the third group, that is, those with more complicated interiors, with many branches off, also constitute characteristic cult places. The grotto at Psychro[12] is a double one, consisting of an upper and a lower chamber. No doubt at one time the upper part (Figs. 39,41) was dark. The floor is comparatively flat, and inclines gently inwards. No stalactites or stalagmites have been observed in this part. The upper chamber is relatively flat, and inclines gently inwards. No stalactites or stalagmites have been observed in this part. The upper chamber is relatively dry. In the next lower chamber, this part of the grotto is dark and damp, and the presence of a large number of stalactites and stalagmites make a splendid impression. This cave is one of the biggest of the cult grottoes in Crete. The Idaean Cave[13] has a wide entrance which lets daylight into the front part of the cave (Fig. 44). Apart from the two principal chambers — one of which measures 20 m × 7 m — there is also a side branch and an upper chamber (Fig. 42). The latter can be reached only with the help of a ladder. As regards the interior, the cave at Melidoni[14] is one of the most picturesque of all (Fig. 43). The grotto consists of three main chambers. From a broad entrance a steep passage leads to the first chamber, which is 40 × 50 m wide with a height of 10-25 m. Daylight penetrates the greater part of this first chamber. The next parts of the cave (Chambers II and III) are long, completely dark passages. Chamber II, which measures 32 × 6 m, is on several levels, and there is a tiny hall in it, at a depth of 12 m. Chamber III, which is 85 m long and 10-15 m wide, is damp. It has four levels, the last of which opens out into a little hall 7 m × 14 m. This cave is famous for its fine stalactites. The cave at Chosto Nero,[15] on the slopes of Jouktas, has an entrance 2.70 m high and 1.80 m wide (Fig. 45). This is one of the dampest caves. From the entrance, where there are four boulders, one passes along a narrow corridor (10 m long) and enters a small room on the right (6 × 2 m). The middle chamber is wider. On the left the corridor forks out into

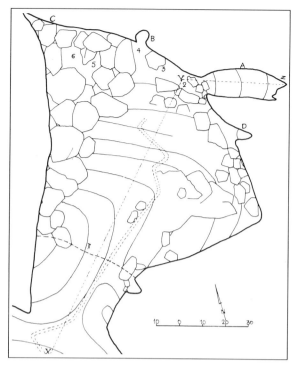

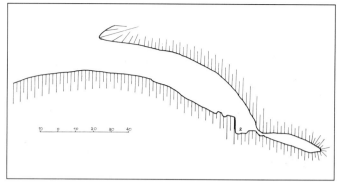

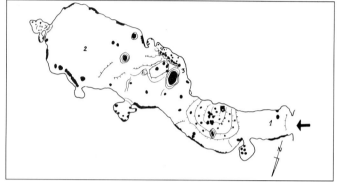

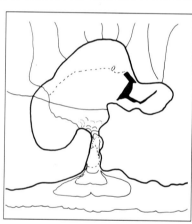

36. *(top left)* Kamares. Plan of the cave. BSA 19, 1912/3, Plan 3.

37. *(far top right)* Kamares. Section of the cave. BSA 19, 1912/3, Pl. 3.

38. *(top right)* A. Phaneromeni. Plan of the cave. E. Platakis, in: Tyree, Pl. 1.

39. *(centre left)* Psychro. Entrance to the cave.

40. *(centre middle)* Arkoudia. Plan of the cave. AD 22, 1967, 496 Fig. 1.

41. *(centre right)* Psychro. Plan of the cave. BSA 6, 1899/1900, Pl. 8.

42. *(left)* Ida. Plan of the Upper Chamber. E. Platakis, To Idaion Antron (1965), Pl. 3.

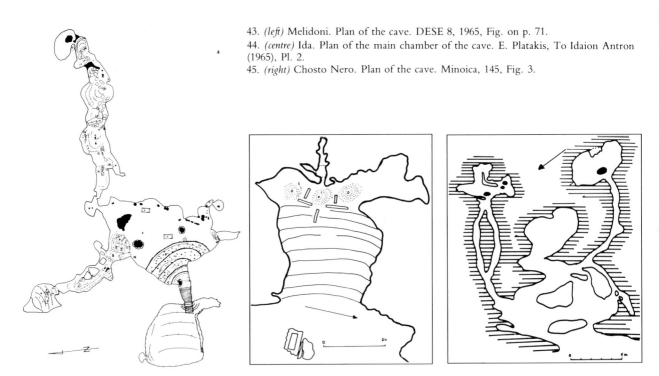

two galleries, one at a higher level than the other. Six metres further on these galleries join and give access to a tiny chamber 1.20 m high. On the slopes of Jouktas, at Stravomyti[16] there is another cave, this time with five entrances. This cave consists of an upper and a lower chamber connected by a narrow passage. Through several narrow, winding galleries one can descend to a depth of 40-50 m (Fig. 48).

The cave at Kera Spiliotissa (Kydonias) with seven chambers (Fig. 46) inclines inwards. The main chamber is connected by corridors and shafts to smaller rooms (cf. below, p. 69). Another cave also is situated close to Chania, namely the cave Mameloukou Trypa. There are seven chambers (Fig. 47) in a labyrinthine system (cf. below. p. 70).

As has been said before, the stalactites and stalagmites as well as other rocks must have been one of the most important features of the caves that made the people of ancient times attribute a sacred character to them. These concretions are to be found in practically every cave. They

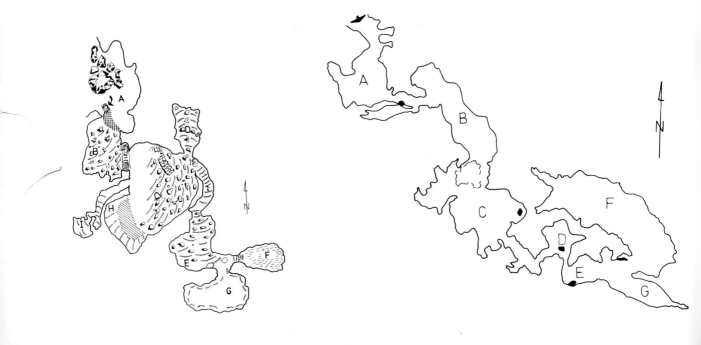

assumed fantastic shapes, and sometimes even resembled human beings or animals. The pilgrims who visited the grottoes occasionally fashioned the rocks to give them a more desirable shape, and in Christian times some of the stalagmites were cut down and destroyed by axes. But in ancient times the stalactites and stalagmites which nature herself had formed into the shape of humans and animals were looked upon as miraculous, and were worshipped like idols. This supposition is corroborated by the fact that rocks shaped like human beings have also been found in the domestic sanctuary in the Little Palace at Knossos (see below p. 138), and in the tholos tomb at Apesokari, where they must have been used as cult idols; see p. 23. There are other examples, too, of fragments of stalagmites having been brought into the Minoan houses.[17] So properties must have been attributed to them. In other Mediterranean cultures, too, stalactites and stalagmites were often brought into the homes. At Çatal-Hüyük[18] one of the statuettes, representing an old goddess, was made of a piece of stalagmite which someone had roughly fashioned to give it human form. Bits of stalactites were also found in one of the sanctuaries.[19] In the seventh millennium B.C. these were no doubt believed to have magic properties. This all goes to prove that some of the stalagmites and stalactites, and other concretions in the caves as well, were regarded as cult images. On the lengthwise axis of the cave at Amnissos,[20] about three metres from the entrance, the rocks form an oval elevation 0.78 m high and 2.20 m wide at the base. It is thought that the ancient Cretans may have regarded this 'mound' as a belly with a well-marked navel (omphalos). The stone referred to here is as smooth as marble, in contrast to the nearby limestone rocks which are very uneven in surface. Six metres further west there is a rock 1.10 m high resembling a female figure; the head has been cut off with the blow of an axe. This rock is surrounded by an ancient wall, forming a rectangle (4 × 3 m), buttressed on the south side. In the middle of the cave, 18 m from the 'woman's figure', there is a stalagmite 1.40 m high and 1.17 m in circumference. This is encircled by a stone wall 0.45 m high, whose horizontal dimensions are 4.30 and 3.00 m. The upper part of this stalagmite has been deliberately cut off, but the discerning eye can still make out the legs and abdomen of a woman. The pilgrims who visited this cave must have believed that this stalagmite had miraculous powers. For it has obviously been smoothed and rubbed by many fingers. Nearby there is another stalagmite of the same height. It is attached to the west wall of the peribolos, dated probably to the Minoan period. These were not the only cult stalagmites in this grotto. For 48 m from the entrance there was another large stalagmite 4.8 m high, also shaped like a female figure and also with the upper part cut off. Not far from this latter stalagmite there was another shaped like a column.

It is not only the scholars of modern times who see a resemblance between these stalagmites and figures of humans or animals. For local country people, too, frequently told travellers that the stalagmites in the caves were like men or animals. No doubt the ancient Cretans were fully

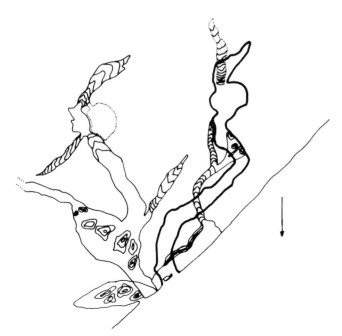

46. *(far left)* Kera Spiliotissa. Plan of the cave. DESE 1967, Fig. on p. 63.
47. *(left)* Mameloukou Trypa. Plan of the cave. PAE 1968, 135 Fig. 1.
48. *(this page)* Stavomyti. Plan of the cave. PAE 1950, Fig. 1 facing p. 252.

aware of this similarity. In the cave of Panagias mentioned above, which the country folk also call the Arkoudias or 'She-Bear', there is a large stalagmite which has a striking resemblance to a bear. This was already noted by travellers in the nineteenth century (e.g. Pashley, 1837). In the important cave at Skotino (see p. 71) in the first chamber there is a big pile of travertine rock which may have played an important part in the cult. This pile is situated along the axis leading in from the entrance. It looks like a bear or a dog. Another, which has the appearance of a four-legged creature, has the eyes indicated by vertical incisions. On each of the side walls the surface rocks are so shaped that they clearly call to mind various groups of human beings, consisting of a child, a woman and other figures. Evans and Pendlebury carried out excavations near this spot. They came across the ashes of sacrificial pyres, and also many potsherds dating from MM and LM. The fact that sacrifices were made as far back as MM proves that at least from that time onwards the pilgrims believed in the miraculous qualities of these concretions. Nature has also given the profile of another rock the shape of a woman's face. Still another rock in the vicinity resembles a man's face.

In the upper grotto at Psychro[21] there are neither stalagmites nor stalactites. One concretion, which is altogether black, shows traces of having been fashioned by some implement and has a likeness to both human and animal shapes. In a straight line leading in from the entrance there is a limestone rock which bears some resemblance to a bull's head. In the lower grotto — in contrast to the upper one — there are numerous stalagmites and stalactites. Apart from a group of stalagmites which give the appearance of holding up the roof of the cave, there is also a hollow filled with water. In Antiquity many votive objects, such as bronze double axes, as well as bronze pins and knives, were imbedded in the stalactite pillars. In all likelihood the pilgrims believed that such stalactites had miraculous properties. In the cave at Melidoni[22] a large number of stalactites had similarly been formed. At the entrance to the first chamber there is a passage with stalactites resembling human heads or hair. In the first chamber itself there are great stalactites shaped like double horns, while one stalagmite resembles a woman with a child. One stalagmite in the first chamber is like a low column, and should have been regarded as sacred (Fig. 49). In the cave at Chosto Nero[23] there is a small, dark chamber (Fig. 45) with three not very large natural limestone smoked pillars (0.50 m high) that look like human torsos. A passage on the left leads into another small chamber which has concretions resembling human shapes. Fragments of pottery dating from MM were found here. Coming now to the cave at Patsos,[24] a concretion shaped like an animal head, and darkened by damp, was discovered 6 m from the entrance. Nearby numerous objects were discovered, the earliest ones dating from LM I.

One of the most beautiful caves on Crete is the Leras[25] grotto near Chania. When we penetrate to the end of the cave (about 37.5 m from the entrance) the floor slopes downwards then leads upwards again. The stalagmites in this grotto may have been regarded as cult images. One of these stalagmites resembles a group of draped figures standing between columns. In western Crete there are other stalagmite grottoes as well. One known as the Korakies Trypa cave,[26] for instance, has a single stalagmite that looks like a baetyl. A passage leads precipitously down into a small chamber on the floor of which there is a stalagmite shaped like a human figure with a cap on his head. The Vigla (Keraton) grotto[27] near Keratokambos is a very damp cave. One of the stalagmites there looks like a mother and child. In another cave discovered not far from Kanli Kastelli (Vitsiles)[28] there is a rock shaped like a giant's face. Then there is, again, a whole forest of stalactite needles in the grotto of A. Phaneromeni[29] in the biggest chamber there. One group of stalactites here looks like double horns, while another suggests a female figure in a sitting position. The stalactites and stalagmites in the depths of the cave at Trapeza (near Tylissos[30] are of the most fantastic shapes.

Apart from the stalactites and stalagmites and other rock concretions, the pools of water found in most of the sacred caves played a very important part in the cult. The qualities admired in water must have been not only its medicinal properties but also its cool, steady temperature. In the cave at Psychro beyond the group of rock concretion that seem to be supporting the roof, towards the back of the lower chamber there is a large lake of pure water whose temperature when measured (on 7 May 1955) was 7°C.[31] The size of this lake varies from one season of the year to another, but at its maximum its dimenxions are 20 × 12 m. It dries up almost completely towards the end of September. A large number of votive offerings, such as several bronze figurines, sealstones, many ordinary bronze rings, pins and knives, were found on the marshy bottom of the lake, near the shore. The water must have been

49. Melidoni Cave. Stalagmite in Chamber I.

regarded as having miraculous qualities, and the lake itself must have been considered a holy place, for in ancient times no-one ever went beyond the lake. The grotto stretches well beyond the lake but no finds have ever been found there. In the first chamber of the grotto at Skotino, not far from the great heap of travertine blocks which were described above, water oozes down the right-hand wall of the grotto, and collects in the hollows at the bottom. It is very difficult to get into the lowest part of this grotto. But there, too, there is a hollow in which water has collected — water which also must have been regarded as having miraculous qualities. As one penetrates into the depths of the Eileithyia cave at Amnissos one reaches the rear part of the cave. Water has collected in the hollows of that part of the cave. In six of them the water is dirty, and in two of them it is pure. It is certain that miraculous powers were attributed to the water here. Chemical analysis has shown that this water was drinkable, but had no special qualities, apart perhaps from the fact that if drunk in large quantities it could have had a laxative effect.[32] In the grotto at Tsoutsouros[33] there is a pool of fresh water which is slightly chlorinated. The water here, too, was held to have miraculous properties. In the Kamares cave as well, water has collected in a small chamber at the back of the cave. At this same spot there were also stalactites, as has been described above. The cave at Melidoni[34] also has a pool. The water in the first chamber is drinkable. Pure water has collected in the second and third chamber of the Leras grotto. The cave at Chosto Nero has a small chamber in which supposedly miraculous water has collected, but entry into this chamber is exceptionally difficult. To get into it one has to go along a long passage with two galleries. In the Patsos cave there is a pool at the very entrance.[35] Further in there is another pool where the water is always of the same temperature. In the case of the cave at Trapeza, near Tylissos, water has collected in a hollow situated not far from the cave entrance.[36] The light from outdoors comes in as far as this spot. The tis Arkoudias grotto has a very important pool which is situated in the middle of the first chamber (30 m in length). A wall has been built around this pool in recent years, for the local people noticed that the water there had special powers.[37] In other caves, such as those at Stravomyti[38] and Phaneromeni,[39] pools of water have been noted too.

Water must have been of special, and even fundamental significance, but contrary to various assertions, it was not the only factor which determined whether a cave was a cult place or not. The fact that water had collected in a cave did not necessarily mean that the cave was a cult place. In order to be a cult place, a grotto had to have all the features mentioned above. It should be remembered that the sacred caves were sometimes very damp. Some of them were unsuitable for use as permanent dwellings not only because of their humidity but also because of their cold temperature, in addition to the fact that sometimes they were snowed up for the whole winter.

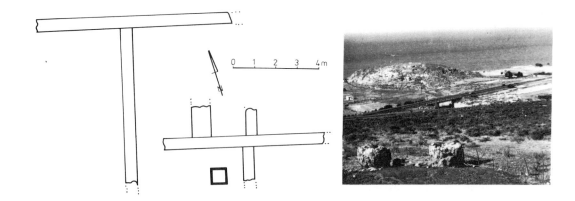

When the configuration of the terrain allowed, the open spaces in the immediate vicinity of the caves were also used for sacred rites. Very often near grottoes there were little dells or open meadows, or gentle rocky slopes where the faithful were wont to gather for cult rites, dances or feasts. This was the case, for instance, at the Eileithyia Cave at Amnissos. The entrance to the cave is on a gentle hill-slope where Marinatos[40] discovered the remains of a rectangular building (Fig. 50), which he called 'the priest's private residence'. Excavations produced few objects, however. The finds consisted mainly of LM III and Geometric sherds and a lead ox figurine, suggesting that the building was used in the aforesaid two periods. We do not know for certain, however, what the building was used for. It may even have been the Eileithyia temple mentioned by Strabo.[41] A little farther west there is a circular area known as the 'plateia ton vomon' (Fig. 51), see p. 68. Sometimes in front of other grottoes there are hollows in the ground, or small terraces. Several instances may be cited here. At Arkalochori, for example, the space directly in front of the cave is small and narrow, but on the hillside above the cave, below the chapel recently built there, is a wider space which would have been convenient for the performance of rituals. At Asphendi Christou there is a circular area measuring about 10 m in diameter, while at Melidoni there is an almost circular depression in front of the cave. At Skotino a depression in the ground before the grotto, as well as the area nearby, may have been used in religious rites. Some other grottoes, on the other hand, were situated on steep hillsides — as at Kamares or Ayia Sophia.

The interiors of the grottoes were so weirdly fashioned by nature that special cult constructions were not really necessary. When walls were erected their sole or almost sole significance lay in the fact that they were built round the cult objects. Stone walls were built around the cult idols fashioned by nature, stone altars were erected, and stone partitions were made, separating the most holy spot from the rest of the grotto.

Few altars have been found in the caves. A small one (Fig. 41) was discovered in a depression in the north-west part of the cave at Psychro,[42] and near this altar diggings revealed four or five layers dating from at least the EM period up to the Middle Ages. The floor of the second chamber of the Idaean cave[43] was covered with a thick layer of ash and charcoal, among which burnt animal bones, several skulls of horned cattle, and a large number of clay lamps were found — dating from later times than the Minoan period. Not very long ago a wall dated to LM III, which may have been part of an altar, was excavated in this part of the cave.[44] In the report of excavations at Arkalochori, mention is made of a small altar, but no details are given as to its location or precise appearance.[45] Taramelli's statement that he found a hearth — or perhaps an altar — in the Kamares cave must be treated with some scepticism. He wrote that inside the cave he found walls made of roughly hewn uncemented limestone rocks, and that these walls formed part of a hearth.[46] Yet a dozen or so years later Dawkins was unable to find the walls described by Taramelli. Dawkins merely reported that at spot 4 he had indeed found the remains of a wall constructed from unhewn stones uncemented together, but these remains were so sparse that they could not be interpreted as suggesting any particular kind of construction, and so he did not mark them on the plan of the cave (Fig. 36).[47] On the other hand in the first chamber of the cave at Skotino, near the travertine blocks which looked like various figures, a large amount of ash was found, which may have come from an altar fire. A large quantity of fragments of Minoan pottery was also found at this same spot. At another place, near a rock 1.80 m high which was used as an altar, a layer of ash was found, mixed with

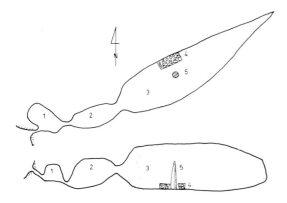

50. Amnissos. Building close to the cave. PAE 1929, 102 Fig. 8.

51. Amnissos. Square of the Altars. In the background Paliochora Hill.

52. Klisidi Cave. Plan and section. AAA 9, 1976, 167 Fig. 1.

the bones of animals (such as sheep, etc.), as well as with stones and with relics which have been dated to the period MM I and later periods as well.[48]

Rocks were also adapted for use as altars. At the entrance to the Idaean cave, on the south side, one's attention is drawn to a great block of rock shaped like an altar (dimensions: 2.80 × 1.95 × 0.88 m) with a high step all round (Fig. 44). Behind it there are large fragments of rock with cracks, into which the pilgrims put their votive offerings.[49] It is not certain, however, whether this natural altar was already in use in Minoan times. Close to the entrance to the cave at Patsos,[50] there is a small, rather flat area measuring 30 × 6 m. Several blocks of stone lie in this area; one of them (measuring 2.50 × 1.50 m) may have been an altar. In front of the Eileithyia cave at Amnissos mentioned above there is a fairly large meadow about 30 m in diameter, which is called the 'square of the altars'. Large blocks of rock more than 1 m high, may have been used as altars. Near these large stone blocks there are also small stones with hollows in them, which may have served as altars as also may a rock in one of the niches in the Spilios (Milatos) cave[51] and a rock in the Vigla cave.[52] Finally, in the Klisidi Grotto[53] (Fig. 52) there is a stone shelf 2.50 by 1.00 m, near a solitary stalagmite, which may have been used as an altar.

Apart from the votive offerings which were brought to the altars, or thrown into the dying embers of the fire, many votive offerings were put as near to the deity as possible, where they could easily be reached: that is in the fissures and cracks of the rocks. In the Kamares cave[54] the biggest number of finds come from areas 2-6 (Fig. 36), where a large quantity of pottery dating from MM was found, along with black earth, under large stones. Areas 2 and 3 were particularly rich in finds. The area marked by these numbers formed a kind of vestibule to the inner grotto. On the left it was bounded by a wall of rock, and on the right by great stones. Areas 5 and 6 were completely dark, being cut off from the rest of the cave by great blocks of rock. Between 6 and C there was a deep fissure, which although low in height penetrated deep into the rock. It contained a large amount of pottery. Clay vessels were found everywhere, but under the great blocks of rock they were found only in spots where they could be pushed or thrown. It is supposed that these vessels contained grain, for in one part of the cave even quite considerable remains of wheat or some other cereal were found. In the lower grotto at Psychro[55] a large number of votive offerings were discovered in the fissures between the blocks of rock. These offerings consisted of bronze figurines, pins and knives. Many votive objects such as bronze double axes, pins, knives, etc. were embedded in the stalactite pillars.

Presumably votive offerings were suspended on the boughs of trees as well. True, we have no direct evidence that this was the custom in Minoan times but it is known that in a later period pilgrims hung various votive offerings on the branches of a poplar that grew at the entrance to the Idaean cave.[56] So it is possible the practice had been already established in Minoan times.

Now we come to the question of what kind of votive offerings were brought to the caves. Probably the most common usage was for the people to bring the deity agricultural products, which they carried in pottery vessels. These vessels were usually everyday ones, and sometimes they were decorated. It has already been remarked that grains of cereal were found in the Kamares cave. Probably at certain times domestic animals, too, were sacrificed to the gods, and perhaps even wild game. We have some evidence about the kind of animals that were sacrificed. In the upper grotto at Psychro, for instance, potsherds and animal bones were found along with charcoal amid the ashes of an altar in layer IV, at a depth of about 1.60 m. One bit of pottery was covered with part of a stalagmite; the vessel in question here had been made on a potter's wheel, which may suggest that the layer containing animal bones should be dated to MM or to MM-LM. The zoologists have identified bones of the following species: the domestic ox (*bos domesticus creticus*), the wild goat, and probably the domesticated goat as well (*capra aegagrus*), sheep (*ovis aries*), deer (*cervus dama*), and the domestic pig. Three boar skulls (*sus scrofa*) were also found in this layer.[57]

In three comparatively well investigated caves, the only or nearly the only finds consisted of clay vessels dating from MM and LM. Probably the vessels in these caves are all that is left of the sacrifices that were made. In the Kamares cave no finds were made just beside the entrance (Fig. 36), with the exception of niche E, where there were potsherds dating from MM lying at the very bottom of a layer of black earth. At the spot marked 1 on the plan pottery dating from MM III-LM I was unearthed. The floor of the cave falls steeply on the left, and it was there that most of the pottery from MM was found. The greatest amount of pottery was discovered in niches 2 and 6. In the northern part of the cave there are small fissures into which one can crawl, but only with difficulty. One of these fissures (A) is actually very wide, but the entrance has been blocked by boulders with the result that there is only a narrow passage left to crawl through. It is in this offshoot of the grotto that Taramelli is said to have found pottery, dating from EM, in the A. Onouphrios style.[58] The finds in this grotto consisted chiefly of pottery vessels — undecorated ones. An exception was a piece of a bowl whose edge was adorned with a bull's head in relief — vessels such as this must have had some function in the cult rites. We also have three clay figurines representing oxen and a pig, bought by Mariani.[59] But as we have said, the pottery was mostly undecorated domestic and storage ware, only fragments of which have survived. Painted and decorated vessels constitute only a small percentage of the finds. The vessels are quite diversified. They were mostly footless jars with two handles and an open spout. The most common forms among the undecorated pottery were lids, jugs, and small pithoi, with plates, little jugs and shallow bowls coming next in frequency.[60]

In another grotto — the Eileithyia cave at Amnissos — again the finds consisted almost entirely of pottery vessels. A great deal of misunderstanding has grown up around the evaluation of the pottery found in this cave, and around the history of the cult practices there. In 1929 Marinatos[61] wrote that comparatively few fragments of MM vessels, that is vessels covered with black wash and white paint, had been discovered in the cave. 'Among the cleaned sherds,' he reported, 'there were no polychrome fragments.' In February 1980 the present author began a close study of material from this cave. He had access to the potsherds exhibited in Room I of the Archaeological Museum at Ieraklion, as well as to sherds belonging to the museum's scientific collection. In addition, he was permitted to examine the pottery in the six boxes (mentioned by Marinatos in 1929), which were stored in the Museum's East Magazine. The pottery fragments in these boxes were very dirty, which suggests they had never been cleaned. Hence it is likely that the aforesaid remarks by Marinatos were based on an examination of a selection of the material — which was subsequently apportioned partly to the scientific collection, partly to the showcases in Room I of the Archaeological Museum and partly thrown back to the boxes — and on a general perusal of all the discovered material, which, it was intended, would be cleaned later. It may justifiably be conjectured that Marinatos, who regarded the Eileithyia cave as one of the most important archaeological sites in Crete, planned at some future date to make a careful study of all the material but in his first report he recorded only the first general impressions he had formed during the field work and he never did manage to make a detailed study of the material. So it was the conclusions Marinatos published in 1929 that became the foundation on which the historians of religion have based their reasoning, in particular, their view that this cave was of no significance in the MM and LM I-II periods. One scholar maintained that only 'a few fragments of jugs and bowls dating from LM III'[62] had been found in the cave, which, he probably thought, meant that the Eileithyia Cave was visited sporadically in that period.

This was the sum total of what was known when the author started a detailed study of the material from the cave. In February 1980 he gave the material a preliminary cleaning. Then, at his request, the Museum had the sherds washed, and he examined them in the autumn of 1980. This examination of the material from the Eileithyia cave is not yet finished. Nevertheless it is already clear that there is more MM and LM pottery than was at first thought. The material includes classical Kamares ware, for example a fragment of a handle of a pithos or jug. There

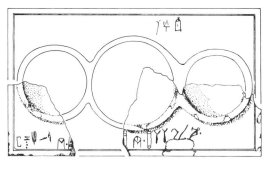
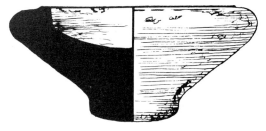
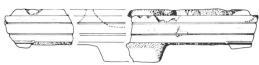

53. Psychro Cave. Offering table. Boardmann, CC, Fig. 28.

54. Psychro Cave. Stone bowl or lamp. Boardman, CC, Fig. 29 No. 271.

was little Kamares ware found here, although it should be borne in mind that even in the Kamares cave itself the vases decorated in this style were few in number. All in all, then, it can be suggested tentatively that the Eileithyia cave at Amnissos was used for cult purposes in the MM and LM Periods. And finally, when we come to the next grotto, at Stravomyti,[63] which has been more thoroughly explored, the earliest finds — consisting of pottery and of objects made of obsidian and animal bones — date from the Neolithic. From MM and up to LM III we have 10-15 large pithoi which no doubt were used for storing grain. Other pottery was found as well — votive offerings consisting of painted bowls with handles, dated to LM III.

About another group of sacred caves contained not only pottery but also other votive offerings. There are eight caves in this group. The upper grotto at Psychro was rich in finds. Near a small altar construction there, Hogarth unearthed four, or rather five layers.[64] A large number of bones were discovered in sedimentary yellow clay which in its upper part was mixed with a small quantity of blackish pottery in the deepest layer (V) at the very bottom of the grotto. Stones polished by water were found under this layer. Layer IV, consisting of black earth mixed with ash and bones and containing pottery, reaches a thickness of about 1.60 m. Kamares ware and stone sacrificial tables were the most valuable discoveries here. Bronze objects were also excavated from the lower part of this layer, about 0.30 m from layer V. Hogarth's description of the next layer (III) is not clear. But at any rate it contained pottery which, judging from his description, would seem rather to have come from the period MM III-LM I. Probably this was a mixed layer, for, apart from Kamares ware, pottery from a later period was found as well. Layer II produced pottery that doubtless came from LM III, as well as bronze artefacts and undecorated clay vessels. Layer I contained objects dating from the Geometric period up to the Middle Ages. In the south-east section of the upper grotto, black earth, in which there was no ash, was found under great boulders; objects which had been preserved almost intact were discovered at this spot. In the lower grotto, too, which as a result of earth movements became closed in LM III, a great many objects were found, including bronze figurines, bronze double axes, pins and knives.

About 500 undecorated handleless cups, as well as a great deal of other pottery, were found in this cave. In addition to these pottery objects, other discoveries were: small stone offering tables (Fig. 53), of which three had inscriptions, the a stone bowl or a lamp (Fig. 54), the stone base of a double axe, votive offerings such as bronze figurines (Figs. 55,56) representing men, women, a child, animals (mainly bulls, rams, a squatting calf, birds, including a duck) and goats horns. The double axes also found were mostly not for use (Fig. 57). Only two massive ones could have been used (Fig. 58). More than 210 other blades, likewise not for use, were discovered. These were swords, daggers, knives, a chisel, a saw, a sickle with a toothed edge, spearheads and arrowheads. Weapons, e.g. MM I daggers were also brought here as offerings. Other bronze finds are also interesting, especially 80 tweezers, needles, fibulae dating from LM III, rings, earrings and bracelets. We know that lead and stone objects were found as well (e.g. figurines), in addition to pieces of clay pithoi decorated with scenes in relief. One very important find was a bronze plaque decorated with various symbols (Fig. 59).

Another cave, that at Arkalochori, produced a wealth of finds. The local country people said

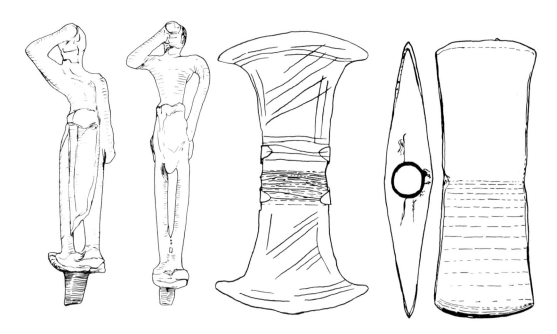

they had taken from the cave about 18 oka, that is, approximately 20 kilogrammes, of bronze objects, mainly knife blades and spearheads, as well as a few beads, which they sold as scrap. When Hazzidakis[65] conducted excavations here, he found that the votive objects were not all collected in one place, but that they were scattered as if in disorder throughout the whole cave. The amount of pottery found was relatively small. Most of it consisted of vessels in the Pyrgos style — a typical goblet on a stem, jugs, a lid, two miniature pots, and a loom-weight. Very few stone artefacts were discovered. Two water-polished stones may have been used for smoothing the pottery, while another one may have been used as a hammer. Bits of a stone lid, and of tools made of obsidian (blades and one core) should also be mentioned.

Most of the objects encountered, however, were made of metal. A piece of bronze sheet-metal may have come from an ovoid vessel. Numerous bronze blades resemble the daggers from EM times, but they were much longer (up to 0.53 m), whereas the daggers dating from the EM period were shorter. Most of these blades were very thin (approximately 1.5 mm). Only two of them were thick enough to have been used. The published reports of these excavations contain illustrations of about 50 blades, although it is very probable that more were found. There are also illustrations of 19 bronze double axes that were not used for any sort of everyday purpose. One votive axe was made of silver. The objects which the country people took from the cave had been discovered in a small area measuring 2 × 4 m. A great many of these objects, such as double axes, knives, bronze daggers, and more than a dozen little gold axes, were recovered. The decoration on the little axes seemed to indicate that they dated from the period LM II. This hoard was situated in the northern sector of the cave, on its lengthwise axis. During excavations in 1935, it was ascertained that the layer was no more than 0.50 m thick.[66] All the objects that came to light were found in two groups, one in the middle of the cave and the other further north, at the back. Marinatos and Platon found still more votive objects, made of silver and gold, in the middle part of the cave. In its northern sector, hundreds of bronze objects consisting of sacred double axes, knives and daggers, were unearthed. It was reported that objects made of precious metals, such as gold and silver double axes, miniature gold swords, and a gold bar (which Marinatos regarded as representing a holy mountain with a grotto)[67] were found lying on a small altar. In the other parts of the grotto, bronze objects (e.g. votive axes) were found thrust into the earth, or fixed onto pieces of wood.

During the excavations 26 gold double axes were discovered altogether, as well as many fragments, scores of swords made of bronze sheeting, and six silver double axes. A lump of copper (probably crude metal)[68] was discovered near a chisel. Most of the bronze objects were obviously not designed for use. Very few of them — such as some double axes — could have been used for work. One of the double axes had hieroglyphic signs carved on it, while another had a Linear A inscription. Nearly all the swords, with the exception of one, had blades which

55 and 56. (far left) Psychro Cave. Bronze figurines. Boardman, CC, Pl. 11 + Pl. 3.
57 and 58. Psychro Cave. Bronze double axes. Boardman, CC, Fig. 201 and Fig. 19 No. 198.
59. Psychro Cave. Bronze plaque. Boardman, CC, Fig. 21.

were too thin to be used in fighting. These swords (1.055 m long) are among the longest found in Crete. In 1935 Marinatos also carried out excavations and, like Hazzidakis, discovered very little pottery. Most of what was found consisted of vessels in the Pyrgos style, but not one potsherd was found from EM II-III or from early MM I. Vessels from MM III-LM I were found in greater numbers. Most of them were domestic ones.

The cave at Patsos[69] contained relics numbering several score at the very least. The decorated horns of consecration (Fig. 61) made of clay which were found here, may have crowned the altar situated inside the cave. A bronze statuette of the god Reshaf (Fig. 60), dated to LM III, was an import from Syria. One of the most intriguing finds was the clay figurine of a man embracing a woman (Fig. 62).[70] Part of a stone offering table dated to LM I was also discovered. Notable among the many other votive offerings in bronze and clay were bronze and clay figurines of worshippers (Figs. 63,64), a clay head with magic signs painted on it, and bronze figurines of a bull, a sow, a ram, a goat (Fig. 65), and a sphinx (Fig. 66). The bronze dagger blades discovered here no doubt also dated from Minoan times. The clay pots represent types characteristic of the periods LM I and LM III. Other vases from the Geometric and the Hellenistic periods were revealed, too, as well as an inscription to Hermes Kranaios.

60. Patso Cave. Reshaf figurine. Evans, TPC, Fig. 15.

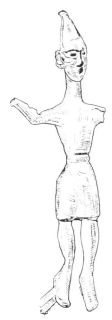

61. Patso Cave. Horns of consecration No. 1167.
62. Patso Cave. Double figurine. Boardman, CC, Fig. 34c.

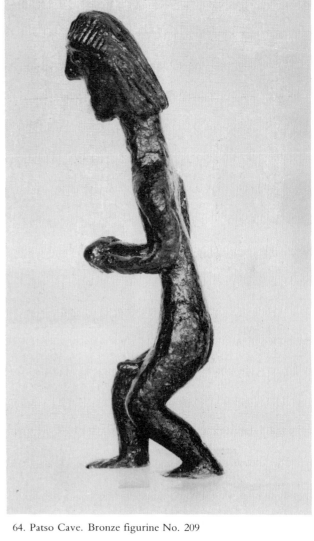

63. Patso Cave. Bronze figurine No. 208.

64. Patso Cave. Bronze figurine No. 209

65. Patso Cave. Figurine of a goat No. 236.

66. Patso Cave. Figurine of a sfinx No. 235.

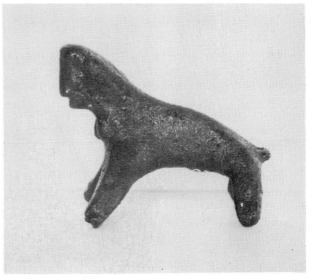

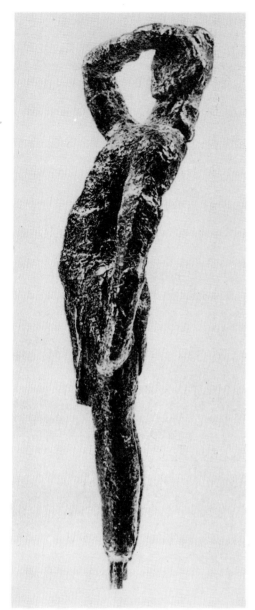

67. Skotino Cave. Bronze figurine. BCH 93, 1969, Pl. XII 1.

68. Skotino Cave. Bronze figurine. BCH 93, 1969, Pl. XII 2.

The grotto at of. A. Phaneromeni[71] at Avdou produced very few relics. Pottery, in particular, was not abundant. Three stone offering tables, three cult double axes, of which one was made of gold, may have been dated to the LM I. Only one bronze figurine can be dated to the Minoan period. The others come from later times.[72] The large cave at Skotino has so far produced very few relics. Apart from numerous potsherds from MM and LM, a single bronze axe, as well as bronze figurines, were found as far back as 1903.[73] In 1962 Davaras recovered from a trial-pit three small bronze figurines (Figs. 67,68), about 0.10-0.12 m high, representing worshippers with their right hands raised to their foreheads.[74] We also know that bronze weapons were discovered in this cave: three daggers, spearheads and various other blades made of bronze. Faure also discovered twenty bone needles as well as sea shells (one of them painted), and part of a pithos or kernos with two tiny vessels.[75]

We now come to the Idaean cave. Its apogee as a cult place was in the first half of the first millennium B.C. A large amount of the pottery found here came from LM I, but potsherds dating from LM III were discovered as well.[76] Two gems, one of which was adorned with a cult scene (see below p. 100) must be dated to LM I. Halbherr also drew attention to the fact that some ornaments, including one made of ivory, and a fragment of obsidian, come from the

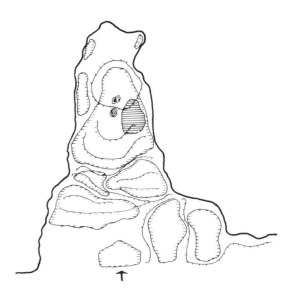

69. Asphendou. Plan of the cave. BCH 96 (1972) Fig. 11.

'Prehistoric' period.[77] A great many studies have been written on the immense number of finds that date from the first millennium B.C.[78] In Roman times there were inscriptions to Zeus.[79] A cave at Trapeza, not far from Tylissos, contained pottery and also two bronze figurines of worshippers — one probably coming from LM I, and the other from LM III.[80] Clay figurines were also found in the Chosto Nero cave in the Jouktas range.[81] The Tsoutsouros grotto produced very few finds from the Bronze Age: five seals, some clay vessels, and a small offering table probably come from LM III.[82] The later finds from this cave testify to the survival of the Minoan cult. Among these are sub-Minoan objects: bronze double axes decorated with a network in relief (No. 2511), a statuette representing a phallic adorant, with a peaked cap on his head (No. 2510), a statuette of a naked worshipper, and possibly some votive double axes made of clay. From the Geometric period come bronze models of double axes, statuettes representing erotic scenes, bronze figurines of pregnant women, etc. There are many votive offerings, too, from the seventh and sixth century B.C. Clay models — mostly dating from the seventh century — of double axes painted with black designs on a yellow ground were sometime fixed on a shaft (also of clay) and decorated with meander and palmette motifs. These axes have holes for hanging them up (No. 13335, 13336) and exhibit a distinct similarity to the Minoan objects, except that clay was used instead of metal.

Recent investigations have brought to light two small caves with decorated walls. One of them is situated close to the village of Asphendou in western Crete. The dimensions of the cave are the following: 8.50 × 3.50 × 2.50 m (Fig. 69), and the engravings were incised only at a height of 0.50 to 0.60 m from the floor. Primitive engravings (Fig. 70) depict mainly animals, weapons and abstract designs. Numerous little hollows are interspersed among the figures. S. Hood supposed it was made by 'a group or groups of hunters invoking magical or divine aid in the chase'. These engravings cover some time, as they overlap each other. Dating of these engravings is disputed. Some scholars suggest the Paleolithic and Mesolithic (that is well before 6000 B.C.), but also the Neolithic, Bronze Age and Geometric periods were suggested as a dating of the decoration of the cave (see below p. 70). The other cave at Kato Pervolakia is situated in eastern Crete. It is called Vernopheto. Contour drawings, about 1.50 m from the floor (Fig. 71) represent animals, human beings, birds and fish, etc. They were executed in different ages, and some of them probably in the LM III B period — as Faure suggested (for the results of recent investigations see below p. 71).

It can be taken as certain that these caves were visited on special festivals, probably once a year. One is led to this conclusion by the very position of many caves, and by the kind of votive objects found in them. Several caves which played a very important role in the cult were situated high up in the mountains, although on the other hand it should be remembered that many of the grottoes were easy to get to all through the year.[83]

The Kamares cave in the Psiloriti massif, at an altitude of 1524 m, could, however, only be reached at certain seasons. In the deeper parts of the cave, there is snow from November until May. Sometimes even later snow makes the deepest part of the cave impenetrable. In June 1894

Taramelli[84] still found it impossible to get into one of the small chambers because his way was blocked by snow. Sometimes, however, the cave could be penetrated earlier in the season. Dawkins,[85] for instance, who visited Kamares in April 1913, found no snow in the grotto, for spring came exceptionally early that year. The tis Voskopoulas cave, which is known as the Idaean cave, is situated at an altitude of 1,538 m in the Psiloriti range. It is very cold inside the cave; indeed it is impossible to spend the night there. The interior of the cave can only be reached in the summer months. But, as I have pointed out above, many other caves could be visited the whole year round — for example the cave at Amnissos, which is situated at an altitude of 30 m, barely 700 m from the seashore.

The nature of the votive offerings, too, tells us that the caves were only visited at certain seasons. It has already been remarked that in the Kamares cave there was a large number of small pithoi which were used for storing grain. It was also pointed out that in one section of the grotto a large amount of grain (most probably wheat) had been collected at one spot. In other caves, for instance at Stravomyti, pithoi were found too. Scholars have wondered whether these pithoi prove that cult rites were performed in the cave. Some have taken the view that because a dozen or so pithoi were found here, this part of the cave was used as the storeroom of a sacred society in LM I.[86] Yet these capacious vessels probably indicate nothing more than that the grain offerings brought to the deity were offered or stored in large vessels.

It may be concluded, then, that the pilgrimages to the cult caves took place at great festival times. The pilgrims must have come after the harvest, that is in early autumn, to some caves, such as that at Kamares where a harvest deity was undoubtedly worshipped as we can see from the offerings in the form of grain. To the other caves, pilgrimages were no doubt made in the autumn or early winter. For the above reasons one can only partly agree with the assertion[87] that from the Neolithic right up to modern times pilgrimages to the caves have been made only in winter.

It can be conjectured that some of the caves were only of local significance, and were visited only by the local population, whereas others attracted pilgrims from the most remote corners of Crete as well. Unfortunately on this point we can do no more than conjecture. Our judgement is based only on what probably occurred, and no definite conclusions can be reached. A cave that attracted worshippers from a wide area is the Psychro grotto. It is large

70. Asphendou. Rock engravings. KCh 24 (1972) Pl. 15:5 (fragment).

71. Vernopheto Cave. 'Paintings'. P. Faure, La vie quotidienne en Crète au temps de Minos (1973), Fig. on p. 160. See, however, a notice on p. 71.

and has an imposing interior. It lies in the Lasitiou plateau, and is reached easily. As a matter of fact, it is situated in a region where there are many hamlets and settlements, such as that at Plati.[88] Undoubtedly the inhabitants of the villages on the plateau would visit this mysterious cave. But the fame of the goddess here attracted worshippers from afar as well, as is proved by the discovery of many inscriptions of Linear A script. It must not be forgotten that the town of Mallia was situated only a few hours' walk from the cave. It is even highly probable that pilgrims from still more distant regions made pilgrimages to the cave. Evidence is at hand suggesting that pottery from the palace workshops at Phaistos was found at Psychro.[89] Thus if we could assume that these vessels were brought to the grotto directly by pilgrims from the Mesara valley we would know that the grotto was a place that was visited by the inhabitants of distant areas, even in MM times.

A natural step from this point is to ask whether other grottoes also attracted pilgrims perhaps even from all over Crete. It is quite likely that Crete had several famous cult caves, but at present too little is known about the cult places for us to be able to prove this conclusively. The cave at Amnissos, where a deity similar to the Greek Eileithyia was worshipped at least in the Minoan Period, was another place whose influence extended far beyond the immediate locality. Greek testimonies indicate that the goddess in the cave at Amnissos enjoyed great fame at this time, although it must be admitted that we have no confirmation of this in the excavated finds. If one of the Linear B tablets found at Knossos has been correctly interpreted,[90] we should know that gifts, including honey, were sent to Eileithyia at Amnissos from Knossos. This source possibly also tells us that the inhabitants of Knossos, and even the rulers of that city, used to take part in the cult rites in honour of the goddess. From a passage in the Odyssey[91] which mentions a grotto consecrated to Eileithyia in the dangerous Amnissos Bay, it can also be concluded that at least at the time the Odyssey was being written the cave at Amnissos was famed far and wide — possibly reports of the cave were also handed down by oral tradition.

The fame of the cave at Arkalochori was probably widespread as well, as seems to be indicated by the number and quality of the objects found in it. It is very likely that the Kamares cave was another one that was visited by pilgrims from various parts of Crete, or at least from the Mesara valley, which is proved by the presence of pottery from the palace workshops at Phaistos. The huge cave at Skotino must also have been widely known. The very fact that the inside of this cave is so huge and imposing suggests that it must have been used for some out-of-the-way purpose. This cave, owing to the proximity of Knossos and the relative ease of communications with the neighbouring towns and villages, was the principal cult place of the entire region. Some scholars take the view that the cave at Skotino was the most important cult place of this kind for Knossos.[92]

When we come to the question of what kind of gods were worshipped in the Cretan caves we must draw a distinction between two different problems. In the first place, we have the question of the name of the gods worshipped there, and in the second place we have quite a different question — that of the real function of the god or goddess. Whether we can find out for certain the names of the deities in the grottoes is of cardinal importance. But so far, with the exception of Ereuthyia (Eileithyia), extremely few gods' names have been ascertained. What we know about the gods who were worshipped comes from the Linear B texts[93] of the Minoan and the Mycenaean Period. But these texts really tell us very little, apart from cataloguing the gods' names and giving us a list of the offerings that were brought to them. As sources for reconstructing what life was like in Minoan times, the Mycenaean texts[94] are not always good. For even if the name of a Minoan deity is known this does not always mean that the cult rites survived in unchanged form from Minoan to Greek times, or that the pre-Greek divinity came down through the ages as an unchanged religious concept. Examples of changes in the form of the divinities and the rites through the ages are widely known in diverse civilisations.

It seems highly probable, then, that the caves were places where the people worshipped a deity, or rather diverse deities of chthonic character, which in later times perhaps became fused in one all-embracing concept as the Great Goddess. Thus in earlier times (in the Neolithic, for example), the goddess who appeared to humans in the grottoes possibly had a very wide range of functions. As time went on, and depending on the cult place, some aspects of the goddess, such as her martial powers, predominated over and obscured her other characteristics. Consequently it sometimes happened that local deities came into existence whose principal characteristic was different from the previous multi-functions of the Great Goddess.

The chthonic character of the divinities worshipped in the grottoes was derived from the nature of these cult places — from the fact that the grotto was a hole in the rock, leading down into the bowels of the earth, and that it was a natural 'bridge' or meeting place where humans could establish contact with the gods of the underworld. We have already quoted examples showing that this desire to approach the divinity, and to get as close as possible to the place where the god dwelled, was of great importance. When the pilgrims approached the grotto carrying vessels with grain or other harvest products as their offerings to the gods, they used to push or throw these gifts into the cracks in the rocks, or at the foot of the rocks leading into the inside of the grotto (e.g. at Kamares).

In some of the caves the gods who were worshipped were deities whose names were no doubt similar to the name of the Greek goddess Eileithyia (E-re-u-ti-ja) of later times. Yet virtually no other relics of offerings other than clay vessels have been found in the places where this goddess was worshipped — e.g. Amnissos, Tsoutsouros, and perhaps Stravomyti. It is quite probable that a stalagmite in the cave at Amnissos (Fig. 31) was an aniconic representation of a deity, and that the water that had collected in the hollows of the rocks was used during the cult rites. These cult elements, in addition to the position of the votive offerings near the aniconic image of a goddess, as well as in the cracks in the rocks, indicate that the cult was chthonic in character. From this example illustrating the changes that took place in the cult between Minoan and Greek times[95] we may justifiably conclude that such changes took place at Amnissos as well. The functions of the Greek Goddess of Fertility were not necessarily identical to those of her Minoan predecessor. Although one may agree with those scholars who say that the passage in the Odyssey in which Eileithyia's grotto at Amnissos is mentioned proves that the Homeric tradition stems from Minoan times[96] it is nevertheless questionable if her cult continued unchanged in character from Neolithic times onwards.[97] All in all, then, it seems likely that in some grottoes, such as those at Amnissos, Tsoutsouros and Stravomyti, similar chthonic deities were worshipped which must have had a fairly wide range of functions, possibly including the easing of birth. On these grounds, too, one can take it that rites connected with the great mysteries of birth and death in the whole realm of man, animals and plants were performed in the caves.

It has already been remarked that the cults practised in the grottoes may have been connected with the worship of lower-ranking divinities, such as nymphs, for instance. In some grottoes — e.g. at the Leras cave — Akkakalis, which, it has been suggested, dates back to pre-Greek times — there is evidence, dating from the classical period, of a nymph-cult. Nevertheless, we can only suppose that it is quite possible that the old name has survived for thousands of years.

In some grottoes the Great Goddess acquired warlike traits apart from her old functions. At least this seems likely judging from the relics found in the cave at Arkalochori,[98] where long swords were offered up to the goddess in the hope that she would ensure long life to the weapons of the local population. But of course this goddess doubtless had other, more general, traits as well.

It has commonly been held that the grottoes underwent a process of evolution, first being used as dwelling-places, then as sepulchres, and later as cult places.[99] Of course students of Cretan religion have pointed out that not every grotto necessarily passed through all three stages. But they have demonstrated how the grottoes were used first as dwelling-places alone, and then as sepulchres alone (occasionally the dwelling phase and the sepulchral phase were successive stages in one and the same cave). They showed that the caves were used solely as tombs in the EM period, and solely as cult places from MM I onwards.[100] Of course it cannot be denied that the grottoes were used for diverse purposes — some, for instance, were first used as dwelling places and then as burial places. It seems likely that in the earliest times the cult places were not only in the grottoes, but above all in the open spaces, in the groves, and in the vicinity of trees. This stage in the development of religion, which is very poorly documented by relics dating from before MM I, was a particularly important one in Crete, where the survival of natural forms of religion can be traced to the end of the Bronze Age.

From Neolithic times and in EM many caves and rock shelters in Crete were used as dwelling places and as sepulchres. Some cult grottoes which were famous in MM and LM times may also have been used as holy places from Neolithic times onwards.[101] The relics from those times consist almost entirely of pottery, but a stone axe was also found at Amnissos[102] and flakes of obsidian were discovered at Kato Sarakino.[103] The problem of why these objects were brought to the Neolithic caves is one that is exceptionally hard to solve. It should be remembered, however, that in the partly explored Pan grotto at Marathon[104] a deposit dating back to Neolithic times was already probably connected with religion. In Crete the matter is specially complicated by the fact that we know very little about the exact place the objects were found. For if the Neolithic pottery and axes were discovered near the sacred stalagmites in the depths of the cave at Amnissos (that is where Marinatos carried out his excavations), then clearly these objects could have been used for a different purpose than the objects found near the entrance to the grotto, that is, a dry place, which at different times of the year could have been used as a dwelling place. It must be stressed here that in Neolithic times pottery — even ordinary vessels such as kitchenware — could have been used as offerings to the gods, for the sacrifices made to the gods were held in these containers. Axes, too, were sometimes used as votive offerings. It will be recalled that in later periods the gifts made to the gods in the grottoes consisted not only of simulacra of bronze axes, but also of ordinary domestic tools whose difference was only that they were generally made of bronze — a fact due to the switch-over to bronze as the metal used in production, in MM and LM times. Possibly, too, the Neolithic inhabitants of the caves brought gifts which they placed in the deeper parts of the cave, near a centrally-placed stalagmite, or at a spot where water gathered. We are unable to prove this hypothesis, however. In the author's studies of the Neolithic material from the cave at Amnissos, nothing so far shows that the pottery found there differed in any way from similar vessels discovered in dwelling-houses.

As has been remarked above, the cave at Kato Sarakino contained not only pottery, but obsidian tools as well. Some scholars have thought that this was a grave, but complete certainty on this matter is unattainable. The Leras grotto produced pottery, flakes of obsidian, and bones and shells, presumably coming from Neolithic times. It is not certain whether this cave, used in Neolithic times as a shelter, was also used occasionally as a holy place. In other grottoes used as holy places in MM and LM, the only remains dating from Neolithic times were pottery. In these circumstances it would probably be an over-simplification to suppose that all these caves were used as burial places. For it must be remembered that the inhabitants of Neolithic Crete frequently changed the site of their camps, and wandered about from one part of the island to another looking for new pastures or for fresh land to cultivate, and that from time to time they most certainly happened on grottoes whose interiors, with their rock formations and pools of clear, cool water, were so mysterious that they gave the impression of being places where the deities made appearances. To the grottoes which they visited more frequently, the people used to bring gifts mainly in the form of grain, etc., which they carried in clay vessels. This is why potsherds were frequently the commonest type of relics left over from those occasional visits to the grottoes.

Clearly although there are rather important arguments to support the view that some of the grottoes were already used for religious purposes in Neolithic times, the present state of our information is such that this view cannot be proved beyond doubt.

The grottoes which were famed as cult places in MM and LM have produced few votive offerings dating from EM times. Relics from the MM period were discovered in several grottoes used later as holy places. Again, these finds consist almost exclusively of pottery. In the Kamares grotto a single pot dating from EM was discovered — in the most inaccessible annexe of the grotto, as was recounted above — and also two potsherds dating from EM.[105] This would seem to indicate that the first occasional offerings were brought to the grotto at this period. The author's examination of the material found in the grotto at Amnissos has confirmed the supposition that EM pottery found there is similar to the pottery discovered in tombs. Among the EM pottery discovered there were two vessels with horn-like ornaments.[106] Similar vases have been found in graves. But this does not mean that vessels with horn-like ornaments were used solely as burial gifts,[107] it merely suggests that this kind of vessel was used very often in ceremonies of various kinds, both burial ceremonies and secular ones. Therefore it cannot be stated with absolute certainty that the cave at Amnissos was used as a burial-place in EM times. It may equally well have been used for a religious purpose. The question of the finds at Arkalochori is not altogether clear either.[108] Apart from pottery of the Pyrgos type, which has also been found in burial grottoes, this cave also contained bronze blades which are like those of the EM period, but longer (maybe they should be dated to MM I). It is doubtful if Arkalochori was used as a burial place in EM times. In the upper part of the grotto at Psychro, however, layer V contained primitive buchero pottery (from the EM period), and a quantity of bones possibly came from a rubbish dump,[109] and so during the EM period this upper part of the grotto may have been used from time to time as a shelter or a tomb.

Our information about the grottoes dating from MM I is meagre. In all the caves, the objects dating from this time consist almost exclusively of pottery. In the Kamares cave there is very little pottery dating from MM IA, but more from MM IB. Whereas most of the ware from MM IA was undecorated, some of the pottery offered to the deities in MM IB was decorated. Ceramic finds have come to light in several other caves as well. Apart from pottery, bronze objects were probably discovered only in a few grottoes.[110] Ordinary everyday daggers made of bronze were found near the altar in the upper chamber of the grotto at Psychro. As the above review shows, the objects found in grottoes used in MM I-II do not tell us much about the forms the cult took.

A word of caution must be given here. We cannot be absolutely definite as to the use that was made of the votive offerings. We have already remarked that the Kamares have contained polychrome vessels dating from MM II, although the majority of the pottery found here came from later — MM III. Most of the pottery consisted of everyday ware used for domestic purposes and for storage, while a small percentage consisted of decorated vessels brought here as votive offerings.

In the grotto at Chosto Nero, potsherds were discovered, as well as clay figurines dating from MM III. It was during this period — MM III — that the cave was renowned as a cult place among the local inhabitants. It was probably at this time that the caves definitely began to acquire greater significance as cult places, as can be seen from the fact that not only pottery, but other votive offerings as well, was brought to the caves. The principal finds have been described above. Here we should also like to draw attention to the bronze votive offerings, such as figurines of worshippers (found at Psychro and Skotino), the votive double axes made of gold or of bronze that were sometimes covered with inscriptions, and finally the large quantity of diverse objects of everyday use or personal belongings, as well as weapons e.g. at Psychro and Arkalochori.

The diversity of the objects brought as offerings to the cult grottoes suggests that perhaps the old beliefs still survived everywhere in the MM III period but that important changes were taking place simultaneously. It looks as though from that period onwards one particular trait of a certain divinity became dominant, or as though the old gods acquired new functions. As has been said before, the Kamares grotto was at the peak of its fame at this time. The large number of votive offerings discovered in it shows that the number of worshippers was large. Yet the only votive offerings found in the cave were the traditional ones, that is, ceramic objects such as small pithoi or beakers or bowls, sometimes richly decorated. The remains of grain found there prove that farm produce was brought in offering to the goddess in the cave.

Changes in the function of the grottoes become fully evident in LM I when many of the cult grottoes were at the height of their glory. Even as early as MM III the deity at Arkalochori was adored as the protector of warriors. A large quantity of exceptionally long bronze swords which were too thin to have been used in battle were discovered in this cave. Only two of them could have been used as real weapons. These swords — both real ones and simulacra — were brought to the gods as gifts, since the people hoped the deity would protect their weapons from destruction. We know quite definitely both from technological examination of a bronze weapon,[111] and from the literary tradition of later times,[112] that bronze weapons could be broken very easily. In times of unrest, when Crete was in great peril,[113] the quality of arms was of capital importance. It will be recalled that the period LM I-II was the time that graves of warriors containing both offensive and defensive arms[114] came into existence. There was a steep increase in the number of sacred grottoes owing to the social changes that took place in LM III, and in connection with the fact that the deities which were worshipped in the grottoes adopted some of the prerogatives of the divinities of the heavens.[115] At this period, over the whole of Crete more than thirty grottoes were used for religious purposes. It is probable that a new concept of divinity emerged at this time, amalgamating the characteristics of the gods of the heavens (appearing in the peak sanctuaries) and those of the old chthonic gods worshipped in the grottoes. This was the idea of a supreme god of universal character.

CATALOGUE I

The caves

1. Agiasmatsi, near Kapsodasos, not far from Sphakia. Discovered in 1963. Grotto with stalagmites; in the second chamber the humidity is 90%; the finds dated to Neolithic, LM III and Classical period.
S. Alexiou, KCh, 17 (1963), 412; Faure, NRT, 135-8; CPI, 317; Tyree, 50, 216.
Asphendou *see* Skordalakkia.

2. Ayia Phaneromeni, cave near Avdou (Pediados). Discovered in 1937. Finds consisted of three stone offering tables, pottery, cult double axes made of bronze and of gold, bronze figurines, etc. The earliest finds come from LM I.
S. Marinatos, AA (1937) 222f.; E. Kirsten, RE, Suppl. (1940), 430; Nilsson, MMR², 59; Faure, Fonct 160; CPl, 32, 133, 319; Tyree, 11ff, 224.

3. Ayia Sophia, near Topolia (Kissamou). Discovered in 1954. Its identification as a sacred cave is uncertain. Pottery comes from Neolithic, LM I, LM III and later periods.
P. Faure, BCH, 80 (1956), 102; Faure, Fonct 189; S. Hood, BSA, 60 (1965), 104f; Faure, NRT, 135; Tyree, 62f, 216.

4. Amnissos (Pediados), the grotto called Koutsouras, Neraidospilios, or Eileityinis speos. Discovered in 1886. It has stalagmites and stalactites, and hollows filled with water; walls were built round the stalagmites. The finds consist almost exclusively of pottery fragments dating from the Neolithic onwards, and clay lamps from Hellenistic and Roman period. On the terrace lead oxen figurine, clay balls and LM and later sherds were found.
Pashley, I, 265; J. Hazzidakis, *Parnassos*, 10 (1886), 339-42; F. Halbherr, *The Antiquary*, 27 (1893), 112; S. Marinatos, PAE (1929), 95-109; (1930), 91-9; Y. Bequignon, BCH, 53 (1929), 520 n.5; G. Karo, AA (1930), 156; S. Marinatos, *Forschungen und Fortschritte*, 10 (1934), No. 28, 341; Pendlebury, AC, 56; E. Kirsten, RE, Suppl. 7 (1940), 27; Nilsson, MMR², 58; K. Lindberg, *Fragmenta balacanica musei macedonici scientiarum naturalium*, 1 (1955), 171; Zervos, Crète, pls. 74-7, 90; P. Faure, BCH, 80 (1956), 96f; P. Faure, BullBudé, Part 3 (1958), 31f; G. Daux, BCH, 83 (1959), 740; F. Matz, *Kreta und frühes Griechenland* (1962), 26; Faure, Fonct, 82ff; E. Platakis, *Kritika Protochronia* (1965) 198ff; S.

Spanakis, *I Kriti* 126ff; Faure, NRT, 133 n.3; M. Gerard, SMEA, 3 (1967), 31ff; L. A. Stella, in *Pepragmena*, I, 254 n.4; Faure, STSS, 204, n.2; CPl, 316; Tyree, 24ff, 217f.

5. Aphendis Christou, or Christou to spilaion, near Kastelli (Pediados). Discovered prior to 1934. There are concretions in the cave. Used for religious (?) purposes from MM III onwards (or earlier).
J. Hazzidakis, *Etcret*, 3 (1934), 76; J. Pendlebury et al., BSA, 33 (1934/5), 80f; Pendlebury, AC, 233; Zervos, Crète, 291; Faure, SpT, 515 n.3; P. Faure, DESE (1958), 115; Faure, Fonct, 185; Faure, STSS, 133; CPl, 48, 128, 318; Tyree, 23.

6. Arkalochori (Pediados), Prophitis Elias grotto. Discovered towards the end of the nineteenth century. Votive gold, silver and bronze double axes, bronze swords, daggers and knifes were found, as well as pottery. Used from EM onwards, mainly from MM III-LM I.
J. Hazzidakis, BSA, 19 (1912/13), 35-47; S. Marinatos, AA (1934), 190, 191, 252-4; AA (1935), 248-56; E. Blegen, AJA, 39 (1935), 134-6; F. Netolitzky, *Buletinul Facultatii de Stiintie din Cernauti*, 8 (1934), 176ff; S. Marinatos, PAE (1935), 212-20; *Rivista di Filologia*, N.S., 12 (1934), 547-9; Evans, PofM, IV, 346, 846; Chr. Alexander, BMMA (1941), 18; Nilsson, MMR², 58; S. Marinatos, *Kadmos*, 1 (1962), 87-94; Faure, Fonct, 160-2; G. Spanakis, *I Kriti*, 82f, E. Townsend Vermeule, BMFAB, 57 (1959), 5ff; CPl, 40ff, 139f, 317; Tyree, 28ff, 216 f.

7. Arkoudia or Arkoudas on Akrotiri (Kydonia); grotto called tis Arkoudas (or Arkouda) or spilia tis Panagias, or Panagia Arkoudiotissa. Discovered as early as the eighteenth century. The grotto has pools and stalagmites. Was probably used for religious purposes in LM III, and later.
R. Pococke, *A Description of the East and some other Countries*, II (1745), 263; C. S. Sonini, *Voyage en Grèce et en Turquie*, I (1801), 387; Pashley, I, 24; V. Raulin, *Description physique de l'ile de Crète*, I (1859), 92; D. Bates, 'The Caves of Crete', in A. Trevor-Battye, *Camping in Crete* (1913), 248; Lindberg, op. cit., 167; Faure, GCr, 98f; Faure, NR, 211f; G. Daux, BCH, 85 (1961), 896ff; P. Faure, KCh,

15 (1961), 897; S. Alexiou, *Archaeology*, 15 (1962), 251; Faure, Cav, 46; Faure, Fonct, 144ff; K. Davaras, AD, 22 (1967), B2, 495f; S. Hood, BSA, 60 (1965), 110; BCH, 93 (1969), 202; 94 (1970), 21, 1156; CPl, 318; Tyree, 54ff, 217; Hiller, 65.

8. Chosto Nero, grotto near the summit of Jouktas (Temenous). Discovered towards the end of the nineteenth century. There are pools of water and stalagmites in the cave, which is very humid. Pottery found almost exclusively; a male figurine of MM III-LM I date and a MM III terracotta animal figurine were discovered. Probably used for religious purposes in MM III and LM I and later.
A. Taramelli, MA, 9 (1899), 356; R. Myres, BSA, 9 (1902/3), 379; Cook, I, 160; Pendlebury, AC, 346; Nilsson, MMR², 57; S. Marinatos, PAE (1950), 250; Faure, GCr, 97; Faure, in *Minoica* (1958), 143; Faure, Fonct, 175f; CPl, 125, 318; Tyree, 33f, 217.

9. Garephallou Spilios, known also as tou Gerouphallou o spilios, at Liliana (Pediados). A bull figurine, a fumigator, two handleless kyathoi from LM IIIB suggest that the cave was used for cult purposes.
A. Kanta, KCh, 23 (1971), 425ff; Tyree, 12, 221f; Hiller, 68.

10. Ida, the Spiliara tis Voskopoulas grotto (Mylopotamou). Discovered in 1884. Inside the cave were stalagmites and concretions, and also a stone altar. Votive offerings, mainly pottery, dated to LMM LM I and LM III, two LM I sealstones. Later abundant votives.
Spratt I, 9 and 19; E. Fabricius, AM, 10 (1885), 59ff, 280; F. Halbherr, MI, 2 (1888), 690ff; P. Orsi, MI, 2 (1888), 769ff; A. Furtwängler, Antike Gemmen III (1901), 47 Fig. 22; L. Mariani, MA, 6 (1895), 178 Fig. 12; G. Karo, ARW, 7 (1904), 123f; Evans, PofM, I, 221 Fig. 167; Cook, I, 649 n.3; II, 932ff; E. Fabricius, *Neue Jahrbücher für Antike und deutsche Bildung* (1941), 165ff; Nilsson, MMR², 64f, 578f; N. Platon, KCh, 10 (1956), 409f; AR (1956), 23; S. Marinatos, EEPhSPA (1956/7), 239ff; N. Platon, KCh, 10 (1956), 409f; Ergon (1956), 108ff; Faure, GCr, 97; S. Marinatos, PAE (1956), 224f; BCH, 81 (1957), 632, pl. 108b; Boardman, CC, 78f; K. Kerenyi, *Frühe Dionysos* (1961), 38f; Faure, Fonct, 99ff; S. Spanakis, *I Kriti*, 189f; E. Platakis, *To Idaion Antron* (1965), 1ff; Faure, NRT, 133; CPl, 124, 198, 318; Tyree, 40ff, 219f.
Jouktas *see* Peak Sanctuaries.

11. Kamares, the Mavri Spiliara grotto (Pyrgiotissis). Discovered in 1890. The second chamber has a large pool of water and also stalagmites. Nearly all the finds consist of pottery dating from Neolithic and EM times onwards, and mostly from MM II. Also three terracotta figurines reported.
L. Mariani, MA, 6 (1895), 333ff; J. Myres, *Proceedings of the Society of Antiquaries*, 15 (1895), 351ff; A. Evans, JHS, 17 (1897), 350; A. Taramelli, AJA, 5 (1901), 437ff; R. M. Dawkins, M. L. W. Laistner, BSA, 19 (1912/13), 1ff; Evans, PofM, I, 238f; Nilsson,

MMR², 65f; Zervos Crète Fig. 337; Buchholz, Herk, 37 No. 12; Faure, Fonct, 178ff; S. Spanakis, *I Kriti*, 196; CPl, 47ff; Tyree, 38ff.

12. Kato Sarakina or Elliniko, near Chania, Kydonia. Discovered in 1957. Its stalagmites and concretions are notable. Contained pottery dating from Neolithic times onwards. Sacred function not certain.
Faure, SpT, 501 No. 4; DESE (1958), 117; Faure, NR, 214f; Faure, Fonct, 189; CPl, 148, 318; Tyree, 59f, 220.

13. Kera Spiliotissa, near Vrysse, not far from Chania. Discovered in 1957. The pool and stalagmites in it are notable. Potsherds from Neolithic and EM, LM I and IIIB discovered.
Faure, SpT, 500; DESE (1958), 117; P. Georgioudakis, *Ta Spilaia tis Kritis* (1961), 27; Faure, Cav, 57f; Faure, Fonct, 189; S. Hood, BSA, 60 (1965), 106; Y. Tsedakis, AD, 22 (1967), 500, 506; KCh, 20 (1966), 331; J. Tsiphetakis, DESE (1968), 1ff; Y. Tsedakis, AAA, 2 (1969), 215; BCH, 94 (1970), 18f; CPl, 318; Tyree, 60ff, 220f; Hiller, 67.

13a. Klisidi, close to Myrtos (Ierapetra). Discovered about 1943. Long and narrow cave, with a stone bench and a cult stalagmite.
Faure, Fonct, 30, 36, 48; J. Younger, AAA 9, 1976, 166ff.

14. Korakias Trypa, in the vicinity of Georgioupolis (Apokorona). Discovered in 1936. Pottery from the Bronze Age was found in this stalagmite cave. Sacred function not certain.
V. Teophanidis, EEKS, 1 (1938), 610; AE (1948/9), 11f; P. Faure, DESE (1955), 98; Faure, GCr, 98 No. 19; Faure, Fonct, 185f; S. Hood, BSA, 60 (1965), 112; CPl, 318; Tyree, 47f, 221.

15. Koumaro (Kydonia). Explored in 1928. The cave is very wet, with stalagmites and stalactites. Pottery from MM and LM noticed. S. Marinatos, *Mitteilungen über Höhlen-und Karstforschung*, 4 (1928), 7; O. Walter, AA (1943), 337; U. Jantzen in F. Matz (ed.), *Forschungen auf Kreta 1942* (1951), 1ff; Faure, NR, 212; S. Hood, BSA, 60 (1965), 110; R. Treuil, BCH, 94 (1970), 21f; Tyree, 53f.

16. Kouroupas, known as 'tsi Meires i trypa'; discovered in 1962. Fragments of pottery from LM III and later.
BCH, 87 (1963), 503; KCh, 17 (1963), 387; Faure, NRT, 135; CPl, 318.

17. Leras grotto by Choraphia, Akrotiri (Kydonia). Explored since 1959. The large pool and the stalagmites there are worth attention. Pottery from Neolithic until Classical discovered, mainly dating from the Neolithic and LM III. Neolithic stone axes found.
S. Hood, AR (1959), 21; Faure, NR, 213f; DESE (1961), 15f; Faure, Cav 46f; KCh, 15/16 (1961/2), 1, 195f; Faure, Fonct, 140ff; Y. Tsedakis, KCh, 19 (1965), 298; S. Hood, BSA, 60 (1965), 110; K. Davaras, AD, 22 (1967), B¹2, 495, 497; BCH, 93 (1969), 202; 94 (1970), 20, 1156; AAA, 2 (1969), 214; P. M.

69

Frazer, AR, 15 (1968/9), 38; CPl, 318; Tyree, 56f, 221; Hiller, 66.

Liliana *see* Garephallou Spilios.

18. Mameloukou Trypa, in the Charodia george by Perivolia (Kydonia). Excavated by Y. Tsedakis since 1967. Three main chambers, and several smaller rooms are noteworthy. A chamber above the cavern was rather connected with the main cave. Pottery from sub-Neolithic until LM IIIB found, and a clay animal figurine. The cave was used for cult purposes at MM II-III and probably at LM I.
Y. Tsedakis, AD, 22 (1967), 506; 23 (1968), 417; 24 (1969), 434; 25 (1970), 469f; KCh, 20 (1966), 331; 21 (1969), 543; Ergon (1968), 102ff; PAE (1968), 133ff; BCH, 93 (1969), 203; J. P. Michaud, BCH, 94 (1970), 1156ff; P. Faure, BCH, 96 (1972), 414; J. P. Michaud, BCH, 97 (1973), 412; H. W. Catling, AR, 20 (1973/4), 40; P. Faure, AAA, 2 (1969), 214; Tyree, 58f; Hiller, 66.

19. Mavro Spilio, at Knossos. Small grotto which contained potsherds from LM times.
J. Forsdyke, BSA, 28 (1926/7), 248f; Faure, Fonct, 183ff; CPl, 41.

20. Melidoni, the Gerospilios or Gerontospilios cave. The stalagmites and stalactites, as well as the large pool, are imposing. Finds include pottery and also a bronze domestic axe dating from LM III. Sacred function not certain.
Pashley I, 126ff; Spratt, II, 85; F. Halbherr, *Rivista di Filologia*, NS 1 (1924), 98; Lindberg *op. cit.*, 169f; Faure, GCr, 98 No. 14; N. Platon, KCh, 10 (1956), 421; S. Spanakis, *Periegetike*, 60 (December 1963), 33ff; Faure, Fonct, 131ff; A. Petrochilou, DESE, 8 (1965), 61ff; J. Deshayes, REG, 79 (1966), 508; CPl, 125ff, 319; Tyree, 43ff, 222f.

21. Patsos (Amariou), the grotto is known as tsi Patso o spilios, or A. Antoniou tou Patsikou pharangiou, or sti Charadra. Discovered in 1886. Noted for its pool of water and its stalactites. Pottery as well as a stone libation table dated to LM I. Clay and bronze figurines, dagger blade, and horns of consecration dating from LM III.
F. Halbherr and P. Orsi, MI, 2 (1888), 905ff; F. Halbherr, MI, 2 (1888), 913ff; AJA, 11 (1896), 593; Evans, TPC, 125, 136f; IC, II, 102f; J. Dunbabin, BSA, 42 (1947), 187ff; Picard, RelPreh, 102; Nilsson, MMR², 67; Faure, GCr, 98; Zervos, Crète, Fig. 723, 724, 793, 801; Boardman, CC, 76ff; Faure, Fonct, 136ff; S. Hood, P. Warren, BSA, 61 (1966), 186f; P. Warren, BSA, 61 (1966), 195f; CPl, 127, 132, 134, 319; Tyree, 45ff, 223f.

Phaneromeni see Ayia Phaneromeni

22. Platyvola, or Skoteini Spilia, Kato Pigadi near Skourachlada (Kydonia). Excavations started at 1964 by Y. Tsedakis. Four main chambers with a steep passage are known. Used as an ossuary and probably also as a sacred cave (?). Skeleton remains and pottery fragments from Neolithic until LM IIIB reported. A double axe sign on a EM I vessel was published.
Y. Tsedakis, AD, 19 (1964), 446; 20 (1965), 569; 21 (1966), 428; 22 (1967), 504f; 23 (1968), 415; KCh, 19 (1965), 297f; 20 (1966), 328ff; S. Alexiou, 21 (1969), 535; AR (1965/6), 24; P. M. Fraser, AR, 15 (1968/9), 38; A. H. S. Megaw, AR, 16 (1969/70), 30; BCH, 94 (1970), 1156; Y. Tsedakis, Pepragmena 2,1, 268ff; CPl, 319; Hiller, 64f.

23. Psychro, grotto known as to spilio tou Psychro. Modern excavations begun in 1883. In the lower grotto are stalagmites and a pool. Very rich finds dating from MM I to LM III and from later times as well. The most notable are: stone offering tables, a bronze votive plaque, bronze and terracotta figurines, bronze votive blades, bronze daggers and knifes, arrow-heads and a fibulae.
A. Evans, JHS, 17 (1897), 350f; F. Halbherr, P. Orsi, MI, 2 (1888), 905ff; A. Taramelli, MA, 9 (1899), 412ff; D. Hogarth, BSA, 6 (1899/1900), 94ff; F. Halbherr, *The Antiquary* (1893), 13f; R. Bosanquet, JHS, 20 (1900), 171; J. Demargne, BCH, 26 (1902), 580ff; W. Boyd-Dawkins, Man, 2 (1902), No. 114, 162ff; G. Karo, ARW, 7 (1904), 118ff, Fig. 1; D. Hogarth, *Accidents of an Antiquarian Life* (1910), 71ff; J. Toutain, RHR, 64 (1911), 277ff; Philologus, 71 (1912), 461; Klio, 11 (1911), 435; Cook, II, 925f; Evans, PofM, I, 162, 438, 625ff; S. Marinatos, *Rivista di Fiologia*, NS 12 (1934), 549; AA (1934), 253f; AA (1937), 22; BSA, 36 (1935/6), 12 and 199; IC, I. 1, III 5-9; BSA, 40 (1939/40), 62f, 76f; Pendlebury, AC, 327f; N. Platon, KCh, 1 (1947), 637; M. Guarducci, *Rivista di Filologia*, NS 18 (1940), 99ff; C. de la Fertè, *Musée de France* (1949), 258ff; Nilsson, MMR², 263, 459ff; Lindberg, *op. cit.*, 9; Zervos, Crète, pls. 253f, 479, 485, 506f, 749, 761; G. Pugliese Carratelli, Minos, 5 (1957), 165 No. 16 and 17; J. Boardman, BICS, 5 (1958), 11f; P. Faure, BullBudé (1958), 34f; Boardman, CC, 1ff; Faure, Fonct, 151ff; S. Spanakis, *I Kriti*, 386ff; L. A. Stella, Pepragmena, I, 255f; Faure, STSS, 204 n.2; CPl, 41ff, 131f, 319; Tyree, 14ff, 225f.

24. Skales (Sitias), grotto known as Stes Skales, or Chelidones, or Riza maronias. Discovered in 1901, new excavations in 1983. Pottery from the Bronze Age discovered.
R. Bosanquet, BSA, 8 (1901/2), 235f; F. Schachermeyr, AA (1938), 474; Faure, GRCr, 95; Faure, Fonct, 187; N. Platon, *Kritomikinaiki thryskeia* (1970), 98; CPl, 319; Tyree, 7ff, 226.

25. Skordolakkia by Asphendou (Sphakia). A small cave with engraved designs with wild goat, bow, spears, plant motifs and ships, geometric signs. Dated to Paleolithic period by Ch. G. Papoutsakis and A. Zois, to Minoan period by P. Faure, and to Early Iron Age by S. Hood. Hiller described it as 'undatable'.
A. Zois, EEEPA, 3 (1972), 456f; A. Zois, *Kriti. Epochi tou Lithou* (1973), 63ff; BCH, 97 (1973), 23ff; Chr. Papoutsakis, KCh, 24 (1972), 107ff; P. Faure, BCH, 96 (1972), 406ff; S. Hood, *The J. Paul Getty Museum Journal*, 1 (1974), 104ff; Hiller, 49f; P. Faure, BCH, 102 (1978), 634f.

26. Skotino (Pediados), grotto known as Spilio tis A. Paraskevis. Visited as early as the seventeenth century. The hollows filled with water and the numerous stalagmites are notable features. Pottery, bronze figurines (LM I) and a double votive axe were discovered and dated to the Bronze Age.
AJA, 5 (1901), 442; Evans, PofM, I, 163; Evans, PofM, IV, 411; Pendlebury, AC, 103, 124, 177, 184; Nilsson, MMR², 57f; Lindberg, op. cit., 171f; Faure, GCr, 96; Faure, SpT, 508ff; BullBudé (1958), 34ff; S. Alexiou, AD, 18 (1963), B, 312; KCh, 17 (1963), 398; A. H. S. Megaw, AR (1962/3), 29f; G. Daux, BCH, 89 (1965), 888; Faure, Fonct, 162ff; S. Spanakis, I Kriti, 347f; Faure, Lab, 315ff; Faure, STSS, 199f; C. Davaras, BCH, 93 (1969), 620ff; J. Joanniou, DESE, 10 (1970), 55ff; CPl, 320; Tyree, 20ff; Hiller, 68.

27. Spilios, grotto in the vicinity of Milatos. There is a hollow filled with water in this cave; pottery fragments dating from LM times found here.
Faure, GCr, 96; Faure, Fonct, 187; CPl, 136, 320.

28. Stravomyti, cave known as spilios tou Stravomyti; situated near Karnari Metochi. A pool and stalagmites are notable features. The finds consist almost entirely of pottery, from the MM-LM period, and later finds.
Evans, PofM, II, 68ff; S. Marinatos, PAE (1950), 248ff; BCH, 74 (1950), 311; BCH, 75 (1951), 126f; J. M. Cook, 71 (1951), 252; F. Schachermeyr, AnzAlt, 6 (1953), 201; Faure, Fonct, 173ff; J. Deshayes, REG, 79 (1966), 508; CPl, 125f, 320; Tyree, 34ff, 227.

29. Trapeza, cave near Tylissos. The first information about this cave was forthcoming in 1934. It has pools of water, stalagmites, and stalactites. Contained a bronze figurine as well as pottery dating from MM III-LM I.
J. Hazzidakis, Etcret, 3 (1934), 75f; Pendlebury, AC, 103, 124; Nilsson, MMR², 58; Faure, CulS, 500f; Faure, Fonct, 176; Faure, NTR, 133; CPl, 42, 133f, 320; Tyree, 10f, 228.

30. Tsoutsouros, cave known as i phylaki tou Vasilia. Discovered in 1959. Contains a pool. The earliest votive offerings come from LM III.
Faure, CulS, 502; Faure, Fonct, 90ff; S. Alexiou, AD, 18 (1963), 2, 310f, 313; KCh, 17 (1963), 397f; G. Daux, BCH, 89 (1965), 884ff; CPl, 142f, 146f, 320; Tyree, 31ff, 218f.

31. Vernopheto or Kato Pervolakia, known also as Vorni Riza (Sitias), altitude 450 m. Painted designs (dated to LM IIIB?) with a goddess with upraised hands and various animals etc. were discovered. Religious significance of the cave is not certain. The author's examination of the 'paintings' in 1984 inclined him to believe that the signs are modern.
Faure, STSS, 196ff; CPl, 318; P. Faure, La vie quotidienne en Crète au temps de Minos (1973), 161f, Fig. on p. 160; Hiller, 67.

32. Vigla, near Keratokambos (Viannou). Discovered in 1935. The cave is damp, and contains stalagmites. Potsherds from the Bronze Age found.
Pendlebury, AC, 148, 178; Faure, GCr, 96; Faure, Fonct, 187; CPl, 320; Tyree, 30f, 217 (Bigla); P. Faure, BCH, 102 (1978), 635.

33. Vitsiles, cave known as tou Diakou ta kellia, not far from Kanli Kastelli (Temenous). There is a very peculiarly shaped rock in this cave. Contained pottery from MM II and from later times as well. Sacred function not certain.
N. Platon, KCh, 9 (1955), 559; Faure, GCr, 101, No. 10; Faure, Fonct, 188; Faure, NRT, 134; CPl, 54, 320; Tyree, 37, 227.

72. Jouktas. Walls of the temenos.

73. Pyrgos. Temenos area.
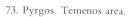

V

Peak sanctuaries

THE SIZE of the temenos area depended on the dimensions of the area available on the mountain peak. Usually this area was small, and it rarely exceeded 600 square metres. There were exceptions, however. The temenos on Kophinas,[1] for example, was at least 80 × 30 m. On Jouktas, too, the temenos area was big, and surrounded with walls (Fig. 72), while the one on Pyrgos was also very extensive (Fig. 73), and occupied the two peaks of that mountain, the distance between them being 60 m. The peak at Traostalos was terraced in ancient times. It measures 22 × 12 m, but the temenos area itself was still bigger, as we can see from the fragments of its wall found on the side of the hill.[2]

The holy place was perched on the peak of the mountain, which very often was reft by fissures and clefts in the rock. The ground was bare, with only a few tufts of moss here and there, and the singularity of the place was augmented by weathering of the rock (Figs. 74,75). This description of the temenos area is confirmed not only by its present-day appearance but also by scenes in art. Bare, steep crags, completely denuded of vegetation, can be seen on a fragment of a rhyton from Knossos — Gysadhes (see below p. 83). Of course there has been some simplification in this scene, there is no sign of the low plants which probably grew on every peak. The supposition that nearly every peak had some kind of sparse vegetation is borne out by other iconographical sources, for example another rhyton found at Zakro (see below, p. 83) where the artist has depicted a rocky area with very sparse vegetation consisting of a few shrubs growing in the cracks of the rocks, or clumps of full-blown crocuses. In another part of the temenos there is even a tree, no doubt a fig tree. The evidence of the iconographical sources, suggesting that the appearance of the peak sanctuaries then was more or less the same as it is today except of course for changes caused by the weathering of the rock, has been confirmed by the latest geological research. Interesting results have been obtained from geological-archaeological investigations carried out in the Mallia area.[3] The experts say that in those regions, which were built of Jurassic and Triassic rocks, there can have been no woods. Consequently, the number of woods in some of Crete in the second millennium B.C. must have been very similar to that at the present day. This view was passionately defended by the greatest expert on mediterranean vegetation, A. Philippson.[4] It should be remembered, however, that the vegetation must have varied from one peak to another, because of the differences of altitude, which ranged from 215 m to over 1,100 m, and so we must bear in mind that there were different vegetation zones in Crete.[5] Region I consisted of an evergreen belt of mediterranean vegetation stretching up to the boundaries of olive cultivation (i.e. up to an altitude of 600-650 m). This region can be divided into a lower and an upper sub-region. In the lower one (altitude 0-350 m) the vegetation was luxuriant and vines and other plants were cultivated. Petsophas Hill lies in this ever green sub-region. In the upper sub-region (altitude 350-650 m), the characteristic vegetation consists of sparse maquis and oak woods. It is in this sub-region that most of the peak sanctuaries are situated.[6] Cereals and vines can be grown in each of these sub-regions. Region II has mountain forests. In its lower sub-region (altitude 650-1,300 m) snow sometimes falls in the wintertime, but frost is rare and the snow does not as a rule last long. Here, too, the main evergreen plants can be found. But instead of Aleppo pines (*Pinus halepensis*) the woods consist of firs and black pines. Cereals and vines can also be grown successfully. There are two transition zones: (a) the zone between 650 and 1,000 m (or between 500 and 900 m), in which the maquis, the Aleppo pine woods, the cypruses and the mulberry trees appear for the last time in the spring and autumn there is heavy rainfall; there are several peak sanctuaries at this height;[7] and (b) an upper zone between 1,000 and 1,300 m (or between

74. Petsophas. Tremenos area. The rocks.

900 and 1,200 m), in which rain occurs at all times of the year, sometimes even in the summer. This area has evergreen shrubs as well as oak and other deciduous trees. Arable farming is practised, and in the summer the sheep are brought to the higher pastures here. At this altitude it is still possible to live year round. The highest temenos, that of Karphi (1,158 m) is situated in this region. In the upper sub-region fir and pine woods can still be found between 1,300 and 1,900 m (or between 1,200 and 1,700 m). Between 1,300 and 1,500 m (or between 1,200 and 1,400 m) the land is still cultivated sporadically, whereas higher up the ground is covered with snow for many months of the year and the cultivation of cereals is not possible. So far not a single sanctuary has been found in the upper sub-region of Region II.

To sum up, the peak sanctuaries were usually situated in the zones with evergreen vegetation. Only very few were located in the upper zone of the lower sub-region of Region II, with its mountain forests. The sanctuaries must have differed from each other in appearance, but on the other hand these differences were undoubtedly of little importance to the Minoan pilgrims, since from the votive offerings we can see that there was great uniformity among the external manifestations of the cult. Of course apart from the differences of altitude at which the sanctuaries were situated, the exposed mountain tops, which were subject to strong winds, were not places that favoured the growth of trees. The strong gusts of wind, and gales coming from the west and north were not only physically destructive, but also caused violent changes of temperature that were harmful to the vegetation. Nevertheless, some trees did occasionally manage to grow, as we can see both from the sanctuaries of the present day and from those depicted in art. For example, in a rather sheltered spot in the middle of the temenos on the summit of Mount Pyrgos (altitude 585 m), there is an evergreen oak (Fig. 75) with all its branches leaning over to one side — to the east — because of a strong wind coming from the west.

75. Pyrgos. Temenos area.

We are therefore led to the conclusion that the cult places on the mountain peaks differed from each other in setting. A few fruit trees — such as olive, or fig — may have managed to grow there. But on most of the peaks between 350 and 1,000 m trees must have been a rarity, whereas stumpy vegetation such as maquis, flowers, etc. grew in profusion among the rocks. Thus in contrast to the sacred enclosures the sanctuaries were usually exposed and bare, with no clumps of trees. The impression was that of a mountain meadow rather than that of a grove.

Little is known so far about the shape of the peak sanctuaries. Yet as we can see from the plan of the temenos on Jouktas (Fig. 76), the cult places were sometimes approximately oval. Generally, however, they were more irregular in shape, as Mount Pyrgos. The temenos depicted on the rhyton from Zakro seems to have been more or less rectangular. The temenos on Kophinas, too, appears to have been of this shape (see below). Hence we come to the important conclusion, that as far as can be judged at present, the sanctuaries varied in shape (as was the case in later times in Greece). They could be oval, rectangular or irregular in shape. Thus in all probability the shape of the temenos was not inspired by any religious rule; it did not need to be of any particular shape.

It was probably the universal custom to mark the temenos boundary. It may have been marked by a mound of stones, or a large boulder, although this has not been confirmed by the Minoan evidence. Another frequent way of marking the boundary of the peak sanctuary was to erect a stone wall. There are fairly well preserved remnants of such a wall round the holy place on Jouktas. The wall is now gradually disappearing, but in the nineteenth century these fragments were still quite well preserved. The first account of this wall dates from 1837, when R. Pashley[8] described the site as follows: 'On the eastern side of the mountain and about a hundred paces from its summit, I found considerable remains of ancient walls (Fig. 72). The construction is chiefly of very large stone, among which a good many small ones were

76. Jouktas. Temenos area. SanctSymp 140 Fig. 3.

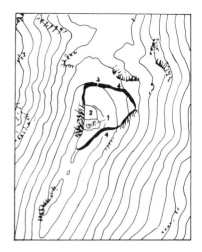

77a. Jouktas. Reconstruction No. 1. B. Rutkowski, Nature Sanctuaries in Minoan Crete: a Catalogue of Sites (1985), Fig. 67.
77b. Jouktas. Alternative reconstruction No. 1. B. Rutkowski, Nature Sanctuaries in Minoan Crete (1985), Fig. 67 a.

intermixed. Some of the latter have fallen out in places. These fragments seem to offer a good specimen of the so-called first cyclopean style. They are four or five in number, and the whole length of ground, which they partially cover, is between four and five hundred paces, of which no more than fifty paces are occupied by the actually existing remains. It is, however, evident that the old walls extended all round the summit, except where, as on its western side, it is nearly perpendicular precipice.' Over sixty years later such walls were also described by A. Taramelli[9] who wrote that the northern of the wall side had been preserved to a height of 3 m, and in a very few places to 5 m.[10] These descriptions are of considerable importance, for at the present time only the northern part of the walls is in a fairly good state of preservation (Fig. 72). The remaining parts of the walls, especially on the eastern side, are almost completely ruined, and look like the stumps of weathered rocks.[11]

These walls have been dated to the MM IA period.[12] Recent investigations have shown[13] that the walls ringing Jouktas, and hence the sanctuary and the Psili Korifi, were 3 m wide, and still stand to a height of between 2.50 and 3.60 m. The circumference of the walls measured 735 m. Part of an offering table dating from LM IA was found just beside the wall. In our opinion it could have been left when repairs were made on the wall. In any case it gives no clue to the dating of the earliest wall of the temenos. The information we have at present about the walls encircling other sanctuaries is scantier still; on Kophinas a wall at one time enclosed a rectangular space; its northern part alone (a section 8.80 m long) has survived.[14] An interesting case was observed on Prinias. The mighty northern rock forms a natural boundary wall of the temenos.

As to the purpose of the mighty ring of walls on the summit of Jouktas, the argument has been raised that the size and thickness of the walls indicate that this place was used as a refuge for the local population in times of danger. Undoubtedly there is much to be said for this view. Nevertheless, let us assay interpretation of this area from another side. It is known that many cult structures — such as those in the Easter Islands, or in Egypt, built above all with religious aims in mind — were huge. Sometimes the might of the god was expressed in the imposing size of great pyramids, monuments or tombs. Hence the most likely explanation of the work put into the construction of the powerful walls surrounding the top of Jouktas would seem to be that it filled a need connected with worship of the divine, with a need to express the might of the divinity.

Thanks to recent investigations we now know much more about the buildings in the temenae. Thus it seems that there were different types of buildings in each particular sacred place, although in other temenae there were only small, modest shrines. Despite the advance of research, it is not yet possible to say anything precise about the development of the sanctuaries. It is thought that sacred buildings first appeared in the sanctuaries at a later stage in their development, that is in MM III, although it is quite possible that most buildings date from an earlier period.[15] The cult place at the top of Mount Jouktas was quite exceptional, as is clear not only from the nature of the walls which we have just described, but also, and above all, from the very varied nature of the constructions there. The sanctuary stood on the lower, northern

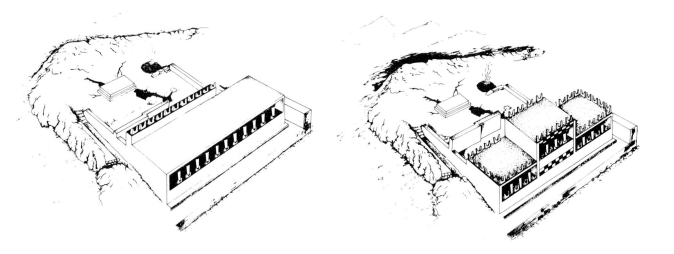

peak of the second summit, and on the south-east side could be approached by a gentle slope. The holiest part of the temenos came almost right up to the edge of a steep cliff facing west.[16] The area with the sacred structures slopes very steeply, for within a distance of about 15 m going from east to west the difference in level is between 2 and 5 m.[17] At the present stage of excavations (1979) it is clear that there are two terraces and a row of rooms (Figs 77a, 77b, 78). The higher terrace, measuring 16.5 by 8.5 m, is really on two levels.[18] A wall was built round it on three sides, the exception being the west side where there was an altar and the entrance to a cave. The terrace wall consisted of several layers of large, irregular stones. The gaps were filled in with small stones. It must have been a complicated task to build this terrace, for in order to make it level, the builders had to put up a supporting wall, which in its northern section is as much as 2.20 m high, and in its south-east part 1.60 m. Karetsou believes that originally the

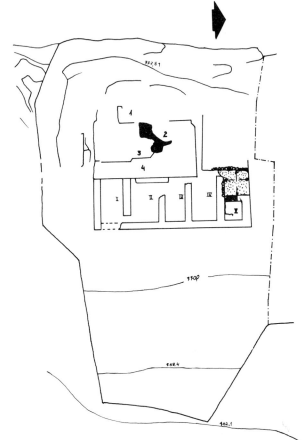

78. Jouktas. Plan of the temenos. Ergon 1978, Fig. 63.

78

79. Piskokephalo. Clay model No. 9815. FGK, Fig. 9.1.

80. Piskokephalo. Clay model No. 9817. FGK, Fig. 8.6.

86. *(far right)* Jouktas. Stone offering table. Courtesy of A. Karetsou.

height of the terrace was the same on both sides. On the external side of the wall, on the east, there is a low, stone bulwark.[19] On either side of the terrace narrow streets lead along the terrace towards the highest part of the temenos. Previously it was thought that there was no wall round the edge of the terrace. But, as the author has explained briefly elsewhere,[20] it is probable that, as has been suggested above, the terrace was in fact bounded on three sides by a low wall which surrounded the holy of holies. This wall was surmounted by stone horns of consecration that were discovered near the east edge of the terrace (Fig. 77).[21] There was a wall round the area in which were the altar and the entrance to the grotto. It is, of course, impossible to say how high this wall was, although similar cases supply us with some indirect indication. For instance, there seems to have been a similar, though smaller construction on the tiny island of Nisakouli, in Methoni Bay, erected at the highest point of the hill there (altitude 171 m). It is likely that the wall excavated on Nisakouli had a similar purpose to that found on Mount Jouktas — it screened off the holy of holies, with the altar. The function of these walls, and their height, may also be deduced from analogy with similar objects depicted in the extant iconographic art. The author has gone into this subject in greater detail elsewhere. Here we shall content ourselves with mentioning that models of constructions from Piskokephalo (Fig. 79), and probably from Knossos, show sacred walls or screens — that is, structures with walls on three sides, the fourth side being open. These structures were unroofed, and on some of the models the structures are surmounted by horns of consecration. In one model (No. 9817) the walls stand to a height of eight rows of ashlars. Another model, No. 9815 (Fig. 80), has a height of four rows of blocks. On the basis of this evidence, we can take it that the walls that screened the holy of holies were not high.

Places of remarkable significance were found at the sacred screen on Mount Jouktas (Fig. 77). At spot No. 2 (cf. Petsophas, p. 80) there is a cleft in the rocks, 3.5 m long and 0.90 m deep, where a number of objects were found, including offering balls of the Petsophas type, as well a great number of other, very small votives, fragments of offering tables of the kernos

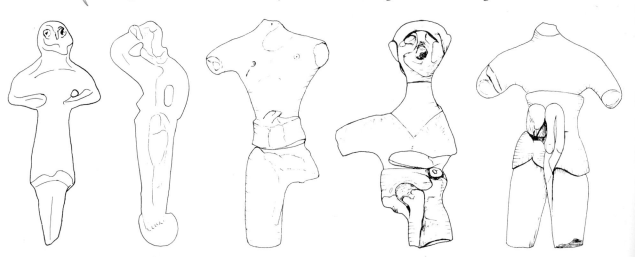

type, offering tables with inscriptions, poros slabs on which star signs have been incised and bronze figurines (Figs. 81-6). A hoard of 30 cult double axes also came to light of which 28 were small (between 0.12 and 0.09 m) and only two of them large (0.24 m in length) (Fig. 87). They were discovered in a pit under a thick layer of remains of sacrifices. A construction found at spot No. 1 was no doubt an altar with a step on its southern side (Fig. 78). Another important cult place was the area near the cave (Fig. 88). The grotto was explored to a depth of 10 m and many votives were found.

Somewhat lower than the most sacred spot on Mount Jouktas, were five rooms which, judging from the objects found there (Fig. 78) were used for the practice of cult. These were the sanctuary proper. In Room V, for instance, there was an LM IA store of conical cups. Fragments of coloured plaster discovered near Room IV tell us how these rooms were decorated. In view of the solidity of the walls, Karetsou believed that above Rooms I-IV there was an upper storey, covered by a roof. This was in use from MM III till LMI. We believe that there are different possible reconstructions of the façade of the sanctuary. One of the reconstructions (Fig. 77) shows an upper storey with columns and horns of consecration. Lower down, Karetsou came upon a long structure which she interpreted as an altar (it is not indicated on our plan). This was a long, step-shaped construction, built at the transition from the Old Palace to the New Palace Period. Numerous stone and clay votives were found here, as well as offering tables, figurines, and clay vessels dating from LM III A2-B.

In some of the sanctuaries the buildings were also quite large, but of course the chapels in the poor sacred peaks were more modest, e.g. on Karphi. The buildings were usually erected at central or prominent places not far from the highest point of the hill or mountain (Fig. 76). Petsophas also seems to have been a very important sanctuary.[22] The walls of the terrace had already been built in the MM I period. At that time only the sacred screens surrounded the holy place close to the rocks of the peak. No sanctuary building stood there then. Later on, probably in the MM III-LM I period, or in LMI, the façade was shown and the walls were covered by a

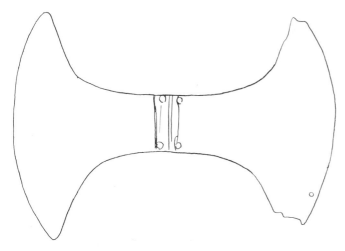

81. Jouktas. Bronze figurine. PAE 1974, Pl. 175 a.

82. Jouktas. Lead figurine. PAE 1974, Pl. 26s c.

83. Kophinas. Clay figurine. AD 18, 1963, Chronika Pl. 363 a.

84 and 85. Jouktas. Clay figurines. Ergon 1977, Fig. 124.

87. Jouktas. Bronze double axe. PAE 1971, Pl. 173 a.

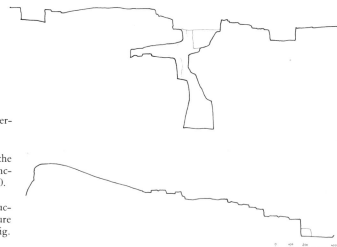

88. Jouktas. Section of the cave at the terrace. PAE 1974, Suppl. VIII.

89. *(bottom left)* Petsophas. Plan of the sanctuary. B. Rutkowski, Nature Sanctuaries in Minoan Crete (1985), Fig. 40.

90. *(bottom right)* Petsophas. Reconstruction. Phase II. B. Rutkowski, Nature Sanctuaries in Minoan Crete (1985), Fig. 72 a.

roof (Figs. 89-91). The best preserved centre part of the sanctuary seems to consist of a narrow vestibule (1) and a sacred room (2). This building was over 18.50 m long, and over 12 m wide. This best preserved part (Rooms 1 and 2) measured approximately 7.20 × 3.70 m. The outer walls were made of large, partially worked stones. The interior of Room 1 was carefully finished. The walls were plastered with a lime mortar and then whitewashed. The floor was made of mortar. Along two walls there was a stone bench 25 cm high, made of unhewn stones bound together with mortar and plastered; it is probable that the cult objects were placed here. Another room to which our attention is drawn is No. 3. One wall is skewed, and another curved. Near it there was a natural cleft in the rock. Unfortunately there are no reports of excavations in this room. Nevertheless, its irregular shape, and the fact that it was built beside the aforementioned, may indicate that this spot had some special significance (cf. the triangular room in the temple at Mycenae, see p. 176, and the rock fissure on Mount Jouktas, Fig. 78, No. 2).

At the summit of Philiorimos mountain (Gonies)[23] a sanctuary with three rooms has been excavated (Fig. 92). There was also a long terrace with an altar. Another altar was noticed in the Room 1, with animal bones nearby. The votives found in the rooms, some of which come from MM I, suggest that the building also dates from that period. On Mount Vrysinas,[24] excavations have brought to light the remains of a temenos wall 9 m long and between 1.20 and 1.80 wide, as well as part of a stone altar which has survived to a height of 0.30 m. On Mount Pyrgos (Fig. 93)[25] a sacred building with an entrance facing the terraces was identified. It seems possible that the cult statue could have been placed in a natural hollow in the rocks. Therefore, when the doors of the sanctuary were opened the pilgrims could have seen the holy figure, just on the rear side of the building. The existence of a sacred building on Mount Modhi[26] is rather doubtful.

91. Petsophas. Sanctuary walls.

At the topmost point of Mount Traostalos[27] (not far from Kato Zakro), traces of building activity have survived in two places. In the first instance, at the highest piece of level ground on the peak — but with a needle of rock jutting up from it — there is a pile of stones, some of which have been partly worked. In front of them five hollows have been made in the rock. Five metres away from this spot, there are the remains of a small building whose inner measurements are 2.50 × 1.65 m.

In the light of the above facts, it can probably be said that the peak sanctuaries differed from each other in ground plan. Some, such as that on Jouktas, had powerful walls, and either the sacred area was built up with terraces, a sacred screen, an altar and a sacred building (as on Mount Jouktas) or terraces formed an open, more or less level space, near which there was a sanctuary with several rooms (as at Petsophas and Gonies), or small shrines (as at Karphi, etc.). The archaeological data tell us almost exclusively about the ground plans of the peak sanctuaries, the outlines of the buildings, but hardly ever about the external appearances of these buildings. Detailed information can be gained from the iconography, however. As a rule only the façade is shown. But in one exceptional case a rhyton depicts a whole temenos[28] situated in the middle of sparse vegetation in a wild mountainous landscape (Fig. 94). The principal element of the picture is the façade of a building inside the temenos, depicted in the foreground.[29] On either side of the building part of a religious structure, consisting of a low wall built of five rows of stone blocks, is still visible. On top of this wall — which no doubt represents the ground floor — we see the first floor, which is crowned with horns of consecration. On both sides of the façade there are pillars not attached to the building, which narrow toward the top and end in a sharp point.[30] The first floor also has large window apertures. This building is shown in very simple, sketchy form. The artist has stressed the most important element in the picture: the façade, which is bigger than the other parts of the temenos. The altar stands in a paved area — the pavement is indicated by long lines. At the side there is another construction. This is an altar built of stone blocks and consisting of two parts: a low construction topped with a plinth, and a higher construction surmounted by sacred horns. Two branches of a tree with big leaves (no doubt a fig-tree) hang over the altar. In the centre of the picture the artist has depicted the façade of a sanctuary which is partly encircled by a wall, part of which is crowned with sacred horns. Since the picture is in linear perspective the various parts of the wall have been placed on different levels, higher or lower. In the centre of

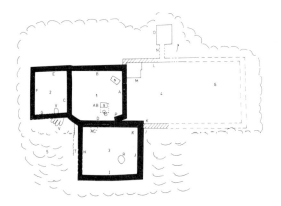

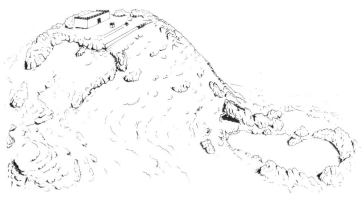

92. Philiorimos at Gonies. Sanctuary. B. Rutkowski, Nature Sanctuaries in Minoan Crete (1985), Fig. 35.

93. Pyrgos. Reconstruction of the sanctuary. B. Rutkowski, Nature Sanctuaries in Minoan Crete (1985), Fig. 73.

the picture we can also see a long and rather low altar made of stone blocks, finished with a double plinth on which there are small, thin slabs. It is probably an altar of the eschara type.[31] Since the artist assigned most importance to the façade of the building, he was unable to depict the temenos in its entirety; the building was undoubtedly situated in the centre of the cult place.

On the fragment on the rhyton from Gypsadhes[32] we can see the façade of a building erected on uneven ground in the middle of a bare, mountainous landscape (Fig. 95). The asymmetry of the building may be due to the fact that the artist wished to show that the ground was rocky. The cult building proper stands on a base with four steps, which is made of large stone blocks. This stone foundation is depicted clearly only on the left, whereas on the right its outline is hardly visible. The sanctuary proper consists of three parts, the middle one being higher. The top of the lower part of the building is finished with a double cornice, which in cross-section is rounded rather than rectangular. It is meant to represent wooden beams. There is a similar cornice on the right side of the building. In the middle, higher part of the building, there are also two beams forming a cornice; no doubt these are longer and thicker. On top of this cornice one can see the remains of three rectangular objects which are probably the bases of horns of consecration. There were horns of consecration on the lower parts of the building, and probably on the higher ones as well (c.f. the picture of a similar building on a seal impression from Knossos, dating from the period LM II.) On the left side, on a stone foundation, there is a pole with a standard hanging on it.[33] There is a similar pole on the right side as well, but it is placed in front of the building.

The façades of sacred buildings present an interesting problem which is complicated partly because of the difficulty of interpreting the iconographic sources, and also because of the difficulty of connecting these sources with the excavated relics. On the one hand it can undoubtedly be taken as certain that the detached shrines and temples situated both in the peak sanctuaries and in other cult places of various types sometimes consisted of three parts; these buildings had a higher middle part, and a lower part on either side; there was also an entrance (or even more than one), and perhaps even an entrance and a portico. On the other hand some façades were all in one part. Especially in the most important shrines, these façades were richly decorated with symbols (Fig. 94) such as aniconic representations of the goddess[34] guarded by agrimia, or with horns of consecration and spiral motifs. Since the goddess revealed herself to mortals at the spot marked by her symbols which denoted that this spot was occupied by the divinity, and was inaccessible to mortals, and since at the side of the façade there were free-standing poles where the rain-producing ceremonies were held, the religious dances, processions, and other ceremonies took place in front of the façade of the shrine. Yet this was not always so, for the shrine was not the most important element of the temenos: the altar was far more important as that was the only object indispensible for cult purposes. The ceremonies sometimes took place near the aniconic image of the divinity, which could take the form of a tree, or a pillar, or a baetyl in some peak sanctuaries, especially the richest of them (and in cult places of other types, too). The façade of the shrine was sometimes the background against which the religious ceremonies took place.[35] Initially this was only because symbols of divinity were to be found on it or in its vicinity. But later on, probably still in the Minoan

94. Zakro. Rython. N. Platon, Zakros (1969), Fig. on p. 167.

95. Knossos-Gypsades. Rhyton. KCh 13 (1959), Pl. 95.

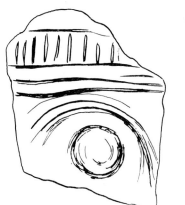 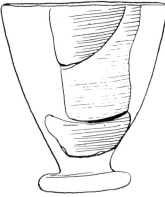 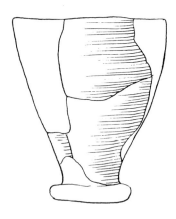

96. Jouktas. Fragment of a LM IIIB statue. Ergon 1975, Fig. 177.   97. Jouktas. MM I cups found in crevices (spot No. 2). PAE 1974, Pl. 179 c.

period, the façade was just the ordinary background of the cult dances, processions, etc., and religious-theatrical performances (Fig. 94).

It is quite certain that altars of various kinds were placed (or made) in the peak sanctuaries. These have been mentioned above: a long, step-like altar (Jouktas), a rectangular stone altar (Jouktas), which was no doubt similar to the altar depicted on the Zakro rhyton (Fig. 94), fire altars,[36] altars of the eschara type (Fig. 94),[37] incurved altars (Fig. 94) and natural stones used as altars. The next question is: were there cult images and sacred emblems in the peak sanctuaries? Undoubtedly there were images in the peak sanctuaries. For instance, an aniconic representation of a goddess in the shape of a pillar can be seen on top of the sanctuary façade on the Zakro rhyton (Fig. 94) mentioned above. This scene is only one of many other similar representations of baetyls. The baetyl resembling a stylised mountain peak, was probably the form in which the goddess of the sky was imagined. No doubt there were baetyls not only in the peak sanctuaries but also in the sacred enclosures,[38] although little information about them has survived.

The problem of the anthropomorphic cult statues in the peak sanctuaries is a more complicated one. On general grounds we may take it as possible that some stone pillars or wooden xoana, occasionally clad in natural clothes, were kept in shrines.[39] This will be discussed below. The existence of clay cult statues, on the other hand, is really quite an open question. Of course the problem of whether a statue is a cult image or not is not a matter of size. Cult statues are sometimes quite small. In general, the characteristic features of the cult image are the arrangement of the hands, the body posture, and the presence of sacred attributes.

At Kophinas,[40] two large statues were recently discovered, no doubt representing votaries. The only difference between them and other figurines is that they are bigger. Large statues said to have been discovered at Plagia have not survived. They were destroyed before the archaeologist arrived.[41] But they are said to have been 0.70 m high;[42] it is not sure whether they were images of votaries, or cult images. Part of a statue (a head fragment) was also found at Petsophas.[43] Upon studying this object, however, the author came to the conclusion that it was part of a head-shaped vessel, similar to some found in other places.[44] On Jouktas, too,[45] a fragment (curls) of a large human figure was found, which has never been illustrated. We do not know, either, where exactly it was discovered. But the excavations on Mount Jouktas have recently produced part of a statue of the Gazi type — that is, a figure with upraised arms (Fig. 96), such as were probably generally used as cult statues.

Among the chief cult emblems that appear in the peak sanctuaries are the horns of consecration. Their functions there are the same as in many other types of sanctuary. Their principal functions were to mark, and crown, the temenos buildings and walls. Another function in the case of the miniature models was to symbolise the presence of a sacred wall and altar. Bronze double axes are also among the symbols that appear in the peak sanctuaries (Fig. 87).

Among the sacred emblems we find also pillars, some of which bore a standard in the form of a square object resembling the capital of a column.[46] In the scene from Zakro (Fig. 94), there are sharp-pointed poles at the sides of the façade of the building, although in other cases such poles stood in front of the sanctuary (Fig. 95). This very essential object, which was probably

98. Petsophas. Female figurine No. 3431.

99. Petsophas. Male figurine No. 3416

100. Petsophas. Female figurine No. 3439.

to be found often in the peak sanctuaries and in the sacred enclosures,[47] had no constructional function but was connected with the rituals.[48]

Very little of the temenae and shrines' furnishings has survived. Apart from those discussed above there were movable sacrificial tables. Many fragments of objects of this kind have been found on Kophinas[49] and Jouktas[50] (Fig. 87). Stone ladles (or perhaps lamps either plain or inscribed) were found on Jouktas.[51] Stone lamps have also been found in other peak sanctuaries — one on Petsophas[52] and several on Kophinas.[53] The rhyta were of capital importance in the ritual. Pottery vessels in the form of a whole bull and others in the form of a bull's head with a hole in its muzzle and another in its back have been found at Kophinas.[54] There are also accounts of a stone vessels decorated with goats, which may have been used during religious ceremonies[55] (Jouktas).

The pottery *in corpore*, which was occasionally reported as having been in the peak sanctuaries (except Jouktas), was not always necessarily used for ritual purposes. But more important, all the vessels, even those used for domestic purposes, may also have been used for cult purposes (cf. Fig. 97b). There was, however, a group of vessels, such as the kernoi, which were used exclusively for religious purposes. One vessel of this type was found at Maza.[56] The small clay balls (found at Petsophas)[57] or the small balls made of rock crystal or steatite (found at Kophinas)[58] were probably used in connection with prayers.

A very large proportion of the votive offerings found in the peak sanctuaries were made almost exclusively of clay. However this great number of terracotta objects does not mean that other votive offerings, especially bronze ones, were not brought to the sanctuaries as well.[59] Among the terracotta objects three groups can be distinguished: human figures, animal figures and miniature objects. As a rule the figurines representing humans (Figs 81, 82, 98-109) do not exceed ten or twenty centimetres in height. It is only in exceptional cases that bigger figurines have been found, and these have been mentioned above. The typical figurines represent women in bell-shaped dresses, wearing jackets, either with their breasts bare or with a very low neckline, and with high caps on their heads (Fig. 98). Whereas the dresses differ little from each other, there is more variety in the headwear, the fantastic hairstyles and caps. The male figurines are also characteristic; they nearly always have a loincloth. Nude figurines, or statuettes with a cloak on their shoulders, are rare. Almost all the figurines are standing in the erect position, with their hands raised as if in supplication. Sometimes one hand is raised above

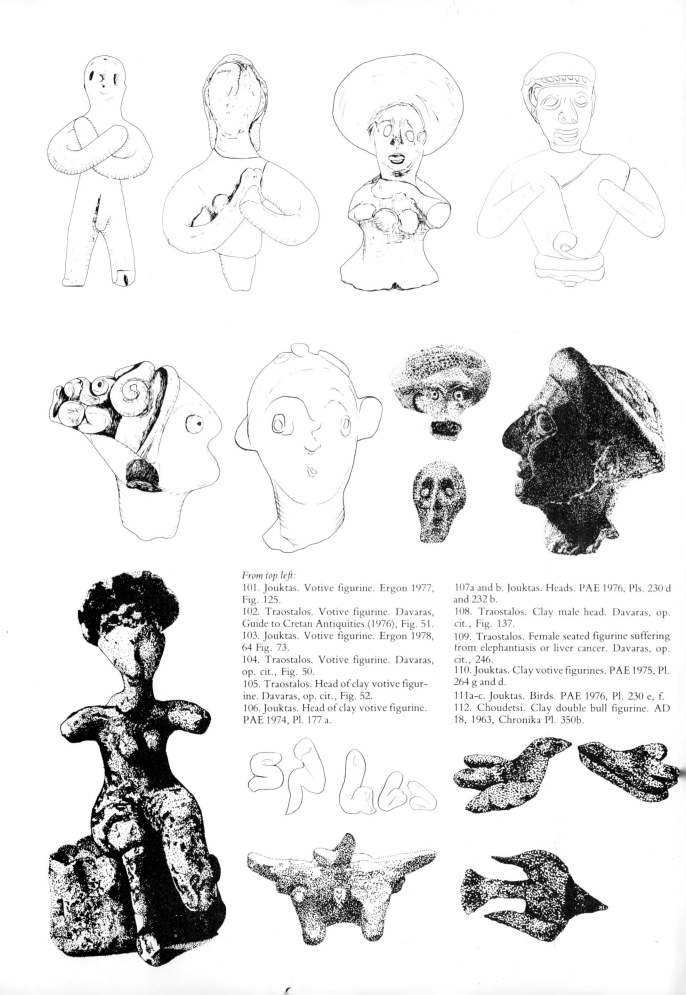

From top left:

101. Jouktas. Votive figurine. Ergon 1977, Fig. 125.

102. Traostalos. Votive figurine. Davaras, Guide to Cretan Antiquities (1976), Fig. 51.

103. Jouktas. Votive figurine. Ergon 1978, 64 Fig. 73.

104. Traostalos. Votive figurine. Davaras, op. cit., Fig. 50.

105. Traostalos. Head of clay votive figurine. Davaras, op. cit., Fig. 52.

106. Jouktas. Head of clay votive figurine. PAE 1974, Pl. 177 a.

107a and b. Jouktas. Heads. PAE 1976, Pls. 230 d and 232 b.

108. Traostalos. Clay male head. Davaras, op. cit., Fig. 137.

109. Traostalos. Female seated figurine suffering from elephantiasis or liver cancer. Davaras, op. cit., 246.

110. Jouktas. Clay votive figurines. PAE 1975, Pl. 264 g and d.

111a-c. Jouktas. Birds. PAE 1976, Pl. 230 e, f.

112. Choudetsi. Clay double bull figurine. AD 18, 1963, Chronika Pl. 350b.

the head, sometimes a hand is held at the level of the forehead, and sometimes both hands are touching the breast (Figs. 98-104). Figurines of seated males were few in number.

Occasionally the divinity was offered a group of figurines. One of the finds at Petsophas was a small base with the stumps of three pairs of legs on it. Probably these were the surviving fragments of a group of dancers. At Kophinas fragments of groups of figurines, placed two or three in a row on a common base, were discovered.[60] Another group which had few specimens was one consisting of votive offerings representing separate parts of the body, such as hands, feet, heads and trunks of the body, with holes inserted for hanging them up. Votive offerings in the form of genitals or in the form of the trunks of pregnant women or those giving birth (Fig. 110) were unique to the site.

It is certainly true to say that the most numerous type of votive offerings consisted of little figurines of animals. As a rule these were tiny, measuring from a few millimetres in length to ten or at the most twenty centimetres. Bigger figurines were exceptional. At Kophinas a fragment of a figurine of a bull was found whose total length would be about 0.80 m,[61] and at Maza part of a figurine which, if the whole of it had been preserved, would have been more than 0.50 m in length.[62] The majority of these figurines represented domestic animals reared as stock. Thus we find statuettes mainly consisting of bulls, oxen, rams and sheep (Figs. 112 and 113), with pigs, dogs, birds (pigeons) coming second (Fig. 111a-c), and in exceptional cases weasels, probably tamed.[63] Statuettes of wild animals were rare, but figurines of wild goats (*agrimia*), for example, occur among the finds. Other characteristic figurines were in the form of beetles which will be discussed at length below. Finally, there is a third group of terracotta offerings, in which we find a large number of miniature vessels, goblets, jars and plates, on which sometimes a loaf of bread, for instance, was represented.

It has already been remarked above that pottery was rarely reported in the peak sanctuaries, with the exception of those on Kophinas, Jouktas and Koumasa. A large number of potsherds has been found in the temenos at Jouktas. Among these are the remains of pithoi and small barbotine vessels dating from MM I-LM IIIB. A great number of pottery fragments were found at Kophinas, too. Most of this consisted of the common, undecorated domestic pottery in which the offerings were brought to the sanctuary. There was also a small quantity of decorated ware from MM III. In shape, these vessels were like the most ordinary, everyday household utensils, such as pithoi, bowls, jugs, plates, etc.[64]

Let us come now to the question of the cult of the gods. The least difficult problem is to describe the type of gods that were worshipped. It is more difficult to establish their names.[65] The general character of the divinity can be gauged from the geographical situation of the temenos and from the kind of offerings brought to the holy place. The salient fact here is that the sanctuaries were situated in relatively high spots (generally between 350 and 800 m), that were bare and unsheltered. The very fact that the Minoans looked for sites at high altitudes shows that they attributed to the god the characteristics of the ruler of the heavens, who was lord of all atmospheric phenomena and, in particular, brought rain[66] and strong, gusty winds.[67] The god ensured the lives and welfare of man and the animals that were his property.

This aspect comes out quite clearly when we examine the votive offerings, and above all the clay (or bronze) figurines representing men and women in supplicating attitudes (Fig. 98) indicating that these mortals were addressing certain concrete pleas to the divinity, giving

113. Choudetsi. Clay double bull figurine. AD 18 (1963), Chronika, Pl. 360d.
114. Knossos. Seal impression. FGK, Fig. 1.1.

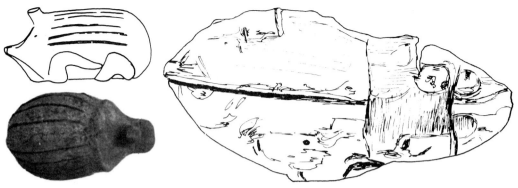

115. *(top)* Prophitis Elias. Beetle.
Etcret. 9, Pl. 45 No. 8666.

116. *(above)* Jouktas. Beetle. Ergon 1978, Fig. 73.
117. Piskokephalo. Clay figurine of a beetle HM 9796

themselves into the god's care, and reminding him of their existence and needs. A great number of votive offerings, as has been pointed out already, represent animals, that is, cattle and pigs, and especially bulls, and oxen, sheep and rams. These votive offerings not only testify to the fact that the god or goddess was offered simulacra instead of the real living animal,[68] but also to the fact that the human being was in the habit of reminding the divinity of the necessity of looking after the most important part of his property, and of watching over and caring for the whole of his flocks. It is therefore perfectly understandable that votive offerings in the form of animals were especially common in the peak sanctuaries, for the god's help, particularly in producing rain, was the very foundation of stockbreeding on the island. Of course the people also believed that the divinity was able to ensure fertility (as we see from the ithypallic figurines)[69] and to facilitate birth, as we can see from the figurines of pregnant women,[70] etc. But it was not just the protective powers of the divinity, or, the preservation of health[71] that made people come to the peak sanctuaries.

One of the most important reasons was that people were convinced that the divinity appearing in the sanctuaries had power over the whole world, and that the divinity transferred part of this power (with regard to worldly matters) to the king, that is, to a human being. It is very fortunate that seal impressions from a gold ring have survived from Knossos (Fig. 114), bearing a scene which may be interpreted as endowment of the king with power.[72] In the middle of the scene there is an outline of a mountain, on which a female figure is standing dressed in a bell-shaped dress and in a jacket which leaves free her ample bust. Undoubtedly a goddess is represented here. In her hand she is holding a sceptre or a spear. On either side of the mountain two lionesses are depicted, facing each other. At the side a man is standing, clad only in a loincloth.[73] Although his attitude is that of a supplicant the size of his figure, and in particular its scale as compared with that of the goddess, convince us that the figure, although a supplicant, is a person of importance, a king. At the side we see part of the façade of a building. This was meant to emphasise the sacred character of the scene. In this particular case, then, the position of the building in the scene was a matter of indifference. This scene which dates from LM II is of immense importance. The goddess depicted on the mountain top is holding a sceptre or a spear in her hand — in either case a symbol of power.[74] Today it does not need to be proved that the spear (and the sceptre) in many early societies were symbols or emblems of the authority of the chief of the tribe, or the king. Here, then, we have a scene showing the king being endowed by the goddess with his royal powers. The shrine at the side of the scene not only symbolises the sacred character of this act, but also indicates that the king's authority, being of divine origin, also extended to the divinity's property on earth, that is, her sanctuary and place of abode. The scene also confirms that the king acted as high priest. It should be remembered that these clay impressions were found in the western wing of the palace at Knossos, one near the Throne Room, and the other near the Temple Repository.

This interpretation of the scene is borne out by ancient testimony.[75] In the Odyssey there is a myth, probably coming from the Bronze Age, that the power of the ruler was of divine origin, and that this power, being a gift from god, had to be renewed periodically. As evidence of this we have the fact that the king had to keep in contact with his divine father, and that every nine years his royalty, or royal power, had to be renewed. This myth must have existed earlier than the gold signet ring showing this scene (LM II). It can no doubt be traced back to the period when the power of the priest-king was being established, that is, before the period MM I. An analogous myth is to be found in the Israelite tradition[76] where God also revealed his laws to Moses on a high mountain — Mount Sinai.

Contacts with the divinity, divine care over mortals and the divine origin of the power of the king are all elements that are found with some frequency in the works of art. For example, the royal chamber in the Palace of Knossos[77] contained a stone throne, the back of which was stylised in the form of a steep mountain, and therefore had double significance, first as a aniconic representation of the divinity, and second as a symbol of the care and protection the divinity extended to the ruler. The back of the throne was a symbol of the ruler's legitimacy and divine origin. This interpretation, as has been stressed above, is borne out especially by the picture of a baetyl in the shape of a stylised hill which is depicted on the rhyton from Zakro (Fig. 94). It will be seen from the above examples how close the links were between the palace and the peak sanctuaries. The kings and the whole of the ruling group had a vested interest in the welfare of the peak sanctuaries.

The scene interests us especially because it dates from a period in which — it is generally believed — Knossos came under the domination of the Mycenaeans, and also a period in which the apogee of the cult in the peak sanctuaries was already past. This can be explained. Despite the decline of the cult in many peak sanctuaries in Crete the continuation of the cult, and the making of sacrifices especially on Mount Jouktas, helped to maintain the continuity of the royal power and the belief in its divine origin. As compared with earlier times, the tradition surrounding the origin of the ruler's power was primarily confined to myth, a myth that played to the advantage of the kings of Knossos. On the other hand, the scene from Knossos has no Mycenaean characteristics; it no doubt adheres to the old iconographic motifs.

The figurines of beetles, too, provide us with valuable information about the lives and religious beliefs of the ancient Cretans. The most interesting fact is that these figurines were found not only in peak sanctuaries[78] and sacred enclosures[79] but also in private houses and in places whose function is not known precisely.[80] The clay models are usually bigger than the average living beetle (Figs. 115-7). The available information suggests that some of these models were placed on the floor of a clay altar (or sanctuary) from Piskokephalo.[81] One clay model was found placed on the back of a clay figurine from Piskokephalo.[82] Vessels were sometimes decorated with models of beetles[83] and in eastern Crete, a vessel in the form of a beetle was found.[84]

The beetles discussed here have a number of traits in common. One clay model found at Piskokephalo[85] can be described as follows:
the body is oval, the horn flat on top and the edge of the shard crenated. It has four pairs of legs, of which two pairs slope backwards and two forwards. The length of this model is 0.105 m. Another model is similar to the one described here, except that only two pairs of legs have been depicted.[86] The third model — discovered at the same place — is very similar, but the head is a different shape and the edge of the shard is not crenated. In contrast to the previous specimens, the abdomen and belly are ribbed (Fig. 117). The legs are not denoted at all (length of this model 0.08 m).[87] Another model is similar in appearance to the one first described here, except that only three pairs of legs are denoted. Of the other examples found at Piskokephalo, nearly all follow the same kind of pattern: the abdomen is oval and sometimes ribbed, the shard is quite separate from the rest of the body, and the horn is bent.[88] A very characteristic specimen was found at Prophetis Elias (Mallia).[89] This model represents a beetle with an oval body, two pairs of legs, a ribbed back and a flat horn (Fig. 115). Another vessel found at Palaikastro depicts a beetle with a slightly bent horn and an oval, grooved body.

It is most interesting to note that the Polish entomologist M. Mroczkowski, whom the author consulted in 1966, said almost without hesitation after seeing photographs of the finds of Prophetis Elias, Petsophas, Piskokephalo and Palaikastro that the models of beetles there could not be models of *oryctes nasicornis* (as has generally been supposed) but were, rather, of the scaraboid species: *copris hispanus*.[90] Mroczkowski pointed out that the ancient Minoans must have observed the beetles very closely, since they depicted not only males (with sharp-ended horns) but females as well (with truncated horns). In view of the characteristics of the copris, he said, and, in particular, the shard, the ribbing of the abdomen and thorax, the species of beetle depicted here was not in question. Some models, without ribbing and with their limbs in the appropriate places, are simply larvae, according to Mroczkowski. Copris, as

118a-b. Petsophas. Clay balls.

119. Copris hispanus L. J. Fabre, Souvenirs
antomologiques (1932), Pl. IV.

has already been pointed out, belongs to the scaraboid species, but in contrast to the scarab (*Scarabeus sacer*) it does not roll the sheep dropping in front of it, but digs a hole under it. In the peak sanctuaries small clay balls (Fig. 118a,b) were found, which may even represent sheep droppings. Apart from the *Scarabeus sacer* the copris is the biggest and most beautiful of the beetles.

The copris leads a sedentary life.[91] If it finds some food during the day then that same night, or at any rate after dusk, it digs a hole under a sheep's dropping. This pit would be big enough to hold an apple. The beetle then drags its sheep dropping into the hole. The dropping serves it as a house, with the entrance at the side. The beetle collects an enormous amount of food in its house and it does not leave until all its stores of food have been eaten up. At night it again begins a search for food, again digs a hole under a sheep's dropping, and again enjoys a period of leisure. In May, or at the latest in June, the beetle lays its eggs. It then digs a hole 0.20 m deep, where it places several sheep's droppings — three or even four. The male and female beetles then remain in this hole. The female lays three or four eggs on a suitably moulded sheep's dropping (Fig. 119). The mother remains in the hole until the larvae hatch, while the male, whose life has been until now conducted under the ground, in the dark, now runs about in the open, in the sun and warmth, for the three months of summer.

After 15 to 20 days the larva hatches. It is not a worm — as is the case with many insects — but a strong, sturdy creature. The larva is white, and has a yellow mark on the dome of its skull. Even at this early stage the crenated shard is well developed. The chrysalis appears about the end of July. It is normally yellow with red spots, although sometimes it is light brown. Towards the end of August the insect breaks its way out of the chrysalis completely, and after 15 days the beetle becomes completely black, and its shell hardens. By the end of September the insect can now come out of its hole.

Although the copris in Crete did not have the same importance as the scarab in Egypt,[92] the fact that numbers of these models of beetles were found in cult places and private houses suggests[93] that the inhabitants of ancient Crete believed that beetles (copris) brought good luck. Although this may be true, it does not exhaust. For the copris was of much wider importance. Since the copris lives on the faeces of domestic animals, its life is connected with the existence of a flock of sheep, the basic source of natural wealth in Crete.[94] The ancient Cretans kept a close watch on the habits of the copris, and drew conclusions from its appearance or disappearance. Where there were copris beetles there were sheep as well. Thus although the copris was not regarded as a sacred animal (and we have no proof of this), undoubtedly it must have been regarded as a representative of the Goddess who was the Protectress of earth and heaven. When they brought the models — which were usually much bigger than the real beetles — to the cult places the supplicants no doubt asked the goddess to multiply their flocks of sheep.

Concerning the types of divinities worshipped, it is reasonable to believe that the ancient Cretans invested the divinity that appeared on the mountains not only with a woman's shape, but also with an aniconic form. This belief is supported by the scene referred to above (Fig. 114). In the peak sanctuaries, the Cretans possibly worshipped not only a Great Goddess but also a minor male divinity. It is likely that in the earliest times only a goddess was worshipped, partly as a rain-giver. Probably at the same period, but surely later, when sanctuaries were erected on the peaks, it became the custom to worship a young male god as well. It was most likely in his honour that high wooden poles were erected in front of the façade of the shrine, or at its sides (Fig. 94). As with the Near East,[95] it is reasonable to suppose that these were an important element in rain magic. It is only natural that a high, vertical pole set on the topmost part of a bare mountain was likely to attract lightning. And lightning was always the forerunner of heavy rains, especially after a long period of drought.[96]

Ceremonies that took place in the peak sanctuaries were no doubt held only at special times — perhaps once or twice a year.[97] Generally when the devotees arrived at the sacred locality they would place their offerings in front of the shrine, inside the temenos area. That is the kind of scene that is depicted on a rhyton from Gypsadhes (Fig. 95). The man in this scene is clad only in a loincloth. He is not in a kneeling position but is bending forward and his left foot is placed in front. His hands are stretched out over a basket into which he is probably putting some objects: these are round in shape and may possibly be fruit. At certain times of the year, as far as one can judge from the Greek festivals of a later period, great ceremonies were held. On those occasions the High Priest, in the presence of the faithful, placed the offerings on the altar. Bonfires were also lit.[98] This was probably followed by the sacrifice of a young sheep which was then consumed by all present, at a feast. The principal ceremonies were accompanied by the strains of music, including music made on triton shells (see below p. 100). No doubt dances took place in the sacred locality in honour of the divinity, as is suggested by the remains of figurines representing groups of people described above. The pilgrims would throw their gifts into the embers of the drying fire — clay figurines representing human beings and animals. Sacrificial animals that had previously been killed were perhaps also cast into the dying fire. The ashes of the fire, along with the votive offerings, were then collected and kept in special places — usually clefts and fissures in the rock (Fig. 75).

The belief that the gods of the sky take up their abode on the mountain tops, or make appearances there, has been observed among many of the people of Asia, Africa and Europe.[99] Primitive man associated the ordinary phenomena of nature, such as the disappearance of the mountain tops into the clouds, with the actions of supernatural forces; they were easily convinced, therefore, that the divinity was able to come down to earth. Other natural phenomena, too, had an effect on man's imagination. The shape of some mountains may have suggested supernatural properties. An example is the Jouktas range, seen from Ghazi or Tylissos, which at first sight looks like the face of a reclining giant.[100] The inhabitants of Crete must have been very familiar with the shape of this mountain range. Travellers in Renaissance times, too, recorded the thoughts of the simple folk on this subject. At the beginning of the fifteenth century C. Buondelmonti[101] reported his observations as follows: 'The mountain is shaped like a human face . . . On the forehead . . . is the temple of Jupiter, while on the nose are three churches. . . . To the south, more or less facing Ida, is the chin.' Jouktas is not exceptional in its shape; many mountains in diverse parts of Greece resemble the human figure in outline.[102] All the phenomena described above — the natural phenomena as well as the shape of the mountains — gave rise to the belief that mountain peaks, especially distant and inaccessible ones — were places where the gods and goddesses appeared or had their abode. This, like the belief that gods and goddesses appear in caves, is a very common and very old form of religion.

The widespread nature of this belief that gods and goddesses revealed themselves on the mountain tops does not necessarily prove the existence of a cult there. We must now examine the circumstances in which a cult was born. The appearance of a cult on the mountain peaks about 2000 B.C., or even somewhat earlier,[103] makes us wonder why it was at this particular period that people began to bring offerings to the holy places on the mountain peaks in Crete.

In seeking the reasons for this explosion — for that is the only word suitable to describe the sudden appearance of this kind of cult — we must consider the question of the peak sanctuaries;

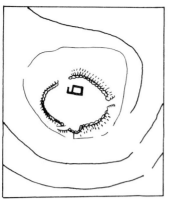

120. *(right)* Vrysinas.
121. *(above)* Prophitis Elias. Plan of sanctuary. Etcret. 19, 1974, Pl. III.
122. *(below)* Prophitis Elias. The hill.

their location and the ease of access to them. From the information that is available, we are convinced that access to the holy places on the mountains was comparatively easy, especially for the local people who from their childhood days were used to wandering in the mountain regions. The sanctuaries were easily accessible in part because most of them were situated at altitudes from 400 to 800 m, [104] and some of the peaks were even lower (e.g. Petsophas, altitude 215 m). In exceptional cases the sanctuaries were situated on the top of very high mountains. For example, there is one at an altitude of 970 m, a little below Kophinas (altitude 1,231 m), the highest peak of the southern range of the Asterousia mountains, which bounds Crete on the south. There is another sanctuary at Karphi on the borders of Lasithiou (altitude 1,148 m). Of course the altitude alone is not enough to determine whether the mountain peak was accessible or not. All the peak sanctuaries have paths leading to them, paths — which must have been easy for the local people — along fairly gentle slopes, where sheep wander in search of grazing land. But any visitor from the town who was accustomed to a peaceful study or monastery cell, was likely to be appalled by the dangers of the ascent to the top of the mountain. These dangers were no doubt magnified but they seemed real enough to the first traveller of modern times, the Venetian monk referred to above, C. Buondelmonti, who made a pilgrimage to the top of Mount Jouktas. [105] He was definitely convinced that the path to the top of Jouktas was an exceptionally difficult one. But from Archanes, on the west side of the Jouktas range, one can reach the lower peak of the mountain (altitude 811 m) in less than an hour. The ascent of Jouktas must always have been easy, as we can see from the fact that the Polish traveller,

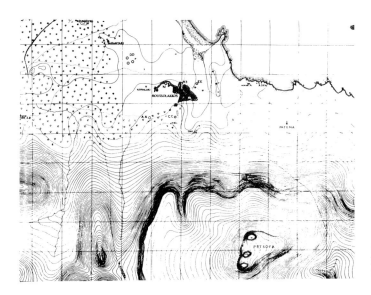

123. Topographical map of Palaikastro and Petsophas. BSA 60, 1965, Pl. 65 (fragment).

Mikołaj Krzysztof (Sierotka) Radziwiłł started to climb it from Candia at a time of the year (December 1583) when the day was short.[106] The mountains which had sanctuaries on their peaks usually had at least one easy side. For instance, one can climb to the top of Mount Pyrgos (altitude 685 m) from Tylissos in a little less than 45 minutes (or at any rate under an hour) by a fairly easy path. The climb to other sanctuaries confirms this general rule. Even sanctuaries that are built at high altitudes — such as the one on Kophinas — are not especially difficult to reach, as we can see from the fact that there are villages not very far from the temenos.

In the second millennium B.C. the highest mountain peaks (e.g. Mount Ida) were not cult places; it was only later in the Greek myths and legends that the gods and goddesses inhabited the highest points of the mountains. During the Mycenaean period, there was no cult place on Olympus, for example; we really only have the first evidence of a sanctuary here in the Hellenic period and later.[107] During the Bronze Age the highest mountain peaks were not the sites of religious ceremonies. We can therefore rule out the hypothesis that the main reason for the emergence of a cult on the mountain peaks was a disinterested desire to worship and pay tribute to the divinities of the heavens. The principal reason for the emergence of the cult must have been one closer to the everyday needs of the people.

Another possible indication of the accessibility of the peak sanctuaries is the distance between the cult place and the nearest town or village. All the peak sanctuaries were situated near inhabited areas, and usually at a distance of not more than an hour's walk. Sometimes, too, the cult place were easily seen from the town or village (Figs. 120-122). A few examples will suffice to illustrate this point. At a short distance from the town of Palaikastro (Fig. 123)[108] there are two peak sanctuaries, one on the top of Mount Petsophas (Fig. 89) and the other on the top of Mount Modhi. The former is about twenty five minutes' walk from the town, and the latter about an hour's walk. The mountain peak of Traostalos is situated only a few kilometres from the wealthy town Zakro and other settlements.[109] The village of Koumasa was situated on a neighbouring peak[110] just beside the temenos. In ancient times there were many villages below the peak of Kophinas, especially not far from the present-day village of Kapetaniana.

In order to determine the reasons why peak sanctuaries developed in the period MM I, we must study the kind of environment in which the cult places were situated. It has already been pointed out that the mountain slopes whose higher parts or peaks were occupied by sacred places dedicated to the gods bordered on natural pastures (this was the case at Jouktas). Even today the temenos there is contiguous with pastures on which sheep graze. This is also the case on the peak of Mount Pyrgos. On the side facing Tylissos there are typical mountain meadows. During the summer flocks of sheep have their grazing grounds here. A little down from the top of the mountain there are caves, at the entrance to which the shepherds seek shelter from the cold of the night. Even the temenos on Mount Pyrgos is not on an isolated peak. Towards the west and south-west the temenos area passes into gentle slopes that are high mountain pastures. It is probable, then, that before this place was regarded as holy the later temenos site must often have been visited by shepherds. There is a similar situation at Koumasa and many other settlements. Features of the same kind can be observed at cult places (especially rural sanctuaries in Hellenistic times) at a later period. From these remarks it may be concluded that all the sacred areas on the mountain peaks were places that were not cut off, but rather were continually penetrated by man in connection with his work (chiefly stockbreeding), places which were well known and easily accessible to the nearby inhabitants.

The votive offerings in the peak sanctuaries provide the best testimony about the faithful who made pilgrimages there. Taking into consideration what has been said above, namely that most of the figurines brought to the sanctuaries were models of animals, we may presume that the sanctuaries were created largely to meet the needs of cattle and sheep breeders. For the fact that the mountain sanctuaries were always within the reach of permanent penetration by the shepherds and their flocks is significant. Even in Hellenistic art we have a myth about Paris on Phrygian Ida; Paris guards his flock on meadows bordering a cult place that is not even walled off; no-one hinders his sheep from wandering over onto sacred land.[111] This myth, too, then illustrates the circumstances surrounding the cult places of these early peoples.

Today there are arguments that may enable us to solve the problem of the origin of peak sanctuaries. Apart from the statuettes of bulls and sheep, models of beetles (copris) were also typical votive offerings. It is logical to believe that a folk cult like this, with pastoral motifs, must have arisen in regions that both in Antiquity and today were pastoral.[112] One is struck by the comparatively large number of peak sanctuaries in the eastern part of Crete. It was *par excellence* a pastoral region. Thus it seems that the peak sanctuaries were established mainly to relieve the fears and cares of the shepherds and cattle breeders.

The development of the cult in the peak sanctuaries, stemming from the needs of the cattle breeders and shepherds, can also be traced back to the changes that took place in Crete from about 2,000 B.C. onwards, that is, about the time when the palace-urban civilisation emerged. The changes that took place in the form of power and in the social and political system led also to an increase of economic needs; against this background, cattle and sheep raising developed rapidly in Crete.

It is probable that the cattle and sheep breeders were not the only group of people who visited the peak sanctuaries. No doubt the arable farmers, too, brought offerings in the form of arable produce, especially grain. We have evidence of this in the remains of pithoi, vessels discovered at Kophinas, whose purpose was the storage of grain.[113] Miniature clay votive offerings representing plates with loaves of bread also testify to the idea that arable farmers were among the pilgrims to the mountain sanctuaries.[114]

In conclusion, it may be said that the peak sanctuaries probably first came into existence in MM I or earlier. Their appearance was spontaneous, being mainly a reflection of the economic needs of the inhabitants of Crete, especially the cattle and sheep breeders and the agrarian farmers. Although a deeply-rooted belief in the power of the divinities who were wont to appear on the mountains undoubtedly fostered the emergence of the peak sanctuaries, nevertheless the principal causes leading to the emergence of these cult places should be sought in the social and economic changes that took place in the period EM-MM I.[115] The rapid growth of stockbreeding and agriculture made the people want to be secure of the possession of their property. Since, of course, no scientific methods for safeguarding cattle and sheep and the crops were known in those days, these early people were forced to have recourse to those other methods — magic and religion — which in primitive societies take the place of science.

As has already been emphasised above, at the time when the peak sanctuaries were being established, that is about 2,000 B.C., Crete was in the final stages of the formation of the palace-urban civilisation. Gradually, from the period MM I onwards, power became consolidated in the palaces. The kings, e.g. at Knossos, became more and more anxious to extend their influence to the cult places, which until then had developed spontaneously. Consequently in the course of a doubtless slow process the local, peasant cult places gradually became transformed into places of a more general character, which served the whole population — the inhabitants of town and country alike. The causes of this process have been explained above, but the principal one among them was the king's desire to strengthen his own position.

By being supported by divine authority, the royal power was not only strengthened, but was also consolidated. The myth formulated during the rise of the new pattern of society,[116] to the effect that the king was of divine origin, the rule (already referred to above) that the king's authority had to be renewed periodically by the gods, and the contacts between the king and the divinity on the mountain top, all meant that the peak sanctuaries gradually came within the orbit of royal power in Crete.

Probably from the period MM III onwards the cult became institutionalised through the appointment of permanent priests who guarded the cult place and represented the royal authority. As the royal protection became extended to the peak sanctuaries, these sanctuaries were made increasingly beautiful. Important sanctuary buildings were erected in MM III although usually they were built in MMT. This was probably also the time when people first began to worship the goddess's spouse. He was accredited with some of her functions, such as producing rain by lightning.

It is interesting to note that in Israel as well the king took over the task of protecting the peak sanctuary, and that a change took place in the social function of the mountain cult places, for we know that during the reign of Solomon the 'high places' came within the orbit of the king's influence. In the period preceding Solomon these rural sanctuaries were modest places sparsely furnished with an altar; in Solomon's reign they became part of the royal political system. When this happened the first temples — often costly and imposing buildings — were built on the sites.[117]

In Crete, the way in which the peak sanctuaries were incorporated into the system of royal power probably varied according to where the sanctuaries were situated. The important sanctuaries must have been treated differently from the small, provincial ones. The large sanctuaries, such as those on Jouktas, Petsophas, Modhi, and Traostalos, their subordination to the central authority and their transformation from places of local, rural significance to places of general significance to all groups of society was complete in the period MM III at the latest. The small provincial sanctuaries, on the other hand, which were situated far from the seat of centralised power, retained their original character as cult places of local significance, serving the local peasant population. The votive offerings found in some of the peak sanctuaries appear to bear out this hypothesis.

In the Minoan civilisation, however, important changes took place in LM IA. During this period, the main reasons for these changes are to be found in the natural events which then took place. Probably in LM I there was a violent eruption of a volcano on the island of Santorini (Thera).[118] Such disasters must have had an important effect on the lives and beliefs of the population of Crete. In our opinion, the importance of volcanic eruptions on the history of forms of thought and belief has hitherto been underestimated.[119] It should be remembered, however, that at this time fundamental changes were taking place in many cult places. These provide us with indirect evidence of how far reaching were the effects of the events described above.

As a result of the disasters that occurred in LM I the cults in the peak sanctuaries declined. It is quite characteristic that, with few exceptions (mainly on Jouktas), no objects from the Late Bronze Age have been found in the peak sanctuaries. This suggests that later, from LM II onwards, the number of pilgrims who worshipped divinities on the mountain tops diminished. This decline of faith in the divinities of the heavens is quite understandable; they had been powerless to prevent disasters so their authority had weakened. Often the people turned away from the gods because they could not help them. So at this time the inhabitants of Crete must have turned for aid to the underground deities in the caves. As a matter of fact, we know that the cult caves grew in number and popularity from LM I onwards. Presumably the inhabitants of Crete appealed to the deities there to save them from the disasters of further volcanic eruptions.

The rejection of the mountain-top deities was not final and irrevocable. For on Mount Jouktas[120] much LM I-III pottery has been found. On Modhi, too,[121] LM pottery has been reported. From the votive offerings discovered on Kophinas[122] and Petsophas,[123] too, it may be concluded that in LM I, and perhaps later, pilgrims visited sanctuaries there. On Koumasa[124] as well, the sanctuary came into use again for a second time in LM IIIB.

One wonders if the revival — although limited and on a small scale — of the peak sanctuary cults was due only to the force of tradition in Crete. It seems probable that it stemmed not only from the everyday needs of the rural population, but also from their belief in the divine origin of the king's authority, which was conveyed to him by the deity on the mountain summit. This motif still occurs in seal impression dating from LM II (Fig. 114). The myth that the king had contact with the divinity on the mountain peak was no doubt one of the basic reasons that led to the revival of this cult in the LM II-III periods, after the disasters caused by the eruption of the Santorini volcano.

There were cult places on the mountain tops right through Antiquity, sometimes even on the same sites as the Minoan sanctuaries. Throughout all the subsequent changes in religion — e.g. the cult of other gods, such as Zeus, or, later, the cult of saints, such as Elias — these same spots were always consecrated to the gods or visited by the gods.

CATALOGUE II

Peak Sanctuaries

1. Ai Ilia, in the vicinity of Sybia (Sitias). A rhyton discovered as well as pottery. It is not certain, however, if the site was used in Minoan period.
Faure, Cav, 38; Faure, Lab 29; Faure, NRT, 121; CPl, 320.

2. Ai Lias, altitude 470 m, not far from Vorrou, near Megali Vryse (Monophatsiou). Pottery found; a votive double axe probably came from this site (MM III-LM I).
H. G. Buchholz, Kadmos, 1 (1962), 166ff; Faure, NRT, 124; AD, 23 (1968), 403; CPl, 320; Hiller, 173.

3. Ambelos (Xerokampos), Sitias. Discovered and excavated by C. Davaras (1971). Some figurines found.
C. Davaras, Ergon (1971), 264f; PAE (1971), 302; AD, 27 (1972), 651; CPl, 320; Hiller, 168.

4. Ankouseliana, o Karavellos (A. Vasiliou). Clay figurines dating from MM period are said to be discovered.
S. Alexiou, KCh, 17 (1963), 401; AD, 18 (1963), 316; Faure, NRT, 127f; CPl, 320.

5. Ayia Triada. Figurines at the hill slopes probably belonged to the peak sanctuary or a rural shrine on the top.
Ann NS, 31-2 (1969/70), 413f; Hiller, 172.
Chamaizi see Domestic sanctuaries p. 150.

6. Choudetsi (Pediados), at Korphi, not far from Vathypetro. Clay figurines and parts of a building found. Dating from MM.
Faure, CulS, 504; S. Alexiou, AD, 18 (1963), B, 310, 313; KCh, 17 (1963), 399; Faure, NRT, 123.

7. Demati, in the neighbourhood of Skinias (Monophatsiou), altitude 180 m. Clay figurines dating from MM I discovered, as well as pottery vessels.
Faure, STSS, 180; AD, 19 (1964), 443; 21 (1966), 409; KCh, 18 (1963), 406; 20 (1965), 289; CPl, 320; Hiller, 173.

8. Drapanos, at Drapanokephala (Apokoronou), altitude 528 m. Research made in 1964 and continued in 1968. The finds included pottery as well as a votive double axe made of bronze (dating from MM III-LM I). Remains of a building (?) found.
BCH, 89 (1965), 56f; Faure, STSS, 186; AD, 24 (1969), 434; BCH, 94 (1970), 11; CPl, 321; Hiller, 172.

9. Etia (Sitias), at Etiani Kephala, altitude 715 m. Clay figurines dated to the MM period discovered. The site was excavated by C. Davaras in 1971.
N. Platon, KChr, 13 (1959), 391; G. Daux, BCH, 84 (1960), 882; F. Schachermeyr, AA (1962), 136; Faure, NRT, 121; Ergon (1971),264f; PAE (1971), 320; AD, 27 (1972), 652; CPl, 321; Hiller, 169.

10. Gialomonochoro at the gorge of Ayiopharangos not far from Odeyitria Monastery. Surface finds. Cult use of the site is uncertain.
K. Branigan, D. J. Blackman, AR, 18 (1971/2), 23; BCH, 96 (1972), 395; Hiller, 173; BSA, 72 (1977), 41ff.

11. Gonies, at Philiorimos (Maleviziou), altitude 797 m. Excavations carried out in 1966. A building, an altar, and numerous clay figurines dating from the MM period were found.
N. Platon, Atti (1967), 402; S. Alexiou, KCh, 18 (1964), 282; Faure, NRT, 125f; S. Alexiou, AD, 20 (1965), 552; KCh, 20 (1966), 322; AD, 22 (1967), 484f; Faure, STSS, 184; CPl, 321; Hiller, 172.

12. Jouktas (Temenous) the tou Zia to mnima site. Archaeological surveys from the early nineteenth century. Explorations revealed cult objects, votive offerings (e.g. clay figurines), walls of a terrace and the walls of a temenos. Excavations by A. Karetsou which started in 1974 revealed an open-air area with an altar, a building, a cave, poros horns of consecrations, stone offering tables, bronze double axes, bronze and numerous clay figurines, sealstones, objects of gold and ivory. Pottery dated to MM I/III, LM I and III. Used mostly in MM-LM times, and later.
C. Buondelmonti, Descriptio insulae Candiae, ed. by Legrande, (1897), 148f; M. Radziwiłł, Hierosolymitana peregrinatio (1601), 242; C. Savary, Lettres sur la Grèce faisant suite de celles sur l'Egypte (1788), 194; R. Pashley Travels in Crete (1837) I, 210ff; A. Taramelli, MA, 9 (1899), 350ff; Evans, TPC, 23f; G. Karo, ARW, 7 (1904), 124; W. Aly, Philologus, 81 (1912), 465; Cook, I, 160ff; Evans, PofM, I, 153ff; II, 939ff; A. Lawrence, JHS, 62 (1942), 84; Nilsson, MMR², 71f; Platon, IK, 144f; 153ff; KCh, 6 (1952), 480; BCH, 77 (1953),

241; P. Faure, in *Minoica* (1958), 133ff; C. W. Brice, *Inscriptions in the Minoan Linear Script of Class A* (1961), 14 No. I 15 pl. 20; S. Alexiou, AD, 18 (1963), 312; KCh, 17 (1963), 399; A. Karetsou, Ergon (1974), 112ff; (1975), 176ff; (1976), 184ff; (1977), 181ff; (1978), 62ff; (1979), 29f; PAE (1974), 228ff; (1975), 331ff; (1976), 408ff; (1977), 419ff; Sanct Symp. 137ff; AR, 21 (1974/5), 27; 22 (1975/6), 29; KCh, 17 (1973), 470; BCH, 99 (1975), 964; 100 (1976), 732; Hiller, 170f; B. Rutkowski, *Acts of the International Archaeological Symposium*, 'The Relations between Cyprus and Crete, *c.* 2000-500 B.C.' (1979), 225f; FGK, 24f.

13. Kalamaki at Kephala near Vai (Sitias), not far from the monastery Toplou. Many figurines found by C. Davaras in 1971.
C. Davaras, AD, 27 (1972), 651; CPl, 321; Hiller, 168.

14. Karphi (Lasitiou). Excavations carried out in 1939. They brought to light fragments of clay figurines, as well as miniature vessels dating from MM times.
H.W., J. Pendlebury, M. B. Money-Coutts, BSA, 38 (1937/8), 97f; Pendlebury, AC, 102; Platon, IK, 142ff; Faure, NRT, 122; CPl, 321.

15. Kato Zakro, at the Gorge of the Dead. Pottery dated to MM IA and fragments of figurines found.
N. Platon, Ergon (1975), 188; BCH, 100 (1976), 723; AR, 22 (1975/6), 32; Hiller, 172f.

16. Keria, not far from Gonies (Maleviziou), some distance down from the summit (altitude 1,160 m). Many pottery vessels and clay figurines from MM discovered.
Faure, STSS, 183f; AD (1967), 486; CPl, 321.

17. Kophinas (Monophatsiou), at Metsolati tou Kophina. Discovered in 1955. Finds comprised wall of a temenos, as well as cult objects, and votive offerings made of clay or of bronze. Temenos used in the MM period and later.
N. Platon, KCh, 9 (1955), 567; 10 (1956), 420; G. Daux, BCH, 80 (1956), 343; S. Hood, AR (1956), 22; G. Daux, BCH, 81 (1957), 617; N. Platon, KCh, 13 (1959), 387; N. Platon, C. Davaras, KCh 14 (1960), 526; Faure, NR, 200; G. Daux, BCH, 84 (1960), 833; AR (1961/2), 24; F. Schachermeyr, AA (1962), 136; Faure, CulS, 501f; N. Platon, C. Davaras, AD, 17 (1961/2), 283, 287f; S. Alexiou, AD, 18 (1963), 310, 313; KCh, 17 (1963), 384, 399; G. Daux, BCH, 19 (1965), 882; S. Alexiou, AD, 19 (1964), pl. 514d; Faure, NRT, 124f; Faure, STSS, 181; CPl, 321.
Korakies *see* Koumasa

18. Korphi tou Mare, in the neighbourhood of Ziros (Sitias). The local inhabitants are reported at one time to have found clay figurines here.
Faure, NRT, 128; CPl, 321.

19. Koumasa (Monophatsiou), altitude 420 m, the summit of Korakies Hill. Excavations carried out in 1906 revealed the remains of a sanctuary, sacred objects, and votive offerings including pottery. The site is dated to MM II and LM IIIB.
S. Xanthoudides, *Panathenaia*, 7 (September 1906), 32; AA (1907), 108; AA (1909), 99; S. Xanthoudides, VTM, 1, 49; D. Fimmen, *Die Kretisch-mykenische Kultur* (2nd Ed.), (1924), 19; Evans, PofM, IV, 140f; Platon, IK, 145ff; S. Marinatos, AE (1937), 284 n.3, 289; Platon, MOl, 457; Faure, CulS, 502. Faure, NRT, 125; Faure, STSS, 181; CPl, 319; Hiller, 173.

20. Krasi, at Entichti (Pediados), altitude 800 m. Walls of a temenos and of a building discovered, as well as pottery dating from MM I.
Faure, STSS, 177, CPl, 321f.

21. Lastros (Sitias). Possibly a figurine dated to MM II comes from this site.
Platon, IK, 147, pl. 7:13; Faure, NRT, 122, CPl, 322.

22. Linarou Selli (Monophatsiou) near Kapetaniana. The ruins of a building, as well as fragments of clay figurines dating from MM, were discovered at this site.
S. Alexiou, KCh, 17 (1963), 384; Faure, NRT, 128; CPl, 322.

23. Maza, on the summit of Stou Maza or Korphi, in the vicinity of Kalo Chorio (Pediados). Excavations carried out in 1947. Numerous clay figurines from MM discovered.
N. Platon, KCh, 1 (1947), 639; Platon IK, 96ff; F. Schachermeyr, AnzAlt, 4 (1951), 15; N. Platon, KCh, 12 (1958), 479; G. Daux, BCH, 83 (1959), 733; F. Schachermeyr, AA (1962), 2, 136; Faure, NRT, 122f; CPl, 322.

24. Megaloi Schinoi at the Gorge of Ayiopharangos near the Odeyitria Monastery. Surface finds. Found in the same area as site No. 10. Cult uncertain.
K. Branigan, D. J. Blackman, AR, 18 (1971/2), 23; BCH, 96 (1972), 395; Hiller, 173; BSA, 72 (1977), 42ff.

25. Modi, altitude 539 m, between Palaikastro and A. Photia (Sitias). Excavated by C. Davaras. Many clay votive offerings and bronze knifes found. The walls of a sanctuary noted.
Faure, NR, 192ff; BCH, 84 (1960), 192f; Faure, Cav, 37f; C. Davaras, AD, 27 (1972), Chronika, 652; Faure, NRT, 118; CPl, 186, 188, 322; Hiller, 168.

26. Perivolakia (Sitias), in the vicinity of Kapparou and Kephala. Clay votive offerings found. Cult uncertain.
Faure, NRT, 128.

27. Petsophas (Sitias), altitude 215 m. Excavated already by J. L. Myres in 1903, when many clay figurines from EM III/MM I-LM I and later were found. New excavations by C. Davaras in 1971 brought large number of clay figurines (some large figurines of beetles), inscribed offering tables, stone vases and lamps and bronze daggers.
J. L. Myres, BSA, 9 (1902/3), 356ff; Evans, PofM, I, 151; Pendlebury, AC, 103, 116; Platon, IK, 120ff; Faure, NRT, 116; K. Davaras, AD, 27 (1972), 652; CPl, 159ff; 170ff, 183, 322; Hiller, 168.
Philiorimos *see* Gonies.

28. Plagia (Sitias). A temenos discovered in 1962 was later destroyed. Many votive offerings, including large clay figurines, are said to have been discovered.
    Faure, CulS, 496 n.1; P. Faure, BCH, 89 (1965), 28; S. Alexiou, KCh, 17 (1963), 399, 406; AD, 18 (1963), Chronika 313; Faure, NRT, 119; Faure, STSS, 176; CPl, 322.

29. Pobia (Kainourgiou) at Vigla. Many figurines dating from MM were found here, at an altitude of 300 m.
    Faure, STSS, 181; CPl, 322.
    Prinias see Zou

29a. Prophetis Elias, Mallia, on a hill 99 m high, where were traces of temenos wall, a terrace wall, MM I sherds and pithoi fragments and a figurine of a beetle. Sacred function probable but not certain.
    P. Demargne, BCH 58, 1928, 505; Pendlebury AC, 102, 123; Platon IK, 140f; P. Demargne, Etcret 9, 1953, 4ff; Faure NRT, 115; CPl, 47f.

30. Pyrgos (Maleviziou), altitude 685 m, at a site where there are two peaks, one called Korphi tou Pyrgou, and the other called Pera Korphi. Site discovered in 1962. Walls of a sanctuary discovered here, as well as many clay votive offerings from the MM period.
    Faure, CulS, 500f; AR (1962/3), 31; S. Alexiou, KCh, 17 (1963), 404f; Faure, NRT, 125; G. Daux, BCH, 41 (1967), 789; CPl, 153f, 322; Hiller, 172.

31. Sklokas, on the Akrotiri peninsula, at an altitude of 528 m. Large amount of pottery from MM I-II found here in 1968. Site destroyed.
    Faure, STSS, 187; CPl, 322.

32. Thylakas, altitude 521 m, at Goulas (Lato), not far from Mesa Kakkonika (Mirabellou). Fragments of clay figurines were found.
    A. Evans, BSA, 3 (1896), 169; J. Demargne, BCH, 25 (1901), 283; Evans, TPC, 100; G. Karo, ARW, 7 (1904), 145; A. Reinach, RA (1913), 289ff; P. Demargne, BCH, 53 (1929), 407ff; Faure, NRT, 122; J. Sakellarakis, AAA, 3 (1970), 1, 252ff; AD, 27 (1972), 647; Faure, CPC, 393; CPl, 322; Hiller, 169.

33. Traostalos (Sitias), at Gallou Skopeli. Discoveries made in 1962. Sanctuary excavated, as well as many clay votive offerings and bronze figurines.
    Faure, Cav, 38 n.2; Faure, CulS, 493ff; Ergon (1964), 148; S. Alexiou, AD, 18 (1963), 313; KCh, 17 (1963), 399, 405f; Faure, Lab, 30 n.1; C. Davaras, Kadmos, 6 (1967), 101ff; Faure, NRT, 116f; Faure, STSS, 181; CPl, 322f.

34. Vigla, not far from Epano Zakro (Sitias). Discoveries made in 1966, excavations — 1972. Votive offerings from MM found.
    Faure, NRT, 118; C. Davaras, AD, 28 (1973), Chronika 592; CPl, 323.

35. Vrysinas, altitude 858 m, near Rousospiti (Rethymnou). Finds from surface survey (1962 and earlier), excavated by C. Davaras (1972-3). Many votive offerings found, statuettes of men and women, figurines of bronze and bronze knifes, two miniature bronze axes, offering tables etc. At the nearest top of Ammoudaroporos remains of walls of a shrine.
    Faure, CulS, 504ff; S. Alexiou, AD, 18 (1963), 315f; BCH, 87 (1963), 504ff; S. Alexiou, O Kretikos Politismos (1964), 126; KCh, 17 (1963), 401, 412; P. Faure, BCH, 89 (1965), 49ff; C. Davaras, AAA, 7 (1974), 210ff; Kadmos, 16 (1977), 5f; Faure, STSS, 185; BCH, 96 (1975), 694; AR, 21 (1974/5), 28; CPl, 323; Hiller, 172.

36. Xykephalo (Sitias), altitude 705 m, in the vicinity of Katelionas. Fragments of clay figurines discovered in 1962, excavations carried in 1971 (C. Davaras).
    Faure (1963), 496 n.1; P. Faure, BCH, 89 (1965), 30; Faure, NRT, 119ff; Faure, STSS, 180; K. Davaras, Ergon (1971), 265; PAE (1971), 302; AD, 27 (1972), 652; CPl, 323; Hiller, 168f.
    Ziros see Korphu tou Mare

37. Zou (Sitias), on Prinias, between Zou and Katsidonia, altitude 803 m. Discovered in 1965, excavated 1971 by C. Davaras. Clay votive offerings, among others a vessel in the shape of a beetle.
    Faure, NRT, 118f; BCH, 91 (1967), 167f; C. Davaras, AD, 27 (1972), 651; CPl, 323; Hiller, 169.

VI
Sacred enclosures in Crete

STUDIES on the sacred enclosures, as was mentioned above, meet serious difficulties because archaeological evidence is scarce as yet. The most important information comes from iconographical sources, and especially from the glyptic art. The scenes on the rings, seals, clay seal impressions, and stone vases commonly depict elements of religious ceremonies or beliefs which may have been enacted in the sacred enclosures. It is not always easy to establish the exact location of these scenes; the cult rites were usually depicted as taking place against an indistinct topographical background which was sometimes hardly indicated at all. This vagueness can be attributed to the fact that delineation of the background was only of minor importance to the owner of the ring. Sometimes roughly sketched vegetation is the background to the religious scene. These iconographic sources provide very little information about the kind of trees and plants that grew in the sacred enclosures, since they are represented in such a simplified way. But at any rate trees, bushes and other plants always formed part of the cult scene (Figs. 124-135). One might think that the kind of trees depicted in these scenes would help us to identify the place where the rites were held. For instance, we can identify fig trees (Fig. 125), olive trees (Fig. 133), and perhaps even palm trees (Fig. 126). Nevertheless, identification of the species of tree or plant is insufficient to enable us to say just where the given religious rite was being held. For these species were to be found in a wide variety of places and altitudes, even above 600-700 m,[1] as we can see from the vegetation at some of the actual peak sanctuaries. For instance, on the summit of Mount Pyrgos (685 m) an oak tree can be found today, having survived many savage winds (Fig. 75). Thus the vegetation which we see on the iconographic sources could equally well have grown in the coastal zone, or right in the interior of the island, or at various altitudes (with the exception of the high mountain zone), and either in the towns and villages or right out in the country (Figs. 124-126). This sparse information about the location of the sacred enclosures and the kind of vegetation to be found there has been supplemented by observations made on the spot. But at any rate the kind of scenes that are depicted on the iconographic sources indicate that the sacred enclosures were situated out in the country, away from the towns and villages. In this respect they are similar to the open-air sanctuaries depicted in Hellenistic and Roman art which were outside the towns, perhaps sometimes near settlements.[2]

In Greece, as in many other countries, the places where there were sacred trees, or baetyls, were often in natural surroundings untouched by man. From the relics found *in situ* on Crete[3] and from the scenes depicted in representational art (Figs. 124-126), it may be concluded that some of the forest clearings or some of the rocky spots where trees grew were once cult places. These places, at which the remains of chapels have survived, could also be on the slopes of low hillocks[4] or the summits of small hills. All these places which we mention must have been fairly accessible.

It is difficult to say how big the sacred enclosures were. The archaeological finds provide us with no clue. All we have to go on in guessing the size of the sacred enclosures is a possible comparison with the peak sanctuaries (Fig. 76). As a rule, however, we can take it that the area they occupied was not big. We know nothing about their shape either. By examining peak sanctuaries,[5] however, we can conjecture that the sacred enclosures occupied a space that was irregularly-shaped or sometimes fairly oval, as we see from part of the wall of a sacred enclosure discovered at the Kephala site near Episkopi, Pediados[6] and a model of sacred enclosure found at Vounous on Cyprus (Fig. 137).[7] It is worth recalling that the sanctuaries portrayed in Hellenistic representational art were sometimes oval.[8] But by examining the peak

124. Archanes. Gold ring. FGK, Fig. 1.2.

125. Kalyvia by Phaistos. Gold ring. FGK, Fig. 13.5.

126. Idaean cave. Rock crystal seal. FGK, Fig. 12.1.

sanctuaries we can also assume that some of the sacred enclosures were rectangular, or nearly so.

Representational art tells us very little about how the god's domain was separated from the area round about. This was probably done in two main ways. The most common way, although we have no direct proof of it in the finds, must have been some conventional manner of dividing off the sacred area from the land surrounding it. Gradually, then, the place where the deity made appearances began to be regarded as that deity's property. This practice dated from the time when the belief that the god resided there, or visited there, became consolidated; a spot may be said to be a cult place from the time people started to bring offerings. The size of the god's domain could then be more or less fixed, especially if it was situated in waste land where there was no conflict with the farmers or shepherds. It was not necessary to mark the spot by a sign because popular memory and tradition were sufficient to make people remember the boundaries of the god's property. In inhabited areas, or in areas which were used by the cultivators or herdsmen, a conventional way of marking out the area belonging to the deity was generally used, the way commonly used to mark out the pieces of arable land or pasture land belonging to different individuals or different tribes. Sometimes the sacred area marked out in a more visible way by putting a large stone or heap of rough pebbles on the boundary-line. We have no direct evidence of this custom, but the commonness of the practice of marking the boundary between different plots of land by means of stones — a practice which is confirmed by the ancient texts[9] — inclines us to the view that this custom goes back to the Bronze Age. In other words, we believe that in the Bronze Age the method of marking the boundaries between the various plots of arable land and the pastures, and that of marking the boundaries of the deity's property, were one and the same. This conviction is corroborated by other, indirect evidence dating from the Bronze Age. For there was a common custom — although we rarely have evidence of it in the finds — of marking the site of a tomb by means of a stone. This stone not only made it easier for people to find the place where the deceased had been interred, but also marked the spot as an area which was visited from time to time by the departed, and as a place to which only the departed person had the right to possession.[10]

The fact that the cult place was cut off from the rest of the terrain by a wall is confirmed by the finds, such as the wall fragment discovered *in situ* mentioned above,[11] and by the scenes depicted in art. The variety of walls surrounding these sacred enclosures is evident in the iconographic finds alone. They were probably low walls, made in the simplest way of rough, generally unhewn, stones found in the fields (Fig. 135). These walls are similar in type to the present-day ones that keep people out of the fields belonging to Greek farmers; it even looks as if there is no difference at all between these present-day farm walls and the walls that once marked the boundaries of the sacred enclosures. Of course sometimes they may have been different. For instance, the more important sacred enclosures may have been encircled by more solidly constructed walls that were higher, and thicker, and that may even have been used for defence. This view would seem to be borne out by the solid construction of a wall depicted on a gold ring found at Archanes (Fig. 124). Sometimes, too, the walls surrounding the cult places

127. Knossos-Gypsadhes. Bronze ring. FGK. Fig. 2.7.

128. Knossos. Gold ring. FGK, Fig. 1.11.

129. Mochlos. Gold ring. FGK, Fig. 2.10.

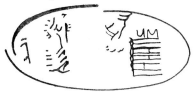

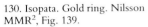

130. Isopata. Gold ring. Nilsson MMR², Fig. 139.

131. Zakro. Seal impression. FGK, Fig. 1.6.

132. Ayia Triada. Seal impression. FGK, Fig. 32.6.

may have been built carefully, as seems to be the case in a scene on a ring found at Knossos (Fig. 128). The fact that the wall in this case is crowned by a double cornice indicates that it was very carefully constructed. A similar isodomic construction of a wall surrounding a sacred enclosure — that is, it too has a distinct cornice — can be seen on a bronze ring found at Knossos-Gypsadhes (Fig. 127). A quite similar wall construction is also shown on a gold ring discovered in grave 11 at Kalyvia at Phaistos (Fig. 125). What looks like a wall can be seen on both the left and the right sides of this scene.[12]

Walls were used not only to mark off the sacred area but also to surround and protect certain objects, such as the holy tree. This custom is quite similar to the isolating of holy trees from the environment, as depicted in Hellenistic and Roman paintings.[13] There is also evidence that even inside the sacred area the holy trees were separated from their surroundings in diverse ways. In Dodona, for instance, this is done by setting up a circle of bronze tripods.[14] A number of interesting finds dating from Minoan Crete provide us with convincing indications that the sacred trees were protected by surrounding walls. A gold ring from Mochlos, for example (Fig. 129), clearly shows a wall built round a tree. A rhyton from Gypsadhes (Knossos) shows a sacred olive tree encircled by a low wall (Fig. 135), whereas the altar is outside the most holy place. We have further proof in a scene found on the Ayia Triada sarcophagus (Fig. 136) that the sacred trees were surrounded by walls. We see on the sarcophagus a tree ringed by a wall whose construction must have been careful and extensive. The wall, as has already been mentioned, was not left in its raw state but was covered with plaster and painted. The geometrical designs, and especially the spirals, were not a matter of accident but must have had a symbolic meaning, as emblems of the Great Goddess.

On the gems we sometimes see constructions whose meaning is not clear (Fig. 130). In these cases we cannot be at all certain whether the artist intended to depict a wall round a sacred enclosure, or a wall round a sacred tree. The walls round the sacred trees must have been built there not only for sacred but also for practical purposes, especially in the case of those enclosures where access was not protected by walls round the whole area. Sacred enclosures, which as a rule were adjacent to pastures and meadows, ran the risk of being devastated by the sheep and cattle grazing nearby.

The famous painting, of much later date, of Paris with his flocks of sheep in an open-air sanctuary at Troas on Mount Ida,[15] provides us with an excellent illustration of the situation we have described here. Paris's sheep can be seen to be grazing right beside the holy place. Of course in ancient Greece it must have been quite typical for shepherds to graze their sheep in the areas consecrated to a deity.

The walls round the sacred enclosures and those round sacred trees were sometimes crowned with horns of consecration. This cult emblem can be seen, for instance, on the wall depicted on the bronze ring from Gypsadhes (Fig. 127). The scene on the Ayia Triada sarcophagus gives us more information still, for on it the wall round the sacred tree is also crowned with horns of consecration.

133. Ayia Triada. Seal impression. FGK, Fig. 2.11.
134. Knossos. Clay matrix. FGK, Fig. 2.3.

102

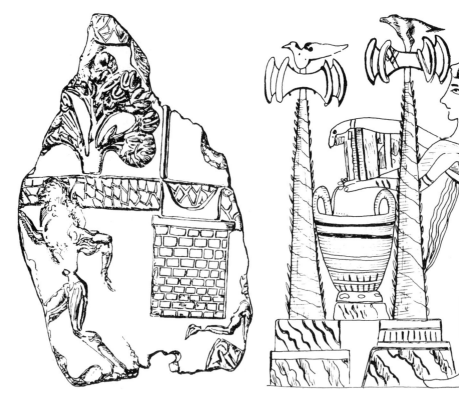

135. Knossos-Gypsades. Fragment of a rhyton. Evans TPC, Fig. 2.

136. Ayia Triada Sarcophagus. A sacred place. Evans, PofM, I, Fig. 317.

137. Vounous, Cyprus. Model of a sacred enclosure. Courtesy of the Department of Antiquities, Nicosia.

138. Archanes. Model of a sanctuary.   139. Kamilari. Model of a sanctuary. Courtesy of D. Levi.
FGK, Fig. 5.3.

In the glyptic art, the scenes generally show gateways into the sacred enclosures (Fig. 128). These are shown so sketchily that it is difficult to guess how they were constructed and how they were ornamented. It can be taken for granted, however, that the gateway into the sacred enclosure, like that into the peak sanctuary, was not only an ornamental structure but an imposing one as well which left visitors suitably impressed.

Probably not all of the sacred enclosures had cult buildings, for these were not needed in poor, seldom visited places. Of course it is just possible that holy buildings made of perishable materials did exist, but we have no evidence of this. On the other hand, what we do know for certain is that some of the enclosures had modest cult buildings made of stone. Most of those were rectangular sanctuaries,[16] although one cannot altogether rule out the possibility that oval buildings meant for sacred purposes were erected as well.[17] We have evidence of this in a clay model found at Archanes (Fig. 138) dating from the Protogeometric period. Others were rectangular (Figs. 139 and 142). The remains of a building excavated at Sphakia (Patela), near Zou (Sitias) belonged to a sacred enclosure. Here, on a hill with an altitude of 375 m, a small, partially preserved building (dating from MM IIIB) has been unearthed. None of its rooms has survived completely, but we can see that the building at one time had two rows of rooms, with narrow entrances. Some of the rooms may have been paved with stone.[18] The remains of a sanctuary have been found too, at the site at Kephala (Pediados)[19] at an altitude of 295 m. This was a building measuring 5.00 × 4.20 m, and dating from LM III. The remains of a very poorly preserved building discovered at Plai tou Kastrou near Kavousi, at an altitude of 410 m, no doubt date back to the sub-Minoan period (Fig. 140).[20] Probably at the same period the people also visited another cult place, near Kavousi at Pachlitsani Agriada, at an altitude of 200 m. The remains of a small sanctuary measuring 4.45 × 3.50 m, built or large, irregularly hewn stones, have also been excavated there. There was a stone bench inside the building (Fig. 141).[21] Two different kinds of building give us further insight into the topography of the sacred enclosures. One is at Gazi, near Iraklion, situated on a nearly flat ground (see p. 104). Only part of the cult building was excavated, but the uncovered room was small and nearly square (Fig. 143). The other sanctuary, at Kato Symi, is situated high in the mountains, on the south slopes of Dikti, beneath the perching rocks and close to an abundant spring, which could have been held as sacred in Antiquity (see p. 104). We believe that the sacred enclosure was founded because of the sacred spring, and later developed into an extensive cult complex. It is not yet quite clear what the plan of the sanctuary looked like in the initial period, that is in MM III-LM (Fig. 144). It seems that already in the Bronze Age the temenos occupied an extensive area, with several rooms used for cult purposes. But, curiously enough, it seems that the stone built altar in the open-air was first erected in the Geometric period.

Well-preserved models of sanctuaries indicate what the rectangular type of building was like. A clay model of a sanctuary from Kamilari (Fig. 139)[22] is especially rich with information. From this model we can assume that some sanctuaries had two rooms. Apart from a columned portico, there was also the cult room proper. This room had thrones instead of the usual bench, and altars stood nearby. Probably cult idols were set on the thrones, although in this particular

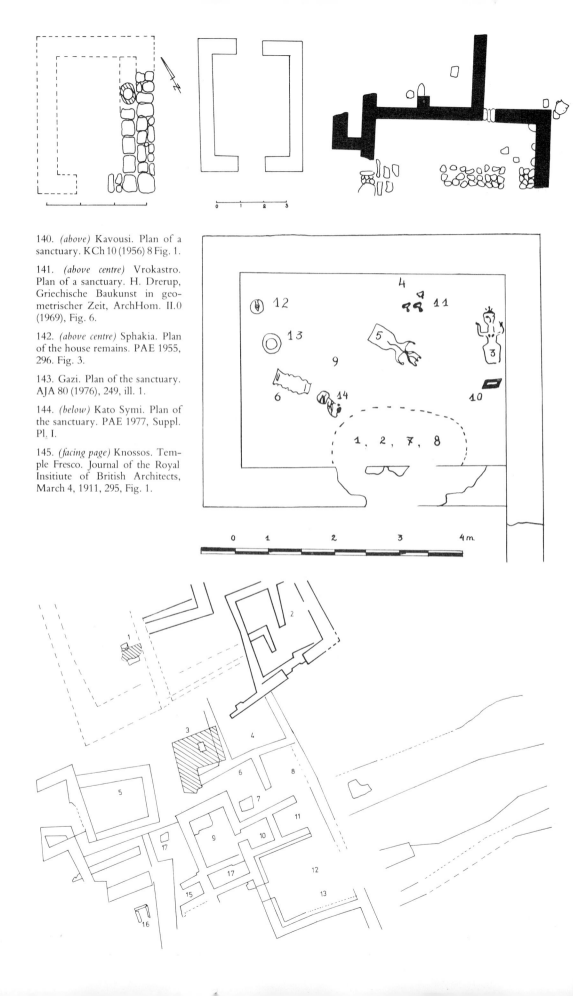

140. *(above)* Kavousi. Plan of a sanctuary. KCh 10 (1956) 8 Fig. 1.

141. *(above centre)* Vrokastro. Plan of a sanctuary. H. Drerup, Griechische Baukunst in geometrischer Zeit, ArchHom. II.0 (1969), Fig. 6.

142. *(above centre)* Sphakia. Plan of the house remains. PAE 1955, 296. Fig. 3.

143. Gazi. Plan of the sanctuary. AJA 80 (1976), 249, ill. 1.

144. *(below)* Kato Symi. Plan of the sanctuary. PAE 1977, Suppl. Pl. I.

145. *(facing page)* Knossos. Temple Fresco. Journal of the Royal Insitiute of British Architects, March 4, 1911, 295, Fig. 1.

model the artist's intention was probably to represent the deity itself, rather that the deity's image (cf. Fig. 138). A minor detail of this model is worth noting: on the one extant wall of the model there are as many as three windows, high up, just under the ceiling. Buildings of this kind, as we know from the model of a house[23] or sanctuary[24] found at Chaniale Teke, near Knossos, dating from the eighth century B.C., were covered with a flat roof. The clay model found at Phyties (Archanes),[25] mentioned above, represents another type of building. Probably in this case the building was oval in shape, and had a steep roof that flattened out somewhat at the bottom. Inside this building there was no doubt a bench that held a cult statue and other holy objects (Fig. 138).

We must repeat, then, that the material evidence indicates that the sanctuaries built in the sacred enclosures were small. These buildings were usually rectangular, but sometimes oval. The sanctuaries had few rooms; generally one was sufficient for all the needs of the cult, such as for storing the objects used in the rituals, but occasionally there were several rooms, one of them being a portico or sacristy. One of these rooms, especially from LM III onwards, generally held the cult statue, while the others were used for keeping the cult objects and the votive offerings. Thus some of these rooms were really storerooms. Occasionally the magazines belonging to the sacred enclosures were situated outside the sanctuary altogether, just as the proprietors of richer houses sometimes built magazines outside the house. Excavations have also revealed magazines inside the sacred enclosures. At Poros, for instance, a small artificial grotto was found, with stone stairs leading down into it.[26]

Some other details can be added to this information about the ground plan, appearance and function of the buildings in the sacred enclosures. The sacred buildings doubtless consisted of a ground floor only (Fig. 145),[27] although examples of buildings with a ground floor and first floor did occur (Fig. 131).[28] The roof was generally surmounted by horns of consecration (Fig. 127). The entrance to the building, as we can see from the scene on the A. Triada sarcophagus, was sometimes richly decorated with motifs which had a symbolic meaning (Fig. 146) such as spirals.[29] Usually these were buildings of simple construction (Fig. 146, cf. 127)[30] but occasionally they had an open portico (Fig. 139),[31] and the existence of more complicated buildings with tripartite façades cannot be excluded. A tripartite façade can be seen, for instance, on a miniature fresco found at Knossos (Fig. 145). This building has two lower parts, and one higher part (the middle one). In the middle part, the ceiling is supported by a single column, but the ceiling of the side parts is held up by two columns on each side. The remains of horns of consecration have been preserved between the columns. On the basis of comparison with other finds,[32] Evans though that all three parts of the building had been surmounted by

146. Ayia Triada. Sarcophagus. Temple and Cult Statue. Evans PofM, I, Fig. 316.

horns of consecration.[33] On either side of the façade, and at a certain distance from the building, wooden pillars once stood probably quite detached from the main building.[34] Similar pillars, also standing in isolation, were also erected in the peak sanctuaries (Fig. 94).

Owing to the very nature of the place, one of the most important features of the sacred enclosures must have been the altars. The scenes depicted as taking place in the sacred enclosures are frequently being enacted in front of an altar. A fragment of a rhyton from Gypsades (Knossos) for instance, shows a rectangular altar (Fig. 135)[35] built of hewn stones arranged in even rows. On the cornice of the altar there are horns of consecration. Based on information from other scenes, particularly one on the A. Triada sarcophagus (Fig. 146) one would expect the altar on the rhyton from Gypsadhes to have steps which, however, the artist has not indicated. Altar constructions are known from other evidence,[36] such as structures standing on their own outside the holy building.[37] This is corroborated by scenes in the glyptic art,[38] too (Fig. 126).[39] We know from the paintings on the A. Triada sarcophagus (Fig. 146) that the altars were sometimes plastered and decorated with paintings. The spiral, which had the same symbolic significance here as on the façades, was the foremost motif, but the iconographic finds tell us that another type, the incurved altar, was used as well. A sealstone from the Idaean cave, for instance (Fig. 126), shows us an altar resembling in shape two cones imposed one on top of the other, with their apexes meeting, probably standing in the middle of a sacred area. This altar is surmounted by horns of consecration.[40] Similar stone altars were found in the 'Summer Palace' at Archanes.[41] Almost every time an altar was needed, this was the type used.[42]

It is possible, of course, that other kinds of altar were used as well, although there is no evidence of them in the archaeological or iconographic finds. Mention must be made, in particular, of the simplest type of altar, that is flat stones on which sacrifices were laid. It would be quite easy for such altars not to be noticed by the archaeologists engaged in excavations, although they have sometimes been noted in the sepulchral cults — for instance near a tholos tomb at Kamilari and Apesokari (Fig. 11).[43] The votive offerings could also simply have been placed on the ground, in some holy part of the sacred enclosure area. Although there is no direct material evidence available, it is also highly likely that fires were made in the sacred enclosures, hence fire altars were possibly used; no doubt the faithful put their offerings into the dying embers. The sacred enclosures doubtless also has sacrificial tables on which the votive offerings were placed, or the victims killed.[44]

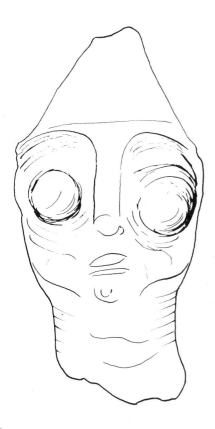

147. Kato Symi Sanctuary. Head of a statue. PAE 1975, Pl. 257b.

The sacred tree was undoubtedly held in high honour: as we have said, it was usually surrounded by a wall. It is seldom possible to determine the species of trees depicted in the iconographic art, for they have been simplified too much. Exceptions do occur however: on the rhyton from Gypsadhes (Knossos), for instance, we find a scene (Fig. 135) in which a huge fig tree[45] can be seen behind a wall. This can be recognised as *Ficus caprica L,* which was especially esteemed in Greece in later times.[46] The A. Triada sarcophagus has a scene with an olive tree growing behind a wall. Olive trees are to be seen growing, too, on a fragment of a miniature wall painting found at Knossos, showing dancers in a place which we think is a sacred enclosure. Unfortunately, this painting is fragmentary and it is impossible to say whether the tree was held in special honour or not. One interesting thing to note is that a building of some kind, perhaps even a sanctuary, stood near these trees.[47] But there is nothing to suggest that the olive trees in this painting were protected by a fence or wall. Finally, a sealstone from the Idaean cave shows a tree which could be a palm tree (Fig. 126).[48] It must be stressed that there is nothing at all to prove that the palm was of any special significance in the sacred enclosures. We do know, however, that the palm tree was held in special honour in the classical period in Greece.[49] Some of the scenes dating from the Minoan period suggest that the palm was of special significance in those times as well. For instance, we occasionally find one on the top of a stone mound, or crowning a symbolically represented hill.[50]

It is characteristic that most of the trees mentioned here, especially the olive and the fig, played an important part in the everyday lives of the Cretan inhabitants. After all many people's lives largely depended on the way in which these trees were cultivated and on the kind of crops they gave.[51] Thus one aspect of the cult in the sacred enclosures was no doubt connected with ensuring and maintaining the sources of existence; other aspects were probably connected with the birth and death of plants, and therefore with human life and death as well. We shall come back to these matters later.

It is almost certain, then, that the trees in the sacred enclosures had a sacred function. But they must have had another important one — that of adorning the buildings and objects there. Branches were used to decorate the altars (Fig. 126)[52] or, as we can see in the paintings on the A. Triada sarcophagus, the sacred pillars standing in isolation in the cult places (Fig. 136).

There is no reason to doubt, then, that both gods in an aniconic form and cult statues of the anthropomorphic type were worshipped in the sacred enclosures. But the evidence for the

148. Phaistos. Clay dish. Matz Gött. Pl. 5.

149. Sachturia. Clay statue. Courtesy of Y. Tsedakis.

existence of anthropomorphic cult images comes mostly from the temples and domestic sanctuaries.[53] We know a little about the LM cult images (Fig. 147) in the sacred enclosures.[54] Of course although the evidence of idols in the archaeological and iconographic material was of a comparatively late date, this by no means proves that the concept of anthropomorphic deities first emerged in the Late Bronze Age. We must clearly separate two concepts here — one that anthropomorphic deities could be represented as cult images, and the other the Bronze Age people's belief that deities when they appeared did so in human form. Both these concepts can be perceived in the iconographic sources. In the Middle Bronze Age we find several representations depicting deities in human form appearing to human beings (Fig. 148), and we also find some evidence of the existence of cult images. Before the Middle Bronze Age there were usually cult images of a different kind — baetyls. This aniconic aspect of the cult may have become disseminated as a result of the influence of the sacred grottoes. A gold ring from Archanes (Phyties) shows a baetyl (Fig. 124) shaped like a pillar, which occurs on the ring along with other symbols such as an eye, a chrysalis and a butterfly. The baetyl is vertical in shape, and has a short cross-bar with two protuberances. The fact that the pillar is depicted as being outside the sacred enclosure may be due to the conventional character of the scene, in which the emphasis, as usual, is placed on the actions performed in connection with the cult, whereas other matters, such as the place and the character of the action, are merely subsidiary. The baetyl may also have been used here as a hieroglyphic sign.[55] A baetyl slightly different in shape can be recognised on a gold ring from Mochlos (Fig. 129)[56] where it can be seen floating free in space, above a figure sitting under a sacred tree. The true function of the baetyl can be seen on a ring found at Knossos (Fig. 128).[57] In this scene, inside a gateway leading into the sacred enclosure there is an object which should be interpreted as a baetyl inside a cult place. And finally, a baetyl-stone of a different kind again, most probably a stalagmite or a stalactite roughly esembling the Cycladic idols,[58] is depicted on a sealstone from the Idaean cave (Fig. 126). But we must stress once more that both types of idols referred to above must have been used as hieroglyphic signs.

A clay seal impression from A. Triada shows a scene, the site of which is not altogether certain (Fig. 132). It depicts a table in front of which a woman stands with her hands raised in a gesture of adoration. There are conically-shaped objects which are probably stalactites brought from a grotto.[59] Of course this scene may equally well be taking place in diverse kinds of cult places, such as a domestic sanctuary or a sacred enclosure.

Apart from those pillar-shaped baetyls, baetyls in the form of natural, oval-shaped stones were also worshipped.[60] Scenes connected with this sort of cult can be observed e.g. on two gold rings from Archanes (Fig. 124) and Kalyvia (Fig. 125). Each of these scenes shows an oval object which a woman, in a dance of ecstasy, is touching. It was universally the custom to stroke or touch the baetyl. This was similar to the customs obtaining to the sacred caves, where the concretions — stalactites and stalagmites — were also treated with special adoration, and were stroked by human hands so often that the marks can still be seen.[61]

We have already emphasised that the existence of cult statues is proved by the material evidence of a very early age. We may recall the finds at Gazi,[62] which are typical of the furnishings of a domestic sanctuary and probably of a sacred enclosure, dated to LM IIIB.[63] Very large statues of deities may have been relatively more common, judging from some finds, e.g. Sachtouria (Fig. 149) and Pankalochori.[64] On the other hand the iconographic sources depict not the statues of deities but the deities themselves. For instance, inside a clay model found at Archanes (Phyties), there is a statuette representing a goddess with her hands raised in blessing (Fig. 138).[65] Here we probably have a representation of a goddess as a living being, rather than a cult image. It has been thought that the female figures (Fig. 130)[66] and sometimes the male figures as well (Fig. 128, and 131) were meant to represent deities appearing to humans in a holy place.[67] This supposition cannot be ruled out, although of course the human figures here cannot be cited as proof that the Minoans set up anthropomorphic statues of their gods. Sometimes, however, the figures shown on works of glyptic art as sailing through the air may have been meant to represent idols. A seal impression from Zakro (Fig. 131)[68] can be cited as a particular example of this. The tiny figure represented in this scene is reminiscent of the bell-shaped idols. This resemblance is not complete, however, for the deity in the scene referred to here is portrayed in full movement, whereas the bell-shaped idols are more static.[69]

We have already remarked that vertical pillars, which sometimes had other symbols stuck into them, were often erected in the cult places. High pillars with no emblems were probably erected in the sacred enclosures as well.[70] From the evidence of a rhyton from Zakro (Fig. 94) we see that the pillars were constructed as vertical wooden beams with sharp points at the top. They stand at the side of the scene, at quite a distance from the sanctuary façade. The same is clear on the rhyton fragment from Gypsades (Fig. 95).[71] Inside the wall built around the sacred tree, part of a high, and probably sharp-pointed pillar is also visible (cf. Fig. 126). Another scene has survived on a gold ring from Knossos (Fig. 128).[72] In front of the wall of a sacred enclosure behind which is a sacred tree, an exceptionally important, solemn ceremony is taking place — a male deity is appearing to a female worshipper. Between the worshipper and the wall of the sacred enclosure is an object which is possibly a pillar. Part of a sacred enclosure with two pillars is also depicted on the A. Triada sarcophagus (Fig. 136). In the centre of a scene there a priestess is pouring some kind of liquid (probably wine) into a crater. The presence of two tall pillars wreathed with ivy and surmounted by double axes shows that the place is holy.[73] Birds which are probably doves[74] are perched on the double axes, thereby indicating that a deity is present during the offering up of the sacrifices. A pillar is depicted on the other side of the sarcophagus as well. This iconographic evidence can be used to support the thesis that pillars, whether with or without sacred emblems, were of great importance in the sacred enclosures.[75]

The sacred double axes surmounting the pillars in the sacred enclosure pictured on the A. Triada sarcophagus (Fig. 136) are the only example of their kind in Minoan pictorial art. Nevertheless they served as symbols of divinity in the sacred enclosures more often than the material evidence would seem to indicate. The horns of consecration were generally set on the walls of sanctuaries (Fig. 127)[76] or on the altars (Fig. 135) are visible indications that the deities often appeared in the sacred enclosures.

Apart from the altars and tables, we know very little about the furnishings used in the ceremonies that took place in the sacred enclosures. A sealstone from the Idaean cave (Fig. 126) shows a woman holding an object to her mouth which undoubtedly was a triton shell, which in Antiquity and at the present time is known and used in Crete as a musical instrument.[77] The finds give us less information about the other furnishings. Judging from the evidence of a clay

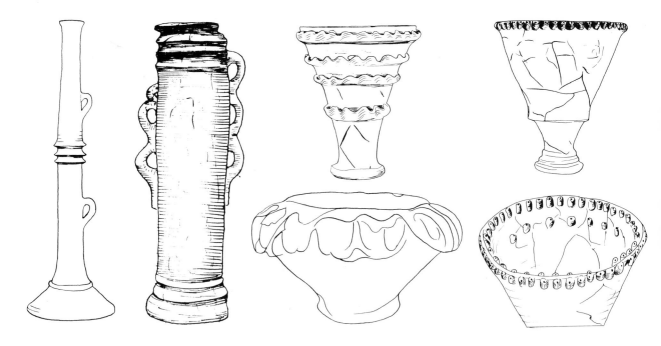

matrix found at Knossos (Fig. 134),[78] we know that sacrificial vessels shaped like a bucket with two large, circular, ornamental handles must have been used in the rituals. Of course there must also have been rhyta and pitchers (Fig. 137) in every cult place.[79] And there were tube vessels supporting the sacrificial bowls and stands commonly used in the sacred rites (Figs. 150-151).[80] An important example of cult implements and votive objects used in the sacred enclosures is given by the excavations at Kato Symi; for example a stone offering bowl (Fig. 153) and clay offering vessels (Figs. 154a,b, 152-7).

The function of the persons who appear in the scenes in the sacred enclosures is not always entirely clear. But certainly the woman portrayed on the sealstone from the Idaean cave (Fig. 126)[81] must have been a priestess whose function was to invoke the deity. This priestess, dressed in a bell-shaped skirt, with her breasts, head and feet bare, is blowing a trumpet to draw the goddess's attention to the fact that the faithful are waiting for her to appear in the sacred enclosure. Clearly we have here an invocation scene taking place in a holy spot.

In other scenes (e.g. Figs. 127,133), it looks as if the deity is being summoned solely by an invocation dance performed by the priestesses or female worshippers. An example of this, which is already regarded as a classic one, can be seen on the scene portrayed on the gold ring found at Isopata (Fig. 130) where we see four women dancing in a meadow full of flowers and bushes.[82] From the position of the various women, it looks as if they are performing a ring dance. The gestures of their hands and arms, which must have been dictated by the figures of the dance, express adoration and expectation. The purpose of the dance is a very solemn one: they are summoning the goddess. Her arrival has been indicated by the artist through the convention of placing her tiny figure in the upper part of the scene.

(*Above from left to right*)
150. Kato Symi. Stand for a sacred symbol. PAE 1973, Pl. 198b.
151. Gazi. Stand for an offering bowl. AJA 80 (1976), 251 Pl. 41 Fig. 2.
152. (*top*) Kato Symi. Clay offering vessels. PAE 1973, Pl. 198c.
153. Kato Symi. Stone offering bowl. PAE 1973. Pl. 201a.
154a b. Kato Symi. Clay offering vessels. PAE 1973, Pl. 199a.
155. (*right*) Kato Symi. Interior of the vase. Fig. 153. PAE 1973. Pl/ 199b.
156. (*far right*) Kato Symi. Small stone vases. PAE 1973, Pl. 200a.
157. (*top facing page*) Kato Symi. Offering table. PAE 1973, Pl. 200b.

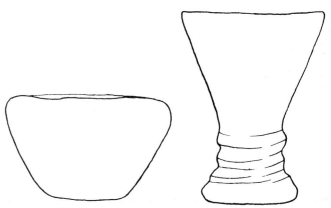

The number of women taking part in the ceremonial dances varied. Of course what we see on the rings is only a small part of the festive occasion. It represents only the most important, culminating moment, since on this miniature scale it would have been impossible for the artist to include the crowd of onlookers. A seal impression from A. Triada (Fig. 133)[83] depicts three women, one taller than the others. They are clad in traditional dress. The moment caught here is one where the dancers appear to be whirling round, with their hands on their hips. This dance must have consisted of rapid movements of the arms and the body, as is confirmed by the scenes on other rings as well (Fig. 124).[84] A gold ring from Kalyvia (Fig. 125)[85] shows a woman who is perhaps completely naked, rapidly whirling round, her arms raised above her head. At the same time, another woman, in a kneeling position, is bowing in front of a baetyl, and a third woman is shaking a tree — or maybe in the heat of the dance, she merely touches it with her hands.[86] Sometimes the gist of the scene is that, as a result of protracted supplications, the god or goddess makes an appearance in the holy place. In such a context, as we learn from a gold ring from Knossos (Fig. 128),[87] a priestess welcomes the god with great ceremony. It has already been remarked that for lack of space the artist was not in a position to represent the entire ceremony. He had to use symbols to indicate what he wanted to say, and he had to select those features of the ceremony which represented its very essence. Only in the scenes painted on the frescoes did the artist have an opportunity to develop his subject. The miniature fresco from Knossos, for instance,[88] shows us a large group of dancers and a crowd of spectators.[89] The dance being performed by a group of women near sacred olive trees in a specially segregated place seems to be a very energetic one.

But it was not only women who took part in these dances. Men took part, too, as we can see from a scene on the rhyton from Gypsades (Fig. 135) where two men are executing vehement dance movements in front of an altar in a sacred enclosure. Both of them seem to be clad in loincloths only. The head of the almost erect male dancer has been lost[90] but it has been suggested that he was wearing a mask. The other man, who most probably wore no mask, is almost kneeling, and his arms are held out in front of him in a gesture which perhaps indicates that he was casting something on the ground. Majewski believes this is a dance in which 'the leader was masked, and the other dancers were going through dance movements symbolisng the sowing of seed'.[91] It may, therefore, have been a vegetation dance. This interpretation goes far beyond the evidence provided by the scene, but it is not contradictory to the character and function of the sacred enclosures, in which ceremonies designed to ensure good crops of grain, as well as of tree fruits such as olives and figs (Fig. 135), must have been of prime importance.[92]

Another interesting scene is displayed on a clay seal impression from Zakro (Fig. 131).[93] A man seems to be bending over a sacred tree. One interpretation is that he is dancing at a

consecrated spot. We expect that lack of space alone compelled the artist to depict this solemn moment so summarily. Other male dances, too, could have taken place in the sacred enclosures. An interesting example is provided by a clay model from the tholos tomb at Kamilari, depicting four dancing men (see p. 113). They were probably naked, apart from caps on their heads. They were performing a ring dance — that is, all the men formed a circle and then, holding hands, moved round in that circle. The horns of consecration in the model indicate that the dance was taking place in a consecrated spot, in this case a sacred enclosure.[94]

We have very little information about the kind of gifts that were brought to the sacred

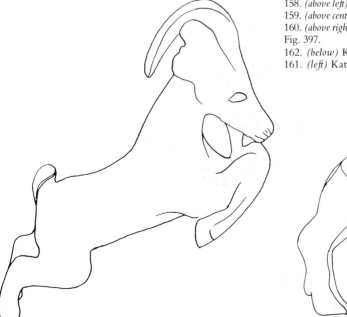

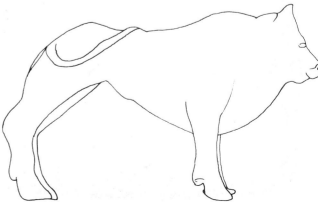

158. *(above left)* Piskokephalo. Clay figurine. Zervos, Crète, Fig. 395.
159. *(above centre)* Piskokephalo. Clay figurine. Zervos, Crète, Fig. 396.
160. *(above right)* Piskokephalo. Female clay figurine. Zervos, Crète, Fig. 397.
162. *(below)* Kato Symi. Animal figurine. PAE 1975, Pl. 256a.
161. *(left)* Kato Symi. Agrimi. PAE 1975, Pl. 256b.

163. *(above)* Zakro. Multiple clay figurine. Courtesy of the Department of Antiquities, Ashmolean Museum, Oxford.

164. *(left)* Kamilari. Group of dancers. Courtesy of D. Levi.

enclosures. But at any rate clay votive offerings, in the form of figurines of men (Figs. 158 and 159),[95] women (Fig. 160)[6] and animals (Figs. 161 and 162) such as oxen (Fig. 163) and sheep,[97] were prominent among them. Sometimes these votive offerings were very similar to those found in the peak sanctuaries[98] and some of the domestic sanctuaries.[99] A stone lamp[100] was also found in addition to the figurines mentioned above, and in all the sacred enclosures the discoveries have included fragments of ceramic vessels. In exceptional cases there have even been vessels with horn-like protuberances on the rims[101] and clay balls.[102]

When we take all these facts into consideration, we are led to the conclusion that the

165. Kalamion. Pyxis. AAA 3, 1970, 111 Fig. 1.

166. Kotchati. Clay model of a shrine. Courtesy of the Department of Antiquities, Cyprus Museum, Nicosia.

principal deity worshipped in the sacred enclosures was the Goddess of Fertility, to whom the sacred trees, that is the olive and fig trees (Fig. 135) which are of fundamental economic importance to the inhabitants of Crete were dedicated. No doubt rituals imitating the actions designed to bring about good crops, such as the sowing of seed (Fig. 135) were performed there. This aspect of the cult is endorsed by the discovery of figurines of men dancing naked, for this kind of dance was undoubtedly also associated with good harvests (Fig. 164). It is also quite likely, although we have no direct proof of it, that religious mysteries associated with sadness at the death of the vegetation at certain seasons, or with joy at other seasons in connection with the new burgeoning of plant life, were held in the sacred enclosures (Fig. 165).

It is likely the inhabitants of Crete believed that the goddess's husband could cause rain, and for this reason vertical wooden pillars were erected in the sacred enclosures. These were placed either near the god's dwelling, that is, the sanctuary, or on the most holy part of his property.

The position of the sacred enclosures as well as their significance as places where cults and rites answered to the people's fundamental needs made them one of the oldest types of cult places on Crete. Although the earliest traceable evidence is from no earlier than the Middle Bronze Age (Fig. 166),[103] it seems likely that these cult places, although in a far more modest form, existed much earlier than the time when the palace-urban civilisation came into being, that is, about MM I.[104] There are numerous relics from primitive times as well. Significantly, most of the people who attended the religious ceremonies were farmers. When authority over all Crete became centralised under a king, the new rulers, too, retained a lively interest in the prosperity of agriculture, which was under the patronage of a goddess. For these reasons it is likely that all groups of the population took part in the religious ceremonies and mysteries, at least in some of the more important sacred enclosures.

CATALOGUE III

Sacred enclosures

1. Arkokephalo (Viannou). Remains of a building, as well as sea shells found.
BSA, 59 (1964), 87.

2. Aski (Pediados) at Amygdokephalo not far from Kastelli. Walls of a sanctuary(?) and one clay figurine were found.
KChr, 10 (1956), 119f; AR (1956), 22; Faure, Fonct, 97 n.3; Faure, NRT, 143f.

3. Epano Zakro, at para to Epano Zakro, ypo epikremamenon vrachon. The earliest excavations date back to 1896. Clay figurines were discovered. See, however, a note on p. 116.
MA, 6 (1895), 183; Platon, IK, 122; Faure, NRT, 115.

4. Kalochorio (Pediados). Clay idol discovered.
Ann, 10/12 (1927/9), 619; Faure, NRT, 145.

5. Kamiliari, the Sta Elia site. Fragments of two clay figurines, which once probably belonged to a cult place, discovered.
KChr, 17 (1963), 406; AD, 19 (1964), Chronika, 443; Faure, STSS, 209.
Kastelli see Keramoutsi

5a. Kato Symi (Viannou). The temenos is situated just by a spring. Rooms of a MM III-LM I sanctuary were discovered, and from LM I-III the area was probably used as an open temenos. Stone offering tables, a funnel offering vessel, a votive bronze double axe, many figurines and other objects were reported.
A. Lembesi, PAE (1972), 193ff; (1973), 188ff; (1974), 222ff; (1975), 322ff; (1976), 400ff; (1977), 403ff; B; Rutkowski, Acts of the International Archaeological Sympsium, 'The Relations between Cyprus and Crete, c. 2,000-500 B.C.' (1979), 223.

6. Katsaba (Temenous). Votive offerings dated to MM II-LM I.
Faure, STSS, 209.

7. Kephala, in the vicinity of Episkopi (Pediados). Remains of a sanctuary, and walls of a sacred enclosure dating from LM III found here.
PAE (1952), 621; KChr, 6 (1952), 474; Faure, NRT, 144.

8. Keramoutsi Kavrochoriou. Potsherds and vases of MM I found. Clay figurine discovered previously.
KCh, 17 (1963), 406; AD, 19 (1964), Chronika, 443; Ergon (1966), 153, 155; KCh, 20 (1966), 323; PAE (1966), 191f; AD, 22 (1967), Chronika, 486; Faure, STSS, 181, 210; Hiller, 173.

9. Kostili (A. Vasiliou), near Miksorouma. A clay figurine and a lamp dating from MM discovered.
Faure, NRT, 146.

10. Kremasma, in the vicinity of Kato Sisi (Mirabellou). MM figurines discovered, as well as pottery from LM III.
BCH, 53 (1929), 529; BCH, 73 (1949), 307ff; KCh, 17 (1963), 405; Faure, NRT, 142f.

11. Pachlitsani Agriada, near Kavousi (Ierapetras). Remains of a sanctuary were found, as well as votive offerings from the sub-Minoan and Archaic periods.
KCh, 10 (1956), 7ff; Faure, NRT, 142.

12. Pankalochori (Retymnou). Clay idol found in 1932.
AA (1933), 297; AD, 15 (1933), Par, 55ff; KCh, 12 (1958), 188; Faure, NRT, 145.

13. Phyties (Archanes). Remains of a sacred enclosure discovered.
Faure, NRT, 146 n.4.

14. Piskokephalo (Sitias), at Katrinia. Remains of a building discovered, as well as clay votive offerings dating from MM.
MA, 6 (1896), 171; BSA, 12 (1905/6), 37; AA (1932), 171; AA (1938), 474; BSA, 40 (1939/40), 43; Platon, IK, 124ff; KCh, 6 (1952), 475f; 7 (1953), 484f; 9 (1955), 413; PAE (1952), 475f; 7 (1953), 484f; PAE (1952), 631ff; Faure, NRT, 115; Faure, STSS, 206.

15. Plai tou Kastrou, near Kavousi (Ierapetras). Remains of a sanctuary found.
AJA, 5 (1901), 149f; Faure, NRT, 142.

16. Poros (Temenous), in the vicinity of Katsaba (Iraklion). Objects dating from MM IIIB-LM IA came to light.
KCh, 10 (1956), 416; AR (1957), 17.

17. Sachtouria (A. Vasiliou), the Ai Jannis site. A clay statuette found here.
BSA, 62 (1967), 203ff; Faure, STSS, 210.

18. Skinias (Monophatsiou). Objects belonging to a sacred enclosure were found here.
KCh, 17 (1963), 406; KCh, 18 (1964), 283f; Faure, NRT, 146; Faure, STSS, 180.

19. Skopi (Sitias). Remains of an oval-shaped building perceived. Figurines and pottery dating from MM discovered.
PAE (1953), 297; Faure, NRT, 121.

20. Sphakia, in the vicinity of Zou (Sitias), at Patela or Pateles. A sanctuary was discovered, as well as objects dating from MM IIIB.
KCh, 9 (1955), 563; Ergon (1954), 101f; PAE (1955), 296f; Faure, NRT, 140.

21. Stous Athropolitous, near Epano Zakro (Sitias). Remains of a building and clay figurines discovered. Note. Recent research proved that the sites Nos. 3 and 21 are one and the same locality.
BSA, 7 (1900/1), 147; 9 (1902/3), 276; 33 (1932/3), 99; Platon, IK, 122; Faure, NRT, 115.

22. Vaveloi, near Nea Praisos (Sitias). Clay figurines probably dating from MM were found.
AJA, 5 (1901), 384ff; Faure, NRT, 146 n.5.

CATALOGUE IV
Iconographic sources

1. Ayia Triada, sarcophagus decorated with pictures of ceremonies being held in a cult place. LM IIIA, Museum: HM.
R. Paribeni MA 19, 1908, 1ff; Nilsson MMR², 426ff; Matz Gött, 396ff; B. Rutkowski, *Larnaksy egejskie* (1966), 126 No. 109; B. Nauert, *Antike Kunst*, 8 (1965), 91ff; Ch. Long, The Ayia Triadha Sarcophagus (1975); FGK, 132.

2. Ayia Triada. Fragments of an ivory vessel. Scene taking place in front of a cult building. Museum: HM 58.
B. Rutkowski, *Levi Studies*, I (1978), 148ff; FGK, 56, 58, 60, 62, 72, 84, 124.

3. Ayia Triada. Seal impressions. Three women dancing near a structure. Museum: HM 505.
F. Halbherr, MA, 13 (1903), 42f; Evans, PofM, II, 341; D. Levi, Ann, 8 (1925/6), 141; Nilsson, MMR², 286; FGK, 30.

4. Ayia Triada. Seal impressions. A woman stretching out her hands towards a table on which there are stalactites(?). Museum: HM 487.
F. Halbherr, MA, 13 (1903), 42; D. Levi, Ann, 8/9 (1925/6), 139; N. Platon, AE (1930), 168; Brandt, GG, 2; FGK, 29, 84.

5. Amnissos. Round naiskos with domed roof, dated to LM IIIB.
G. Daux, BCH, 91 (1967), 777f.

6. Archanes, at Phourni. Gold ring from tomb A. Three dancers, a construction, and a sacred tree. LM I. Museum: HM.
J. Sakellarakis, Kadmos, 4 (1965), 177ff; ILN, 26 March 1966, 33; Archaeology, 20 (1967), 280; PAE (1966), 174ff; FGK, 26.

7. Archanes, the Phyties site. Clay model of an oval sanctuary from the Protogeometric period. Museum: HM.
S. Alexiou, KCh, 4 (1950), 445ff; Marinatos-Hirmer, Kr, 103; N. Platon, KCh, 11 (1957), 338; S. Alexiou, KCh, 12 (1958), 277ff; H. Drerup, 'Griechische Baukunst in geometrischer Zeit', ArchHom, II (1969), 75; FGK, 19, 20, 108.

7a. Chania. Seal impression. Two women dancing close to sacred buildings or altars. Museum: Chania.
I. A. Papapostolou, *Ta sphragismata ton Chanion* (1977), 69; FGK, 28, 84.

7b. Chania. Seal impression. A woman dancing close to a sacred structure and a tree.
I. A. Papapostolou, *op. cit.*, 68; FGK, 28, 84.

8. Idaean cave. Rock crystal sealstone. A priestess before an altar. Museum: HM.
L. Mariani, MA, 6 (1895), 178; Evans, TPC, 141f; Vallois, REA, 28 (1926), 122, 128; Evans, PofM, II, 607f; F. Chapouthier, BCH, 52 (1928), 311f; Evans, PofM, IV, 141; Nilsson, MMR², 153; V. Kenna, KrS (1960), 65 no. 9; Brandt, GG, 1f; FGK, 42, 78.

9. Isopata. Gold ring found in a tomb. Four women dancers. LM I. Museum: HM.
Evans, TDA, 10; Evans, PofM, III, 68; Nilsson, MMR², 279; S. Alexiou, KCh, 12 (1958), 231f; D. Levi, PP, 14 (1959), 383; Brandt, GG, 5; S. Alexiou, Gnomon, 39 (1967), 612.

9a. Isopata. Gold ring. Two dancing(?) women close to a sacred building. Museum: HM.
Evans, TDA, 31; FGK, 28, 84.

10. Kalamion, near Chania. A pyxis has a scene on which we see a temenos surrounded by a low wall. A man is playing a kitharos, while nearby there is another wall and horns of consecration. Between them is a double axe. LM IIIB. Museum: Chania.
Y. Tsedakis, AAA, 2 (1969), 365; 3 (1970), 111f; FGK, 82.

11. Kamilari, tholos tomb. Clay model of a sanctuary. MM IIIB-LM IA. Museum: HM 2632.
D. Levi, Ann, 23/4 (1961/2), 129ff; FGK, 16, 18, 40, 108.

12. Kamilari, tholos tomb. This clay model represents a group dancing in a cult place which is symbolised by horns of consecration. MM IIIB-LM IA. Museum: HM.
D. Levi, *op. cit.*, 139ff.

13. Karphi. Clay models of sanctuaries from LM IIIC.
J. Pendlebury *et al.*, *op. cit.*, 84.

14. Knossos, palace. Fragments of a miniature frescoe depicting a tripartite building with isolated pillars standing on either side of it, and also a crowd of people, probably in a sacred enclosure. MM III-LM I. Museum: HM.
Evans, BSA, 6 (1899/1900), 46; Evans, TPC, pl. V; H. Bulle, *Orchomenos*, I (1907), 78;

Evans, PofM, II, 597; Evans, PofM, III, 46ff; Nilsson, MMR², 175; Matz, Gött, 386ff; D. Levi, PP, 14 (1959), 328f; S. Alexiou, KCh, 17 (1963), 349; Ch. Kardara, AE (1966), 176, Fig. 26; FGK, 133.

15. Knossos, palace. Miniature frescoe with an olive grove, female dancers, and a crowd of spectators, and a part of a building. MM IIIB. Museum: HM.
Evans, PofM, III, 66; Matz, Gött, 8; M. Cameron in *Europa*, 65ff.

16. Knossos, palace. Fragment of a wall painting showing a tripartite sanctuary. Museum: HM.
BCH, 80 (1956), 341; F. Schachermeyer, AA (1962), 77.

17. Knossos, 'Underground Spring Chamber'. Clay model of a sanctuary. LM IIIC. Museum: HM.
Evans, PofM, II; 128ff FGK, 19.

18. Knossos, palace. Two models of sacred screens. Museum: HM.
Evans, PofM, II; 128ff FGK, 19.

19. Knossos, palace. Fragments of a rython with a scene depicting a procession filing past a building. LM I. Museum: HM.
A. Evans, BSA, 9 (1902/3), 129; Evans, PofM, III, 752f; K. Müller, JdI, 30 (1915), 269; Nilsson, MMR², 183; Evans, PofM, IV, 65; Zervos, Crète, Fig. 483; S. Alexiou, KCh, 17 (1963), 349.

20. Knossos, Gypsadhes, near Hogarth's house. Fragment of a serpentine rhyton. Peak sanctuary: a man in front of a holy building, bent over a basket. MM IIIB-LM IA. Museum: HM 2397, 257.
Platon, IK, 154ff; Zervos, Cr, Fig. 482; S. Alexiou, KCh, 13 (1959), 346ff; *idem*, KCh, 17 (1963), 338ff; Ch. Kardara, AE (1966), 176f.

21. Knossos, Gypsadhes. Fragment of a serpentine rhyton. Sacred enclosure: a sacred tree and pillar, and dancers before an altar. MM IIIB-LM IA or LM I. Museum: AM AE 1247.
Evans, TPC, 101ff; G. Karo, ARW, 7 (1904), 144f; K. Müller, JdI, 30 (1915), 260; M. Mobius, JdI, 48 (1933), 14f; Evans, PofM, III, 65; Nilsson, MMR², 120; FGK, 135.

22. Knossos. Gold ring. Epiphany of a deity in a sacred enclosure. LM I. Museum: AM.
Evans, TPC, 170; Karo, ARW, 7 (1904), 144; Evans, PofM, I, 160; R. Vallois, REA, 28 (1926), 121f; Persson, RelGr, 376; Nilsson, MMR², 256; Biesantz, KSG, 114f; Matz, Gött, 391f; Kenna, CrS, 125, No. 250; FGK, 26, 30, 116.

23. Knossos, Gypsadhes. Bronze ring. A scene representing a sacred enclosure. Museum: HM.
S. Hood, AR (1958), 19, Fig. 30; G. Daux, BCH, 83 (1959), 736, Fig. 6; FGK, 29.

24. Knossos, palace. Clay matrix. A sacred enclosure. LM IB. Museum: HM.
A. Evans, BSA, 7 (1900/1), 19 and 101; Evans, PofM, III, 767, Fig. 498; Evans, PofM, IV, 395; Nilsson, MMR², 349; V. Kenna, Kadmos, 4 (1965), 75 No. 1; FGK, 26, 84, 108.

25. Knossos, not far from the Sacred Repository. Clay sealings. A goddess on a mountain top, a worshipper, and a sanctuary. LM II. Museum: HM.
A. Evans, BSA, 7 (1900/1), 28ff; *idem*, 9 (1902/3), 37; Evans, PofM, II, 806ff; F. Chapouthier, BCH, 52 (1928), 322; Evans, PofM, III, 463; Evans, PofM, IV, 608; E. Herkenrath, AJA, 41 (1937), 416; Nilsson, MMR², 352; Biesantz, KSG, 135; Matz, Gött, 394; E. Spartz, *Das Wappen in mykenischen und frühgriechischen Kunst* (1962), 12f, 99 No. 1; A. Furumark, OpAth, 6 (1965), 94; FGK, 26.

26. Knossos, Little Palace. Seal impression. Façade of a building surmounted by a baetyl. LM I-II. Museum: HM.
Evans, PofM, III, Fig. 327; Evans, PofM, IV, 605 No. 2, Fig. 597 Ai.

27. Knossos, Little Palace. Seal impression. LM I-II. Museum: HM.
Evans, PofM, IV, 605 No. 1.

28. Knossos, palace. Seal impression with a scene interpreted as the interior of a grotto (Evans).
Evans, PofM, I, 273; N. Platon, AE (1930), 7; Evans, PofM, II, 453.

28a. Knossos. Seal impression. A man before a sacred façade. Museum: HM.
CMS, II.3 (in press); FGK, 29, 66, 84.

28b. Knossos. Seal impression. A woman dancing close to a sacred structure and a tree. Museum: HM.
CMS, II.3 (in press); FGK, 30.

28c. Knossos. Fragment of a vessel with columns and horns of consecration. Museum: HM.
Evans, PofM, I, 494; FGK, 84.

28d. Lebene. Clay model of a house or shrine used as a lamp dated to EM III.
K. Branigan, *The Foundation of Palatial Crete* (1970), 40; FGK, 18.

29. Ligortino. Seal with a scene showing a building and a sacred tree was found in a tomb. Museum: Paris, Cabinet des Medailles, AM 1844.
Evans TPC, 184 no.2; Nilsson, MMR², 182, 270, 413f; CMS, IX, 163; FGK, 78f.

29a. Makrygialos. Seal. A scene with an altar or a cabine(?) on a boat. Museum: Ayios Nikolaos.
C. Davaras, *Guide to Cretan Antiquities* (1976), 326f; FGK, 28 n.56.

30. Mochlos. Gold ring. Sacred enclosure: a sacred tree, building and boat. LM I. Now lost.
Seager, Moch, 90; Persson, RelGr, 82ff; Nilsson, MMR², 269ff; FGK, 30.

31. Petsophas. Part of an oval vessel. Museum: AM 1938, 426 (as coming from Palaikastro). Red clay, traces of brown paint. Two figures are sitting on a bench, and in front of them are traces of objects which have not been preserved. Cf. Kamilari model (with figures sitting in front of altars, Fig. 139). Length 0.044 m, width 0.04 m, thickness of base 0.006 m. MM. A new fragment, which we identified recently in the HM among the Petsophas material makes it certain it was found not at Palaikastro but at Petsophas.
CPl, 199, Fig. 81.

32. Phaistos, at Kalyvia, tomb 11. Gold ring. Sacred enclosure: a sacred tree, a baetyl, and a religious dance. LM I. Museum: HM 45.

     L. Savignoni, MA, 14 (1905), 577ff; Persson, RelGr, 35f; Nilsson, MMR², 268; Biesantz, KSG, 142; Matz, Gött, 23; V. Kenna, KCh, 17 (1963), 330.

33. Phaistos, at Kalyvia, tomb 2. Gold ring. Scene of adoration in front of a holy building. LM IB (Kenna). Museum: HM 44.

     L. Savignoni, MA, 14 (1904), 585ff; Persson, RelGr, 50f; Biesantz, KSG, 167; Nilsson, MMR², 257, 346; V. Kenna, KCh, 17 (1963), 330; FGK, 30, 52, 54.

34. Phaistos. Clay model of a house or sanctuary. LM III. Museum: HM.

     L. Pernier, MA, 12 (1902), 128; S. Alexiou, KCh, 12 (1958), 279 n.392.

35. Piskokephalo (Sitias), the Katrinia site. Clay models of sacred screens found in a sacred enclosure. MM III. Museum: HM.

     N. Platon, KCh, 6 (1952), 475f; 7 (1953), 484f; *idem*, PAE (1952), 631ff; D. Levi, Ann, 41/2 (1961/2), 128; FGK, 22, 24, 47, 86, 124.

36. Zakro, palace. Serpentine rhyton with traces of gold plating. Peak temenos with a gateway and walls, as well as altars and a sanctuary set in a mountain landscape. LM I. Museum: HM.

     N. Platon, Ergon (1963), 172f; ILN, 7 March 1964, 352; S. Alexiou, KCh, 17 (1963), 343f; S. Alexiou, AAA, 2 (1969), 85; N. Platon, *Zakros* (1971), 160ff; J. Shaw, AJA, 82 (1978), 432ff; FGK, 133.

37. Zakro, House A. Two sealings. Sacred enclosure with a building, an altar with horns of consecration, and a tree. LM I. Museum: HM 47.

     D. G. Hogarth, JHS, 22 (1902), 76f No. 1; Nilsson, MMR², 268, 272, 283, 323; Biesantz, KSG, 129; Matz, Gött, 14f; Ch Delvoye, BCH, 70 (1946), 120ff; FGK, 133.

38. Zakro, House A. Seven seal impressions. Portal of a gateway surmounted with a baetyl. LM I. Museum: HM.

     D. G. Hogarth, *op. cit.*, 87 No. 112; G. Karo, ARW, 7 (1904), 153; Evans, PofM, I, 307; FGK, 105.

VII

Cretan sanctuaries in the
towns and settlements

THE CULT places varied in kind in the towns and settlements. Here they have been classified according to their function in the lives of the inhabitants. First we have the public cult places, that is temples and open-air shrines with altars in the town or village squares. Second, we have the private cult places. Some of these were situated inside the palaces; the most prominent were the domestic sanctuaries — with repositories for the cult paraphernalia[1] the lustral basins, the spring sanctuaries and the enclosures in the palace courtyards. Other cult places, which were similar to the aforesaid in appearance, were the sanctuaries in private houses, in the villas and country properties, in town houses, and also the sacred enclosures in the courtyards.

The public cult places in the settlements must have been of two kinds: temple buildings situated in the central point of the town, and sacred precincts in the town's open spaces and squares. The temples are discussed in Chapter VIII. Although we have no proof yet that the squares in settlements or towns were used for sacred purposes, it is highly probable that religious ceremonies did take place in the open spaces used for trading and for public gatherings. The evidence we have about later times in Greece[2] tells us that religious ceremonies were inseparably connected with everyday life.

At the highest spot in the town of Gournia (Fig. 167)[3] there is an open space next to the palace or chief's house. This space, which measures 30 × 20 m, was paved with a kind of concrete. On the left side of a rather narrow street leading into this square is a stylobat 5.60 m long, on which there are two pillars. Nearby, we find what look like steps, although they may also have been used for sitting on. Not far from the stylobat fragments of posts were found, and beside these were limestone horns of consecration that may have come from an altar in the corner of the square.[4] Many scholars are agreed that the town square in Gournia must have been used as an agora[5] or market place. It is even possible that the buildings whose remains were found along the western and eastern sides of the square housed shops. If we assume that the horns of consecration belonged to an altar, we can surmise that the religious ceremonies begun near the temple were continued in the square. The town square was not only the place where sacrifices were made. It was also the place where bullfights were held, as well as processions and other sacred ceremonies in which almost the whole population of the town took part.

Apart from Gournia, where the town square dates from LM I, we also know of another square, that at Philakopi on Melos.[6] Although this square dates from a somewhat later period than the 'agora' at Gournia, it was likewise situated not far from the ruler's residence. At Plati,[7] on the Lasiti plateau, we find the remains of a square surrounded by houses in a settlement dating from LM III. Its functions can be guessed at only from a comparison with other squares. At Mallia, too, new excavations are revealing what public life was like in the town. Adjacent to the palace there is a large, almost rectangular open space which is known as the northern square. To the north-east of the palace, too, is another square which some archaeologists refer to as an agora.[8] But it is thought that this square may have had only a few of the functions of the later agora in Greece; and there is no indication that it had any sacred function. In the vicinity of the squre there are buildings of various types. One of them is a hypostyle crypt which, H. van Effenterre thinks, was used as a buleterion.[9]

We must also mention here the open-air shrines in the courtyards, situated both in the centre of the palaces and elsewhere. Whether they were used for private worship or played a part in the court ceremonial, in which the town inhabitants took part, is a matter of controversy. The altars stood either in the middle of this, or at the side. Some cult places, too, were situated

167. Gournia. Plan of the town. H. Boyd Hawes, Gournia (1908), Pl. I.

outside the palaces in paved open spaces on the outskirts of the town. The best example of an altar standing in the centre of a courtyard can still be seen, not at Knossos where remains of one were destroyed during excavations at the Neolithic site, but at Mallia.[10] A structure in the central courtyard there has been interpreted as an altar (Fig. 168,169). It is situated on the axis of Room VII 3-4, which is one of the best rooms in the west wing (Fig. 170). This was a pillared structure, like an eschara — an altar for sacrifices,[11] such as were known in the later culture of Greece. Other structures, of which only stone slabs remain (although they are somewhat bigger than those belonging to the eschara at Mallia), can still be seen in the central courtyard of the palace at Mallia[12] (Figs. 170,171), and in the central courtyard at Zakro (Fig. 173).[13] Remains of altars were also discovered in the west courtyard of the palace of Knossos, near Magazines 1 and 13,[14] and in an outdoor courtyard belonging to a villa at Nirou Chani (see below p. 27, Fig. 19). At lease some of these structures seem to have been altar-towers — that is, relatively high constructions, such as have been found at Myrtos-Pighades in Cyprus (Fig. 172).[15] This supposition is borne out by a scene on a fragmentary rhyton from Knossos (Fig. 135), showing an altar made not of brick but of stone ashlars. The altars or altar-towers were no doubt surmounted by horns of consecration. In view of the great height of the altar-towers — for on the basis of the scene on the rhyton from Knossos (Fig. 135) its height has been reckoned as being between 1.50 and 2.00 m, or even more — they may have had a symbolic function, as bases for the sacred emblems. If, on the other hand, they were altars in the strict sense, the top of them must have been reached by means of a ladder or some other wooden structure, for there is no evidence of any stone steps, with the exception of the stepped structure in the central courtyard of the palace of Phaistos (Fig. 174) (cf. the shrine opened to the court Figs. 175,176),[16] which is similar to the structures shown on the A. Triada sarcophagus (Fig. 146).[17]

It is highly probable that the theatral areas at Knossos[18] and Phaistos, and probably in other towns as well were used mainly as meeting places for political and other secular occasions.[19] On the other hand it cannot definitely be stated that religious ceremonies were not held there as well. It is also possible that there were some other sacred enclosures in the towns and villages, like those close to the tombs (cf. Fig. 177). We have no direct evidence of these but some of the iconographic sources do not rule out such an interpretation.[20]

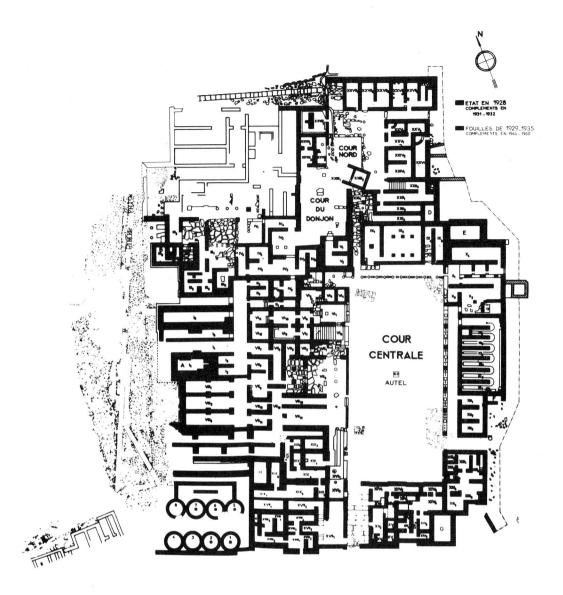

168. Mallia. Plan of the palace. Etcret 12, Plan 1.

169. Mallia. Eschara at the palace court-yard.

170. *(above left)* Mallia. Palace, south-west corner. Plan of Room XVI.1 and the altar. Etcret 19, Pl. IX.

171. *(above right)* Mallia. North-west angle of the palace with an altar. Etcret 19, Pl. VII (fragment).

172. Myrtou-Pighades. Altar-tower. FGK, Fig. 25.8.

173. Zakro. Plan of the palace. S. Hood, The Minoans (1971), Fig. 33.

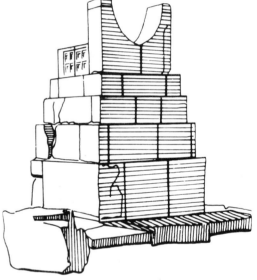

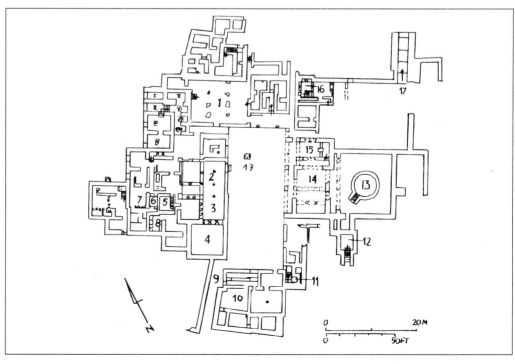

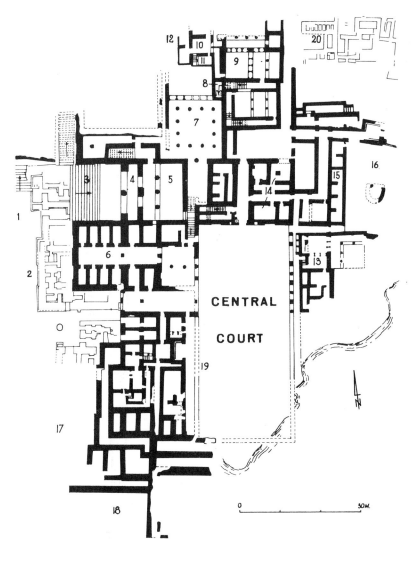

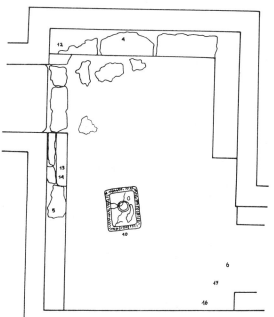

174. *(above)* Phaistos. Plan of the palace in the LM I period. Hood, op. cit., Fig. 35.

175. *(left)* Phaistos. Plan of the sanctuary. Festos, I, Fig. 82.

176. Phaistos. Sanctuary. Plan of the later phase. Festos, II, Fig. 306.

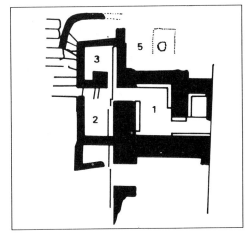

177. Kamilari. Altar close to the tholos tomb. Ann. 39/40, 1961/2, 81 Fig. 106.

We must bear in mind, too, the probability that cult statues and cult emblems were placed in the open spaces of the towns, palaces and squares. These would not be cult places in the real sense but, like the altar-towers, they would mark the presence of a divinity. We can take an example of this in the stands for double axes that stood in the corridors of the magazines (Fig. 178),[21] or the statues, sometimes of more than natural size, which were probably set up under the open sky, although in the midst of the palace buildings.[22]

The spring sanctuaries may also be counted among the natural cult places. Their traditions go far back. There is little archaeological evidence for them, but two distinct instances may be cited here. At the Caravanserai lying below the palace of Knossos is a quite exceptional discovery of this type. In the western part there was a foot-bath, and next to it was a room where many fragments of bath-tubs, with motifs dated to LM IIB, were discovered.[23] As for the second instance, we may cite the neighbouring building[24] placed diagonally to the Caravanserai. It measured 1.90 by 1.70 m and had a basin, two benches and a niche (Fig. 179). It is thought that in the period LM I–IIIA1 it was a fountain-house, built round a natural

178. Knossos. Long Corridor. Double axe stand (not in situ).

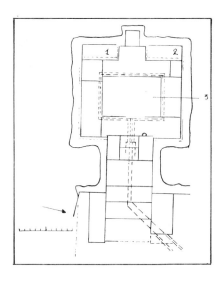

179. Knossos. Plan of the Spring Chamber. Evans PofM II, Fig. 60.

180. Knossos. Spring Chamber. Offering vessel.

spring.[25] Perhaps not till LM IIIC did it become a shrine, as is suggested by the presence of an LM IIIC urn-hut, which has a figurine of a naked goddess whose hands are upraised, and sacrificial vessels dating from LM IIIC and the Sub-Minoan period (Fig. 180).[26] At Zakro a small room, LXX,[27] measuring approximately 3.00 by 3.50 m,[28] had been built round a well (Fig. 173 No. 12). It had been erected at the back of the palace, with an entrance from the outside. The fact that horns of consecration were found nearby probably shows that this small room was sacred.[29] In this same palace (Fig. 173), there is another room, close to the central courtyard, in which a well was discovered.[30] Its diameter is 1.40 m and its depth about 2 m (Fig. 173, No. 11). It is sometimes known as the 'Sacred Well'.[31] Fragments of tripod offering tables, clay animal figurines, animal bones, pumice, cups holding carbonised material (there were olives in one of them) and other vessels, were all found in it. However, the author's view is that these objects could have landed up in the basin by chance. The well must have been in daily use and since it took up a fairly large area, dirt and refuse must easily have got into it.

Even up to the present day the cult places in the palaces remain a subject of controversy

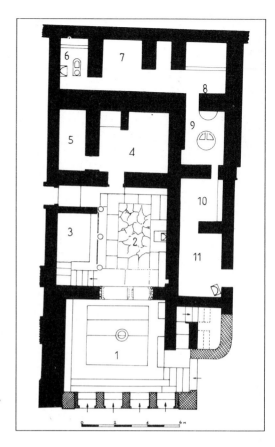

181. Knossos. Throne Room Complex. Evans PofM, IV, Fig. 877.

182. Knossos. Temple Repository

among archaeologists. In the early days, owing to the influence of Arthur Evans, archaeologists were inclined to regard quite a lot of the rooms in the palace as sanctuaries. But the arguments put forth in those days were not always altogether convincing, and lately it has been felt that it would be wise to subject the evidence to careful re-appraisal.

We have already pointed out that it is extremely difficult to establish what use the various rooms were put to, except in those cases where whole groups of finds of a sacred character were discovered. The sacred emblems are very important, but some of them, such as the double axes, could in certain cases merely be expressions of piety and not testimony to the existence of a sanctuary.[32] Finally, those objects which were of unusual appearance or outstanding value (such as the rhyta) were not necessarily objects used exclusively in the cult. In the system based on a palace culture, objects of unusual appearance or of great value could have been used by the king, or by rich villa owners. Thus to say that all unusual or valuable artefacts were made for use in the cults is to simplify the picture of Minoan society.

We have already drawn attention to the fact that the cult places in the palaces, rich houses or villas were heterogeneous. They consisted of shrines at altars in the courtyards and squares, sanctuaries at the sacred wells or springs and also domestic sanctuaries and lustral basins. Apart from cult places, that is, places where the gods were worshipped, emblems representing divinities were also set up in open spaces in the palaces, such as rooms or corridors, as expressions of piety, and to indicate that the people there gave themselves into the god's care.

In discussing the cult places in the palaces, it is necessary first of all to draw attention to the function of the west wing of these edifices. Previously it has often been asserted that the entire side of the palace lying west of the central courtyard was given over to cult purposes and to sacred and official ceremonies.[33] For instance, there was a row of rooms along the western side of the courtyard in the palace of Knossos, dating from MM IIIB to LM II. During MM IIIB a sacred repository had been built, as well as large pillar crypts, while in LM II a Throne Room and adjacent rooms were added (Fig. 181). The room in which a repository of sacred objects was found undoubtedly formed part of a sacred area. In this small chamber (Fig. 182) there were two shallow, empty pits and two earlier, deeper ones containing a large number of

objects including figurines of snake-goddesses,[34] votive robes, a marble cross, and sea shells painted red. West of this were two crypts which, however, were probably not used for sacred purposes,[35] despite the fact that many double axe signs were carved on the pillars there. Seal impressions, some of them bearing the figure of a goddess standing on a mountain top (Fig. 114), were discovered in one of the nearby rooms. This narrow room, which is next to a courtyard, has been interpreted as a sacred façade. Further north lies the Throne Room and adjacent rooms.

It seems possible that the Throne Room complex[35a] had a religious function, either direct or indirect. A brief account of the material found in these rooms will therefore not come amiss here. From the central courtyard, several steps lead down to an antechamber with benches along the side walls. Remains of wood were found between the benches on the right side. It is thought that perhaps this came from chairs similar to the stone throne in the neighbouring room (Fig. 181). The walls of the antechamber are decorated with frescoes, of which a fragment depicting the hind leg of a bull has survived. In the next room, that is the Throne Room, there were benches along the walls except on the left side where there was a lustral basin (see p. 136). Between the low benches was a gypsum throne which at one time had been covered with red paint. On the wall above the throne was a large painting representing wingless griffins and objects generally held to be altars. The lustral basin was a small room to which eight steps lead down. Behind the Throne Room was still another chamber, completely windowless. This was thought to be a sanctuary because the raised platform was believed to be an altar. Horns of consecration were also reported. The floor was laid with stone slabs, whereas in the Throne Room the stone floor was covered with stucco painted red. Evans was of the opinion that the stone basin found outside this antechamber in actual fact belonged to this room. Several alabastra and a single jug were found in the Throne Room, and various ornaments in the lustral basin. What is known as a kitchen may also have been a cult room. All in all, then, two or three rooms around the Throne Room may have been used for worshipping the gods.

It is more difficult to arrive at a convincing interpretation of the Throne Room itself; it is not

128

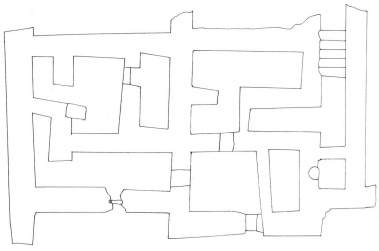

183. Mallia. Palace, plan of
the south-west area. Etcret
19, Pl. 10 (fragment).

known for certain whether it was a sanctuary or merely a royal chamber. The objects
discovered there provide no clear indication that the Throne Room was used for cult purposes,
but there is more indirect evidence that it was put to such use. At any rate the throne, and
especially its baetyl-shaped back, merely indicates that the person sitting on it was under divine
protection.[36] Following this train of thought, it seems likely that the griffins on the wall had
symbolic significance as animals protecting the king, although their main purpose, like that of
so many other frescoes, was to decorate the wall.[37] Evans took the view that the alabastra and
the jug were objects used during the ceremonial anointment of the king. Thus the author finds
it difficult to decide whether the Throne Room was wither a sanctuary or a royal state
chamber.[38]

In other palaces, such as at Phasitos, Mallia (Fig. 168) and Zakro (Fig. 173), the west wing of
the palace could have served these same purposes. But at Mallia it is more difficult to prove that
the west wing of the palace (Fig. 183)[39] was used for cult rituals. We may arrive at an idea of the
function of the two main sets of rooms, VI 1 and VII 3-4, by referring to comparisons with
Knossos and Phaistos.[40] There is no direct proof that the other Mallia rooms were cult
places.[41] The only possibility is that Room XVI 1, in the side part of the west wing, could have
been a sanctuary at the entrance to the principal dwelling apartments, while the sanctuary
proper was situated in a side section of this area (XVIII 1-2).

It must be said that in the Minoan palaces the number of rooms devoted to religious
purposes was small. In the Palace of Knossos, apart from the sacred repository (forming part of
the sanctuary) mentioned above, which dates from MM IIIB (Fig. 182), we know only of the
Dove Goddess Sanctuary, which dates from MM II and which lies underneath the Loom
Weight Basement of later date,[42] and of the famous Sanctuary of the Double-Axes, dating
from LM IIIA 1.[43] The lustral basins may also have been used for cult purposes in addition to
the enclosures in the town or village squares, where there must have been altars, and the theatre
areas and the enclosures in the green open spaces. In the palace at Mallia[44] it is probable that,
apart from the lustral basins, only two rooms (XVIII and XIV) were used as cult places as well
as enclosures situated in the open spaces (Figs. 169-171). At Phaistos[45] apart from the lustral
basins there is only one sanctuary (Fig. 176). In one of the lustral basins at Zakro[46] the wall
decorated with altars indicates that this room may have been used for sacred purposes. Near
the central courtyard in the same palace was a spring around which a stone construction
forming a shrine was built (Fig. 173, No. 12). In the central courtyard there was a small
construction that probably served as an altar, although this interpretation is not substantiated
by any material evidence, apart from the west wing and the sacred repository. Altogether,
then, the sanctuaries in the palaces were few in number. The reasons for this will be discussed
below.

The position of the sanctuaries in the palace area is likewise characteristic. Knossos is the
only palace where the Sacred Repository (and the sanctuary above it) is in the centre of the west
façade of the palace facing the courtyard. In the other palaces, the sanctuary is situated in one of
the side sections. There are some characteristic examples of this rule. First, the no longer extant

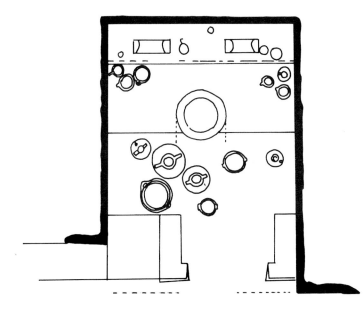

184. Knossos. Shrine of the Double Axes. Evans PofM, II, 338 Fig. 190.

room on the first floor of the Dove Goddess Sanctuary in the northern part of the palace at Knossos, and second, the Double-Axes Sanctuary in the south-east part of the same palace. Rooms XVIII and XIV (Fig. 168) in the southern quarter of the palace at Mallia are also good examples. These sanctuaries were sometimes on the ground floor (e.g. sanctuary XVIII at Mallia — Fig. 185), and sometimes on the first floor (e.g. the sanctuaries at Knossos already mentioned above, and Room XIV at Mallia). All these sanctuaries are in the midst of other rooms used for domestic and everyday living purposes, and there is no evidence to show that the Minoans made any attempt to isolate the places where they kept their sacred objects from their everyday environment.

As a rule sanctuaries had few rooms. In the majority of cases there was only one room (e.g. in the Shrine of the Double Axes, Fig. 184), but sometimes there were two (as in Sanctuary XVIII at Mallia, Fig. 185), and on occasion even as many as four (as at Phaistos, late phase, Fig. 176). All these sanctuaries were very small, as we can see from the following dimensions: the Shrine of the Double Axes (Fig. 184) measured approximately 1.50 × 1.50 m (not counting the vestibule), whereas Sanctuary XVIII at Mallia measured about 3.80 × 3.50 m (without the annexe it measured 3.80 × 1.50 m),[47] and Room VIII at Phaistos measured 3.62 × 2.57 m (Fig. 175).

In considering the question of the ground plan, the function of the various rooms, and the ease of access, the rooms at Phaistos (Fig. 174)[48] are the best example to study. In the earliest phase, the two small rooms VIII and IX were isolated from the west courtyard, and access to them was possible only from a small inner courtyard of the palace. Room VIII was reached

130

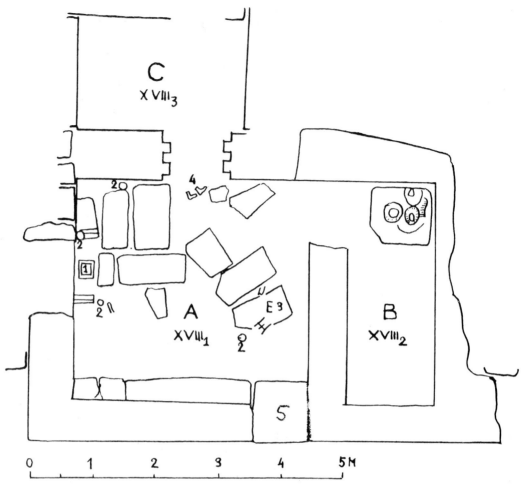

185. Mallia. Palace. Plan of Sanctuary XVIII. Etcret 12, 9 Fig. 2.

through vestibule IX, which formed a connection between the building and the eastern part of the site. In phase II (during the existence of the first palace), a door was made in the wall of Room VIII to give that room access to the west courtyard, and two small rooms, V and VI, were added. A doorway 0.75 m wide connected Room VI with this courtyard. To the north of Room V, a small lean-to was built. Also in MM (phase III) other changes were made (Fig. 176). Room VII was added; it was reached from the courtyard, but had no connection with any of the other rooms. During the construction of the second palace, Rooms V–VII and VIII–IX were knocked down, and other buildings put up on the same site. It is thought that only Room VIII was used for cult purposes, and that the other rooms served either as a vestibule or a sacristy (IX) or for some other purpose.

The other sanctuaries also generally have a cult room as well as a vestibule (or sacristy, or annexe); see the Shrine of the Double Axes at Knossos, and Sanctuary XVIII at Mallia (Fig. 185). At Mallia it is not certain whether the sanctuary was entered from the outside of the palace, on the south side, or whether it was reached from the inside, through Room XVII 3 (Fig. 185). It is supposed that the gap in the south wall was walled up, and that there was a window[49] in the now non-extant wall above the gap. It sometimes happens, too, that in the sanctuaries with several rooms the repository of holy objects was situated on the ground floor, whereas the main rooms were on the first floor (e.g. the Sacred Repository at Knossos, Fig. 182). In some palace sanctuaries, the façade of the building was contiguous with the courtyard (e.g. the Sacred Repository at Knossos), like the façades of the peak sanctuaries and of the shrines in the sacred enclosures. Where this is the case, it is probable that the façade of the sanctuary was the background against which the cult ceremonies took place. But as a rule, the sanctuaries in the palaces formed part of the palace complex, and were situated inside the

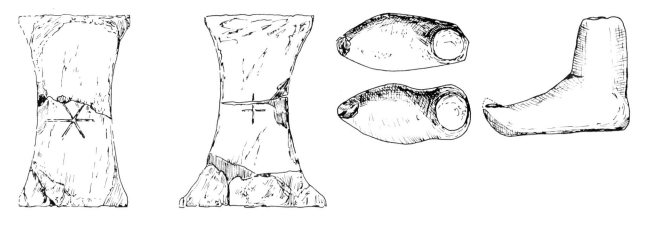

building, and generally the cult room was reached through neighbouring rooms used either as living quarters or for domestic purposes.

A quite characteristic furnishing of the interior of the sanctuary was a stone bench or shelf with an altar close by (Fig. 184), although (as in Sanctuary XVIII at Mallia) it was not always necessarily present;[50] wooden tables may have served the same purpose. This was a very important piece of furniture, for upon it stood the most important cult objects (Fig. 187).

Not all the rooms believed to be sanctuaries have been found to contain objects that provide us with sound evidence about the cult images and sacred emblems. It should be remembered that in the palace sanctuaries statues of deities — or priestesses or attendants — have been found in only two shrines (the Sacred Repository and the Shrine of the Double Axes at Knossos), and sacred emblems in only one (the Shrine of the Double Axes). The other sanctuaries produced only sacred implements and votive offerings. The question of what kind of divinities were worshipped in these shrines, and the question of the uses to which the various rooms were put, will be dealt with at greater length below.

Some interesting problems emerge when we study the lustral basins (Table III). These were small rectangular or square rooms, whose characteristic feature was their sunken floor (Figs. 188-190).[51] Steps always led down into the basins, the inside of which was carefully finished, being often lined with gypsum slabs or stuccoed rock or cement. The walls above the dado were equally well finished, as we can see from the surviving fragments of frescoes or stucco work. Running along the side of the stairs was a parapet, on which stood either a pilaster or a column. Nearly all the lustral basins that are extant were found in Crete; the only exception being one on Thera (Figs. 191-192). The question of their date is an interesting one. Most of the lustral basins date from the period MM III-LM I; there are far fewer dating from the period MM II and LM II-IIIA. For the most part the lustral basins were situated in the complex e.g. the Residential Quarter or near the principal room, known as the Cretan Megaron and its anteroom, although at Knossos they are near the Throne Room complex. They constitute a typical element of the palaces, although very few lustral basins have been found: five at Phaistos, three or four at Knossos, one at Mallia, and two at Zakro. They also occur in rich houses and villas, although in some big complexes, such as at A. Triada, none has been found. Occasionally a change took place in the use to which these rooms were put. For instance, in the period LM I, they were filled in, and sometimes, as was the case with the Fetish Shrine in the Little Palace at Knossos at a later period (that is, LM III B), the lustral basin became a sanctuary (Figs. 193-195).

The most likely explanation of the function of the lustral basins would seem to be that they were used for ritual ablutions, this consisting of pouring water over a person. The absence of drains indicates that perhaps the basins were not filled with water, and that the rituals involved pouring water over a sitting or standing individual. We know that such rituals took place in Egypt. The fact that, as at Akrotiri (Fig. 192),[52] the walls were lined with wood, and that gypsum (which is impermeable) was used in the building work, do not preclude the possibility

Table III: Lustral Basins

1 No.1	2 Locality	3 Date	4 Dimension of basin	5 Stair	6 Collonnaded parapet	7 Gypsum lined
1.	Amnissos	LM I	2.80 × 2.04	wooden		
2.	Gournia Palace	LM I	1.80 × 2.00	concrete floor, no steps		
3.	Gournia Qr.H	LM I	1.80 × 1.80	cement floor		
4.	Knossos, Palace Throne Room Complex	LM II-IIIA2	2.90 × 2.44	steps	x (gypsum lined)	x
5.	Knossos, North-west Lustral Basin	MM II-MM IIIA	2.56 × 2.45	steps	2	x
6.	Knossos, South-east Lustral Basin	MM III	2.20 × 2.00	steps		x
7.	Knossos, Little Palace	MM III-LM I	2.50 × 2.18	steps	2	gypsum stair
8.	Knossos, House of the Chancel Screen	MM IIIB-LM IA	1.50 × 2.00	steps		x
9.	Knossos, South House	MM IIIB-LM IA	1.50 × 1.90	steps		x
10.	Mallia, Palace Room III 4	MM III-LM I	2.00 × 2.50	steps		stuccoed
11.	Mallia, House Da 7	MM III-	1.75 × 1.75	steps		stuccoed
12.	Mallia, House E, Room IX	MMIII-LM I	2.90 × 2.40	steps		stuccoed
13.	Mallia, House Za, Room 11	LM I				stuccoed
14.	Mallia, Quarter Mu	MM II	4.00 × 2.75	steps		stuccoed
15.	Nirou Chani	MM III-LM I	2.00 × 2.70			plaster floor
16.	Palaikastro Block B, Room 3	MM III-LM I	1.50 × 1.80	steps		paved floor
17.	Palaikastro Block Gamma, Room 3	MM III-LM I (filled in IIIA)	ca. 1.40 × 1.70	steps		x
18.	Phaistos, Palace, Room 19	MM III-LM I	2.20 × 2.20	steps		x
19.	Phaistos, Palace, Room 21	MM III-LM I	2.20 × 2.20	steps		x and stucco
20.	Phaistos, Palace, Room 63d	MM III-LM I and later?	2.03 × 1.47	steps		x
21.	Phaistos, Palace, Room 70	MM II (filled in MM III)	2.30 × 2.30	steps		x
22.	Phaistos, Palace, Room 83	MM III-LM I	2.20 × 2.20	steps		x stucco and bench
23.	Phaistos, Chalara, South St, Room Z	MM III-LM I	2.40 × 1.72			x

1 No.1	2 Locality	3 Date	4 Dimension of basin	5 Stair	6 Collonnaded parapet	7 Gypsum lined
24.	Thera, Akrotiri, Xeste 3	LM IA		steps		gypsum and wood panels
25.	Tylissos, House A, Room 11	MM III-LM I	1.30 × 2.10	steps		
26.	Tylissos House Gamma	MM III-LM I	2.13 × 2.95	steps		
27.	Zakro, Palace, Room XXIV	MM III-LM I	2.00 × 3.00	steps		flagged floor
28.	Zakro, Palace, Room LVIII	MM III-LM I	2.00 × 1.75	steps	2 and other parapets	stucco

No.	8 xoanon	9 faience vase	10 incense burner	11 conical cups	12 niche	13 sacred emblems a) offering table b)	14 stone lamp
1.							
2.							
3.							
4.							
5.							
6.							
7.		x					
8.							
9.			x	x			
10.							
11.							
12.					2	b: 1 with cupule	1
13.							
14.							
15.						4 DA	
16.				miniature jugs and cups inverted			
17.							
18.							
19.							
20.						a: HC (2 miniature)	
21.				x			
22.							
23.							
24.							
25.							
26.					x		
27.			over 30 incense burners or fruit stands				
28.				x			

HC — horns of consecration
DA — double axe

Table III (cont)

	15 fresco	16 a) pottery b) stone vessels	17 oil flasks	18 seals	19 rhyton (a)	20 arms	21 shells	22 other objects	23 remarks
1.									no published objects the floor is slightly lower than surrounding
2.									
3.									
4.					a: stone	crystal pommel	x	x	all objects from above
5.	x	a; b	x						
6.			x						treasure deposit and
7.				(cult scenes)					later cult objects of a LM III sanctuary
8.									no published objects
9.									floor raised in LM IA
10.									no published objects
11.									no published objects
12.						1 dagger			carbon from above
13.		a; b			terracotta conical rhyton from Room 5				carbon from above
14.									probably remodelled from earlier Lustral Basin
15.		a; b							
16.		a							2 female figurines, horn cores of agrimia
17.		a							
18.									no published objects
19.									no published objects
20.		a b: bird's nest bowl			a: terracotta (2) piriform a: terracotta bull's head a: terracotta male head				9 bronze double axes with no traces of use stacked together; stone pestle filled in MM III
21.	x	a							
22.	x								no published objects
23.									
24.	fresco with procession and sanct. fas. with horns of consecr.								
25.									no published objects
26.		a							
27.		a; b						stone saw anvil or curved hammer	all probably from above in Room XXV — Treasury
28.	fresco: a row of HC on altar bases	a: pitchers and possibly a bath-tub rim							

Table IV: Lustral Basins

No.	Chronological Table used in	total number	remarks
5, 14, 21	MM II	3	
5–13, 15–20, 22, 23, 25–28	MM III	21	
1–3, 5–13, 15–20, 22–28	LM I	24	
4, 5	LM II	2	+ probable 1 (No. 20)
4, 5	LM IIIA	2	+ probable 1 (No. 20)

that these rooms were used for cult ceremonies, which involved the pouring of water. For small quantities of water do not damage wood. Another thing to be remembered is that in the wealthy houses there were enough slaves to clean rooms of importance to the owner. It seems that these rooms were not used for ritual immersion, for there is no trace of baths — it is likely that bath tubs came into common use not earlier than MM III–LM IA.[53] Moreover, the discovery of jars for oil tells us that anointing with oil formed part of the ritual. Of course it is quite probable that the religious ceremonies included the ritual pouring of water, followed by anointing with oil. A theory has been propounded according to which some of the bathrooms — for example one in the Royal Megaron at Knossos — may have been lustral basins in earlier times. If this hypothesis were to be proved, we should have perhaps a typical phenomenon, consisting in the fact that an area used for rituals became in the course of time an area of a secular nature. One of the most difficult problems regarding the lustral basins is that of establishing what use they were put to. For we know (see Table III) that many lustral basins produced no sacred objects or important objects used in the practice of the cult. On the other hand, the discovery of groups of sacred emblems — e.g. in Room 63d at Phaistos (see Table III) — may be indirect evidence that this type of room was used for rituals.[54]

In contrast to the temples and domestic sanctuaries (of which there are more below), the rooms and building used exclusively for secular purposes were usually built according to an established plan. Sometimes even the lay-out and size of the interior followed a fixed scheme. The general lay-out of the palace itself (e.g. Fig. 168) and of its rooms followed fixed rules as well. Thus it is often possible to guess the function of the rooms from their lay-out. Sacred architecture, on the other hand, did not follow such rules during the Minoan period. The main conclusion that can be drawn from this is that the diffusion of high material standards led to the adoption of fixed cannons for the design of rooms and buildings of special function. The sanctuaries in the palaces and private houses did not come under these rules, for their role was only a minor one in the lives of the Minoans. The Minoans' principal places of worship were situated not in the towns and villages but out in the country.

The cult places in private houses can be divided into two categories. To one belong those domestic sanctuaries that were situated in the villages or towns, and to the other, those which were to be found in isolated houses or farms or in villas.

The position of the shrines in the town houses is known from examples at Knossos, Palaikastro, Karphi, Pseira, etc. It is quite characteristic that the Fetish Shrine in the Little Palace at Knossos (LM III)[55] is situated near what in the period MM IIIB–LM I were the main living rooms.[56] This shrine was made in a room which from MM III to LM IA had been used as a lustral basin. It was small and also less imposing than the dwelling rooms (Fig. 193). Equally interesting conclusions can be drawn from a review of the position of the various shrines in the town of Palaikastro. Apart from the shrine in block N, from which only the cult objects have survived,[57] there are also several other shrines: one in block A and one in block B. Again it can be said that the extant rooms on the ground floor which were used as a shrine, or as the repository of a no longer existing shrine, are very modest. In house B there is a tiny place about 2.50 m × 0.40 × 0.60 m, between Room 20 and central site 6. From its size it would appear to be a small cellar or repository, rather than a shrine. There was also a shrine[58] in a small

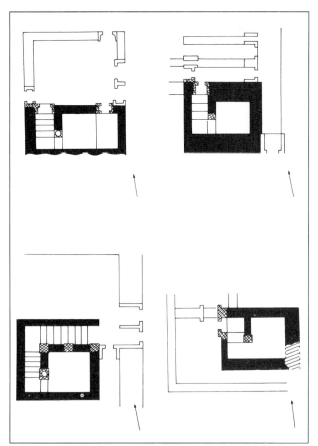

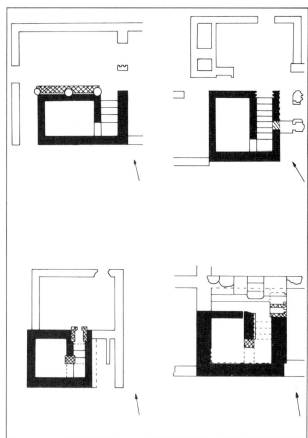

188. *(above left)* Lustral basins
a. Phaistos, Room 83
b. Knossos. South-east basin
c. Knossos. Northern Basin
d. Phaistos. Room 21
Mirie, Pl. 12

189. *(above right)* Lustral basins
a. Knossos. Throne Room Complex
b. Zakro. Room 24
c. Phaistos. Room 63d
d. Phaistos. Room 70
Mirie, Pl. 13

190. Lustral basins
a. Zakro. Room 88
b. Knossos. Queen's Bath
c. Phaistos. Room 19
d. Mallia. Room III.4
Mirie, Pl. 14

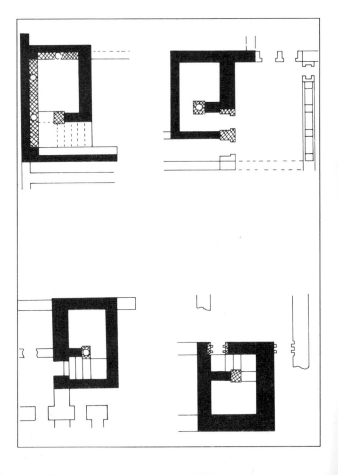

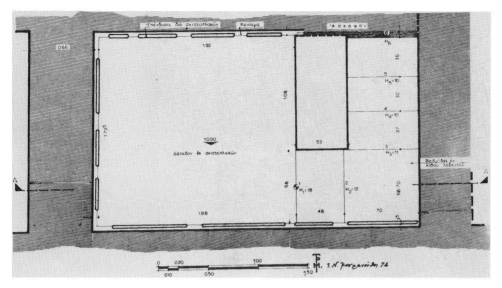

191. Thera. Xeste 3. Plan of the lustral basin. S. Marinatos, Excavations at Thera VII (1976), Fig. 3.

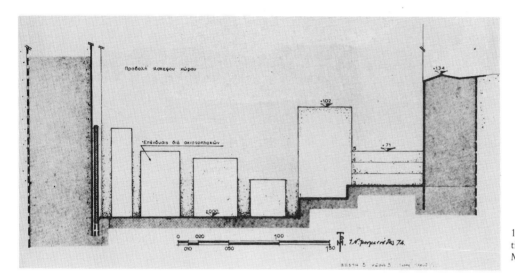

192. Thera. Xeste 3. Section of the lustral basin. S. Marinatos, op. cit., Fig. 4.

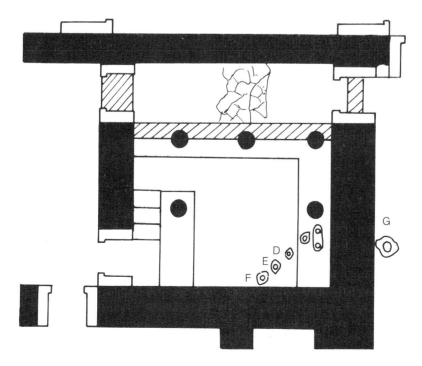

193. Knossos. Little Palace. Plan of the Fetish Shrine. Evans PofM, II, 520 Fig. 321.

 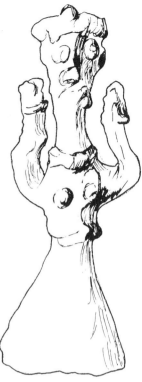

rectangular room (No. 42) in the same block, but in a side wing. This little room belongs to the row of rooms that look onto the street, but the only access to it is from inside the house. In block D, which is known as the 'palace' although it should be looked on rather as several separate houses, a number of large, elegant rooms have been discovered.[59] The shrine here, on the other hand (No. 44), was poor and badly constructed. It was a little room measuring only 3 × 2 m, with an antechamber not exceeding 2.00 × 1.50 m.[60] It is not clear as to how access was gained to this room — whether from the street or from the inside of the house. The latter supposition seems the more likely one.[61]

Finally, two other premises may be cited as examples of small domestic shrines in the LM III-sub-Minoan period. One is a room at Karphi,[62] which is thought to have been a domestic shrine although the entrance is from the street (No. 57), and the other is its neighbour (Room 55). It should be noted that neither of these rooms was more than 9 × 7 m in size, and that they were sparsely furnished. It is not clear whether the former of these shrines was connected directly with what is known as the Priest's House — one of the most important buildings in Karphi — which is just beside it (No. 58-61). On the periphery of this house was a small shrine which was not connected directly with the main part of the building. It is irregular in shape and is directly adjacent to the street. Here again we have another case of a shrine that occupies a small space and that is of no architectural importance.[63] In the excavations at the village of Kephala Chondrou (Viannou), which lies at an altitude of 785 m, a number of houses have been discovered (Fig. 196).[64] In the centre of a large house, four rooms[65] formed a shrine (4-8). Since most of the sacred and votive objects were found in the rooms 5 and on the north-west side of closet 6, it has been thought that only these two rooms were used for cult purposes, and that the other rooms were corridors. A notable feature is that the shrine was placed exactly in the centre of the house, and most probably it was not on the ground floor, but on the first floor. The shrine described here was rectangular. Other shrines of a unique type are sometimes found as well. At Katsaba,[66] for example, a fisherman's cottage dating from LM IIIB-C (Fig. 197) was partly explored and a triangular shrine discovered west of the living room.[67] One wall of the shrine was formed by the living room wall. The other walls were right up against two streets. The shrine's triangular shape, then, was dictated by the cramped nature of the site.

Another problem which requires attention is the position of the shrines in the villas or large

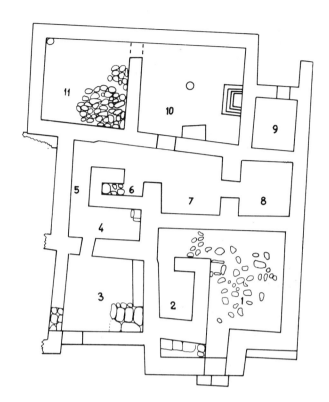

194. *(far left)* Knossos. Fetishes from the shrine. Evans, PofM, II, 346 Fig. 198.

195. *(left)* Knossos. Fetish Shrine. Lead figurine. Zervos Crète, Fig. 769

196. Kephala Chondrou. Plan of the house. Ergon 1959, Fig. 147 (fragment).

farms as well as in isolated houses which presumably were situated out in the country.[68] A villa, or rather farm at Kannia,[69] which is quite exceptional, is very informative. In the excavated part, ground floor rooms that are still in good condition have been found. A characteristic feature is that the biggest and best built rooms were storerooms (Fig. 198, e.g. the top right rooms), whereas the shrines, although quite large in number, were tiny rooms (Rooms 1-6), which were generally very poorly built. It should be noted here that the large number of these rooms (five) has been cited in support of the supposition that this was not a 'villa' with shrines but that the whole building was a temple.[70] Another suggestion may be true: despite the fact that there was no connection between Shrine 6 and the rest of the house, it seems likely that all five rooms, together with Room 4, constituted a single domestic sanctuary consisting of five or even six small rooms. An argument in favour of this view is that all five or six are concentrated in one part of the house. Of course it should be remembered that the main dwelling rooms were on the first floor, while the farm premises were in that part of the farm that is only just beginning to be excavated.

At Chamaizi (Fig. 199) there is a house which belongs to this same category, although it is much smaller. It is situated on the top of a high hill, which in the Minoan period was levelled to form an oval space about 26 m long and 15 m wide. The apexes of this elipse face east and west. The house was nearly oval[71] and had well built walls. Other walls, about which little is known, were also discovered not far from the house. This house, which was built in MM I, contained a number of rooms of which one (No. 4) may have been used as a domestic sanctuary. It was placed at the side of the house. At Rousses,[72] what was believed to be a domestic sanctuary might be regarded as a shrine in a sacred enclosure. (Fig. 1) Sacred objects were found including fragmentary horns of consecration.[73]

It has already been stressed that the domestic sanctuaries were small. They consisted mostly of one to three rooms, or at the most (in exceptional cases) of five rooms, which were situated both on the ground floor and the first floor. Our information about these rooms concerns almost exclusively those on the ground floor. Little is known about the rooms on the first floor, for the evidence is too sparse, especially in the case of the furnishings;[74] or sometimes too vague, as in the case of the wall frescoe. It has already been stressed that access to the shrine was nearly always from inside the house. This is only natural when one considers that the shrine was simply a family sanctuary.[75]

197. Katsaba. Plan of the sanctuary. 1. Shrine. 2. Altar. 3-5. Rooms. 6. Street. 7. Section of the ALtar. PAE 1955, 312, Fig. 1.

Despite the fact that evidence is still scarce, a new problem has arisen from the information that is available. At the entrance to a room at the summer palace at Archanes (see Catalogue VI.1) incurved altars were found which probably stood there at the time the building was in use. At an earlier period, that is, in MM II, an altar was a permanent fixture just beside the entrance to the East House of Quarter Mu, in Mallia. The most interesting find, however, comes from the palace at Mallia, near the south entrance (Fig. 170) This is a small room, measuring 3 by 3.5 m, beside the central courtyard. It contains a kernos and a bench (Fig. 200). The situation of the room near the monumental staircase leading up to the first floor may indicate that this part of the palace was important. The difficulty of interpretation, however, lies in the fact that apart from an altar (cf. Archanes, and Quarter Mu in Mallia), or an object held to be a kernos (cf. Fig. 175, No. 10, see p. 123) no objects of definite sacred signficance were discovered. But if we assumed that there is sufficient reason to define these rooms as cult rooms, then a question arises: whose cult did they serve? We may conjecture that they were used in the worship of divinities who guarded the entrance to the house. We should keep in mind that this cult was the object of universal respect in classical Greece.

In our discussion of cult places in the settlements and palaces, it has already been stressed that temples and palace shrines in the Bronze Age had no established shape and no fixed place in the ground plan of the building, as was the case in classical Greece. A study of the domestic sanctuaries in private houses leads to the same conclusion. Of course if the sanctuary had always been of the same shape, or if it had always occupied the same position in the building, it would have been much easier to identify the Minoan cult places. The quality of construction cannot be used as proof of the existence of a sanctuary either. Quite the contrary, in fact, since high quality construction was not a characteristic of the shrines but was more common in

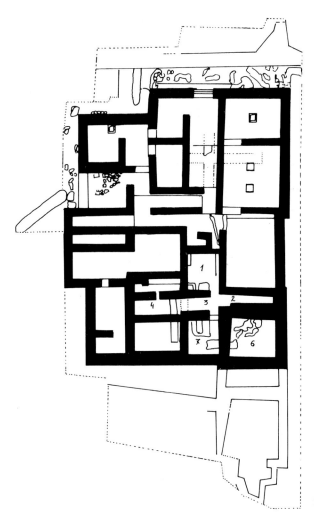

198. Kannia. Plan of the villa. BA 44 (1959), 238, Fig. 2.

secular architecture. The most solidly built and often the biggest rooms were the farm buildings (e.g. at Kannia and at Tylissos, Fig. 13), whereas the sanctuaries were situated in unimportant places and were like farm sheds (e.g. at Palaikastro). Thus the architecture of a building or room cannot be used to determine whether this place served a religious purpose.

The present-day state of the sanctuary interiors is somewhat disappointing. In view of the small dimensions of the sanctuaries, it was not to be expected that there would be any furnishings of importance inside. The rooms in the sanctuaries did not differ in any special way from dwelling rooms or store-rooms. The only construction usually (but not always) found inside was a rather low stone bench, which was a characteristic feature of the interior of the shrines. It was usually placed opposite the doorway or along the side walls (e.g. at Phaistos, Fig. 175 or Kannia, Fig. 198). Of course it would be a mistake to attach too much importance to the part played by this bench, since stone benches are fairly common in the dwelling houses. They have been discovered, for instance, in many houses at Knossos and Palaikastro.[76] They were used not only for sitting on but also for storing various things. It should be remembered that at least up to MM III the houses had extremely meagre furnishings. Indeed, it seems that it was not until near the end of MM III that wooden chests were introduced.[77] When the houses had no chests, the various pottery vessels such as jugs, pithoi, etc., as well as other domestic hardware, must have been kept in special small rooms as well as on stone benches. Thus the stone benches in the sanctuaries provide an example of the practice whereby the furnishings of the sanctuary imitated the interior of the home. Although in the sanctuary the other objects belonged to the deity, the function of the bench in the private house and the bench in the sanctuary was one and the same: it served to store the cult objects, idols or votive offerings.

We could accept that the inside of the sanctuaries, and especially the walls and floors, were

142

covered with paintings or signs symbolising the holiness of the place, but unfortunately few sources are available to confirm this theory. The main find was from the temple in A. Triada.[78] In one of the rooms of the town-shrine discovered at Mallia in 1956,[79] a stucco fragment with a painting of a red bucranion on a blue background was unearthed. The significance of these examples is that the extant sources provide no indication that there were paintings of a sacred character in the sanctuaries. It should be borne in mind that monochrome plaster-work and painting of the walls was probably quite common, especially in the wealthier houses. The marine motifs, whose purpose was not merely decorative, were even more common — so much so that they later became an almost completely conventionalised part of the everyday surroundings of the Minoans. These marine motifs were to be found on almost every object of everyday use, such as dishes, bath-tubs, ornaments, etc. Of course in spite of the fact that the sea, the fresh-water streams and the springs were in some way sacred, this does not indicate that everything (e.g. a pot) decorated with a marine motif was a cult object.[80]

When we address the question of the façade of the sacred building, we again face the problem of a paucity of sources and therefore we cannot reconstruct this part of the sanctuary with any certainty. To start with it should be pointed out that the façades of the domestic sanctuaries were never so important as the façades (or portals) of the sanctuaries in the mountain temenae or sacred enclosures — that is, of detached buildings. For most of the domestic sanctuaries were tiny rooms entered from inside the house. Of course from analogy with the shrines in the peak sanctuaries, the sacred enclosures, the tombs, and even the palace shrines,[81] it can be taken that the entrance of the domestic sanctuary was sometimes richly ornamented (Fig. 200).

The main question concerning the sanctuaries is that of the cult images. The number of finds from which reliable information can be obtained is relatively small. Yet one must reject the view once put forward that anthropomorphic cult images were not yet known in the Minoan period. It must be stressed that the term 'cult image' is very broad since it embraces not only images of the divinities in human or animal form, but also diverse aniconic images.

Undoubtedly the holy places also contained baetyls in various forms. These baetyls are frequently shown in the pictorial art (Fig. 128). At least from the Middle Bronze Age onwards, stalagmite and stalactite pillars in the caves were worshipped. Further, the rhyton found at Zakro (Fig. 94) depicts a sanctuary on the portal of which there is an aniconic image of a goddess in the form of a stylised mountain, guarded by agrimi. Some of the Cycladic idols in

199. Chamaizi. Plan of the house. Pepragmena III vol. I,. 49, Fig. 2.

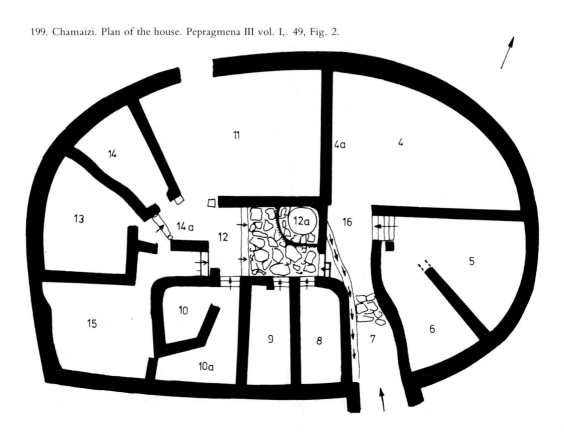

200. Mallia. Reconstruction of Room XVI. 1.
Etcret 4, frontice piece.

the form of conical pillars also indicate this way of thinking. Therefore one cannot preclude the idea that various kinds of aniconic images of the deities were kept inside the sanctuaries.

It is probable that the trend towards anthropomorphic cult images began very early, however. In the sacred grottoes the stalagmites and stalactites shaped like humans or animals may also have had a religious significance since sacrifices were made in front of them. It is known for certain that even in LM IIIB the images of the divinities were sometimes no more than natural stones, possibly taken from sacred grottoes. The only surviving evidence of this comes from the Fetish Shrine at Knossos (Fig. 194). One of the idols discovered there was found on a balustrade that in LM IIIB served as a bench. Others (D, E and F on Fig. 193) had fallen off the bench onto the floor, and one was found outside (G). Human figures can be recognised at first glance. It should be remembered that very little was done to improve the appearance of these idols, although the eyes were chiselled by human hand. Evans thought a mother and three children could be discerned in those forms, but it is more likely that they represent four goddesses.

Not all scholars are convinced that these were cult images. But the discoveries in the tomb chapels,[82] the stalactites found in private houses, and the religious nature of some of the stalagmites in the grottoes has dispersed doubts about the finds in the Fetish Shrine and it is generally accepted that they do in fact have to do with cult images. Possibly stone pillars and wooden xoana were placed in some of the sanctuaries. They were clothed in real garments, which gave them an anthropomorphic appearance. A rather eloquent argument in favour of the idea that these were cult images is that models of votive robes were found in the

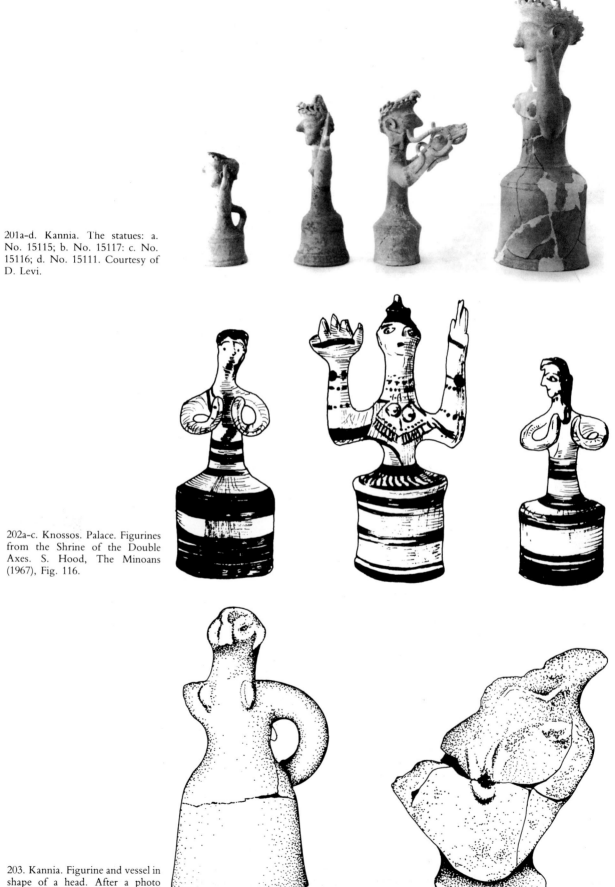

201a-d. Kannia. The statues: a. No. 15115; b. No. 15117: c. No. 15116; d. No. 15111. Courtesy of D. Levi.

202a-c. Knossos. Palace. Figurines from the Shrine of the Double Axes. S. Hood, The Minoans (1967), Fig. 116.

203. Kannia. Figurine and vessel in shape of a head. After a photo supplied by D. Levi.

sanctuaries. Some, dating from MM III, were discovered at Knossos. Of course this indicates that real garments, and not just the models of garments, were brought as gifts to the shrines.

We now have other evidence regarding the development of the cult images, from aniconic to anthropomorphic forms. Interesting material was discovered recently at Kotchati near Idalion in Cyprus, in the form of clay models from the early Bronze Age (Fig. 166).[83] The principal element of one of these models is a vertical wall or wide post with protuberances like breasts — a wall which is surmounted with a bull's head. The important thing is that this is not merely a representation of a deity, but also a cult scene. We see a woman leaning over a tall pithos, making an offering to the idol. It should be noted that in the Vounous clay model of the sacred enclosure (Fig. 137) there is a similar pillar, although in that case the scene does not depict the offering up of a sacrifice to the god. It seems likely that the cult images developed in two directions. One led to the emergence of anthropomorphic statues in which the deity had all the attributes of a human being. A famous example of this is the figurine from Enkomi, representing a god in a horned cap — the zoomorphic form of the divinity now being symbolised solely by the horns on his cap. The other direction led to the creation of flat anthropomorphic figurines of goddesses with no zoomorphic symbols. The figurines of this kind still showed traces of the old, aniconic idols, that is the flat form of the body. We find examples of these in the flat Bronze Age idols discovered in Cyrpus. This tradition still survived in the archaic idols in Beotia.

This is not all that can be said about the anthropomorphic figures, however. In Greece, at least from Neolithic times onwards, the people made small figurines, usually representing women, which may have been images of the gods, or which may have been statuettes used in the religious rites — e.g. in the initiation ceremonies. But with the exception of the discoveries at Nea Nikomedeia (see below), the figurines that have been discovered so far were not found in the sanctuaries. Nor have we any strong reason for thinking that those figurines which were discovered in the MM sanctuaries were cult images. As a matter of fact, in the light of the present evidence, the earliest cult images were found in sanctuaries dating from LM, although some statuettes were found in earlier shrines. The four clay figurines discovered at Chamaizi date from MM I. Two of them were found outside the oval building, near Room 2. These were votive statuettes — a view which is confirmed especially by the hands extended in supplication. The first evidence of cult statues in the domestic sanctuaries comes from LM IIIA or from LM IIIB. It would seem to be a valid supposition that the statues found at Kannia date from LM IIIA.[84] At Kannia (Fig. 201), as at Gournia, Gazi (see p. 164) and Karphi the statues which were found must have been idols. A statue of a goddess was found in Room 6 at Kannia. It bore a close resemblance to a small statuette at Knossos (Fig. 202b), except that its dimensions were bigger. Another statue represented a goddess with snakes. On her head she wore a dentillated diadem, with the heads of snakes writhing out of it as if from a nest (Fig. 201).[85] In Room 2 fragments of statuettes were discovered. One of them represented a goddess with an ornamental headdress whose principal elements were small sacred horns and birds. In Room 5 stood a cult statue representing the Snake Goddess, although this time her hands were in a different position, i.e. palms outward. Her conical-shaped headdress was traditionally decorated with snake-heads.[86] There is no doubt that the Kannia statues described here were simply cult idols. Their function will be described below.

In many sanctuaries no cult images were found, only cult objects (Figs. 203-4) and emblems. The most common emblems were the horns of consecration. These have been found in several sanctuaries. At the town-shrine at Mallia these horns were a permanent fixture on the balustrade of the inner stairway. Horns of consecration made of stucco have also survived elsewhere. The Shrine of the Double Axes at Knossos provides an interesting example of the placing of such horns. The spot where they stood on a bench can still be seen (Fig. 184). In tiny Room 20 in Block B (at Palaikástro), stucco horns were also found. In the same house,[87] other sacred horns (small ones) were discovered in Room 42. It has already been remarked that in Block N at Palaikastro the sanctuary must have been on the first floor. The miniature double horns, measuring no more than 0.05 m, found there must have come from this room.[88] Among the other characteristic finds are double axes. A gold double axe was found at Apodoulou,[89] while in sanctuary N referred to above (at Palaikastro) one of the discoveries was a stepped stone base which at one time supported a double axe on a shaft.

The sacred furniture also remains to be described. The most common objects of this kind were undoubtedly the altars (Fig. 205) and the libation tables.[90] A portable stone altar[91] with

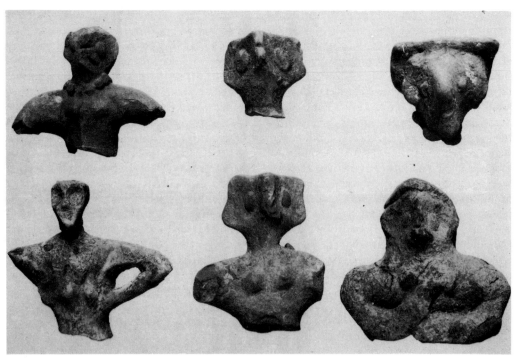

204. Kannia. Figurines. Courtesy of D. Levi.

horns of consecration and hieroglyphic signs carved on its side walls was discovered not far from the stone bench in Room 4a at Kannia. The stone table with linear inscriptions from Apodoulou is a unique find,[92] although fragments of such tables without inscriptions are quite common — e.g. at Rousses.[93] The little clay tables found at Chamaizi were not always necessarily used for religious purposes.[94] However the one found at the temple in Mallia (see p. 160) which has a hole in the middle, was most probably used solely as a hearth. Cult vessels were found there as well. The rhyta and clay tube stands (see p. 161) are undoubtedly among the most important of these. Specimens of the latter type have been found in practically every sanctuary. Sometimes these are objects made in a simple, even primitive way, such as the small vessels discovered at Katsaba. But vessels of a more superior kind are sometimes found and these are occasionally ornamented with snakes.[95] Other finds of this kind include bull rhyta[96] or rhyta in the form of a lion's head,[97] or vessels in the shape of a woman's head.[98] Some stone or clay vessels with sacred signs such as horns of consecration,[99] or double axes may have had a special religious significance,[100] despite the fact that similar vessels, also bearing cult symbols, were probably used for everyday purposes.[101] The goblet found at Apodoulou became a cult object through its Linear A inscription, which perhaps signified magic formulae.[102] Certainly, as the iconographic sources also prove, triton shells must have been used for sacred purposes.[103] They may have been used as musical instruments, such as trumpets for calling the faithful or for summoning the deity (Fig. 126). This last aspect would seem to be confirmed by the discovery of a clay model of a triton shell (Fig. 205b). Further, one may also mention the incense-burners, the stone lamps, the cups and other vessels although similar objects, or even the same ones, were used both in religious premises and for everyday purposes.[104] It is thought that the small inverted bowls may at one time have contained votive offerings (Fig. 205a), although it must be admitted that similar inverted bowls were also found in a dwelling-house.[105]

Among the votive offerings are very characteristic statuettes of votaries, and also animal figurines common in other cult places. For example, the votive figurines found at Kannia (Fig. 204) show the same characteristics as the small objects of this type found in the peak sanctuaries (Figs. 98ff). Yet these figurines, whether made of clay or bronze, are rare. The votive offerings also include pinakes with mythological scenes,[106] or others which no doubt were once covered with painted inscriptions that no longer exist.[107] Finally, nearly all the sanctuaries have been found to contain many objects of everyday use, such as table and kitchen pottery, domestic utensils, tools (e.g. pestles and loom weights), as well as seals, ornaments, etc.

Another question about which we have little reliable evidence is the religious function of the courtyards in the larger dwelling-houses and villas (farms). It should be recalled, as has been remarked above, that in both towns and villages, as well as in the palaces, religious ceremonies were held in the large courtyards, or squares or theatrical arenas. On a smaller scale, the same should hold true of the courtyards in the smaller private houses or isolated farms (villas). But the excavations have only produced one piece of evidence as to this, although a characteristic one. In a small inner courtyard at Nirou Chani (Fig. 19), a stepped base was discovered as well as, nearby,[108] fragments of stone horns of consecration. If it can be assumed that at one time the horns stood on the stone base, then there is no reason to doubt, either, that the base was used as an altar. Thus it is possible that rituals were performed in the courtyard of this farm.

In these sanctuaries domestic deities were worshipped whose attributes can be deduced from the characteristics of the cult statues there. At Kannia, for example, snakes entwine the arms of the goddess (Fig. 201c), or snake heads come writhing out of the nest formed by her headdress. From the chthonic character of the beliefs here, which was such a typical feature of later Greece as well as of other cultures, and from the fact that statues of such deities were discovered in the domestic sanctuaries, it can be reasoned that the snake deities were expected to look after the houses and the inhabitants in them. The goddess whose symbol was the snake was expected to make the grain and the other crops grow, and to protect the house from misfortune. Ethnological examples collected by Nilsson, as well as Greek examples, illustrate the importance of the snake most clearly.[109] Evans made an interesting discovery of objects testifying to the cult of the domestic snake near the south-west corner of the palace at Knossos,[110] in a little sanctuary consisting of no more than a single room which had a pithos sunk in the floor. This pithos, it transpired, contained objects of great interest: cylindrical vessels with snakes attached to their side walls, as well as tubular snake vessels and tiny little vessels no doubt used for milk. The snakes that lived in the sanctuary were fed in these vessels.

Nilsson has very rightly stressed[111] that the household goddess revealed herself in the sanctuaries in the form of both a snake and a bird. The statue at Kannia suggests that the household deity had two attributes — one as a snake, and one as a bird (Fig. 201a). On other statues, these attributes occur separately. For example, the statues at Karphi are adorned with birds. It is possible that the terracotta statuettes of birds found at Gournia constitute part of cult statues which themselves have not survived.[112] The bird figurines may signify that the deity worshipped in the sanctuary was the ruler of the heavens, although on the other hand they may equally well signify that the sanctuary was a place where the deity made appearances.

The deity who appeared in the temples (such as at Gournia and Karphi) was no doubt of a similar character, although her cult was public, not private. Manifestations of the household deity took place in other parts of the palaces and private houses as well — for instance, the goddess, as the giver of life-giving water,[113] frequently appeared to the people in the lustral basins and spring sanctuaries.

From the very brief résumé given above, it can readily be seen that the divinities who were worshipped in the palace and domestic sanctuaries, as well as in the temples, were basically of the same kind, although they appeared in various forms.

It may be concluded that the objects attached to the cult of the Household Goddess, or the Protectress of the town or village, were of a rather modest kind. Both the domestic and the

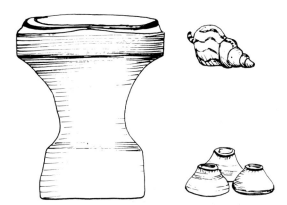

205a-c. Knossos. Finds from a sanctuary. BSA 52, 1952, Fig. 15.

palace sanctuaries were consecrated to divinities that were worshipped within the family circle. There were not even any basic differences between the cult practiced in the residence of the rulers and that in the private house. In only two sanctuaries have objects of a superior quality been found — the Repository of the Central Sanctuary at Knossos with objects of a superior artistic quality, and the domestic sanctuary at Apodoulou where the contents were of a higher level of workmanship. In the other sanctuaries, both in private houses and in palaces, the contents were rather commonplace and sometimes of small material worth. These facts are the best proof that in the private and palace sanctuaries the cult was a matter of private concern, which on the whole was of no interest to anyone outside the confines of the particular house or palace in question. It was only much later that the situation changed and that the cult became a public affair concerning all the inhabitants of the town, although at the same time it retained nearly all the features of a private cult.

The question may also be asked as to whether there was any worship of the ruler. This problem has already been discussed above in connection with the Throne Room at Knossos. Of course if we accept the view that the domestic sanctuaries were places where the household deities manifested themselves, this weakens the theory as to a cult of the ruler. The argument for the existence of a cult of the ruler was based principally on the group of rooms round the Throne Room. But it has been suggested above that it is not certain if the Throne Room was used for religious purposes. It is stressed that the throne did not testify to a cult of the deity or ruler, but only to the fact that the deity was the protector of the king,[114] who was not the embodiment of the deity but rather his representative and High Priest — this situation being a relic of the tenacious traditions of a primitive society.

It will repay us here to glance at similar customs in ancient Israel.[115] In the religion of Israel, as in that of Crete, apart from general oriental elements, there are also traces of chieftainship dating from the time when the Israelites were a pastoral people and the chief was a 'Holy One' and 'Father' who blessed his people. But the chief possessed these attributes more because of his physical identification with the tribe than because of any special relationship with the gods. The god of the tribe was also 'Father' of the chief, but at the same time 'father' of the whole tribe as well. Whereas in ancient Israel there was no mythical connection between the king and god, in Mesopotamia and in Egypt the idea of adoption prevailed, for the kinship between the king and god could be represented in mythical form — in some cases the king was said to have been fathered by a god while in other cases it was said that a new sun god had been born on an unknown mountain in the east.

But in Israel, too, the idea of adoption existed and the authority of the king was derived from the cult rites. The king took part in the ceremonies, dancing and singing at the head of the procession. In the religious dramas he took the part of David, whereas Jehovah was symbolised as an ark, as a stool in front of the throne on which he also sat invisible. David was divine because Jehovah had chosen him and made him his ally. Every new king renewed this alliance through anointment and divine adoption, and also repeated these ceremonies during the New Year celebrations. Therefore if the king fulfilled the will of Jehovah, his blessing fell on the people. The king was god's representative with the people, and he alone had the right to contact Jehovah, for example by remaining in the sanctuary all night. He acted as High Priest and had the gift of foretelling the future. With regard to Jehovah he was both representative and mediator of the people.

Although there are certain similarities to ancient Israel there are no indications that in Crete the king was endowed with divine properties. Indeed, the evidence shows that Minos was in the habit of meeting Zeus on a high hill,[116] which means that the king represented the people in his meetings with the god and that he acted as High Priest and mediator as well. The fact that the king's powers were renewed periodically (every nine years), shows that the fortunes of the entire community were dependent on the king's meeting with the divine being and with ensuring the aid of the gods. Although tribal traditions were too strong to permit a cult of the ruler of the oriental type, nevertheless the power of the king was based on the myth that this power came from the gods.

The early beginnings of the cult places in private houses are shrouded in mystery. But there is no doubt that the earliest cult places in the private houses were to be found near the fireplace or hearth in the interior of the houses. No traces of cult places round the fire have survived in the Neolithic houses in Crete but in view of Nea Nikomedeia this possibility should not be precluded.[117] The cult of household deities lasted right through the Bronze Age. During this same era special rooms were set aside inside the houses as dwelling-places for the gods. We have evidence of this from the excavations at Chamaizi and other places. Despite the changes that took place in the social and economic structure in MM I, the cult of household deities still maintained its old character, whether in the private houses or in the palaces. Other kinds of cult places, such as lustral basins and spring sanctuaries, developed in the villages. Places consecrated to the gods in the open spaces of the village are also a modest type of cult place. As society progressed, the private sanctuary belonging to a single family gradually developed into the public temple.

Thus neither the domestic nor the palace sanctuaries nor the other cult places in the houses or villages were of basic importance in the lives of the Cretans. The reason for this is to be found in the strong traditions of tribal life that persisted in Cretan palace-urban civilisation. For, as has been pointed out earlier, the principal cult places were situated not in the towns and villages but right out in the country — in the peak sanctuaries, the caves and the rural sacred enclosures.

CATALOGUE V

Domestic Sanctuaries

1. Amnissos (Pediadou) at Palaiochora a room, where an amphora with double axe representation and a tube stand dated to LM IIIA were found.
   AD, 23 (1968), Chronika, 402; AR, 16 (1969/70); KCh, 21 (1969), 533; Hiller, 166.

2. Apodoulou (Amariou), at Gournes. A building and sacred emblems, cult objects, and votive offerings. MM III-LM I.
   AA (1933), 297; AA (1935), 246ff; AD, 15 (1933), Parartime, 54f; Evans, PofM, IV, 656; BSA, 42 1947, 188 No. 40; E. Kirsten, *Forschungen auf Kreta 1942* (1951), ed. F. Matz 99; BSA, 59 (1964), 78.

3. Archanes, at Troullos. One of the rooms in a large building here may be a sanctuary.
   AR (1956/7), 22.

4. Archanes, at Troullos the 'summer palace'. Contents of a shrine with offering tables, horns of consecration and other finds were reported. LM I period.
   AD, 20 (1965), Chronika, 560.

5. Atsipades, discovered in 1965. Probably there was a sanctuary here in LM III or in sub-Minoan times.
   BSA, 61 (1967), 178.

6. Chamaizi (Sities), altitude 510 m near the village of Souvloto Mouri. One of the rooms found here was a sanctuary. The statuettes and other votive objects date from MM I.
   AE (1906), 117ff; BSA, 14 (1907/8), 414ff; Evans, PofM, I, 147; Platon, IK, 122fk; AS, 7 (1957), 113; AAA, 5 (1972), 283ff; Pepragmena, III, 467f; AD, 27 (1972), 648; BCH, 97 (1973), 396. In light of the new excavations by C. Davaras, AAA 5, 1972, 283ff, it is no longer possible to support the view that at Chamaizi there was a peak sanctuary (for a different opinion see O. Höckmann, Istanbuler Mitteilungen, 25 (1975), 287).

7. Kannia, in the village of Mitropolis (Gortyn). A sanctuary in a large house found here had five rooms, and was furnished with statuettes and cult objects. It also contained votive offerings. LM IIIA.
   AR (1957), 18; Ergon (1957), 92ff; KCh, 11 (1957), 332; KCh, 12 (1958), 195ff; PAE (1957), 148f; BCH, 82 (1958), 792ff.

8. Karnari (Temenous). Near the cave of Stravomyti a small settlement was discovered, where one room 6.00 × 2.90 m, destroyed in the course of building of a modern road, was discovered. A pit filled with ashes, vessels and two clay animal figurines were found. Used in LM III, and also in the Geometric and Orientalising periods.
   Ergon (1974), 115.

9. Karphi, sanctuary at the High Priest's House (Rooms 58-61, 80). Cult objects from the LM IIIC period found here.
   BSA, 38 (1937/8), 84ff.

10. Karphi, sanctuary at Rooms 55 and 57. Finds included an altar decorated with horns of consecration.
    Ibid., 84.

11. Karphi. The Great House, Rooms 16-17. Cult objects were reported. LM IIIC period.
    Ibid., 77ff.

12. Karphi. The Southern Houses, Room 27. A natural rock and two rhyta were mentioned. LM IIIC period.
    Ibid., 81f.

13. Karphi. The Central West Quarter, Room 85. Five small figurines were discovered here. LM IIIC period.
    Ibid., 90ff.

14. Karphi. The Cliff Houses, Room 106. Two figurines were found here. LM IIIC period.
    Ibid., 94f.

15. Karphi. The Commercial Quarter, Room 116. Fragment of cult statues were mentioned. LM IIIC period.
    Ibid., 88f.

16. Katsaba (Iraklion), near the Drakou bus stop. A sanctuary which contained tube stands from LM IIIC among the other finds.
    PAE (1955), 31ff.

17. Kephala Chondrou, Viannou. Votive offerings and cult objects belonging to a sanctuary. LM IIIA-B.
    KCh, 9 (1956), 417; 10 (1957), 330f; 11 (1959), 368f; PAE (1957), 136ff; (1959), 197ff; Ergon (1957), 85ff; (1959), 134ff; (1960), 202f; AR (1956), 22; (1957), 17f.

18. Knossos, Temple repositories in the west wing of the palace. Many cult objects and votive offerings dating from MM IIIB were found.
    BSA, 9 (1902/3), 38ff; Evans, PofM, I, 425, 441f, 463ff, 556ff; BSA, 60 (1965), 69ff.

19. Knossos, palace, Sanctuary of the Dove Goddess (= Loomweight Basement Deposit). Objects that once furnished a sanctuary. MM IIB.
    BSA, 8 (1901/2), 23ff; Evans, PofM, I, 221f,

248ff.

20. Knossos, palace, above magazines 11-16. Frescoes and vessels decorated with double axes which may have been furnishing of a sanctuary.
BSA, 10 (1903/4), 39ff; Evans, PofM, I, 445.

21. Knossos, palace, Shrine of the Double Axes. Many cult objects and votive offerings from LM IIIA 2 or IIIB came to light.
BSA, 8 (1901/2), 96ff; Evans, PofM, I, 76; Evans, PofM, II, 335ff; KCh, 12 (1958), 202ff; Kadmos, 4 (1965), 44; R. Popham, *The Last Days of the Palace of Knossos* (1964), 14f; Kadmos, 5 (1966), 17ff; Kadmos, 5 (1966), 137f.

21a. Knossos, palace, Vat Room Deposit. Finds including an arm of a faience figurine (a predecessor of a Snake Goddess?), fragment of obsidian, gold plate, beads, faience and shell inlays, clay sealings and pottery were dated to EM III-MMIA. Was there a treasure of a sanctuary, as Evans believed?
BSA, 9 (1902/3), 98ff; Evans, PofM, I,165ff.

22. Knossos, Fetish Shrine in the Little Palace. Natural idols, cult objects and votive offerings dating from LM IIIB were published.
BSA, 11 (1904/5), 2ff; Evans, TDA, 70ff; Evans, PofM, II, 519ff.

23. Knossos, Sanctuary of the Domestic Snake Cult near the 'Treasury'. The only finds consisted of vessels which may have been used for a sacred purpose in LM I-II.
Evans, PofM, IV, 138ff.

24. Knossos, north of the Royal Road. Finds consisted only of cult objects dating from LM IB.
AR (1961/2), 25ff; AD, 17 (1961), Chronika, 295.

25. Knossos, the Gypsades site. Excavations brought to light a room with cult objects dating from LM I.
AR (1957), 22.

26. Knossos, South-East House, Room L1. Cult objects from LM IIIB found.
BSA, 9 (1902/3), 12; Evans, PofM, I, 426; Platon, MOI, 440.

27. Knossos, South-East House, Room C1. Cult objects from MM IIIB-LM IA found.
BSA, 8 (1901/2), 109f; BSA, 9 (1902/3), 3ff; Evans, PofM, I, 425ff; Evans, PofM, II, 481; Platon, MOI, 440.

28. Knossos, room in the South House. Cult objects found, dating from MM IIIA-LM IA.
Evans, PofM, II, 386ff; Platon, MOI, 441f.

29. Knossos, Unexplored Mansion. The finds comprised the furnishings of a sanctuary, with cult objects (horns of consecration and a fumigator) dating from LM III.
AAA, 3 (1970), 93f.

30. Knossos. North House, close to the Stratigraphic Museum. Many vases and children's bones were found in a LM IB level of the house. The finds probably testify to a ritual, which has taken place at the period.
AR (1980/1), 73ff; SanctSymp, 155ff.

31. Kommos (Pyrgiotissis). Household shrine of LM IIIA date.
Hesperia, 47 (1977), 227ff.

32. Mallia, palace, Room XVIII. Excavations brought forth a stone altar and some cult objects.
BCH, 53 (1929), 523; Etcret, 12 (1962), 9ff, 52ff; H. van Effenterre, Le Palais de Mallia et la cité minoenne (1980), II, 445f; Etcret 25 (1980), 213ff.

33. Mallia, palace, Room XIV. Excavations conducted between 1929 and 1935 and between 1946 and 1960. Cult objects discovered.
Etcret, 12 (1962), 3ff; 25 (1980), 207ff; H. van Effenterre, op. cit., 449.

34. Mallis, palace, room 23.2. A sanctuary, probably LM IIIA-B, was constructed here. A terracotta animal figurine was found in the anteroom.
Etcret, 4, 24f; H. van Effenterre, op. cit., 449; Etcret, 25 (1980), 96ff.

35. Mallia, House Delta-beta. Room 14 is sometimes referred to as a sanctuary on the grounds that a rectangle of slabs (for a religious use?) was found here. MM I-LM I.
Etcret, 9, 58ff; H. van Effenterre, op. cit.m 448.

36. Mallia, House E, room 38. There was probably a sanctuary(?) in this area. Two stone offering tables, three lamps, and a fragment of a cup with double axe decoration may suggest a cult room or just testify to the piety of the inhabitants in the Neopalatial period.
Etcret, 9, 110ff; 136; H. van Effenterre, op. cit., 448.

37. Mallia, the border of House E. Rooms II 1 and 2. Figurines (one of a beetle), and a fragment of an offering table was found. The finds may suggest a sanctuary (?) or just testify to the piety of the inhabitants. See also above, p. 000.
Etcret, 16, 40ff, 139; CPl, 55 (doubts as to the religious function of the hall 38 and the nearby rooms; followed by H. van Effenterre, op. cit., 447f).

38. Mallia, Quarter Mu, in one room of the N House was a sanctuary, where votive objects dated to MM II were found.
Etcret, 26 (1980), 99ff.

39. Mallia, Quarter A, Area XVII. Contents of a shrine, among others miniature horns of consecration were reported. LM I period.
H. and M. van Effenterre, *Mallia. Le Centre politique* (1969), I, 103ff.

40. Nirou Chani. A small Room 7a, where the big double axes were found, was probably a workshop or a storeroom of sacred objects. LM I period.
AE (1922), 6f, 10, 12f; Platon, MOI, 449.

41. Palaikastro, Block N. Excavations produced cult objects from LM IB.
BSA, 60 (1965), 252ff; 65 (1970), 215ff, 235ff.

42. Palaikastro, Block delta, Room 44. Cult objects from LM IIIA 2 discovered.
BSA, 10 (1903/4), 216ff; BSA, Suppl. I, 88ff.

43. Palaikastro, Block Pi. The rhytons found in Rooms Pi 105 and 101, as well as in Chi 24 may

attest to the fact that there was a sanctuary here in LM I.
BSA, 40 (1939/40), 39, 66ff; Hood, TS, 167f.

44. Phaistos, West Sanctuary. The offering table and other objects found there may indicate that there was a sanctuary in the western part of the palace in MM II.
MA, 12 (1902), 33ff; 14 (1904), 405; RendLinc, 12 (1907), 286; Festos, I, 195ff; II, 573ff.

45. Phaistos, Palace, Room XXXVI (88). An offering table may indicate there was a shrine in MM II and probably later on.
Festos, I, 338ff, 351, 440; II, 203ff, 586ff.

46. Phaistos, Palace, Rooms LIII and LV. Vessels found here may suggest that a sanctuary existed here in the MM IIA period.
BdA, 41 (1956), 243ff; AE (1965), 46f, 52f, 98f; Gesell, 266f.

47. Phaistos, Palace, Rooms 8-10. Stone offering tables and other finds probably testify to a sanctuary being here in the neo-palatial period.
Festos, II, 104ff, 582f; Gesell, 267f.

48. Prinias. Idols and cult objects from LM IIIB/C discovered.
AM, 26 (1901), 247ff; Ausonia, 1 (1906), 119f; BdA, 2 (1908), 455; Banti, CulM, 43; KCh, 12 (1958), 181ff; PAE (1968), 184f.

49. Pseira, House B, Room 4. The objects found here may attest to the existence of a sanctuary in one of the rooms. LM I period.

Seager, Ps, 14f, 27ff; Hood, TS, 167.

50. Pseira, House in G7 (Room 2). The vessels found here may indicate a shrine in the LM I period.
Seager, Ps, 30f; Hood, TS, 167.

51. Pyrgos (Ierapetra). Contents of a domestic shrine found in a country villa. LM I period.
G. Cadogan, Pepragmena, 1 (1973), 34; AR (1977/8), 70ff; SanctSymp, 169ff.

52. Rousses, Chondrou Viannou. Excavations revealed a small building that may have been used as a sanctuary in LM IA or LM IB, or a room for sacred purposes in the house was used.
Ergon (1957), 89f; (1959), 139ff; PAE (1957), 145ff; BSA, 59 (1964), 82; CPl, 50; Hood, TS, 169.

53. Sklavokambos. Finds which probably fell from Rooms 1 and 4, among others a terracotta foot and a stone rhyton may indicate that a shrine existed here on the I floor in the LM IA period.
AE (1939/41), 72f; Gesell, 273.

54. Zakro, House of the Sacred Deposit, where objects of probable votive significance (e.g. a figurine of a beetle) and LM IB pottery were found.
Ergon (1969), 188ff; (1970), 172ff; (1971), 231; PAE (1969), 232ff; (1970), 223ff; (1971); 264ff; Hiller, 143.

CATALOGUE VI
Sacred places at the house entrance

1. Archanes, Summer Palace. At the entrance four stone altars were found.
AD, 20 (1965), Chronika, 560.

2. Mallia, Room XVI 1, with kernos.
BCH, 50 (1926), 576; 52 (1928), 292ff; Etcret, 4 (1936), 12ff; Nilsson, MMR², 106f; CPl, 55f; Etcret 25, 134ff; the kernos was taken as a gaming table by Evans, PofM, III, 391, see also

H. Van Effenterre, BCH 79 (1955), 545ff; CPl, 55f; H. van Effenterre, Le Palais de Mallia et la cité minoenne (1980), II, 449.

3. Mallia, Quarter Mu. East House. In a room facing the court and by the entrance, there is a table of offering.
BCH, 91 (1967), 885.

CATALOGUE VII
Sanctuaries at springs and water intakes

Kato Symi *see* Sacred enclosures
1. Knossos. Underground Spring Chamber close to the Caravanserai. Used for cult purposes in LM I, IIIC, and later.
Evans, PofM, II, 123f.

2. Zakro, palace, Room XLI. Sacred well. Traces of what seems to be an offering (cups with olives). LM I.
PAE (1964), 158f.

CATALOGUE VIII
Lustral basins

1. Amnissos. Villa. A probable lustral basin. LM I.
N. Platon, *Europa. Festschrift für Ernst Grumach* (1967), 238f; Gesell, 212.

2. Gournia, Room G 28. LM I.
Gournia, 25; Gesell, 215.

3. Gournia, Room H5. LM I.
Gournia, 26; Gesell, 216.

4. Knossos. Palace. Lustral Basin at Throne Room Complex. LM II-IIIA 2.
BSA, 6 (1899/1900), 36ff; Evans, PofM, IV, 902ff; Gesell, 236; Mirie, 69f.
5. Knossos. Palace. North-west Lustral Basin. MM II-MM IIIA.
BSA, 7 (1900/1), 60ff; Evans, PofM, I, 218; III, 8ff; Gesell, 238.
6. Knossos. Palace. South-east Lustral Basin. MM III.
BSA, 7 (1900/1), 63; Evans, PofM, I, 574f; II, 330; Platon, op. cit., 241; Gesell, 239.
7. Knossos. Little Palace. MM III-LM I.
BSA, 11 (1904/5), 6ff; Evans, TDA, 59ff; Evans, PofM, II, 519ff; Platon, op. cit., 241; Gesell, 240f.
8. Knossos. House of the Chancel Screen. MM IIIB-LM I.
Evans, PofM, II, 392f; Gesell, 243f.
9. Knossos. South House. MM IIIB-LM IA.
Evans, PofM, II, 378f; Gesell, 245.
10. Mallia, Palace, Room III. 4. MM III-LM I.
Etcret, I, 13f; XII, 32f; Gesell, 253.
11. Mallia. House Delta. alfa, Room 7. MM III-LM I.
Etcret, IX, 45f; Gesell, 257.
12. Mallia. House E, Room IX. MM III-LM I.
Etcret, XI, 135f, 144; Gesell, 257.
13. Mallia. House Za, Room 11.
Etcret, IX, 94f; 98; Gesell, 259.
14. Mallia. Quarter Mu. MM II.
BCH, 91 (1967), 882; Gesell, 259.
15. Nirou Chani. Villa, Room 7. Remodelled later? MM III-LM I.
Gesell, 261.

16. Palaikastro, Block B, Room 3. MM III-LM I.
BSA, 8 (1901/2), 312f; Gesell, 261.
17. Palaikastro, Block Gamma, Room 3. MM III-LM I.
BSA, 9 (1902/3), 290f, 315f; Gesell, 261.
18. Phaistos. Palace, Room 19. MM III-LM I.
Festos, II, 125ff; Platon, op. cit., 243; Gesell, 268.
19. Phaistos. Palace, Room 21. MM III-LM I.
Festos, II, 129; Platon, op. cit., 243; Gesell, 268.
20. Phaistos. Palace, Room 63d. MM III-LM I.
Festos, II, 171ff; Gesell, 269.
21. Phaistos. Palace, Room 70. MM II.
Festos, I, 327ff; Gesell, 270.
22. Phaistos. Palace, Room 83. MM III-LM I.
Festos, II, 299ff; Gesell, 270.
23. Phaistos. Chalara, South Section, Room Z. MM III-LM I.
Ann, 29/30 (1967/8), 113ff; Gesell, 270.
24. Thera, Akrotiri. Xerte 3. LM I A.
S. Marinatos, Excavations at Thera (1976), VII, 26.
25. Tylissos, House A, Room 11. MM III-LM I.
Etcret, III, 17f; Platon, op. cit., 238f; Gesell, 273.
26. Tylissos, House Gamma, Room 12. MM III-LM I.
Etcret, III, 40f; Platon, op. cit., 238f; Gesell, 274.
27. Zakro, palace. Room XXIV. MM III-LM I.
PAE (1963), 176ff; 1964, 148ff; Platon, op. cit., 239f; Gesell, 276.
28. Zakro, palace. Room LVIII. MM III-LM I.
PAE (1966), 165ff; Platon, op. cit., 240; Gesell, 279.

CATALOGUE IX

Cult places in the squares and courtyards

1. Gournia, town. The horns of consecration may testify that an altar stood in the north-west corner of the courtyard.
2. Knossos. West Court. Northern Altar.
Evans, PofM, II, 612.
3. Knossos. West Court. Southern Altar.
Evans, PofM, II, 613.
4. Mallia. Eschara at the central courtyard. A layer of ash and also some pottery date from MM IIIA and from later times.
Etcret, 12 (1962), 22.
5. Mallia. Palace. Central courtyard. North-west corner. Stone blocks there may have been used as an altar.
Etcret, 12 (1962), 21f.
6. Mallia. Palace, central courtyard. South-west corner. Stone blocks probably were used as an altar.
Etcret, 12 (1962), Plan I.
7. Nirou Chani, courtyard. The remains of a stepped construction (probably an altar) and a fragment of horns of consecration were discovered here.
AE (1922), 1ff.
8. Phaistos, central courtyard. The stone blocks discovered here may have served as an altar, but no traces of offerings have been found.
Festos, II, 585; AJA, 61 (1957), 261ff.
9. Zakro. Palace, central courtyard. Remains of a construction there may have served as an altar.
N. Platon, Zakros (1971), 102.

VIII
Neolithic and Minoan Temples
The problem of the temples

IN ANCIENT Greece the plan and external appearance of the temples basically became settled in the sixth and fifth centuries B.C. Since the dwellings of the gods were quite different in outline from those of ordinary mortals, it is generally fairly easy to ascertain the nature of the sacred buildings from the archaeological remains. But from the very earliest days of study of the pre-Doric cultures, it was regarded as certain that no temples of the classical type could be expected to be found in Minoan-Mycenaean Greece.

Owing to the absence of monumental buildings that obeyed the rules of sacred buildings of the classical type, students of ancient architecture (such as Anderson, Spiers, Dinsmoor, Robertson,[1] etc.) and many of the most eminent scholars of classical archaeology (such as Furtwängler, Karo, Rodenwaldt,[2] and especially Matz)[3] expressed their disbelief in the existence of temples (and often cult idols, as well) in the pre-Doric period. But Nilsson, while denying the existence of temples in the Bronze Age, regarded a building at Gournia (see below p. 163) as a public cult place.[4] The terms 'public cult place', 'town shrine' and 'temple' should all be taken as having the same connotation. The temple is accepted as being a place separated from its surroundings — usually quite isolated from other buildings, and it is the place where a divinity dwells, in anthropomorphic or aniconic form. The isolation of the temple was necessitated by its function and significance, for the open space in which it stood allowed the worshippers to gather before the sacred building or in the open-air not far from the temple.

A number of years ago some buildings were already interpreted as temples: Megaron B at Eleusis (Mylonas[5] and Karo),[6] the sanctuary at A. Triada in its final phase (Banti),[7] the temple at A. Eirene in Keos (Caskey),[8] and one at Mycenae (Taylour).[9] All these investigations provided a wealth of evidence regarding the existence of temples in the Bronze Age, but no general theory was reached.

It should be remembered, too, to what conclusion Evans came regarding the sacredness of the palaces. His efforts went to show that the Minoan palaces were almost saturated with sacred elements connected with the functions of the King-Priest. In a sense, then, according to Evans, the palace at Knossos was a holy place. That question is an extremely complicated one, and is discussed above (see p. 126). Here we shall be content merely to point out that in our view the sacred character of some of the rooms, and the discovery of sacred objects in various parts of the palace do not suffice to mark the whole palace as sacred. This will readily be comprehensible just by comparing the ratio of sacred rooms to secular ones. Even if the ruler had divine qualities — being a god's representative on earth — this does not entitle us to say that his dwelling was a holy place. We contend that in those days, as in the time of classical Greece, there was no hard and fast line between the sacred and secular, especially among the common people. Because of the vagueness of this boundary we must be doubley cautious in our interpretation of buildings or rooms in which sacred objects have been found. For buildings and objects had varying degrees of sacredness — an altar, for instance, would be the property of a god, often proving that the place where it stood was a cult place, whereas something else, an element such as water, for instance, consecrated to the god, or a jug in which this sacred fluid was kept, had only a very general connection with the divinity. Hence not every object with a sacred function that was found in a settlement would testify to the holy character of the place where it was found. Similarities to this situation may be found, for instance, in late Roman houses where there was a cult place in the most important part of the house, on the ground floor, while sacred objects used for religious purposes were also to be found in the bedroom on the first floor. In other words, the presence of an object sacred in

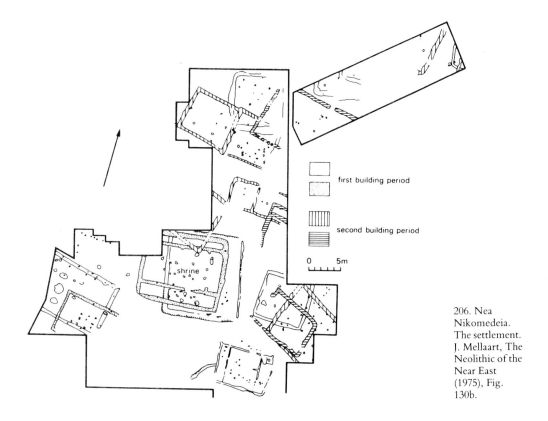

first building period

second building period

0   5m

206. Nea
Nikomedeia.
The settlement.
J. Mellaart, The
Neolithic of the
Near East
(1975), Fig.
130b.

character does not necessarily prove that the place where it was found was a sanctuary. Furthermore, many objects used in the religious cult were also used for practical purposes.

Yet the basic problem rested on a broader base. For archaeologists who studied the development of the Aegean world concentrated mostly on the palaces. So the palaces (not the towns) were the subject of economic and social interpretation. Other scholars, too, propounded theories concerning the temples. Faure[10] interpreted villas at Nirou Chani and Gortyn (Kannia, Figs. 19, 198) as temples, and subsequently regarded palaces as temples, too.[11] Finally, Hood[12] supposed that certain buildings at Gournia, Fournou Korifi (Myrtos), A. Triada, Koumasa, two at Mallia, one at Pseira, two at Palaikastro, and one each at A. Eirene on Keos, at Rousses and at Kannia (Gortyn) were town shrines.

From the above it can be seen that even at the beginning of this century archaeologists questioned whether temples existed in pre-Doric Greece. On the whole their answer was negative. But now the situation is different. New discoveries have been made not only in the study of religion, but also in connection with deeper studies of the entire culture of early Greece, and as a result the questions we ask are of a different nature. We accept that temples did exist from very early times and nowadays we are concerned principally with distinguishing which buildings are temples, classifying them, and attempting to determine their origin.

Neolithic town shrines

The earliest public shrines date back to the Neolithic period. In another chapter we have already pointed out that in central and northern Greece there were sacred grottoes (p. 200) and the remains of open-air cult places with altars (p. 203), testifying to the existence of sanctuaries both out in the country and in the human settlements. A settlement excavated at Nea Nikomedeia[13] in 1961-3 interests us particularly. Here excavations revealed the presence of two layers dating from early Neolithic times and separated in places by soil, indicating that for a time the settlement had been abandoned. This settlement has been dated to about 5500-5300 B.C.[14] (that is, early Neolithic), although we cannot rule out the possibility that partial

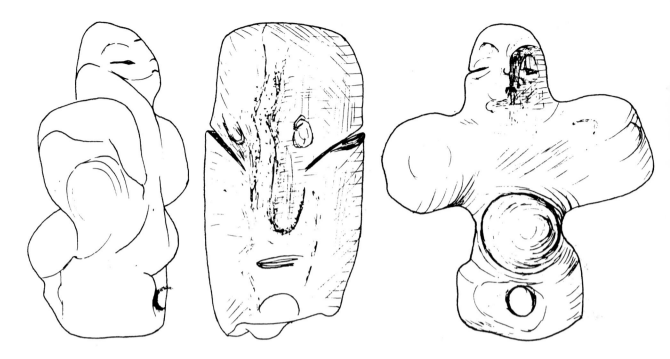

resettlement took place in the late Neolithic period. Certain similarities between this material and that found in Bulgaria (Karanovo) and Asia Minor (Çatal Hüyük) provide us with a better understanding of types of early Neolithic settlements in Macedonia. Excavations uncovered four houses grouped around another building 12 sq. m in area, which was used as a public shrine, or temple (Fig. 206). The interior of this building is interesting. It is divided into three parts by parallel rows of pillars. The building was burnt down but rebuilt later, also in the early Neolithic period, likewise in this tripartite form. This time, however, instead of pillars there were dividing walls. The objects found here — which included five idols representing the goddess of fertility — were of exceptional significance. Three idols were discovered together, next to each other. Broken into pieces, they were found in the north-east corner of the building. Rodden thinks they may have fallen from a table or shelf. Together with them were discovered two serpentinie axes 20 cm long, two large hoards of worked flint blades (about 400 items), two very unusual gourd-shaped pottery vessels, and several hundred clay roundels. At another spot in this building, figurines were discovered. The stylistic characteristics of these figurines, showing that their function was a religious one (Figs. 207-210), is worth noting. Pregnancy is indicated, although not in exaggerated form. The thighs, however, are strongly stressed, being exceptionally rounded. The torso is flat with small breasts (generally breasts are not indicated at all on figurines). Another figurine is made differently, for it looks like an irregular pillar. A hole in it, situated lower than the abdomen, cf. Fig. 207, signifies that the goddess is in the process of giving birth, or that she has just given birth. As for the modelling of the head, the eyes and nose are emphasised, while in another case, where the head alone has survived, the mouth is well marked. Since the height of the head is about 0.06 m, it is presumed that it belonged to a large figurine, and indeed to the biggest of the idols found at Nea Nikomedeia. As a rule the figurines made of dried clay bear no traces of having been painted, with the exception of one, the hair of which had been painted red. In contrast to the human figurines the zoomorphic ones were made more roughly (Fig. 211). The roundels, too, are interesting, for they were discovered in one place.

Rodden's idea that the three idols may have stood on a table or a shelf in the corner of the room is an intriguing one. If we accept this idea, we should have here the earliest case in Greece testifying to the custom of placing sacred objects on a table in the corner of the sanctuary (later on it is more common to find a stone bench instead of a table, but their function is identical). It is also important that the interior of the building was divided into three parts. This can have been no mere accident. And finally the temple's position, in the centre of a group of houses, underlines its importance. No comparable material has been found in Greece,[15] but the similarities between the culture of Nea Nikomedeia and those of Anatolia entitle us to seek

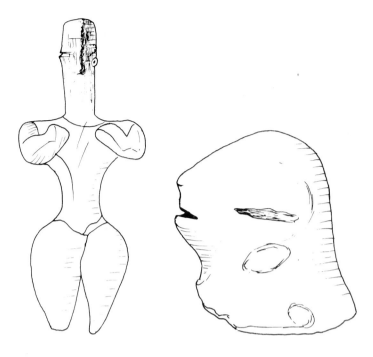

207. *(facing page)* Nea Nik-
omedeia. Figurine. ILL, 11
April 1964, Fig. 3.
208. *(centre)* Nea Nikomedeia.
Figurine. ILL, 11 April 1964,
Fig. 4.
209. *(right)* Nea Nikomedeia.
Figurine (cf. Fig. 207), ILL, 11
April 1964, Fig. 5.
210. *(this page, far left)* Nea
Nikomedeia. Figurine. ILL, 11
April 1964, Fig. 8.
211. *(left)* Nea Nikomedeia.
Head of an animal figurine.
ILL, 18 April 1964, Fig. on p.
604.

analogies in that region. As a general rule, the sanctuary stood in the centre of the settlement, or in an important spot. Several examples may be cited here. At Hacilar IIA, there is a sanctuary, with a courtyard next to it, in the northern part of the settlement.[16] In the culture that developed on the trans-Caspian plateau from the middle of the sixth millennium B.C. to the early fifth millennium B.C., settlements with sanctuaries existed (Fig. 212) — for instance there was a sanctuary in an important part of a settlement at the Geoksyur oasis (Dashliji II and III, Namazga I culture),[17] and one in the centre of the settlement[18] at Pessejik Depe (middle Jeitun culture).

The above examples go to show that in the Neolithic settlements the sanctuaries, as we see from their position in the settlements, played an important role. It is particularly interesting to note the connection between the cult building and the open area near it. Two characteristics developed: the temple was isolated from the buildings around it, and the temple had a courtyard attached to it. In the course of the millennia these two characteristics both developed, in different forms, in the Mediterranean.

This is not to say that in Greece there was an interrupted continuation from the Neolithic to the early Bronze Age Culture. The question of the origin of the early Bronze Age culture lies outside the framework of our subject. As far as the town shrines are concerned, there is undoubtedly a gap from the fifth millennium B.C. to the EM II period in Crete (Myrtos). Models of Neolithic buildings, e.g. at Krannon[19] (fifth millennium B.C.), or dating from the period EM II at Lebena[20] (third millennium B.C.), are difficult to interpret with complete certitude. They may represent either sanctuaries or houses. Nor can the models of sanctuaries found in the Balkans[21] be of any help, despite the interesting finds from that region.

Cretan temples

Myrtos (Fournou Korifi),[22] dated to the EM II period, represents another type of settlement. In the character of its buildings it differs from Nea Nikomedeia: the houses are crowded closely together, and the boundaries between them are not always clear. It may be taken, then, that as P. Warren supposes, the social system was based on community of property. In his view, this type of settlement developed later into Cretan towns like Gournia. At Myrtos, remains of Settlement I have survived only in the centre of the site. Settlement II, which also dates from EM II, covers a bigger area, but was partly destroyed by erosion. Four rooms (89-91) in the south-west part of the settlement formed a sanctuary (Fig. 213), which was probably a public

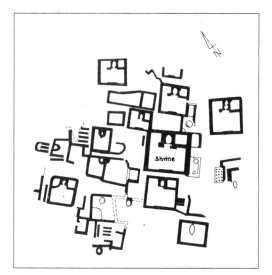

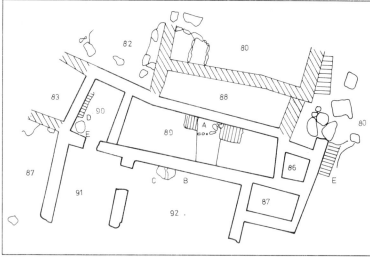

212. Pessejik Depe. The settlement. J. Mellaart, The Neolithic of the Near East (1975), Fig. 130b.

213. Myrtos. Plan of the temple. P. Warren, Myrtos (1970), Plan.

one. They were near an open space. Two rooms (91-92) have partly been destroyed by erosion. The east room had no door, and was entered by means of a ladder. Along the east wall of this room were benches, standing near a hearth that, as Hood supposes,[23] was no doubt used for the offering of sacrifices or for the preparation of ritual food. A fragment of a human skull was discovered on one of the three steps. Room 90, which is small, may have been used for making the ritual wine for a large spouted tub and remains of grapes were discovered here. Room 91, next to it, was no doubt a storeroom. The main cult room was Room 92, in which a figurine representing a woman with a jug (Fig. 214) was found. This figurine was discovered near a stand or altar placed right at the wall.

Quite early on, both in the temples and in the domestic shrines, there was already specialisation of the function of the rooms. Some were used for cult purposes, while others were used for storage. The location of the sanctuary, at the edge of the settlement with direct access to an open space (town square or meadow), shows that in every case there was easy access to the shrine. The figurine mentioned above, representing a goddess with a water jug and decorated with a weaving motif, testifies to some of the main aspects of the goddess: the supply of water and weaving, an important domestic occupation.

Not till we come to the period MM-LM, however, do we find a number of buildings that enable us to trace the history of the architecture of the town shrines. The best, and earliest,

214. Myrtos. The Goddess. P. Warren, Myrtos (1970), Fig. 94.

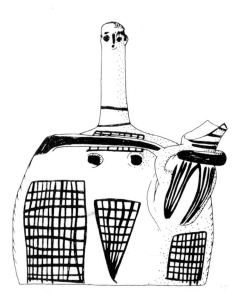

215. Mallia. Topography of the town. Etcret 19, Plan topographique (fragment).

example comes from Mallia where the MM II town shrine stands about 100 m south-east of the palace. Little is known about this area of Mallia as yet, and not much can be said about its buildings (Fig. 215). Undoubtedly, however, the building in question was completely, or almost completely isolated from the neighbouring area. On its north side is a narrow street (approximately 0.80 m wide). The partly excavated room lying to the south of Room 2, J. C. Poursat believed, also belonged to the shrine.[24] The shrine is not large; it measures about 11 × 4-5 m. It consists of three rooms (Fig. 216):[25] a vestibule (1), the sanctuary proper (2) and a storeroom (3) Figs 217-230. The sanctuary proper (Room 2), measured about 4.50 × 3.70 m, and was on a higher level than the other premises. At the left side, just beside the entrance, there was a large libation vessel, with an aperture in its base, buried in the earth up to the handles. Fixed to the ground in the centre of this room was a large hearth altar, with a large cavity in the top (Fig. 217, cf. also Fig. 176). The altar was 0.92 m long. Around this cavity Poursat observed a layer of burnt clay which, he thought, might indicate that burnt offerings were made on the altar.[26] Whether or not one of the stones round the altar was used as the base for a wooden cult statue or baetyl is not certain. In the south-east corner there was a stone bench 0.40 m high and 0.75 m broad. Nearly all the movable objects discovered in Room 2, and in particular the large numbers of vessels, were discovered at this spot. In the north-east corner

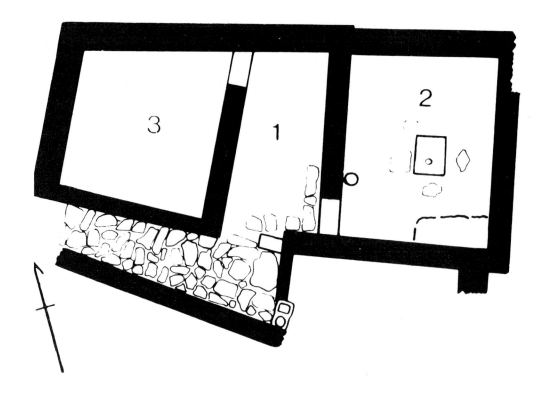

216. *(above)* Mallia. Plan of the temple. BCH 90 (1966) 516 Fig. 3.

217. *(right)* Mallia. The temple. Altar. Courtesy of J.-C. Poursat.

218. *(below)* Mallia. The Temple. Offering table. Courtesy of J. C. Poursat.

219. *(above)* Mallia. The Temple. Offering table. Courtesy of J. C. Poursat.

220. *(right)* Mallia. The Temple. Bottom of a tripod vase with double axe incised. Courtesy of J. C. Poursat.

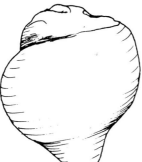

221. *(left)* Mallia. The Temple. Tube-stand. Courtesy of J. C. Poursat.

222. *(centre)* Mallia. The Temple. Clay model of a triton shell. BCH 90 (1966) 534, Fig. 25.

223. *(right)* Mallia. The Temple. Cup. BCH 90 (1966), 534, Fig. 24.

were three small sacrificial tables (Figs. 218, 219), and the base of a tripod vessel on which the sign of the double axe had been incised before the vessel was fired (Fig. 220). The room believed to be a storeroom contained two tube-stands with handles (Fig. 221), a clay model of a triton shell (Fig. 222), a fragment of a small black clay vessel with carefully modelled horns of consecration on the rim (Fig. 224), and numerous jugs and amphorae. Other interesting objects were a fragment of a rectangular plaque (Fig. 226) like a pinax (c.f. that at Kannia), and large thick-walled trace-like vessels (Fig. 227). Animal figurines were few in number (Fig. 225). None was found in the shrine proper. From the pottery vessels (Figs. 228-230) we can say this building belongs to the MM II period, and that it ceased to be used because of a great natural disaster that occurred towards the end of that period. Afterwards this region was completely deserted.

Although many problems concerning the topography of Mallia still remain to be solved, it is highly probable that this shrine stood on a site which was very important in the MM II period. Near it was the Quartier Mu, for instance. The question of what type of cult image stood here, on the other hand, cannot be answered. It may have been a wooden statue or a baetyl.

The shrine at Mallia with several rooms, which has just been described, was part of a large, important town. Gournia,[27] a provincial settlement which reached its apogée in LM I, provides us with an example of a different type (Fig. 167). The shrine referred to here stood in a higher section of the settlement, near the local ruler or governor's palace, and near the public square which led to a paved street. From the main street a smaller, short street led directly and exclusively to the temple (Fig. 231). The stones forming the surface of this minor street (about 1.50 m wide) are very worn. The latest publication[28] suggests that the shrine may have been built later than the beginning of LM I, possibly even towards the end of that period. The shrine is small (the inside measurements being 3 × 4 m), and was approached by a flight of steps.[29] A low dais made of rubble was found along the south wall and part of the east wall. The most important finds (Figs. 232-3) are usually dated to LM III (although this dating is not altogether certain). They consist of the following: one idol with upraised arms, and two heads of other idols, three arms decorated with snakes, the bases of other figurines, and four small birds, five tube vessels with snake-shaped handles, of which the three best prexerved are ornamented with horns of consecration. According to Williams,[30] the base of one of these vessels lay on the tripod altar. On a fragment of a pithos a double axe was depicted, and above it a disc. No pottery that could be used for dating was found, only 'numerous coarse fragments of pottery'.[31]

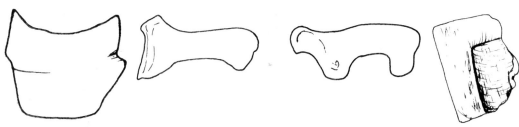

224. Mallia. Horns of consecration on rim of a clay
vessel. BCH 90 (1966)
534, Fig 26.

225a-b. Mallia. Animal figurines. BCH 90 (1966) 534, Fig. 26.

226. Mallia. Frag-
ment of a clay
offering table or a
pinax. (Un-
published).

Nearly all the various types of religious paraphernalia, with the exception of cult statues and snakes, were already in use in the Mallia shrine. They were the tripod altar, the tube vessels, the double axe signs and the horns of consecration. So at Gournia we find a cult which was more advanced in form, although its inner substance had already taken shape in MM.

The dating of the temple equipment is not altogether certain, either. It is generally accepted that the statues come from LM III B, although it has not been proved that no such statues existed earlier. At least one statue, that found at Sachtouria,[32] could possibly be dated to LM III A or earlier. The five tubular stands for small sacrificial bowls which were discovered in the temple, likewise do not provide adequate grounds for dating, since at least the tubular stand[33] from Mallia (Fig. 221) can certainly be dated to MM II, and the Pyrgos finds to LM I (Fig. 234 cf. also Figs. 235 and 236).[34] All in all, then, the dating of this Gournia temple to LM I does not seem likely to be incorrect,[35] although the finds could be from a later period.

Near the town square at Ayia Triada, excavations carried out in 1903[36] revealed a building which was later studied further by L. Banti.[37] This building stands on the gentle slope of the hill there, and at least in its later phase was separated from the other buildings by a small street. Its front elevation faced the Piazzale dei Sacelli. The earliest temple here was rectangular, its inside measurements being 4.05 × 3.25 m (Fig. 237). Double doors formed the entrance. Further in, right against the wall, was a stone bench 0.65 m high and 0.96 m deep (Fig. 238). The floor, bench, and probably the walls as well were plastered and painted (Fig. 239). The floor was decorated with a marine scene that covered the whole area. A large polypus can still be seen in the middle, and near it three dolphins, and then a group of five fish. Other dolphins and creatures can still be seen in fragments. The bench is ornamented with swirls in red, blue and white. Thus 'the surface of the waves were portrayed on the parapet and the underwater scene on the floor'.[38] This decoration has been dated to MM III/LM I.[39] Various other finds have been dated to LM I, such as fragments of tube stands[40] which lay at a distance of about 1.10 m from the bench. One of them was fixed in a layer of stucco, hence its dating seems certain. We must also mention three vessels of the censer type, cups, numerous plaques of glass paste that came from the surface of a wodden box and a gold plaque.

227. Mallia. Vessel from the Temple.

228. Mallia. Jug from the Temple. BCH 90 (1966) 538, Fig. 29.

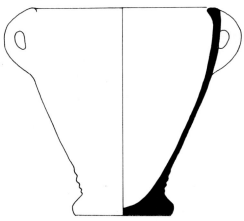

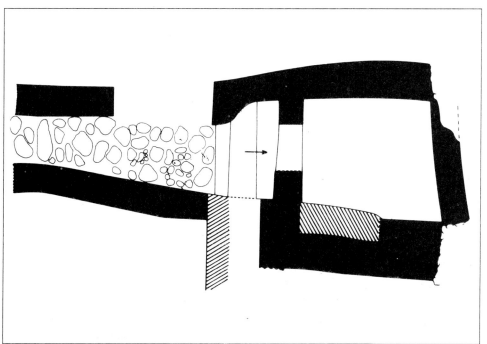

229. Mallia. Lamp or stand from the Temple. Courtesy of J. C. Poursat.

230. Mallia. Jar from the Temple. Courtesy of J. C. Poursat.

231. Gournia. Plan of the temple. B. Rutkowski, Der Tempel von Gurnia (in the press).

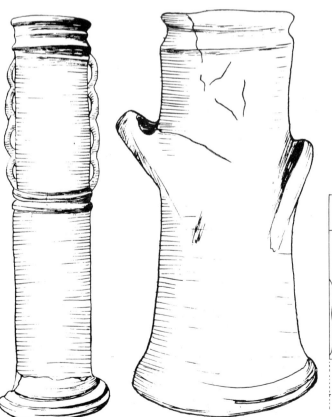

232. *(top right)* Gournia. Offering table. Nilsson MMR², Fig. 14.

233a–i. *(above right)* Gournia. Finds from the temple. Nilsson MMR², Fig. 14.

234. *(above left)* Pyrgos. Tube stands. AA 80, 1976, Pl. 44 Fig. 22.

235. *(far left)* Koumasa. Tube stand. AJA 80, 1976, Pl. 41 Fig. 2.

236. *(left)* Karphi. Tube stand. AJA 80. 1976, Pl. 43. Fig. 16.

237. *(below left)* Ayia Triada. Plan of the earlier phase of the temple. Ann N.S. 3/4, 1941/3, 41 Fig. 27.4.

238. *(below right)* Ayia Triada. Plan of the later phase of the temple adapted from: Hodd TS, Pl. A Fig. 3.

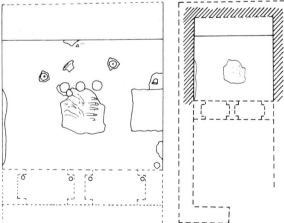

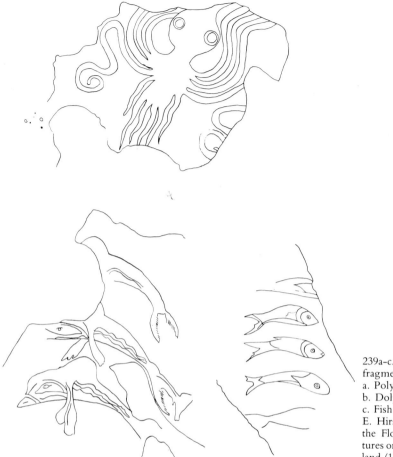

239a-c. Ayia Triada. Painted floor fragments from the temple.
a. Polypus
b. Dolphinus
c. Fish
E. Hirsch, Painted Decoration on the Floors of Bronze Age Structures on Crete and the Greek Mainland (1977), Pl. I.

Trial pits sunk below the floor have confirmed the dating of the early building to the beginning of LM I (as Banti thought) or, if we accept the dating of the wall frescoes, to MM III/LM I. This first building fell into ruins but was restored in LM III. A new temple was erected on the foundations of the old and this time a portico was added. The new temple measured 11.35 × 5.72 m. The walls consist of ashlars on the outside, and of small unhewn stones on the inside. At this phase the walls were covered with white paint, but with a band of red at the bottom. Two fragmentary tube stands and a clay lamp were discovered on the floor, while on the bench there were numerous shallow bowls measuring from 0.03 to 0.45 m in diameter, and small vessels 0.07 m high. This phase may be divided into two periods of use.

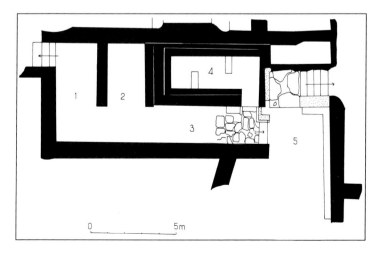

0   5m

240. Mallia. Plan of a temple southwest of the palace. BCH 81, 1957, Fig. 15 by p. 696.

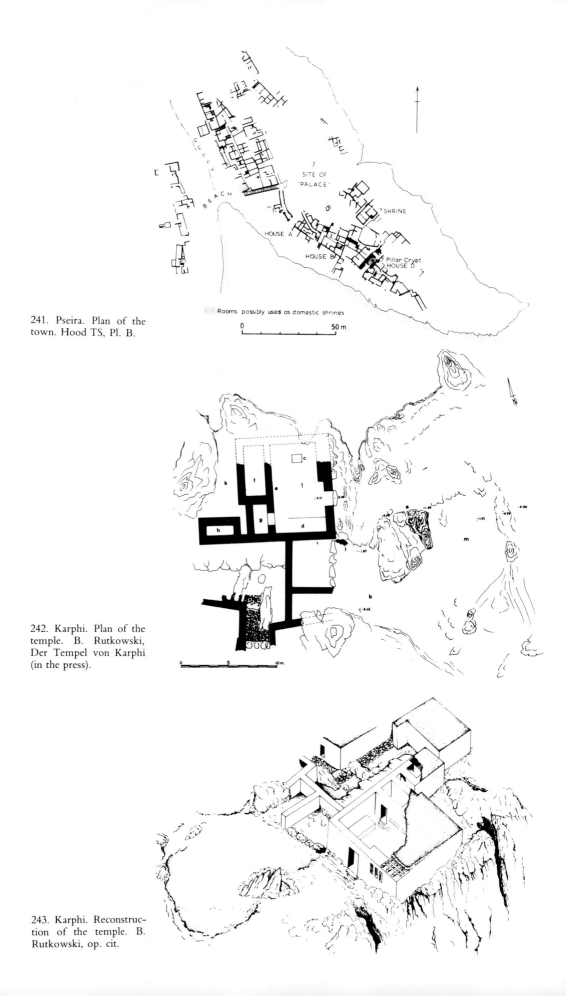

241. Pseira. Plan of the town. Hood TS, Pl. B.

Rooms possibly used as domestic shrines

0   50 m

242. Karphi. Plan of the temple. B. Rutkowski, Der Tempel von Karphi (in the press).

0   5   10 m

243. Karphi. Reconstruction of the temple. B. Rutkowski, op. cit.

Although neither idols nor religious emblems have been found the temple's situation near the town square indicates that it was a public shrine. Another building at Mallia (see Catalogue X 6) was excavated in an area still little explored. The main room was rectangular, and horns of consecration as well as fragmentary frescoes were reported (Fig. 240).

It has been pointed out recently that there may have been a town shrine at Pseira, too (Fig. 241).[41] In the town centre, not far from the site of the palace (?), is a small building measuring approximately 10.0 m × 5.5-7.0 m. It was completely cut off from its surroundings, and was divided into three rooms. The biggest one was, according to Seager, a small courtyard with a portico on its north side. It is thought that this temple consisted of both a ground floor and a first floor. Pieces of frescoes depicting two women (probably a goddess and her attendant) that were found here probably fell from the upper floor. The high standard of these frescoes is comparable with that of the frescoes at Knossos. Seager believes that no objects other than the fresco fragments were found because this building was plundered more thoroughly than others. There was a town here from MM to LM IB. Nevertheless it is necessary to say that despite those interesting aspects — such as the building's isolation from other buildings and the wall paintings of possibly religious significance — there is no certainty that this building was a town shrine.

And finally we have another example at Karphi[42] (Fig. 242) a town in the high mountains, which dates from LM IIIC and the sub-Minoan period.[43] It lies in the highest part of the saddle between Karphi and Mikri Koprana. The temple has been partly destroyed as a result of erosion. It borders a precipitous cliff which had eaten away the northern part of the building. A road, which we have called Main Temple Road, runs towards the place where the temple is situated.[44] It leads onto a square before the temple and from here a main doorway gave entry inside (Fig. 243). The temple consisted of a large main room — a cella (ca. 10.0 or more × 6.0 m), and of several small rooms, which served as storerooms. A statue of a goddess was stored in a treasury (f). Some of them were found on the bench in the southern part of the cella.[45] They were six of even more in number. In the northern part of the cella a small altar was built like that on Keos (see p. 170).

CATALOGUE X

Neolithic and Minoan Temples

Neolithic

Nea Nikomedeia. The building probably contained a table or bench. Figurines and other objects were reported. Neolithic period. *Balkan Studies,* 5 (1964), 110ff; ILN (11 April 1964) 564ff; (18 April 1964), 640ff.

Minoan

1. Anemospilia (Archanes). A cult building surrounded by a temenos wall. An altar, clay feet of a possible wooden cult statue and many other objects were found. MM period.
   Ergon 1979, 31f; 1981, 71; *The Athenian* (March 1980), 22ff; *National Geographic*, 159 (February 1981), No. 2 205ff. See also Addenda, p. 234.
2. Ayia Triada. A building was unearthed, as well as cult objects and votive offerings from LM I and LM III.
   RendLinc, 12 (1903), 318; AA (1913), 119ff; Banti, CulM, 28ff; JHS, 59 (1939), 203; Nilsson, MMR², 96f; CPl, 239f, 245; Hood, TS, 163.
3. Gournia. A building, as well as cult statues and cult objects came to light.
   Gournia, 47f; Evans, PofM, IV, 160ff; S. Marinatos, AE (1937), 289ff; Pendlebury, AC, 191ff; Yavis, Alt, 1f; Nilsson, MMR², 80ff; S. Alexiou, KCh, 12, 185ff; *idem* in Pepragmena, I, 108; CPl, 56, 215, 217, 219, 256; Hood, TS, 160ff; *Temple University Aegean Symposium*, 4 (1979), 27ff; B. Rutkowski, Der Tempel von Gurnia (forthcoming).
4. Karphi. A building, clay statues, cult objects, and votive offerings are dated to LM IIIC —

   sub-Minoan.
   J. Pendlebury *et al.*, BSA, 38 (1937/8), 75f; B. Rutkowski, Der Tempel von Harphi (forthcoming).
5. Mallia. Close to the palace a temple with three or possibly four rooms was discovered. An altar, tube-stand, offering tables, various vases, double axe sign and horns of consecrations modelled on a vessel were reported. MM II period.
   BCH, 90 (1966), 514ff; CPl, 235, 248, 251; Hood, TS, 164f.
6. Mallia. South-west of the palace. A building with several rooms and horns of consecration was found. MM II or later.
   BCH, 81 (1957), 695ff, CPl, 236, Fig. 105; Hood, TS, 165; FGK, 76.
7. Myrtos, at Fournou Koriphi. The temple consists of several rooms. An altar, a hearth, a figurine of a goddess, and many vases were reported. EM II period.
   P. Warren, *Myrtos* (1972), 81ff; Hood, TS, 162f.
8. Pseira. A small building might have served as a temple. Fragments of relief frescoes only were reported by excavator. Used in LM I period.
   Seager, Ps, 15; Hood, TS, 165ff.

IX
The Mycenaean Temples

THE SETTLEMENT of Ayria Irini in Keos throws further light on the question of the temples. An excavation led by J. Caskey[1] has revealed a fortified settlement lying in the bay there, which has been partly destroyed by the sea. Keos, lying on the route between Attica, the outer Cyclades, and Crete, was of great importance not only because of its trade but also because of its manufactures, such as metallurgy. Towards the end of the Middle Bronze Age, when the settlement was ringed with fortifications,[2] A. Irini was at the height of its prosperity. Despite the strong influence of Crete — seen in A. Irini's adoption of the Linear A script, and its numerous imports of Minoan pottery — the Keos town retained its own, local character.[3] The entire space inside the town walls was covered with buildings. Near the defence walls there was a sacred area with a temple, as well as two other buildings used for religious purposes: a group of small rooms extending along the line of the fortifications, and building B. Near the main town gate, within this area, were a small courtyard and narrow streets. The area was bounded on one side by the sea. The temple, which stood apart from the neighbouring buildings (Fig. 244), was rather long and narrow (Fig. 245). In its present state it is 23 m long and more than 6 m wide. It was frequently altered, and its inner decoration and furnishing was changed as well. It is not precisely rectangular, for the back wall is slightly skew — presumably because two of the oldest parts of the structure (Rooms XI and XII) were originally built on another axis. The pottery shows that part of the building, Room XI (perhaps a smaller temple?), dates from the early part of the MH period. The earliest finds of a religious character come from a later period: LH IB, but it was used to the end of the Bronze Age (Figs. 246-252). The internal division of the building into three large parts with a series of smaller rooms (especially in the vicinity of Room IV) is typical of dwelling houses. The earliest part of the edifice was no doubt the holiest place: the treasury was housed in this area.

These statues were made of local clay. Traces of ochre on them indicate that at least some of them were painted. Most of them were up to 1 m high, although some were taller, and one was even of natural height. They all represent women in Cretan dress: bell-shaped skirts, and bodices revealing the breasts (Fig. 246). Garlands can still be found around the neck of some of the statues. In each case the position of the hands is the same: the arms are bent and hang down at the sides, while the hands either point to or are resting on the hips. In this they are similar to the goddesses and priestesses depicted on the rings — e.g. one from Isopata (Fig. 130), and in particular a ring from Mycenae (see below p. 206)[4] Their hands are not raised up.[5] Apart from the terracotta statues, other objects have been found as well.

Thus the temple we are discussing here was built as a small sanctuary in the MH period. In period LH IB, the sanctuary was enlarged, and other rooms added. During the same period, statues were added. In LH IIIA, that is, about 1400 B.C., the temple was destroyed by a great earthquake. It is possible that for some time later it was not used at all, or was only partially reconstructed. A new temple was built in LH IIIC (that is, between 1200 and 1100 B.C.). At the same time it was enlarged by the addition of several rooms. Yet the walls were only partially restored. The objects dating from this period indicate that the building was used for religious purposes. Sacred objects were also discovered in Room XI. They come from a later time: the Proto-Geometric period, about 1000 B.C. We have here a very interesting series of finds testifying to a continuance of religious practices right up to Hellenistic times. From each period we have finds — pottery of a religious nature, and terracotta figurines — indicating that the building was used for religious rites. Another most unusual object testifying to the continuation of the cult practices here dates from the eighth century B.C. It is the head of a

244. *(right)* Keos. The town. Hesperia 40, 1971, 361 Fig. 3.

245. Keos. Plan of the temple. Hesperia 33, 1964, 327 Fig. 2.

Bronze Age statue, found on a clay base, which tells us that its presence here was not merely fortuitous, but was intended for cult purposes (Fig. 247). The statue's skirt was used as a vessel for wine. By the sixth century B.C. there is evidence of the cult of Dionysios here.

Another intriguing question arises. It is known that some of the temples, such as those at Mycenae and Philakopi, had two or more buildings. Was this the case at Keos, too? There is some hint of this in the finds that have been discovered in Room I, which opens onto the long street bordering the temple and is completely cut off from the other rooms that follow the line of the fortifications. For in Room I five terracotta feet were found, three belonging to the left leg and two belonging to the right, but not forming pairs (Fig. 248). They were discovered in Room I, in a fill under the floor near the entrance.[6] Did they belong to the original furnishings of this room or were they brought here, from somewhere near at hand, when the area was being tidied up? The feet vary in length from 0.12 to 0.20 m, and the toes are not indicated. In Caskey's view this may mean that the feet were supposed to be shod. They are well made, and above the ankle they end in a flat, finished surface, which indicates that they are not fragments that have been broken off from statues. On one of them there is a small hole, which may have been used for fixing something, or for hanging up the foot. Caskey does not think these feet were made for statues of the type we are familiar with in the temple, for the edges of the skirts of such statues were executed in such a way that obviously the statues did not need to be supported by anything underneath. There is no proof that these feet were even meant for statues. Nevertheless Caskey inclines to the view that they might have been meant for statues that were prototypes of statues of the Karphi type.[7] Naturally another fact that has to be taken

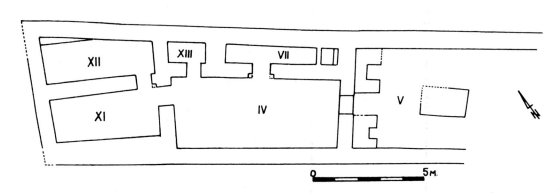

246. Keos. Female statue K.3.611. Courtesy of J. Caskey.

into consideration is that large feet may have belonged to small statues. The feet discovered in Keos have, on the basis of the pottery found there, been dated to a period somewhat earlier than the layer corresponding to LM IIIA, when Room XI in the temple was destroyed.

Yet the feet might have had other purposes still. In the first place, they may have been left over from wooden statues (p. 235). We know of other cases, outside the Aegean, where wooden statues had clay feet. Another possibility is that they were simply models of feet, such as those in Antiquity which were often brought as gifts to the gods.[8] Their true purpose is not altogether clear.

172

247. *(top)* Keos. Head of terracotta statue K.3.611 found in an archaic Greek shrine. Courtesy of J. Caskey.

248a-c. *(above left)* Keos. Clay feet. BCH 91, 1967, 755 Fig. 13.

249. *(right)* Keos. Fragment of a bronze figurine. Hesperia 33, 1964, Pl. 56.

250. *(bottom left)* Keos. Jug. Hesperia 33, 1964, Pl. 56.

251. *(bottom centre)* Keos. Jug. Hesperia 33, 1964, Pl. 56.

252. *(bottom right)* Keos. Goblet. Hesperia 33. 1964, Pl. 56.

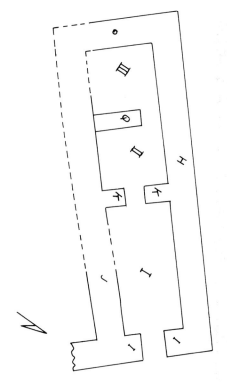

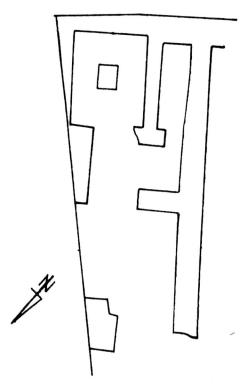

253. Keos. Plan of House B. K. Abramovitz Coleman, A Study of Painted Wall Plaster Fragments from the Bronze Age Site of Ayia Irini in the Island of Keos (1976), 224, Fig. 5.

254. Mycenae. Plan of Tsountas House (level II). I. Mylonas Shear, Mycenaean Domestic Architecture (1968), III, Pl. XXII (fragment).

We began this topic by raising the question of whether the various objects found under the floor of Room 1 came from a room or building that belonged to the early temple complex. There may be another answer to this question. Since the back wall of the temple (Rooms XI and XII) is skew, it might well be asked whether the original temple was limited to the area it occupied at the time, or whether it extended onto the area on which Room 1 was later built. In the latter case, the alteration in the direction of the temple walls would not be surprising. It could have been that when the temple was being reconstructed and enlarged after the great earthquake in period LH IIIA, its position was altered slightly to its present state. If that were the case, the supposition that the cult statues in Keos were made of wood would acquire greater plausibility.

Coming now to another problem, we must ask whether the entire row of rooms running the length of the temple constituted a separate entity, or whether they formed part of the temple complex. Room I also yielded a sherd of a jar with a monophon composed of two incised Linear A signs: L.82 and L.53, which probably indicated great quantities of wine.[9] Almost nothing in the published reports tells us anything more about the significance of the rooms bordering the fortifications.

House B is a large building (Fig. 253 cf. Fig. 254) only part of which (13.20 by 4.70 m) is still in existence. The house was originally smaller than it was later on, since it consisted only of Rooms I and II. Only in the last period of its existence was it enlarged, and Room III was added onto part of Room II. The house was in use from the Middle Bronze Age onwards. But the information published so far contains very little mention of sacred finds. We are told, however, that there were numerous Late Bronze Age conical cups. Many fragments of painted plaster bear parallel bands, while only a few fragments have depictions of human beings. One fragment (F. 49) shows a man apparently holding a stone rhyton. Another (F. 50) carries what is no doubt part of the left profile of a half-sized figure that may have belonged to a processional scene.

The temple on Keos poses several interesting questions. On the one hand the temple, which is elongated in shape, with many rooms inside, is similar in plan to the Bronze Age dwelling houses. On the other hand, it bears some resemblance to the kind of building which later developed into the Greek temple (see p. 195). The Keos temple was not the sole building

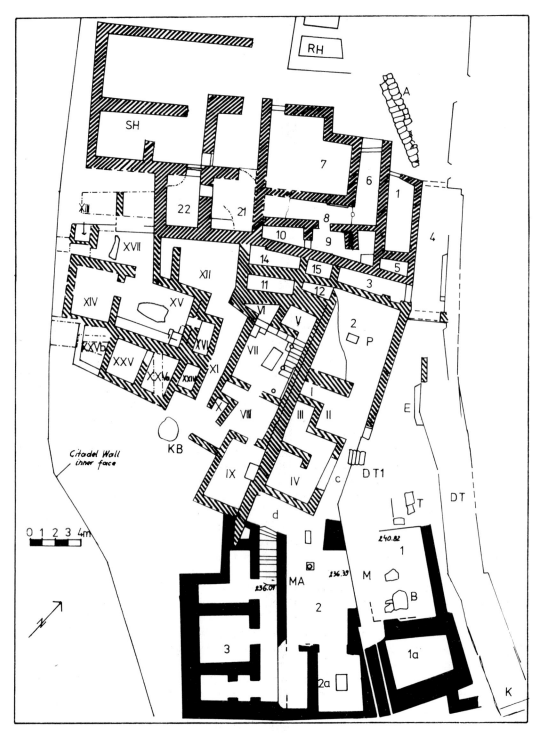

255. Mycenae. Sacred Area. BSA 71, 1976, 78, Fig. 1a.

in the cult area but was its focal point. Another important fact is that it continued to be used, either entirely or partially, from the Middle Bronze Age to the Hellenistic period. As for the interior, benches stood along the walls for the duration of the temple's existence in the Bronze Age. The earliest ones, dating from the Middle Bronze Age, were in Rooms IV and V. They have survived to a height of 0.40 m: originally they were higher, and one was stepped. Room V also contained the remains of a large altar from the LH II level, and traces of burnt sacrifices. Another interesting fact is that fragments of statues were discovered in all the rooms, but mainly above Room XI. But the function of Room XI changed, for as early as LH I it was still a cellar or a storeroom.

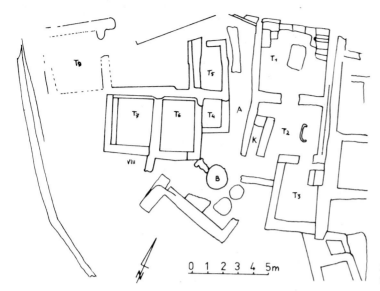

256. Mycenae. Area close to the temple. PAE 1973, 100, Fig. 1.

According to the Caskeys, the head on an eighth century B.C. ring would seem to represent the anodos of the god Dionysios. A scene depicted on a plate from Phaistos (Fig. 148) has been given a similar interpretation. During the Bronze Age, Dionysios was worshipped in the form of a xoanon in the Keos temple. The clay statues representing standing or dancing attendants are not menaeds, since some of them wear garlands round their neck, worn as amulets against the noxious vapours of wine. Such garlands are called hypothymis by Athenaios (678 d). These statues, of which there were about 55, began to be made about the LH I period, new ones gradually being added later. Damaged statues were repaired and repainted, instead of being thrown out. Dionysios was worshipped in Keos, and according to the discoverers he was not only a chthonic divinity, but also a patron of metallurgical production. Traces of this were discovered in the temple and in the town.

An interesting example of a temenos with cult buildings inside an acropolis has been found at Mycenae. Excavations carried out under the direction of Ch. Tsountas in 1886, A. Wace in 1950, W. Taylour in 1968 and 1969, and by G. Mylonas in 1966-74 uncovered nearly the whole space in the south-west part of the acropolis between the House of Tsountas and the South House (Fig. 255).[10] This space is next to the defence walls on one side while higher up, in the direction of the palace, it is bounded by a steep hill-slope. The temenos is on three levels. On the lowest level there is a temple and another sacred building (the House of the Frescoes). East of it, and more than 2 m higher, is level II, which is contiguous with the House of Tsountas (MA). Still higher is level III, which consists of the Processional Way (DT), a small courtyard (DT1), and the sanctuary in the House of Tsountas (M). There is still another sacred building (Figs 255, 256) beyond that area, but on level I which is lower and further south-west. The difference in height between levels I and III is more than 5 m.

Several roads led to the temenos. One led from the Shaft Graves Area along the House of the Ramp, while another led along the defence walls. It seems that a road led also along the hillside from the palace. Then there was a 'monumental stairway', and another road, of which about 10 m has survived, leading to a structure which Mylonas called a vestibule with a big stone threshold (K). The inside walls of the vestibule were covered in painted plaster, with decoration which has survived on the lower part of the wall. On one side we can still see part of a scene showing a procession of chariots and a figure, while on the other side there are coloured wavy bands. The size of the vestibule has not been ascertained. It may have been used as an imposing portico leading into the Sacred Area. The road, 1.90 m wide, continues west for a distance of about 30 m. It is flanked by heavy walls, and its floor is covered with lime plaster. In Mylonas's view this was a processional corridor leading down to a lower level where there were altars and sacred buildings. Yet it is quite possible that this 'corridor' was a specially made, unroofed road with high walls on either side. The road then bends, and opens out into a wider space. On the left there is a bench (E), and somewhat further on a rectangular structure 2.50 by 1.10 m, standing 0.30 m high (T). It is covered with stucco, three layers of which

257. Mycenae. Sacred Area. A view of the upper terrace.

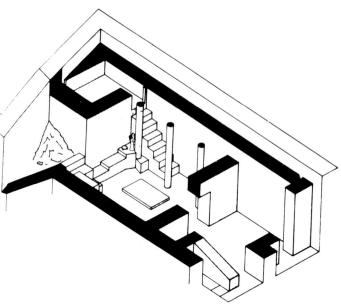

258. Mycenae. Isodomic reconstruction of the temple. AAA 3, 1970, 75 Fig. 2.

survive. In addition, there are three stone blocks here, with square dowel holes, probably for holding some kind of light wooden construction. This was an altar with a prothysis. The courtyard with altar T lies next to part of the House of Tsountas (M).

The House of Tsountas, or rather, that part of it which lies on Level III (M), was a sanctuary. It is probably here that Tsountas discovered the famous plaque with a depiction of the War Goddess. Excavations by Wace (verified later by Mylonas) led to the discovery of a horse-shoe altar (B) measuring 1.29 by 1.33 m, standing 0.20 m above the floor (Fig. 255 M,B1). It had a projection with a depression for libations. The purpose of the cylindrical projection in front of it is unknown. The sides and top of the altar were coated with many layers of plaster. About 0.82 m further on, there was a huge boulder 1.15 by 0.65 m, which Mylonas took to be a slaughtering stone (Fig. 255). Along the side of Room M.1 was a shelf, and in the north-east corner the remains of a pavement; Room M.1, then, was a shrine. It measured 6.45 × 4.50 m,

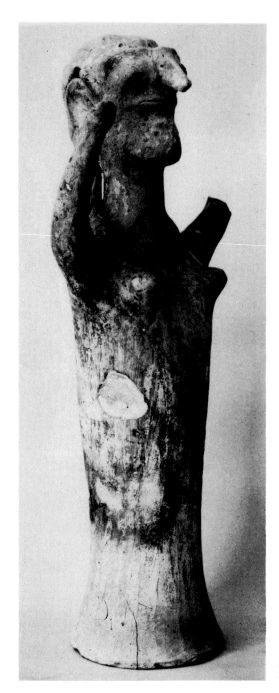

259. Mycenae. Cult statue from the temple. Courtesy of Lord W. Taylour.

and was open towards the north-west. It was a later addition to MA, which was annexed to the new building. Mylonas thinks it was used as an adyton. It is still uncertain whether Room M.1 was an unroofed space, like a sacred court, surrounded on three sides by a wall (hence like a Cretan construction — Fig. 78), or whether it had a roof.

The transition from Level III to Level II (P) was by means of a staircase. Level II falls into three parts: the northern and the southern part of complex P, and the House of Tsountas (MA). The northern part of area P is higher (2), the southern part being about 0.90 m lower (I-IV). Part 2 consists of a large room (4.14 × 5.53 m), with a floor made of a light-coloured mortar. Remains of this mortar are also to be found on the north wall. The south wall of this room is very thick (about 1.55 m thick, and 3.34 m long). In the narrow passage (1.10 m wide) between part 1 and part 2 there may have been wooden steps. Rooms I-IV form two sections: Room II (2.54 × 3.58 m) with its annexe Room I (1.18 × 1.36 m), and Rooms III-IV, which have no

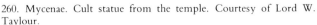

260. Mycenae. Cult statue from the temple. Courtesy of Lord W. Taylour.

261. Mycenae. Cult statue from the temple. Courtesy of Lord W. Taylour.

distinct traces of doors. This later section is only partly built of stone walls. The north and east walls of Room III are made of brick. This irregularly shaped room is divided into two parts. Rooms 2 and I-III are recently restored as a meganon. No significant objects were found there, but the basements were full of material. M. Cameron identified fragments of a processional frescoe, found close to the meganon. Running along Rooms III-IV is a corridor which between Room IV and the House of Tsountas (MA 2) widens into a small courtyard. We can assume that originally there were stairs here, which were removed when Room IX was added on to the Vestibule (VIII) of the Temple (Figs. 255, 256). It seems likely, then, that in the earliest period all three levels of the temenos were directly connected with each other. Not until a later phase was the temenos divided into two sections, one consisting of Levels I and II along with the neighbouring House of Tsountas, and the other consisting of Level III. Of course the palace still had access to Level III by means of Road DT, by a narrow road leading along the eastern edge of the House of Tsountas (Fig. 257), and by means of the steps situated behind the House of Tsountas. The temple (VII) stands in a densely built-up area. The entrance is on the south. The building measures 10.60 × 4.25 m, and is not quite regular in outline. One enters a vestibule (VIII) and passes through into a small chamber (5.10 × 4.20 m) with three columns at one side, and with steps leading up to a small cell (Fig. 258). In the middle of the room there is a rectangular dais with rounded corners, covered with a veneer of white clay. This cannot have been used as a hearth, for there are no signs of fire. It is thought that there were cloth hangings on the walls. There was a wooden shelf on at least one of the walls. The most interesting feature of the furnishings consisted of platforms constructed along the north side of the room. Their height varied, but was always considerable. On one of them (Fig. 258) stood an idol (Fig. 259) in front of which was a small offering table made of mud plaster. According to Taylour the goddess found here is 'the most formidable and forbidding of all the idols'. Steps lead up to

262. Mycenae. Fresco from Room XV. Antiquity 43, 1969, 95 Fig. 2.

a little cell about 2 × 2 m, where numerous clay objects were found. The most important of these were clay idols up to 50-90 cm high (260-261). The gestures and the arrangement of the hands of those idols varied. One figure is holding a double axe or hammer. Some of figures may have been bald; on others the hair has been denoted, sometimes even in the form of spirals (Fig. 261). At least eight large figures, and as many smaller ones, have been found here. One of them (height 0.28 m) is painted, with a rosette on the face, and wears a robe decorated with a pattern similar to an LH IIIA/IIIB motif. The large figures are in monochrome and were probably dressed in long robes. They have all been dated to the period IIIA/LH IIIB and with one possible exception, they are all female figures. Among the pottery, which was mostly found along the north wall, was a small two-handled bowl containing many objects: a small ivory figurine, a scarab of Queen Tiye, a cowrie shell, beads of amber, rock crystal, lapis lazuli, carnelian and other stones, and many made of glass paste. These are thought to have been used for adorning the idols. The pottery consisted of common objects: kylikes, small bowls and cups, as well as a lamp, two braziers, and three offering tables of unbaked clay with a stucco overlay. There were one or two unusual objects: figurines representing curled-up snakes, two of them measuring 0.22 and 0.28 m respectively in diameter. Nearby there was a small triangular alcove, where several other figurines were found. This group of idols lay on a rough ledge of stones, near the uncut rock. Two male idols were among them. The next two idols are unusual. One has upraised arms and a painted face while the other, which had a total height of 0.80-0.90 m, had a terrifying expression (Fig. 261).[11] The faces of these idols really do look like masks. It may be remarked here that the Mycenaean idols, masks could have been copies of the masks placed on wooden idols. The priestesses also wore such masks during the religious ceremonies.[12] In addition to these, two other, smaller idols were found as well, and fragments of model snakes. The alcove was separated from the main room of the temple by a stone still.

Taylour stresses that there must have been special religious reasons for separating this rock chamber from the main room of the temple. Room IX seems to be a later addition to the temple.

Close by there is another sanctuary. Originally, the entrance to it was through a narrow passage, but later on the sole entrance was from the north-west. This sanctuary is an irregularly-shaped building rather like the temple at Mallia (Fig. 216). It measures approximately 11 × 4 m, and was divided into three rooms (if Rooms XXV and XXIV do not belong to this complex). One entered the anteroom from the west side. Here there is a conglomerate threshhold, the only one in the whole area, which, according to Taylour, emphasises the importance of this building. The large room (Room XV) measures 5.30×3.50 m. The centre of the room is taken up by a large oval hearth, on the western and northern edges of which are two large stones that tell us a post or small column stood at each of these spots; a third column is indicated as well. In Taylour's view these columns supported the roof. Close to the entrance stood a larnax or bath-tub. Nothing was found in it, but nearby were a jug, a kylix, a miniature jug, a hydria fragment and an alabastron. A stone bench 1 m high and 0.70 m wide stood along the south wall. There were no objects on it. A fresco was discovered in the south-east corner of the room.

A thin layer of white plaster, about 2 m long, on which there is a fresco (Fig. 262), existed on the east wall. At right angles to the wall there was a platform of rubble and clay about 0.65 m high. In the corner between the wall and the platform was a low step about 0.10 m in height. Both the step and the platform were coated with clay. Part of the platform constitutes a ledge several centimetres high, on which were three discs which are possibly rather like small hearths: ash was found here. The purpose of these hearths is not certain. Nearby there was place for a post. North of the platform coarse and fine clay vessels were found, some of which had fallen from a shelf. These have been dated to late LH IIIB. The remains of a large leaden vessel, and an Egyptian faience plaque with a cartouche of Amenophis III, were unearthed as well. South of the platform, the most important objects were a serpentine bird's nest vase dated MM I-LM I, a unique ivory lion figurine and the ivory pommel of a sword. The fresco on the east wall was divided into three parts. On the middle one there is a goddess facing right. She is standing just above the platform mentioned above. In front of her on the fresco is a pole, narrowing towards the bottom, on which possibly an emblem of some sort is depicted. On the right, a smaller figure depicts a man in female dress. Between these two figures, a small male figure is stretching out his hands towards the goddess. Presumably the most important figure was that of the goddess in front of whom stood a lower-rank divinity dressed in female garb. At the side of the scene were posts adorned with garlands. Next to it this part of the fresco is a panel with nothing surviving on it, while below it is another panel depicting a Royal Priestess with a characteristic headdress[13] and a garment made of grey leather (the animal's legs are depicted below). Taylour believes that the royal priestess is offering fruits to the earth goddess. Black and red discs were painted on the platform, while above them there were horns of consecration. This would seem to be an abbreviated representation of a sanctuary[14] in front of which a religious ceremony, involving cult idols, is taking place. On the platform there is a hole for the shaft of an emblem — no doubt a double axe. It is certain that the platform was added a little later, but the time interval is small — only a matter of a few days, in Taylour's opinion. At a later period the platform, on which horns of consecration had originally been painted, was covered with white paint that obliterated these sacred symbols. This suggests that the platform, like the whole room, ceased to be used for religious purposes. To the left of the upper room there was a storeroom, and to the right (Fig. 255) was a shrine known as the Room of the Ivories (Room XVI), which was found to contain fragments of partly carved ivories, and also an unworked cube of ivory (these objects may have belonged to a sacred deposit). Clay vessels were found as well. The shrine proper was situated in the southern part of the room. Here a figurine with upraised hands, dating from LH IIIB2, was discovered *in situ*, and nearby were 44 beads or buttons, and numerous vessels.

The space nearby, between the Temple and the Shrine (Fig. 255 No. XII) was probably a workshop. A hexagonal matrix for making ornaments was found here, as well as other objects. The supposed workshop's proximity to the holy places was no accident; this implies that the sanctuary supervised the production of artefacts here.

There was another important communications system leading from the Grave Circle along the defence wall. This was a very narrow road, about 1 m wide (or slightly more in places), which on the one side was flanked by the defence wall, and on the other by the high walls of the

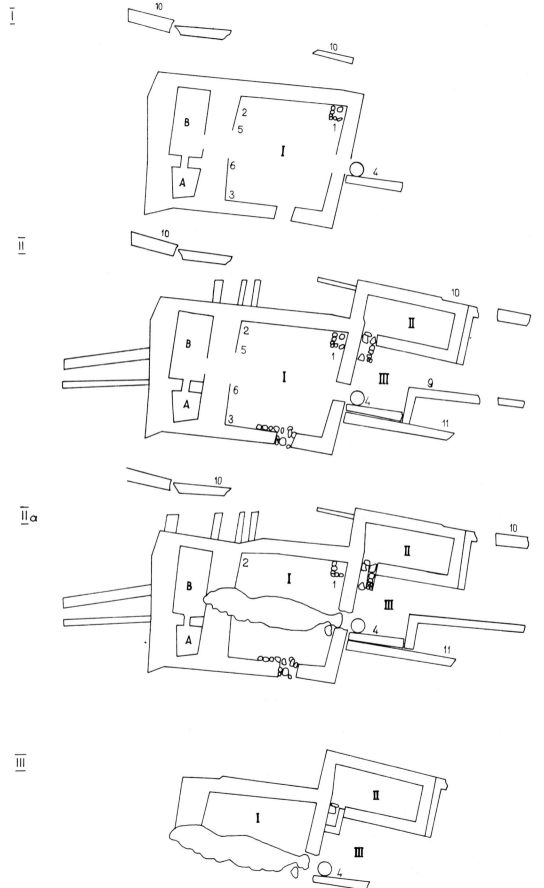

263. Philakopi. a-d. Main phases of the Temple. Adapted from: Antiquity 52, 1978, 8 Fig. 1.

264. Philakopi. Figurine of Reshaf. Antiquity
52, 1978, Pl. IV.

265. Philakopi. Figurine of Reshaf.
Antiquity 52, 1978, Pl. IV.

South House and then the walls of the Shrine with the Fresco. In some places this imposing road, which was like a deep corridor, expanded into little open spaces. This was the case, for instance, before the entrance to the Shrine with the Fresco, and just beyond the south-east part of the Shrine. Information about the area south of Taylour's excavations is not altogether clear, but we do know that it contained structures dug up in 1975.[15] A little further on, past the House of Tsountas, there is another building, South-East House,[16] where two interesting frescoes were discovered. This building, according to Mylonas, was possibly used as the priest's house, or 'for minor cult purposes'.

Interesting questions have arisen as a result of the excavations at Philakopi in Melos (Fig. 263).[17] During the period LM IIIA, a temple was erected near the defence wall (as at Mycenae), in the southern part of the town. A street ran along at a higher level than the temple, but the land to the south and east was not yet completely built up. There were probably fortifications east of the temple. The entrance to the temple was through a small paved square, which very likely originally occupied a bigger area than it does now (Fig. 263I). Thus to begin with this space was about 8 m wide (N-S), and later about LH IIIB1, approximately 4 m, while in the

266. Philakopi. Lady of Philakopi. Courtesy of C. Renfrew.

267. Philakopi. Clay bull-shaped rhyton.
Antiquity 52, 1978, Pl. VII.

east to west direction it measured 10 m or more. The original temple, whose dimensions were approximately 11.00 m by 6.5-7 m (Fig. 263I), was perhaps even partly isolated from its surroundings. The entrance was on the east side, and led into a room 6.60 by 6.00 m. A few objects (including a seal) have been found from phase 1 of the period LH IIIB, but there were already three altars in the corners of the room (with the exception of the south-east corner) and in the door leading to Room B there were two apertures 0.70 m high. Two small chambers A and B were built on.

In phase 1 b/c of the later period LH IIIA, the square took on a different shape and function (Fig. 263 II No. III). The space in front of the buildings was diminished by the erection of wall No. 9 in the south section of the square, and by the erection of Room II (approx. 4.90 by 2.10 m). At the entrance to Room 1, along Wall 9, a low bench was placed, and, beside it, a stone baetyl 47 cm high, which stood so near the door that it partially blocked the entrance (No. 4). Thus the Temple consisted of three units: two roofed rooms (I,II) and the courtyard (III).

The temple was destroyed in LH IIIC. Two figurines of the Reshef type (Figs. 264, 265) and ten seals come from this phase. The north-west part of Room I contained an altar or bench (2), from which some male figurines and an unusual figurine of the Psi type probably fell. Another male figurine was discovered on an altar (bench 3), as well as a female figurine and a stone column 44 cm high, which may have been used as a lamp. The small room (probably Room A) yielded a figurine of the Lady of Philakopi (Fig. 266), 45 cm high, with her head slightly tilted upwards. A figurine made of badly fired clay and the head of another figurine were discovered as well. A group of objects, consisting of four figurines of bulls or cows, and a grotesque head, were discovered in a niche or a hollow of the wall, dating from an earlier period. A rhyton shaped like a bull (Fig. 267), a bronze male figurine (Fig. 268), and another figurine whose eyes were rendered in gold, were unearthed in the vicinity of the temple.[18]

The temenos buildings changed in appearance again in phase 3 of the later period, LH IIIC (Fig. 263 IIa). A blocking wall was built in the south part of Room I. Then Rooms A and B were filled in with great stones, and ceased to be used. These changes reduced the size of the temple almost to that of Room II (Fig. 156 III). How Room I was entered is not clear, for the blocking wall almost completely hides the entrance to it. Nor do we know whether the baetyl and the bench at the entrance continued to be used. Two male figurines were discovered near the altar of Room I. Room II was used in a similar way. Later on, too, building work went on, but this was of no particular significance to the history of the temple. Few objects have come down to us from phase 3c, towards the end of period LH IIIC; most of the surviving objects have come from the preciding phase. A terracotta bull, the gold head of a wooden idol (the head, made of gold sheet (Fig. 269), was no doubt mounted on a wooden shaft), an ostrich egg, and a clay human figurine came from phase 3c.

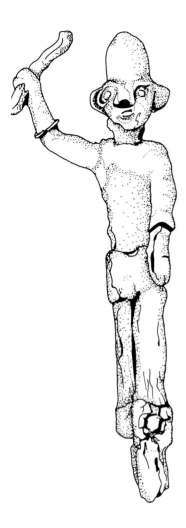

268. *(right)* Philakopi. Bronze male figurines. Antiquity 52, 1978, 11 Fig. 2.

269. Philakopi. Head in sheet gold. Antiquity 52, 1978, Pl. VIa.

Various problems arise as a result of the discovery of the temple at Philakopi, which may have been part of a holy area. The similarity of the position of the sacred area at Philakopi, Mycenae and Tiryns (see below), in that they were all adjacent to the defence walls, is striking. The conjunction of the sacred buildings with an open, unroofed area is equally important. Two buildings at Philakopi and four at Mycenae were connected with an open-air space. Those at Philakopi were linked with a place where sacrifices (?) were made, and those at Mycenae were linked with open-air terraces and an open courtyard. The fact that the sacred buildings at Tiryns are situated near an open square is not fortuitous (see p. 487). There are other questions as well. During period IIIB there were at least two statues of goddesses, one complete (Fig. 266), and the other fragmentary. They were probably cult idols. The statue of the Lady of Philakopi,[19] standing 0.45 m high, represents a young goddess with her head turned slightly upwards, as if in expectation. This is a depiction of a virgin goddess (see below). Apart from this statue, coming from the end phase of period IIIC, there is also a xoanon with a gold mask (Fig. 269). The male figurines represent a Reshaf type warrior with a club (Fig. 268). The male figurines have very prominent genitals, and are almost ithyphallic (Fig. 270). It is probable that these two elements, male and female, are indications of fertility cults whose existence and importance are emphasised still further by the figurines of bulls or cows, and bull-shaped rhyta. The question arises: do the Reshaf-type figurines and the bovine figurines represent local elements? It should be recalled how important the role of bull figurines was in the Bogazköy religion. The possibility of Hittite influence on the development of Mycenaean religion in later times cannot be ruled out.

A cult centre came into existence, too, in the lower citadel of Tiryns.[20] After the cataclysm that took place in LH IIIB a new communications system emerged, as well as a new approach to the syrinx. Three phases may be perceived in the history of this cult centre. In the early

270. Philakopi. Clay male figurine. Courtesy of C. Renfrew.

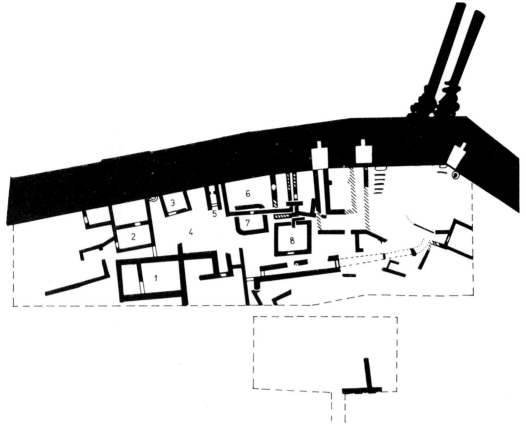

271. Tiryns. Plan of the Sacred Area. AA 1979, 380 Fig. 1 (fragment). (1: VIa, 2:106, 3:112, 4:111, 5:110a, 6:115, 7:119, 8:97).

part of LH IIIC a small cult chamber was built (119), but it fell into ruin before the end of the same phase (Fig. 271), that is, when the first temple was erected (117, on top of 110a). At that period a large open place (H1), about 15 m long, with an almost square temple on it (117), measuring 2.92 × 2.80 m, came into existence right beside the defence wall. A cult bench, coated with a pale lime plaster, stood beside the wall of the fortifications. On a stone base there are bricks which walled in a small niche measuring 86 × 34 cm. There were three layers of stucco on the niche and the floor. The top one was white, and in 117 it was ascertained that the first, lowest, layer still bore traces of red paint. It seems likely that the entire interior was painted red. Later on the niche was filled with small stones and brick rubble, and at a later period it was used as the foundation for the bench in the temple (110). In the corner of the room, in front of the cult bench, there is a low platform 5 cm high, made of stucco. Traces of a wooden, square-shaped object, possibly a column, were visible in the middle of the room. At this period the façade of the building was a tripartite one. The temple contained miniature vessels, a rhyton in the shape of an animal, the upraised arms of a figurine which when whole must have been 0.35-0.40 m high and Psi idols of normal size.

An altar measuring 2.08 × 1.00 m, standing on a stone foundation discovered north of 117 also comes from the early phase when the first temple was built. Apart from ash, a fragment of a large idol with hands upraised, and part of an animal-shaped rhyton, were discovered here. East and south of 117 about 22 idols of normal size were found.

Building VIa stood in the southern part of the square. No objects were found in the main room, but in the vestibule (116) four animal figurines, one miniature tripod and one male idol were discovered near the door. This is no doubt an example of a cult place existing at the entrance to the house. Other examples have been found in Crete (see p. 143). But here a hearth (possibly a summer kitchen) was situated outside Room VI.

At that time, work was begun on the erection of a large building (115), 14 m long, in the north section of the square. During its construction an offering, placed in four miniature

272. Tiryns. Figurine of a young goddess. Courtesy of K. Kilian.

273. Tiryns. Figurine of a young goddess. Courtesy of K. Kilian.

vessels, was deposited in the corner of one of the rooms. A group of human and animal figurines dating from the same time was also found in area LXI 41/22-4.

A new temple (110a) was erected during an advanced stage of LH IIIC. It was bigger than the previous one, since it measured 5.10 × 2.20 m, and its inner walls were covered with a fine lime plaster. A large figurine representing a goddess with upraised hands, of the Lady of Asine type, was found in front of the cult bench.

Somewhat later — in the middle phase of LH IIIC — building 112 ceased to be used, so the

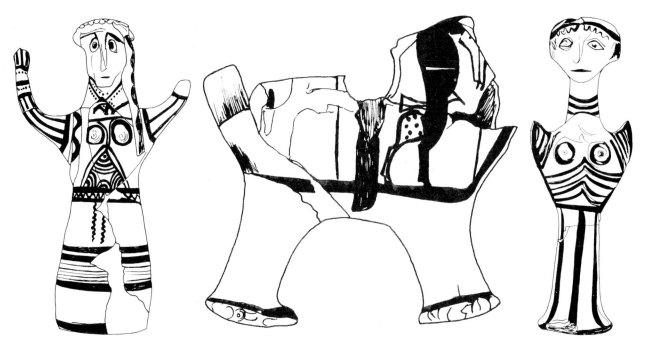

274. Tiryns. Figurine of an old goddess. AA 1978, 461 Fig. 17.

275. Tiryns. Animal-shaped rhyton. AA 1978, 465 Fig. 22.

276. Tiryns. Figurine of a young goddess. AA 1978, 465 Fig. 23.

courtyard may have become larger. Temple I 110 measures only 3.00×1.28 m. Its entrance is on the east side. The floor was carefully paved with lime, and the cult bench was covered with lime plaster. It is thought that various objects discovered here stood originally on the bench: two cult idols (Figs. 272-3, compare how different the goddesses look Fig. 274),[21] fragments of five other idols, a bowl and a skyphos. Four of the idols were large, and the arms were upraised. One idol that also had its arms upraised was executed in a primitive way. Pieces of animal figurines, a steatite pearl and a bone needle, are also recorded. A bull-shaped rhyton (Fig. 275) was decorated with figures of demons. All these objects have been dated to an early phase of IIIC.

Building R 115, which (6×10 m) is bigger than the temple, is interesting. Traces of four columns in a row were found in it. In the south-east corner, the excavators found a stone slab lying at floor level, and beyond it another stone slab standing vertically. A faience pearl, a glass pearl, and a terracotta idol 0.12 m high of the Psi type were discovered here. Nearby were two small terracotta horses and one terracotta bird preparing for flight. It is not certain whether this room was used for religious rituals, although it is probable that the objects mentioned above belonged to an altar. A figurine of a young goddess was also found (Fig. 276). During the latest excavations, another place of worship has been identified in the fortifications, near the entrance to the well.

Now we come to Eleusis. Before the time of excavations (that is before 1883) it was submitted by many scholars (e.g. by Baumlein[22] in 1832) that the cult of Demeter at Eleusis was of pre-Greek, i.e. of 'Pelasgian', origin. Lenorment wrote in 1864 that the pantheistic conception of the mysteries at Eleusis was of Pelasgian and Asianic origin.[23] Naturally enough speculations on the beginnings of the sacred precinct at Eleusis remained more or less at a dead-end until excavations were started. The man who instigated this was Philios, who excavated the telesterion as well as tombs from the earliest periods.[24] Although Philios's excavations show that the earliest telestrion could not be dated to earlier than the seventh century B.C., the tradition that this cult place was of pre-Greek origin by no means died out; indeed, as we shall see, it was to revive in various forms right up to the present day. Persson, for instance, wrote in 1922: 'At any rate it is certain that even in pre-Hellenic times Eleusis was a place of some significance; it is likewise certain that the oldest telesterion was of pre-Greek origin'.[25] Persson was writing at a time when attempts to reconstruct the telestrion could not yet benefit from the knowledge that under the Greek telesterion there were walls dating from LH times. All Persson had to go on then was analysis of the myths that had been handed down

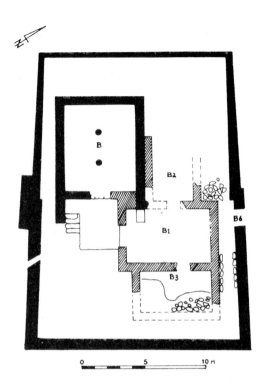

277. Eleusis. Plan of the temple. G. Mylonas, Eleusis and the Eleusinian Mysteries (1961), Fig. 11.

from one generation to another. In particular, he studied the etymology of the name Eleusis, which also seemed to be of pre-Greek origin. He also put forward a new conception concerning the genesis of the cult at Eleusis. This cult, in his opinion, had come from Crete. Persson mounted many other arguments to support his thesis about associations with Crete. For instance, he compared the shape of the telesterion in Archaic and later times with the shape of the theatral areas in Knossos and Phaistos. These facts about Persson's reasoning are less important today. The main point that concerns us here is the fact that he consistently advocated a view which by the first half of the nineteenth century had become a canon: that the cult of Demeter could be traced back to pre-Greek times. Persson embellished this idea from many different angles — for instance, he sought out archaeological analogies which were unknown in the first half of the nineteenth century — but with it all, the essence of the idea remained unchanged.

The work of Noack reveals a different approach.[26] In 1927 he published a study of the architecture here, and put forth succinct arguments to prove that the origins of the sanctuary dedicated to Demeter reached no further back than the eighth century B.C. He argued that during this period an artificial terrace, supported by a wall, was built on the east slope of the hill, at the spot where the telesterion was constructed in later times. Originally, on this terrace an altar stood where Demeter was worshipped with sacrifices and religious ceremonies. At the beginning of the seventh century B.C. the first temple was built on the hill-top — a fact which is mentioned in a Hymn to Demeter composed about 650 B.C. The religious mysteries themselves were held in the open air, near an altar. The first temple, surrounded with a peribolos, was erected in Archaic times. Noack accepted the previously advanced view that the temple of Demeter and the telesterion were two separate buildings. Since no temple was revealed by the excavations, Noack thought that before the Persian invasion it had been knocked down to make room for a new temple (known as temple F).

Later excavations, however, brought forth evidence which made a revision of Noack's views necessary. For today it is now certain that the Demeter temple and the telesterion were one and the same building. Temple F dates from Roman times. The only part of Noack's views that can still be defended is the idea that Demeter's temple was built towards the end of the eighth century B.C. As has been mentioned above, Noack's suppositions were published before the new excavations at Eleusis were begun. In 1930 and 1931 prehistoric graves and walls of houses were discovered near the stoa of Philon. In 1932 the explorations of the area were completed; the earth lying at a depth of from 0.40-7.5 m was removed.[27] The earth that in

Antiquity had been transported from various parts of the hill to make the terraces had been thrown there. During the same expedition, under the telesterion from Pisistrates time building B (Megaron B) was discovered. Its walls were about 0.60 m high and 0.50 m wide (Fig. 277). Only two parallel walls made of rough, unhewn stones were discovered. Judging from the lay-out of the site, say the excavators, the building probably measured about 9.50 × 5.70 m. It consisted of one room with a portico. In the middle of the room was a column base, which was all that was left of the column that at one time supported the roof. The floor was made of limestone mixed with small stones. There was a platform before the entrance (2.90 × 2.00 m). On both sides space was left for staircases leading to the portico. The building was surrounded by a peribolos wall 0.85 m wide, only part of which is preserved. The purpose of this wall was either to fence off the place, or to protect the house from rainwater running down the hill. Fragments of pottery found in the building and around it are dated to LH II or MH and in particular LH II to the end of III C. A three-roomed building adjoins the original Megaron B. The dimensions of the middle room were 7.00 × 4.40 m. Room B.2 was already explored towards the end of the nineteenth century, when no special attention was given to the stratigraphy of the place. It was again was the subject of excavations in 1930-1, but nothing was found. In Room D.3, however, many potsherds dating from LH IIIC were discovered. One wall — b1 — had been built up against the portico of Megaron B. It is possible that the new building was merely an addition to the older one (Megaron B). As far as can be reckoned from the pottery from LH IIIC — which was found both in the megaron of earlier times and in the later one — it is possible that the entire building was used in the final phase of the Bronze Age.

Two handles of a vessel from the Geometric period were found in the south-west corner of Room B.1, about 0.5 m above the floor. Mylonas holds that they prove the telesterion was used in the Geometric period. Under the floor of rooms B-B.3 small fragments of walls were found, as well as pottery from MH and graves from MH II.

As early as 1932, Mylonas and Kouroniotis[28] supposed that Megaron B was the first temple (telesterion). This view was accepted by many other authors, including Karo, who in 1935 wrote that Megaron B was the first example of a Mycenaean temple and temenos on the Greek mainland.[29]

Later on, however, after the most important remains of the sanctuary had been excavated, Nilsson[30] advanced another theory. Despite relics of early settlement, there are no traces of cult places. Nevertheless, it can be assumed that an agrarian cult was indeed practised in Mycenaean houses, although not universally. It was not until the eighth century B.C. that it became transformed into a cult of wider significance, and it was only then that mysteries began to be practised. It was only then, too, that the first cult building was erected.

Nilsson's theory is based on the assumption that the changeover from a private, domestic cult to public cult started in a later period. When the cult had developed to this stage, a special temple became necessary. According to Nilsson, Megaron B was the dwelling place of a rich man, or perhaps even a palace.[31] Yet this opinion bears the seeds of another idea, namely, that the development of the Greek temple can be traced back to its beginnings in the palace of the Mycenaean ruler. This was the view that was put forth at the beginning of the twentieth century and made use of ideas propounded much earlier.

We therefore find two mainstreams of thought concerning the genesis of the telesterion. These had their source in two different conceptions as to the development of religion from the Mycenaean to the Greek period. According to one theory, the cult of Demeter persisted from pre-Greek times; after the archaeological discoveries, a corollary of this view was that even the cult building had survived from those times. According to the other theory, a house or a palace that in Mycenaean times had belonged to the King (who at the same time was High Priest), was in Greek times transformed into a temple, the result being that what had previously been a domestic cult now became a public cult. This second concept has its adherents even in more recent times. Mylonas in 1961 supplemented this view with new arguments.[32] He contends that Megaron B was the first temple built at Eleusis, and that in the Bronze Age important features of this cult took shape, which were passed on to the Greek civilisation of later times. Thus although the Hymn to Demeter, taken by itself, suggests that the temple was built in the eighth century B.C., Mylonas argues that the sanctuary dates back to an earlier period. For this he produces many arguments.

The first group of arguments he uses are based on the legends. These arguments are as

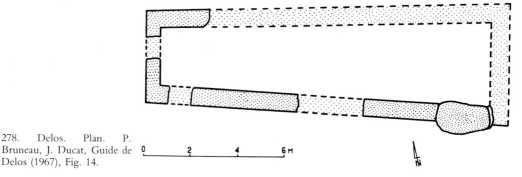

278. Delos. Plan. P. Bruneau, J. Ducat, Guide de Delos (1967), Fig. 14.

0   2   4   6 M

follows: 1. It can be deduced from the Parian Chronicle that the beginning of the mysteries can be traced back to the fifteenth century B.C. 2. The Hymn to Demeter, which represents the official local tradition, mentions that her cult began in the time of Eumolpsos, who was contemporary to Erechteios. The latter, according to Mylonas, is a historical figure from the second half of the fifteenth century B.C. 3. From the traditions handed down concerning the wars between Athens and Eleusis, it can be concluded that the cult of Demeter began in the fifteenth century B.C. 4. What is said by Herodotus about the spread of the cult of Demeter Eleusinia to the south-east part of Asia Minor also attests to the early origin of the cult. The cult of Demeter Eleusinia was brought to Asia Minor by the Ionians when they were colonising that part of the world. It must, therefore, have been much earlier than the eighth century B.C., when Phillistos — one of the companions of Neleus, the founder of Miletus — erected a temple to Demeter Eleusinia on the summit of Mount Mykale; the Ionians, on the other hand, colonised Miletus in the eleventh century B.C. 5. From another source (Aristotle) we learn that the Eleusinia mysteries were first celebrated and then spread in popularity in the time of Pandion, who according to Mylonas lived at the turn of the fourteenth century B.C. 6. The widespread dissemination of the cult of Demeter Eleusinia in the Peloponnese also testifies to an early date; for instance, the cult of Pheneos was firmly consolidated by Naos, the grandson of Eumolpsos, which justifies us in placing these events in the fifteenth century B.C.[33]

Mylonas's next group of arguments is based on the material remains found at Eleusis. He says that for the celebration of the cult a temple was needed which could not be erected on top of the hill (because there were already other buildings there) but only on one of its slopes. All the important architectural features suggest that Megaron B was a temple. Mylonas goes on to say that it could not have been a palace, since remnants of such a building were found on the top of the hill. Even from its size it could not have been a royal residence, for to begin with, it had only one room. The idea that Megaron B may have been a dwelling-house belonging to ordinary people must also be ruled out, for it has a peribolos, an artificially built platform, and remains of wall decoration (fragment of painted stucco). Mylonas puts forth two arguments that lead him to think Megaron B was a temple. First, the dimensions of the building were small, and it was situated outside the walls of the town. Secondly, Megaron B stands on the same place as a telesterion of later days, that is, in a holy place. The site where Megaron B was built was an inconvenient one, whereas only a little further north there was a spot where a building could have been erected without any difficulty. The question arises then as to why it was built here in particular. The answer is clear: because the place was a holy one. The Hymn to Demeter contains a passage in which it is said that the Temple of Demeter was situated above the Kallichoron well. Mylonas argued this was not the well mentioned by Pausanias, but that the name Kallichoron refers to a well discovered in the north-east corner of the wall that supports the construction of the stoa of Philios. The dating of this well is not certain, but the entire area here comes from the eighth century B.C.; after the Persian invasion the wall was filled in, while the name Kallichoron was transferred to the well situated outside the sanctuary. Hence the passage in the Hymn which says that the temple to Demeter was situated above the well clearly refers to Megaron B. Mylonas goes on to argue as follows: 1. although no traces of a cult were found in Megaron B, it should be remembered that Megaron B was excavated at a period when attention was not yet paid to details. 2. there are no monumental works in any of the Mycenaean sanctuaries. 3. the holy objects were taken away by the priests when the Megaron had to be abandoned. 4. the fragment of a temple dating from the end of the seventh century B.C. has been identified with the telesterion, yet no traces of a cult were found here either. To sum up, Mylonas believes that the temple was already constructed in the LH II period.

Another building worth mentioning is one at Delos.[34] Under the Arthemision dating from the Archaic period, excavations revealed the remains of a building probably dating from LH III. Its ground plan measurements were about 4.00 × 15.30 m (inside width 2.27 m). Although only a small part of the walls still exist, the reconstruction of the plan published by Brunneau and Ducat seems to be accurate (Fig. 278). What is less certain is whether the building was completely isolated, since the ruins of a room or building dating from the same periof were found on the west side of Arthemision C. It has been conjectured that the treasury of ivory and other objects[35] found there forms part of a building dating from up the Mycenaean period.

Excavations at Pylos[36] have revealed an altar in the courtyard beside the palace, and, north-west of this, a small shrine with antae, measuring 3.10 × 3.40 m (Fig. 279). The floor of this shrine as higher than the level of the courtyard, and steps led up to the shrine. No objects were found that would indicate this place was used for a holy purpose. The supposition that it is a sanctuary is based only on the position of the altar in the courtyard (it lies precisely on the axis of the entrance to the sanctuary), and on the exceptionally careful construction of the building.

We now come to some general conclusions on Minoan and Mycenaean temples. One of the most important problems is that of the genesis of the temples. Although little material evidence has survived, we can assume that the temple is a product of an earlier age, and had already made its appearance in the Neolithic in the form of a building of the dwelling-house type. Weinberg's supposition that the temple at Nea Nikomedeia may at the same time have been a chief's dwelling-house deserves serious consideration. The acceptance of such a hypothesis would make our approach to the problem of the appearance of temples much easier, for it could then be assumed that the house of the chief, who no doubt also acted as priest, incorporated a cult place, which in the course of time developed into a separate building.

A constant feature of the Aegean temple was that it imitated the architecture of the Aegean dwelling house. But occasionally the temples differed slightly from the houses (Fig. 254)[37] and as time went on temples with distinctive ground plans began to be built, as can be seen in Keos and at Eleusis (Figs. 245, 277). The temples were generally small; their size depended on the religious needs of the inhabitants of the given town.

It would appear that two basic trends in temple architecture emerged fairly early. In one of them the temple was completely, or almost completely, cut off from its surroundings (Fig. 244). In the other, it was only partly isolated from the other buildings in the town. But both

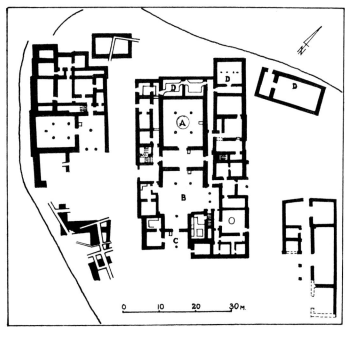

279. Pylos. Plan. C. Blegen, M. Rawson, The Palace of Nestor at Pylos (1966), I, Fig. 417.

0   10   20   30 M.

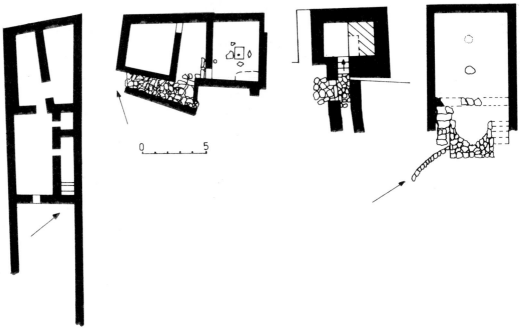

280. Types of Minoan and Mycenaean temples. a. Keos b. Mallia c. Gournia d. Eleusis.

trends had one characteristic in common: in the towns the temples always had an open space adjacent to them, where the religious rites took place. This was often the town square, as at Gournia (Fig. 167), or a meadow next to the temple, as at Myrtos, or an open space outside the town, near the defence walls, as in Keos (Fig. 244).

It is our contention that the temples can be understood properly only if they are viewed in conjunction with the open-air, frequently empty space near them. This — the link between the temple and the open area next to it — is one of the most significant problems concerning all the cultures of the Mediterranean. Originally, that is in the Neolithic and in the Early Bronze Age, this space was possibly always a small area round the temple (e.g. at Nea Nikomedeia, Fig. 206), or a meadow next to the temple (e.g. at Myrtos). But later on a much bigger, more complex entity — a well-developed cult centre — came into existence, as at Mycenae (Figs. 256-7), in Keos (Fig. 244), or at Tiryns (Fig. 271), corresponding in some measure to the cult centres on Cyprus, such as that at Kition.[38] It is still too early to expect a complete answer to this question, which has emerged only recently as a result of excavations at Kition, Mycenae, Keos and Tiryns within the last few years. Nevertheless it already seems quite certain that the Aegean sacred areas are the forerunners of the Greek sanctuaries of later times, which took over the lay-out of the old cult areas, and adapted it to the requirements of their own times.

The main holy building (the temple proper) does not seem necessarily to have been the

281. Early Hellenic temples. a. Delos. Building Gamma   b. Dreros. Temple of Apollo   c. Perachora. Temple of Hera Limenia   d. Zagora. Town Temple   e. Asine. Temple of Apollo Pythaios   f. Tiryns. Temple. Drerup, op. cit., Figs. 2, 3, 5, 47, 7 and 14.

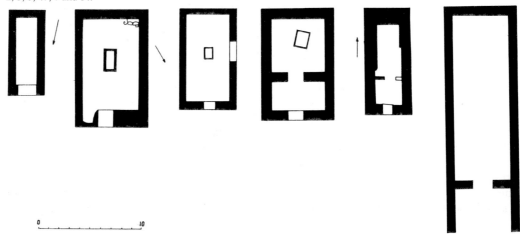

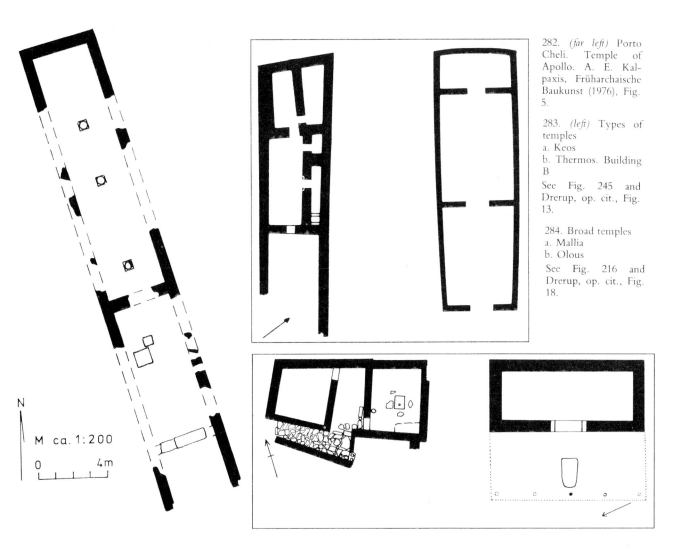

biggest building in the complex. An example of this may be seen at Tiryns. The temple was, however, the place where the cult idols were kept (though there may have been more than one). Other buildings which, like the building with the Fresco room at Mycenae, may also have been used as temples, stood not far from the main temple. The simultaneous existence of several temples in the one sacred area is also evidenced at Kition. But in the Aegean world this is not so clear as it was at Kition. On the other hand in the Aegean there were not only holy buildings, but also altars — sometimes, as at Mycenae, standing on their own out in the open-air space. The position of these structures (that is, the temples and altars) is not such to suggest any conscious planning. The requirements of the cult, not aesthetic considerations, were the deciding factor. Of course we can decipher very little about the organisation of the religious cults at these places, although certain moveable finds — such as frescoes and scenes on rings — suggest that the cult places were looked after by priests or priestesses (see p. 204). Some information on the functions of the priests or priestesses, the running of the temple, and the bringing of sacrifices has become available to us from passages in Linear B script — especially texts referring to Pakijana,[39] a cult centre near Pylos or a separate part of Pylos.

The newest studies of temples are beginning to reveal the exciting possibility of a link between the temples and the production of artefacts, such as metal work (on Keos), or of jewellery and ivory objects (at Mycenae). This problem has been studied most thoroughly at Kition where a fair amount of evidence has survived.[40]

Since more and more material has been amassed about the temples, the time is ripe for an attempt to classify the buildings. It seems likely that in both Minoan and Mycenaean times there were two main temple types (Fig. 280). On the one hand we have a building consisting of a single room, with a portico (Eleusis, Kamilari model, Figs. 277, 139), or, without a portico

285. Mycenae. Bee-hive Tomb.

286. Mycenae. Lion Gate.

(Gournia). In the other type we find elongated buildings (Keos). In between there is an intermediate type (Mallia and the sanctuary at Mycenae). All in all there seems to have been a great variety of architecture, even within each type. Only towards the end of the Bronze Age was there any definite tendency to standardise the buildings.

It is also interesting to note that both these types of Aegean temple have their equivalents in Geometric and Archaic architecture (Fig. 281). As examples of the former one may cite buildings of the Dreros type (Fig. 281b),[41] and a model of Argive Heraion,[42] while the other type is represented by temple buildings at Thermos and Porto Cheli (Figs. 282 and 283b cf, also the examples on Fig. 284a,b).[43] Despite the difficulties of tracing the history of the temple in the Dark Ages it is undoubtedly true that continuation of the temple from the Bronze Age to the Iron Age is documented in Keos. Another recent development in this field is that the previously accepted theory concerning the function of the megaron in the development of the Greek temple has now been undermined.[44] It is now clear that the origin of the Greek temple is more complicated than was previously believed.[45] The sources of the Greek temple are to be sought not only in the dwelling houses of the Geometric period, but, above all, in the two types of Bronze Age temples.

Hence it is highly likely that temples appeared fairly early in Greece, parallel with the development of the settlements. The Bronze Age temple was not especially different from the other buildings in appearance. It always looked like a dwelling-house, although it no doubt acquired a more imposing façade that symbolised the presence of a deity. There is some evidence, though indirect, of such symbolism in the iconographic material that has come down to use form these times (see p. 196). The temple façades were like those of the palaces and the tombs (Figs. 285-6), which no doubt in their turn had some resemblance to the façades of dwelling-houses. Yet the link between the façades seen in the iconography, and the buildings which have survived is still insufficiently documented. Although extant specimens of temples are scarce, it can nevertheless be presumed that there was a temple in every town and village, although these edifices differed greatly in size and appearance.

It may seem strange that the Minoans and Mycenaeans did not erect monumental buildings. The explanation may be as follows. In the Minoan and Mycenaean world, the tradition of rural life was very strong; it in fact permeated the entire structure of beliefs and cults. We see this reflected in the existence of manifold sanctuaries of the natural type. Since nature was the dominating factor in the lives of the people of the Bronze Age, the towns and villages whose life was based on handicrafts, trade and sometimes seafaring, were really of less significance than the countryside. So while the old, rural ways of living changed over to urban fairly rapidly, the beliefs and cults retained their rural character. Hence it was only natural that, as on Mount Jouktas, the old, rural cult centres should become drawn into the life of the town and the palace. To begin with, then, the urban cult centres were of less significance. But their importance grew in measure with the development of urban life in the Middle Bronze Age, with the increase of royal power and influence, and with the growth of social bonds organised by the state. It even seems likely that the smaller urban settlements, which, like Gournia, were little more than villages, were tied by tradition to the natural cults. In LM I, when the village was developing, these cults may have played an important role, if only because the inhabitants were so involved in agricultural pursuits. Hence in small settlements like Gournia, imposing architecture was not necessary for the cult; in each village no more than a small temple was needed. It is the view of the author that only by learning much more about this complicated system of Minoan and Mycenaean life will it be possible to understand the places of worship in the Bronze Age.

At the same time we do not wish to give the impression that cults during the Bronze Age developed in isolation from the influence of neighbouring areas. Although temple buildings tended to be in the local style (but comparable to the Middle East architecture), the actual cults themselves may have succumbed to external influences (as may be seen, for instance, in the fact that the cult idols at Tiryns clearly bear the mark of Minoan influence — Figs. 272-3). There may even have been some Hittite influence, as is suggested by the animal rhyta discovered at Philakopi (Fig. 267), which resemble those found at Bogazköy,[46] dated to the sixteenth century B.C.

It is not known whether the direction of the temples' façade depended on custom or not. In some places their orientation may have been determined by the position of a sacred stone or rock. This is particularly evident at Mycenae, where the natural rock is shielded by the main room of the temple. But the temples whose orientation (indicated by the side the entrance is on) is determined by the points of the compass fall into two groups. In the one group (e.g. at Gournia, A. Triada, and probably Myrtos) the entrance faces west, or (e.g. at Mallia, Eleusis, Pseira, Mycenae, Philakopi and probably Keos) north-west, while in the other group (Tiryns), the entrance faces east. It would be hard to believe that such a distinct orientation of the temples was a matter of pure chance. It seems more than likely that the avoidance of north-facing entrances was in some way connected with reasons involving the cult. It could be that the temple was built to face a certain direction because the sun's rays would then light up the temple entrance at a certain point in the cult rituals — perhaps at the start of the procession when the cult statue was being brought out of of the temple. At the moment, we can do no more than conjecture on this point.

As a rule, the temple interior was divided into several sections. The main section, distinguished by a bench, consisted of the cult chamber proper, which contained a permanent (or sometimes moveble) altar, a bench and a cult statue (if such survived), while the other rooms were store-rooms or vestibules etc., whose function is sometimes difficult to define. The rooms in the temple were sometimes on two levels — this was the arrangement of many dwelling houses as has been confirmed by frescoes (Fig. 145) and by the gold plaque from Mycenae. The inside walls were painted red, blue or white (A. Triada, Tiryns), or hung with cloth (Mycenae) and the floor was adorned with paintings depicting waves and underwater scenes (A. Triada). The main room of the temple generally contained a bench on which the sacred paraphernalia stood. The bench may very well have been a cult substitute for the natural rock, thereby emphasising the temple's association with chthonic divinities. The origin of the bench probably reaches far back to the customs of Neolithic times, when the sacred paraphernalia were placed on a wooden table (Nea Nikomedeia). An important feature of the temple was the altar, or sacrificial table, which was generally moveable but sometimes (e.g. at Mallia) a permanent fixture with a hollow in its top surface (Mallia). Both at Mallia and in Keos (during LH III) ash was found, possibly left from the making of sacrifices on the altar inside the temple. The moveable altars, on the other hand, are low stands resting on three feet.

The cult statues no doubt took different forms, ranging from aniconic to acrolithic and anthropomorphic. There is much evidence to show that in Keos an aniconic statue of Dionysios was venerated. At Mallia, too, there is a stone near the altar, which may have supported a pillar which was an object of worship. At Philakopi there were small idols, probably made of wood, with gold masks covering the face. It seems likely that in some temples at this same period (e.g. at Philakopi) there were clay statues and xoana, although in other temples (e.g. on Keos or at Mycenae) the idols were made of either wood or clay. The size and number of the idols varies. Generally each temple had more than one, and it seems evident that the idols varied in importance. Taylour has made the interesting observation that the variation in height of the postuments of the idols at Mycenae corresponded to the difference in rank of the deities in the Mycenaean pantheon. Those deities which stood on a higher level were the more important. The range represented by the statues within a single temple is striking. For instance at Tiryns one statue (Fig. 274) represents an old goddess, whereas others (Figs. 272-3, 276) are rather of the young, virgin goddess type, such as a prototype of the early Athena or Artemis.[47] The gooddess whose statue is at Philakopi is likewise youthful in appearance. The fact that in some of these statues the head of the goddess is tilted a little upwards, as if in expectation, is not without significance. The goddesses are probably awaiting the appearance, or re-appearance, of a divinity, who seems usually to have been depicted in the form of a xoanon. The deities whose images we see at Mycenae differ markedly from each other in type. There are goddesses, male gods, and hermaphrodite divinities as well. Some of the statues at one time wore robes (Fig. 259), as may be deduced from the fact that some parts of the body are rendered only roughly.[48]

The painted faces of these idols are like masks. This ties up with the custom of putting masks on the faces of statues to convey different types of personality. Some divinities have a frightening appearance, while others look benign. Some divinities are protective — they ensure the supply of water, or are patrons of weaving (Myrtos, Fig. 214). But sometimes it is difficult to draw the line between the cult images (which were objects of worship), and the statues of divinities (which did not have this religious purpose). Some of these representations — for instance the figures at Mycenae, or the goddess at Philakopi, or the idols at Tiryns — were undoubtedly not just ordinary statues, but cult statues (that is, they were objects of adoration), which is obvious because they stand on postuments (at Mycenae) or on a bench (at Tiryns). On the other hand the male figures at Philakopi, which are naked and almost ithyphallic (Fig. 270), or which are of the Reshaph type, may not have been objects of worship. All in all, these seem to be statues of divinities of a chthonic character, and to have had a limited religious purpose. They merely represent gods associated with nature — with change and rebirth in nature — but were not worshipped. No doubt the statues of different divinities represented different aspects of nature, or different elements in the cycle of religious events.

As for the clay figures, as has been remarked above, they may have been votive offerings. That is surely how we should interpret the finds on Keos, where over 50 such figures were discovered. It may be assumed that they represent priestesses, or attendants of the god (Fig. 246). The animal figurines, and animal-shaped rhyta were likewise usually votive. But it may be that the Philakopi rhyta (Fig. 267) symbolised renewed strength, so should be classified rather as objects used in the practice of the cult.

Apart from the tripod altars which have been mentioned above, we must also, among the moveable finds, discuss the tube-stands. Those at Mallia were simple (Fig. 221) while those at Gournia were decorated with snakes and horns of consecration (Fig. 233). Gesell's work,[49] confirmed by finds at Kommos[50] where a tube-stand with a small offering vessel was discovered, has shown that the tube-stands were used as supports. No doubt offerings of fruit, grain, etc. were placed on small cups or plates. The origin of these stands is not yet altogether clear, although it is certain that they go as far back as the Old Palace Period, and not just the Neo-Palatial Period, as was hitherto supposed.[51] Triton shells, or imitations of them in clay (Fig. 222), or pinaxes (Fig. 226), and perhaps large vessels (Fig. 227) were also used in the rituals. The model of a ship found in Keos is more likely to have been a votive offering. The temples (e.g. on Myrtos) may have had vessels for making ritual wine.

The vessels used in the cult rituals were of the ordinary domestic type. Occasionally their function as objects used in the cult is denoted by the presence on them of cult emblems, such as horns of consecration (Fig. 224) or double axe signs (Fig. 220), marked on them before firing. In another case it is clear that a libation jug sunk deep into the ground was used in the performance of the rites (Fig. 216) Room 2, close to the doors).

CATALOGUE XI

Mycenaean temples

1. Delos. A probable temple of Mycenaean date under the Artemision.
   Ph. Bruneau, J. Ducat, *Guide de Delos* (1966), 2nd ed., 100.
2. Eleusis. Megaron B. Probably used as a temple in the Mycenaean Age.
   G. Mylonas, *Eleusis and the Eleusinian Mysteries* (1961), 12ff; B. Rutkowski, *Euhemer*, 8 (1964), 30ff; P. Darque, BCH, 105 (1981), 593ff.
3. Keos. Ayia Irini. The temple was used from MH period onwards. Hesperia, 34 (1962), 263ff; (1964), 314ff; (1966), 363ff; SancSymp, 127ff; Hood, TS, 168f.
4. Mycenae. Sacred area close to the defensive wall of the citadel was used in LH IIIB period.
   Antiquity, 43 (1969), 91ff; 44 (1970), 270ff; Mylonas, CCent, 36ff; SanctSymp, 48ff.
5. Phylakopi, Melos. Tempel of LH IIIB and C date.
   Antiquity, 52 (1978), 7ff; SympSanct, 64ff.
6. Pylos. A probable shrine, possibly a tempel close to the palace.
   C. Blegen, M. Rawson, *The Palace of Nestor at Pylos*, I (1966), 301ff.
7. Tiryns. Sacred area at the lower citadel was used in LH IIIC.
   AA (1978), 449ff; (1979), 379ff; SympSanct, 49ff.

X
Natural Sanctuaries of the Greek Mainland and the Nearby Islands
Caves

AT PRESENT we have very little evidence about the function of the sacred caves in the lives of the inhabitants of the Greek mainland and nearby islands. The paucity of the material available is due to the fact that so far there has been little interest in cult places of this kind. All we can do at present, then, is to summarise the work that has been done on the sacred caves. We must remember, however, that caves were important in the cults of Classical and Hellenistic times, and so it is quite possible that in earlier periods still, the sacred caves were more important than would seem to be the case from the material evidence.

Undoubtedly the most interesting of the caves is the Pan grotto at Ninoi on the Marathon plain (Fig. 287).[1] This cave has several different chambers, in which there are many stalagmites and stalactites. The walls are covered with a red and blue precipitate, and the ceiling, too, is blue. On the floor of the grotto there are a number of holes with water. Fragments of Early Neolithic vases, and human skeletons which are the remains of burials here, were found in a recess in a chamber on the left of the entrance. A bronze axe dating from LH III, as well as Neolithic clay beads and also potsherds dating from the Neolithic right up to Roman times, were found at a spot just beside the main entrance. Neolithic pottery which ranged from Middle Neolithic up to the Dimini style was discovered in a pit in the first chamber. Two fragments of a large Neolithic statuette were discovered here. They had a red surface and matt decoration executed with black paint. Neolithic pottery was also found in the first chamber to the right of the entrance. One monochrome vessel, covered with a lid belonging to another vessel, was found to contain blue glass beads and also larger beads made of monochrome stone and of beautiful rock crystal, as well as two stone axes and five painted sea shells. Another group of pottery objects was covered with stone slabs. According to Papadimitriou, who explored this cave, it can be deduced from the above fact that there was a holy place in the cave. The pottery comes from Early Neolithic times (Arapi II style); earlier pottery, too, was discovered, dated to Early Neolithic I. Between the Neolithic and LH III, the first two chambers right beside the entrance were the only ones that were in use. As the above review of the finds indicates, there is very little material evidence to prove that the cave was used for a religious purpose between the Neolithic and LH III, although it certainly seems probable that the deposit of objects under the stone slab was connected with a cult. It is clear, however, that the cave was used for burials from Neolithic times onwards.

The evidence that has been discovered in other caves is more meagre still, and the view that the objects were used for religious purposes is even less certain than in the case of the cave at Ninoi. But one cave that is worth noting is the Lychnospilia[2] grotto, or Spela Lychnarite, not far from Chasia (Fig. 288). This cave is situated in an almost inaccessible spot high up on one of the walls of a very precipitous gorge. It is so difficult to reach that it could not have been used as a dwelling-place. At the very entrance to the cave there is a great stalagmite that almost bars the entry; although the interior of the cave measures about 15 × 52 m, the entrance is so narrow that only one person can pass at a time. The finds which were unearthed here included a single fragment of a matt painted vessel from the MH period, and some other vessels dating from LH and in all likelihood especially from LH IIIC times, as well as from later periods. A large number of lamps from Classical and from Late Roman times were excavated as well, in addition to clay figurines, a miniature gold bed, and gold ornaments, etc. Although the pottery remains come exclusively from MH and from LH, the other evidence — the cave's inaccessibility and the fact that it was used for a religious purpose in the first millennium B.C. — shows that we cannot rule out possibility that it was already being used for a religious purpose even earlier.

287. Marathon. Cave of Pan. Ergon 1958, Fig. 14.

Another cave that might be mentioned is the partially destroyed one on Polis Bay on the island of Ithaca.[3] A small paved area inside this cave may have been used for some cult purpose. LH pots which were not typical grave gifts have been found here. When we consider that this cave was being used as a place of worship in the first millennium B.C., we cannot exclude the possibility that it was also used in association with religion in LH times as well.

In another part of the Aegean world, near Katapoloi at Kato Akrotiri on the island of Amorgos, there is a place which is regarded as a grotto.[4] Diverse votive offerings, such as a marble phiale, animal bones, and potsherds, were found in the rock fissures there. Broken fragments of pottery, for instance, were discovered in a pit measuring 2.80 long, 2.30 m broad, and 1.00 m deep. The description of this place given by C. Tsountas is not clear.[5] The most likely explanation may be that he came upon a ruined grotto, although from his description of the place one gets the idea rather it was part of a sacred enclosure, with fissures where votive offerings were placed, and with a pit where such gifts were kept, too.[6]

High Places

The importance of the Minoan peak sanctuaries is proved by archaeological discoveries made in Crete. But the question remains as to whether the mainland people also worshipped their gods on hills. This supposition seems highly probable in light of the fact that the cult on mountain summits played an important role in the religion of many European and Asiatic peoples. In fact, all information about the cult on mountain summits in Hellas dates from the Geometric period onwards. The Greeks erected altars and other structures to their gods, often locating them on the highest summits of mountains e.g. on Olympus.[7] From earlier periods, however, there were no cult places similar to the Minoan peak sanctuaries. This can be explained in part by the little interest shown by archaeologists in the cult on mountains. Furthermore, on the Greek mainland the cult on mountains could take place in a natural environment different from that of Crete's. Therefore, to avoid confusion we use the term 'peak sanctuary' for Cretan cult places, and we introduce the term 'high place' (taken from the Bible)[8] for the Greek mainland to mean a cult place on an elevation or hill. If we accept this

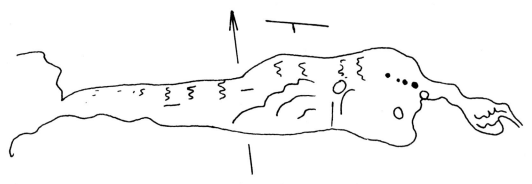

288. Lychnosphilia. Cave. DESE 1, part 4, Fig. on p. 150.

proposal we can regard some sanctuaries from the Bronze Age as 'high places'. Before going on to describe one identified example, we would like to add that the high place is often similar to the sacred enclosure and the classification of a site to one or another group may sometimes be the result of subjective opinion.

One example of a high place, which we present here, comes from Epidauros. The topographical location of the sanctuary is of interest. The highest area of Kynorthion Hill was a dwelling-place which existed presumably as early as the Early Helladic period, but also in MH and LH I-IIIB.[9] On a gently sloping area, below the summit of the hill, there is a Classical temple dedicated to Apollo Meletas, Asklepios' father, and a few metres to the north of it there are altars from the Geometric and Mycenaean periods situated on the northern, steep slope of the hill. In respect to the topography we can observe important differences between Epidauros and the Minoan peak sanctuaries. First, the peak sanctuaries in Crete were not

289. Epidauros. Sanctuary of Apollo Maleatas. PAE 1976, Suppl. Pl. I.

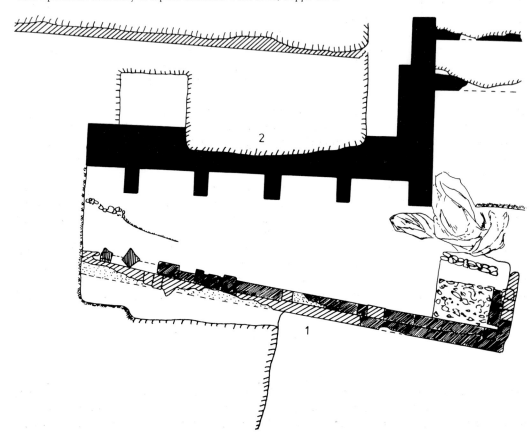

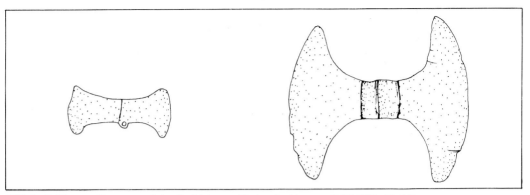

290a-b. Epidauros. Sanctuary of Apollo Maleatas. Votive double axes. PAE 1975, Pl. 149c.

situated near to settlements and second, they always occupied places which could be seen from far away. Third, they were always located in places where there were crevices in the rock. This last element is absent in Epidauros. Excavations have shown that at least from LH I there was a cult place (Fig. 289).[10] The altar measured 10.50 m and was built in the Early Mycenaean period. It was presumably long and narrow judging from the published information on it. An abundance of black ash together with burnt animal relics, potsherds and other offerings were discovered on this altar, as well as near it. The animals most often sacrificed were bulls and goats. Clay vessels were broken in small pieces, which may perhaps prove that they had been thrown onto the altar; among these fragments were early types of Vapheio cups, stemmed cups, and later figure styled vessels. There were numerous clay figurines dated to the later (LH III) period's use of the altar. These are mainly small and large figurines of oxen and bulls; some of them are up to 0.50 m high. Seals and fragments of a chariot group were also unearthed, and fragments of the human figurines of the phi and psi types were a very common find. The bronze weapon discovered at the site is interesting. It has good Mycenaean parallels: swords, both *in corpore* and votive, daggers and spearheads. Two rhyta are worthy of special interest. One of them, a steatite rhyton discovered in the ashes of the altar[11] is decorated with a scene depicting an assault on a city from the land and sea. The second rhyton (of bronze) is preserved in fragments and is in the shape of a life-size bullhead. Among the religious symbols the most important are numerous bronze double axes both in the Minoan type[12] and others, which are presumably locally-made copies of the foreign shapes (Fig. 290a). They include two main types: first, axes with a double edge, as those derived from the Papadimitriou's excavations,[13] and second, axes with a simple edge. These axes do not always have a typical edge (Fig. 290b), and sometimes they are a simple piece of a rectangular bronze sheet.[14] Similarly, the making of the axes varies greatly from fine and carefully manufactured to coarse, irregular, and primitive workmanship. A decoration on the surface of the axes is also quite interesting. As a rule, it is simple, in the form of incised lines. In one example, however, the decoration recalls a stylised holy palm tree.[15]

Nearby, i.e. to the west of the above described altar, there were other buildings. Under the pavement of the Classical temple parts of three rooms dated to the Mycenaean period were uncovered, one of which was paved. With regard to Lambrinoudakis, they must have been derived from a cult building which is indicated by pottery similar to that discovered in the altar area. To sum up, we can imagine that in boundaries of the temenos there were cult buildings and altars, whereas religious ceremonies[16] took place near the Mycenaean sacred building. The sanctuary at Epidauros described above illustrates a type of high place. In the future we hope to be able to identify other sites; presumably we will be able to include some of the sacred enclosures in the group considered here.

Sacred enclosures

As a rule the iconographic finds on the Greek mainland (Figs. 291-302), like the Cretan glyptic art, cannot help us very much in determining the exact location of the sacred enclosures. But at any rate even the meagre indications of trees and bushes on these scenes shows that they were set in the open air, in some open space out in the country, away from the towns and villages,

291. Mycenae. Gold ring. FGK, Fig. 1.3.

292. Mycenae. Gold ring. FGK, Fig. 33.3.

citadels and other settlements. The material evidence found *in situ* tells us that the sacred enclosures must have been located in a variety of sites — for instance, on the slopes or summits of hills, or equally well on the plains. Near the modern little chapel of Ayia Triada, not far from the locality of Ayios Vasilios, are the remains of a sacred enclosure, which at one time was situated on the slopes of a hill beside a Mycenaean road that led from Mycenae to Corinth.[17] Probably the best known example of a sacred enclosure was one discovered at Delphi. The remains of a cult place dating from LH was discovered at Marmaria, in the grounds of what was at a later date a sanctuary consecrated to Athena Pronaia,[18] and therefore on a rather flat terrace lying at an altitude of over 500 m on the slopes of Mount Elapho Kastro. Relics from this period were discovered in a small area lying between the terrace where the altars were, and a temple made of tuff. At Amyklai[19] there is a cult place dating from the LH period about 1 km from the village. There was also a sacred enclosure on a hilltop.[20] Judging from the glyptic art it can be conjectured that the areas where the sacred enclosures were situated must have been rocky ones (Fig. 301), which of course is quite natural.

It is difficult to say just how big an area the sacred enclosures occupied, for no information can be gleaned on this subject from the iconographic finds (Figs. 291-301), and not all of the sites of the sacred enclosures have been investigated completely. One of them which has been fairly thoroughly investigated by the archaeologists, however, is that at Delphi. The dimensions of the sacred enclosure at Delphi can be deduced fairly accurately from the distribution of the LH objects found there.[21]

Similarly, not much can be said as yet about the way in which the sacred area was marked off from its surroundings. The way in which the dividing line between the sacred and the secular terrain was indicated was probably the same on the Greek mainland as it was on Crete. It is likely that the sacred area was marked off not only by custom, or by setting up a large stone (there is no evidence of this method in the finds), but also, very commonly, by ringing the cult place with a stone wall. The scene on a gold signet ring in the Berlin Museum most likely

293. Pylos. Gold ring. FGK, Fig. 2.6.

294. Dendra. Gold ring. FGK, Fig. 1.12.

295. Mycenae. Gold ring. FGK, Fig. 33.2.

296. Mycenae. Gold ring. FGK, Fig. 1.4.

depicts part of the wall of a sacred enclosure, built of regularly shaped hewn stones. As usual (and also in Crete, see Fig. 128), the wall was topped by a cornice. A gold ring from Mycenae shows two constructions of this kind (Fig. 300).[22] It has been argued that both constructions were topped by a cornice, which meant (it is said) that in reality they belonged to a single whole. To make this clear, let us consider a bronze ring from Knossos (Fig. 127), which shows a cornice on the top of the wall encircling the sacred area. In this scene, despite the cornice, we do not expect that the wall was continued on the other side of the action taking place, for on that side we see another tree and altar. In the scene on the gold ring from Mycenae the important point to notice is the hierarchy of importance of the elements depicted. The main features worthy of notice are the dancers and the sacred tree in the enclosure, whereas the construction on the left, of which more will be said below, was perhaps the least important feature of the scene. It was suggested that the figure on the left was not leaning on the 'altar', but was performing one of the figures in the dance — and hence was bent half-forward. The structure on the left is really part of the wall of the enclosure, seen from the inner side.

We can not rule out the possibility that diverse cult objects were suspended on the external side of the peribolos wall. Looking at the scene on the gold ring from Vaphio (Fig. 298), we can see something on the right of the scene, and possibly a shield and a double garland hanging on the wall (not visible). On another big gold ring also found at Mycenae (Fig. 292) six objects are ranged along the edge of the scene, on the left-hand side. They may have been bulls' skulls.[23] Although it is reasonable to believe that the oval line in which these objects are ranged did not reflect the real situation but rather was due to the oval shape of the gem, we cannot exclude the possibility that the oval line symbolised the wall of the enclosure. In that case, although one cannot be sure, one can presume that animal skulls were sometimes hung on the inside of the enclosure wall. One of these gems is exceptional in that it seems to show the lay-out of the area inside the sacred enclosure.[24] It depicts a whole series of intersecting paths running over an area which does not seem to be altogether level. Apart from the walls built round the whole sacred

297. Mycenae. Gold ring. FGK, Fig. 2.8.

298. Vaphio. Gold ring. FGK, Fig. 13.6.

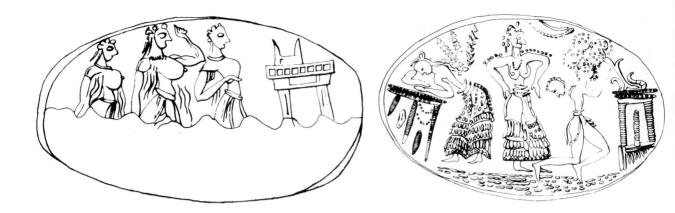

enclosure, other walls were also erected round the sacred tree for protection (Fig. 300), as was also the case in Crete (Fig. 125).

There is little direct evidence about the appearance of the gateways to the sacred enclosures. We know that the gateway into the sacred enclosure played an important part as a symbol of a cult place, as we saw when considering the sacred enclosures in Crete. Some of the scenes depict the façades of buildings, but there is no evidence to show that these were buildings in sacred enclosures. It is suspected, however, that the object on the scene on the ring from Mycenae (Fig. 299) is a gateway, although a different interpretation of the construction is possible as well.[25] The habitations of the gods and the dwellings of human beings were similar in many ways. The holy places in Crete were surrounded by powerful walls which were used for practical purposes as well, just as the citadels on the Greek mainland were protected by massive fortifications. In both cases the entrance was through a great gateway. This was probably not built for defence purposes alone, but also, because of the symbols on it, to denote the importance of the holy area and the might of the god (cf. see also Fig. 76). At Mycenae the lion relief above the magnificent entrance to the citadel expressed the power of the ruler. The lions that guarded the residence of the king, god's representative on earth, symbolised the belief that the whole of the king's residence was under the god's protection (Fig. 284).[26] Of course many more examples of this kind can be given. The façades of the beehive tombs (Fig. 283) which were decorated with motifs of symbolic significance, such as continuous spirals and scenes with figures, reveal to us the kind of ideas which the Mycenaeans also expressed on their great tombs, citadel gates and sacred enclosures. When we reflect on the connection between the sacred enclosures as the property of some deity, and the citadels as the property of the king, we are forced to the conclusion that the massive gateways constituted an important feature of the sacred enclosures, for they were adorned with symbols or figural scenes which not only conveyed an idea of the might of the deity, but which also had an apotropaic purpose.

Naturally there must have been special places set aside in the sacred enclosures for the performance of the rites. It is thought that these were mostly paved areas or areas where the ground had been tramped down. But no answers to this question can be derived from the iconographic art. At various times it has been suggested that the scene on the gold ring from Mycenae depicts a dance being performed on a cobbled area. The cobble stones, it was thought, were represented by horizontal rows of small oval shapes filling in the very bottom part of the scene. But however likely this interpretation seems at first glance,[27] it must nevertheless be rejected. For at the bottom of the scene on several other rings there is rectilinear or triglyph ornamentation whose purpose must have been to fill in the space.[28] This feature did not necessarily have any connection with the rest of the scene.

There are grounds for supposing that cult buildings were erected inside the sacred enclosures, although as has been pointed out above, this was not always the case. It looks as though the excavations at the Marmaria site, at Delphi, where the remains of a sacred enclosure were discovered, prove that not all the sacred enclosures had sanctuaries built in them. But it is true that buildings were erected in many cult places and sacred enclosures, particularly those situated near the more important wealthy towns and villages. It is quite possible, of course, that these buildings may have been made of wood or other less durable substances which later simply disintegrated. Other buildings, however, were of stone, as we know from the finds *in*

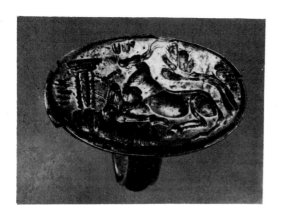

299. Mycenae. Gold and silver ring. FGK, Fig. 1.9.

300. Mycenae. Gold ring. FGK, Fig. 1.8.

301. Thebes. Gold ring. No. 2079. Courtesy of Benaki Museum.

302. Mycenae. Glass plaque. Evans TPC, Fig. 12.

situ,[29] and from the pictorial art. It is conjectured that these were buildings with several rooms, and sometimes with more than one floor. But the iconographic finds depict only the façades or parts of those buildings. On a gold ring found at Dendra (Fig. 294), for instance, we see what seems to be a building in profile.[30] The portico is clearly visible — with a single column — as is part of the cult room proper, which is almost certainly built of large ashlars. On the gold rings found at Mycenae (Fig. 295), the details of the façades of the buildings are not entirely clear. On one of these rings we can see the upper part of the façade of a building; in the middle there is a column with a capital. In front of the sanctuary there is a bench on which a woman is sitting.[31] On the other ring the details are even less clear but in the general outline the same elements of construction occur as before. Thus we find the façade of a building whose roof is supported by a single column which gets narrower towards the bottom and is surmounted by a capital. One gold ring from Thebes has a scene in which a cult building is represented.[32] A woman is sitting on a broad bench in front of the building. This building, too, is possibly depicted in profile. Another gold ring from Thebes[33] shows the façade of a building made of two posts surmounted by a couple of beams, one on top of the other (Fig. 301). This structure looks as if it was meant to represent a building, rather than an altar.[34] It is probable that the sanctuaries in the sacred enclosures were sometimes tripartite.[35] We can see an example of this in the gold ring which is now in The Berlin Museum. This ring has a scene that includes a fragment of an edifice which looks as if it was one part of a façade. It is quite possible that this central part had a section on either side of it, forming the other two elements of a tripartite façade. This kind of representation is typical of glyptic art. The appearance of the façades, and no doubt the buildings in the sacred enclosures as well, can be seen on the gold plaques from Mycenae[36] and also from similar scenes on Cretan frescoes (Fig. 145). One of the scenes shows a tripartite building (Fig. 295) in side view. In another scene (Fig. 291) we find a structure which can be interpreted as the façade of a building in a sacred enclosure.[37] It is symbolised by trees and branches. This scene is extremely simplified. One can see the façade of a building in the centre of the scene, which is a very unusual place to find it in glyptic art, as the sanctuaries most often occupied the side parts of the scene. This façade consists of a central part with a column holding up the roof: the column is designated by dots, while this central part is surmounted by a square-shaped beam with a triple cornice. Beyond the façade there are marks representing trees. As we have said, the whole of this building is depicted summarily. Some of the details cannot be seen clearly at all, but must be guessed at. It is notable that the upper part of the façade has been depicted in great detail whereas the lower part is merely sketched in. The designation of the column by means of short strokes one on top of the other is illustrative of the Mycenaean artists' love of decoration. The foliage of the tree on the left part of the scene is likewise represented by dots. One cannot rule out the possibility, either, that the lower part of the building was supposed to be a tripartite one, although it had only one column.

One of the main furnishings of the interior of the sacred enclosures must have been the altars. The strange thing, however, is that on none of the scenes seeming to show the inside of the sacred enclosures is there an altar clearly depicted.[38] Of course a large number of finds have scenes where sacrifices are being made at an altar, but the actual place where the action is taking place is not indicated in any detail at all. It seems likely that the altars could have been situated anywhere, and that the libations and ceremonies (Fig. 292) could have taken place anywhere as well — in a sacred place, or in a town square, and either inside the town or in a sacred enclosure right out in the country. Obviously all the altars must have been of more or less the same shape, regardless of whether they were in a sacred enclosure, or in one of the diverse cult places in the towns, or in a citadel. The simplest kinds of altar cannot be seen in the archaeological material,[39] but we have evidence suggesting that it was fairly common for natural stones to be used as altars. In the sacred enclosure found at the Marmaria site at Delphi,[40] several votive offerings were discovered on a large flat stone which may have been used as an altar. The iconographic finds show us another, more primitive kind of altar as well. For instance there is a scene on a glass plaque from Mycenae (Fig. 302) showing a heap of rough stones on which a libation is being poured.[41] At a later period this kind of altar became more frequent in scenes depicting the cult of Priapos.[42]

Some of the altars were polygonal. When this was the case ordinary stones were sometimes used in their construction as well. These altars were probably connected with the cult of baetyls.[43] However, other shapes occured as well. These altars, for instance, were sometimes conical in shape, and surmounted with horns of consecration,[44] or occasionally they were separate, square constructions, probably of stone, also surmounted with horns of consecration.

The holy tree was one of the basic elements of the landscape in the sacred enclosures. It is to be found in numerous scenes. Even if the artist had placed the trees outside the wall of the sacred enclosure (Fig. 301), we have no reason to question that they were sacred. Other trees inside the cult place have special walls built round them (Fig. 300), although in some of the enclosures the trees may have had no walls round them (Fig. 292). Some of the idols found at Delphi Marmaria[45] had holes in the body — it is possible that they were suspended on trees. Trees grew in the sacred enclosure at Marmaria; at the present time there are orchards of olive trees on the slopes below the sanctuary. It is not always possible to determine the species of tree. What is shown on the gold ring from Mycenae (Fig. 292) was no doubt a fig tree. On other rings the species of tree is less clear, but it is possible they were all olive trees.[46]

Neither the iconographic finds nor the other objects found in the sacred enclosures indicate in any way that anthropomorphic statues were placed there,[47] although of course such a possibility cannot be ruled out. Probably in the sacred enclosures the gods that were worshipped were mainly represented in an aniconic form. A scene on a gold ring from Mycenae, for example, shows a sacred enclosure with not only a sacred tree but a baetyl as well (Fig. 300). Yet as we can see the evidence at hand is too meagre for us to be able to say anything certain about a baetyl cult. These scenes often have symbols heralding the presence of the deity. The most important of these symbols are the double horns of consecration surmounting the cult building (Figs. 295, 299) or altar. The double axe symbol which likewise signifies that the place in which it occurs is holy (Fig. 292) is found less often. Of course other symbols, such as the sacred knot, may also indicate that epiphanies of the deity occurred in the cult place (Fig. 298).

From the material evidence very little information can be gained about the utensils and other cult objects used in the sacred enclosures. Apart from the rhyta commonly used in the cult, other everyday vessels must have been used as well, such as jugs (Fig. 302) etc. On a gold ring[48] we have a unique scene in which a woman is sitting on a bench and holding a mirror or a standard. It is likely that other objects generally used in the religious ceremonies, such as knives, were in common use as well. The information about the votive offerings brought to the sacred enclosures is meagre. Most of these objects date back to LH IIIB-C times. There are numerous reports, then, of figurines of the Phi and Psi type, and of other kinds of votive offerings — for instance, figurines of animals such as oxen and pigs,[49] and of pottery, too. Of course only some of the votive offerings brought to the sacred enclosures have survived to our times. Another source of information on the votive offerings brought to the cult places is the Linear B tablets, which in particular tell us about gifts being sent from Pylos to a holy place outside the town.[50]

Three kinds of scene are depicted in the glyptic art — invocation dances, adoration and the making of sacrifices. It is difficult to say for certain whether the female figures in these scenes are priestesses or votaries. But on the gold ring from Mycenae (Fig. 292) it seems more likely that the women approaching the figure sitting under the tree are priestesses. They are attired in rich ritual robes — long flared skirts with frills and bodices that leave their breasts bare. Their long hair is plaited, and adorned with lilies. One of the women has nothing in her hands, for no doubt she has just presented three poppy heads to the figure sitting under the tree. It should be noted that the votary (or rather, in all likelihood, the priestess) who is holding the lilies, is also pictured on a gem seal discovered at Routsi, and in that scene is approaching the altar. These scenes, then, testify to the use of lilies and poppies in the religious ceremonies, probably to symbolise ripening corn.

The cult ceremonies, especially the processions and dances, were held in the sacred enclosures, as we know from the iconographic finds. A gold ring from Mycenae, for instance, shows three women[51] attired in skirts and short-sleeved bodices. They are making their way, probably barefoot,[52] in the direction of the sanctuary,[53] and each of them has one hand held high, holding a flower, while in the other hand each is carrying a branch.[54] This scene is meant to represent part of a ceremonial procession in which a large number of worshippers are taking part. On another ring from Mycenae (Fig. 299), we see three women going towards the sanctuary.[55] They are dressed in long skirts and in bodices that leave their breast bare. Long tresses hang down their backs. Each of the women is making some gesture. The one in front has her right arm sharply bent at the elbow, with her forearm extended forwards. The one in the middle is raising her left hand to her forehead, and the third one has both arms hanging down at her sides. We see from the waving hair of the first two votants that all three women were in movement. Again, then, here we have a scene portraying a procession. The artist has been able to suggest the whole procession by indicating only two or three of the people taking part in it.

The deities who made appearances in the sacred enclosures were worshipped not only by means of processions, but also by means of dances. One of the gold rings found at Mycenae (Fig. 300) shows a very energetic dance being performed by two women and one man.[56] The female dancer in the middle of the scene is in the upright position, her elbows extended outwards, and her hands almost on her hips, and she is whirling round. There is a person on either side of her. On one side there is a woman who is bent forward sharply from the hips, while on the other side there is a man so given up to dance that he is almost kneeling.[57] A similar scene has been carved on a ring from Vaphio (Fig. 298),[58] and likewise on a ring from Dendra (Fig. 294), where the dancers are in front of the façade of the sanctuary.[59] The scenes described above give us only a fleeting image of the ceremonies that must have been held in the sacred enclosures, which in actuality must have been of much greater variety.

The divinities who were worshipped in the sacred enclosures were doubtless the gods of nature, who ruled over birth and death in the world of plants, animals, and people. Evidence frequently comes to the fore suggesting that cultivated trees such as the olive and fig were the objects of worship. The decoration of the altars with branches likewise demonstrates one of the deity's principal traits. It is possible that in LH times some of the sacred enclosures were dedicated to the principal god of the Mycenaean pantheon, Poseidon, as well as to other gods or goddesses.[60]

The sacred enclosures on the Greek mainland, like those on Crete, probably belonged to one of the most common types of cult places. It is very likely that they existed much earlier than would seem to be the case from the archaeological and iconographic finds. These primitive cult elements, which connected with the necessity of ensuring good crops and protecting the flocks, persisted much longer, since at least up until MH I the community was almost entirely dependent on agriculture and stock-breeding.[61] Yet they persisted even to the time when radical changes had taken place in the economic foundations of Mycenaean society, and when the economy was based not only on the traditional farming and stock-breeding, but also, to no small extent, on sea trade and piracy as well. The people continued to be devoted to the old cult places in the sphere of the Mycenaean religion even at the dawn of the palace civilisation,[62] that is, from MH III on. The people's devotion to these places is also confirmed by the Linear B tablets found at Pylos,[63] which tell us that votive offerings were sent from the palace at Pylos to sanctuaries out in the country, which means to the sacred enclosures. Since this was the case, the sanctuaries in the palaces and the temples in the towns were of relatively little importance.

CATALOGUE XII

Caves

1. Ayios Nikolaos (Atikia), not far from Klenies (Korinthia). The pottery found here may have come from a sacred grotto.
RE, Suppl. 6 (1935), 606; Hope Simpson, Gaz, 28 No. 51.

2. Amorgos, at Kato Akrotiri. The potsherds discovered in a small cave may indicate that it was used for a religious purpose.
AE (1898), 166; AM, 38 (1913), 166.

3. Ithaca, cave in Polis Bay. Pottery found here may indicate that the cave was used for a religious purpose.
BSA, 35 (1934), 45ff; BSA, 39 (1938), 1ff; BSA, 44 (1949), 307ff; Hope Simpson, Gaz, No. 325; Hägg, MKult, 51.

4. Ninoi, Pan cave at Marathon. Neolithic idol found here as well as pottery which is thought to indicate that the cave was used for cult rites from the end of the Neolithic period onwards.
AR (1957), 6; AR (1958), 4; Ergon (1958), 15ff; BCH, 82 (1958), 681, 685; 83 (1959), 587; DESE (1961), 31; Hope Simpson, Gaz, No. 379; Hägg, MKult, 50.

5. Parnes, grotto near Chasia. Potsherds discovered here may indicate that the cave was used for a religious purpose.
AE (1905), 99ff; AE (1906), 89ff; PAE (1900), 13, 38ff; (1901), 12, 32ff; JHS, 21 (1901), 350; AE (1918), 1ff; Nilsson, MMR², 67f, 72; Hope Simpson, Gaz, No. 384; Hägg, MKult, 49f.

CATALOGUE XIII

High places and sacred enclosures

1. Ayia Kyriaki (Amyklai), near Sparta. Fragments of walls discovered, as well as about 75 figurines of the Psi type and others. Period LH IIIC.
AE (1892), 1ff; A. Wace, A Catalogue of the Sparta Museum (1906), Nos. 550, 798, 802; JdI, 33 (1918), 109ff; AM, 52 (1927), 1ff; BSA, 51 (1956), 170; BSA, 55 (1960), 74ff; BSA, 56 (1961), 164, 170 and 173ff; F. Grace, AJA, 44 (1940), 105 (who declares there was no cult place here in the Bronze Age); Nilsson, MMR², 470, 556; Hope Simpson, Gaz, 42 No. 97; Hägg, MKult, 54; Dimakopoulou, p. 259 n. 19.

2. Ayia Triada, not far from A. Vasilios, near Corinth. In one small area over 200 figurines, mostly of the Phi and Psi type, were discovered. Period LH IIIB.
AA (1913), 116; RE, Suppl. 6 (1935), 600; Hope Simpson, Gaz, 28 No. 49; Hägg, MKult, 52.

3. Delphi, Marmaria, at a temenos later dedicated to Athene Pronaia. A large stone there may have been used as an altar; several score figurines also found there, including some of the Psi type. Period LH IIIB.
Fouilles de Delphes, II, fasc. 5 (1926), 5ff; Nilsson, MMR², 467f; BCH, 81 (1957), 708ff; Hope Simpson, Gaz, No. 446; Hägg, MKult, 54.

4. Egina, objects found at the temenos of Aphaia included many figurines, of which some were of the Psi type, and pottery from LH IIIA and B.
H. Tiersch, in A. Furtwängler (ed.), Aegina (1906), 370ff; Nilsson, MMR², 471f; Hope Simpson, Gaz, No. 393; Hägg, MKult, 53.

5. Epidaurus, at the summit of Kynortion. Many clay figurines discovered in a temenos where Apollo Maleatas was worshipped in later times. Period LH IIIB and earlier.
PAE (1948), 90ff; (1949), 91ff; (1950), 197ff; (1951), 204; (1974), 96; (1975), 167ff; (1976), 202ff; (1977), 187ff; Hope Simpson, Gaz, 20 No. 22; Hägg, MKult, 53.

6. Samos, Heraion. In a village which existed here there was an open-air shrine close to the gate of the settlement. A circular stone platform probably held an altar. Walter believes that a lagos (a willow-like tree) was growing in the middle of the platform, dated to second millennium B.C.
H. Walter, Das Heraion von Samos (1976), 14ff.

7. Samos, Heraion. In the village there, which had flourished since the third millennium B.C., an open-air cult place existed close to the megaron and a gate of the settlement. It consisted of a

basin, a circular platform, and a semi-circular construction. In that area many broken jars were found.

Walter, op. cit., 14.

8. Troullos, at Ayia Irini, Keos. On the summit, some 65 m above sea level, a building with one room (2.25 × 4.75 m) and possibly a second room or porch was excavated. Adjoining this was an enclosure ca. 11.50 × 15 m, with a projecting wall, where there may have been an entrance. The northern part of the enclosure is paved with large irregular slabs of local marmor, elsewhere there are remains of coarse plaster flooring. In the centre there is a circular construction, ca. 5 m in diameter, of rough stone masonry. Close by there is another circular construction, ca. 6 m in diameter. Fragmentary libation tables and a stone ladle may suggest religious practices.

J. Caskey, Hesperia, 35 (1966), 375f; 40 (1971), 392ff.

CATALOGUE XIV

Iconographic Sources

1. Athens, Agora. A crater found here is decorated with a scene depicting an altar or sanctuary. Period LH IIIA. Museum: AgM.
Archaeology, 13 (1960), 8; AJA, 65 (1961), 157; AJA, 66 (1962), pl. 40, No. 12; Mylonas, MycMA, 141.

2. Berlin (Museum). A gold ring said to have been found at Kilia bears a scene depicting a sacred enclosure. Period LH I.
BCH, 36 (1912), 297; Persson, RelGr, 177; Nilsson, MMR², 266; FGK, 26, 30.

3. Dendra. A gold ring discovered in tomb No. 10. It has a scene showing a holy building, a sacred tree, and women dancing. Period LH II. Museum: NM 8748.
A. Persson, *New Tombs at Dendra near Midea* (1942), 81 and 132ff; Persson, RelGr, 40ff; Nilsson, MMR², 157, 178, 268f; CMS, I, 218 No. 191; Mylonas, MycMA, 140; FGK, 18, 28, 29, 84.

4. Eleusis. A steatite matrix. Two women dancing before a sacred façade. LH II-III. Museum: Eleusis, unnumbered.
PAE (1953), 80f; CMS, V, No. 422; FGK, 12, 26.

5. Mega Monasteri. A gold ring. Two women before a sacred façade. LH IIIA. Museum: Volos, M 107.
AD, 19 (1964), Chronika, 257; CMS, V, No. 728; FGK, 20, 29, 84.

6. Mycenae. Gold plaques found in shaft graves. Each of them depicts a holy building. Period LH I. Museum: NM, 26, 242-244.
H. Schliemann, *Mycenae* (1878), 267f; Evans, TPC, 191; G. Karo, *Die Schachtgräber von Mykenai* (1930), pl. XVIII 242-244, XXVI 26; Mylonas, MycMA, 138; FGK, 18, 25, 29, 34, 84.

7. Mycenae. A gold ring found in a 'hoard' near shaft graves, (or in a destroyed shaft grave). It has a scene with a sacred enclosure on it. Period LH I. Museum: NM, 992.
Evans, TPC, 107f; Evans, PofM, II, 339; H. Thomas, BSA, 37 (1936/7), 79ff; Nilsson, MMR², 281ff; CMS, I, 30 No. 17; Mylonas, MycMA, 149; FGK, 94, 96, 108, 110.

8. Mycenae. A gold ring with a scene representing a sacred enclosure (with a sacred tree and dance rites) was discovered in chamber tomb No. 91. Period LH I. Museum: NM, 3179.
Evans, TPC, 177f; CMS, I, 142 No. 126; Mylonas, MycMA, 141; FGK, 30.

9. Mycenae. A gold ring with a scene depicting three women in front of a holy building was found in a chamber tomb. Period LH. Museum: NM, 2853.
Evans, TPC, 189; Persson, RelGr, 56; Nilsson, MMR², 181; CMS, I, 102 No. 86; Mylonas, MycMA, 139, FGK, 26, 84.

10. Mycenae. A gold ring with a scene depicting a sacred tree was discovered in chamber tomb No. 84. Period LH. Museum: NM, 3148.
Evans, TPC, 182; Persson, RelGr, 52f; Nilsson, MMR², 258; CMS, I, 135 No. 119; Mylonas, MycMA, 141; FGK, 30.

11. Mycenae. A gold ring with a scene of a holy building and worshippers was found in chamber tomb No. 91. Period LH. Museum: NM 3180.
Evans, TPC, 141, 183ff; Evans, PofM, III, 137; Nilsson, MMR², 182 and 287; CMS, I, 144 No. 127; Mylonas, MycMA, 144; FGK, 14.

12. Mycenae. A gold ring said to have been found at Mycenae. It has a picture of a woman sitting holding a looking-glass or a standard. Museum: Berlin, Antikensammlung.
Furtwängler-Loeschcke (1879), p. III and 78; A. Furtwängler, II (1900), 10 No. 21; Evans, TPC, 190; Persson, RelGr, 43; Nilsson, MMR², 180; Mylonas, MycMA, 140; FGK, 26, 84, 108, 110.

13. Mycenae. A gold ring said to have been discovered at Mycenae. It has a scene showing a building in a sacred enclosure. Period LH I. Museum: AM.
Evans, TPC, 182; Persson, RelGr, 54ff; Kenna, CrS, 154; Mylonas, MycMA, 141; FGK, 14.

14. Mycenae. A silver, gold-plated ring with a scene showing three women in front of a holy building was found in tholos tomb No. 71. Period LH. Museum NM 2972.
Evans, TPC, 184; Nilsson, MMR², 181; CMS, I, 124 No. 108; Mylonas, MycMA, 142; FGK, 29, 84.

15. Mycenae. A seal bearing a scene with a sacred tree and a building was found in chamber tomb No. 88. Period LH I. Museum: NM 3154.
Evans, TPC, 153; Nilsson, MMR², 285; CMS, I, 139 No. 123.

16. Mycenae. A glass plaque with a scene depicting demons pouring out a libation at a stone altar. Period LH. Museum: NM.
Evans, TPC, 117; Evans, PofM, IV, 455; Nilsson, MMR², 146; FGK, 40.

17. Mycenae. A glass plaque from the Tomb of the Genii with a scene showing a sacrifice being made over a pillar. Period LH. Museum: NM.
Evans, TPC, 117; Evans, PofM, IV, 455; Nilsson, MMR², 146.

18. Mycenae. A glass plaque from the Tomb of Genii with a scene showing a sacrifice being made at an altar. Period LH. Museum: NM.
Evans, TPC, 117; Evans, PofM, IV, 454; Nilsson, MMR², 146; Mylonas, MycMA, 148f.

19. Naxos, Aplomata. A flat cylinder from Tomb A. A man with a spear is worshipping a sacred tree in front of an altar. Probably a scene in a sacred enclosure. Period LH IIIA.
Ergon (1959), 127; PAE (1959), 184; CMS, V, No. 608; FGK, 47, 49, 52.

20. Pylos, palace. Fragment of a wall-painting with a scene depicting a sanctuary. Period LH IIIB. Museum: Chora Triphylias.
Archaeology, 13 (1960), 37; AJA, 57 (1961), 157; M. Lang, *The Frescoes: The Palace of Nestor at Pylos in Western Messenia*, II (1968), 136ff; FGK, 10, 83.

21. Pylos, royal beehive tomb. A gold ring with a scene representing the epiphany of a deity. Period LH II. Museum: NM 7985.
CMS, I, 292; FGK, 26, 44, 84.

22. Pylos, palace, Room 98. A clay sealing no doubt from a gold ring with a scene showing a procession of three women, and a small cult building. Period LH. Museum: NM 8479.
CMS, I, 349 No. 313; FGK, 26.

24. Routsi (Myrsinachorio), near Pylos. Scene on which a priestess is approaching an altar or sanctuary. Period LH II-LH IIIA 1. Museum: NM 8323.
CMS, I, 315 No. 279; FGK, 44.

24. Thebes. Tomb not far from the town. A gold ring on which there is a bull in front of a sanctuary. Period LH. Museum: Athens, Benaki Museum, 2079.
CMS, V, 198; FGK, 29, 84.

25. Thebes, tomb near the town. A gold ring found there has a scene of a woman sitting in front of a sanctuary or altar. Period LH. Museum: Athens, Benaki Museum 2075.
CMS, V, 199; FGK, 54, 84, 108.

26. Thera, Akrotiri. Parts of a frescoe which shows a construction with horns of consecration belonging to an altar or a sanctuary or a palace building, and also a column. Period LM/LH I.
S. Marinatos, *Excavations at Thera* (1969), II, 53.

27. Thera, Akrotiri, West House. On a miniature frescoe a hill sanctuary (?), a building with horns of consecration, probably a temple and a temenos out of the town are represented. Period LM/LH I. Museum: NM.
S. Marinatos, *Excavations at Thera* (1974), VI, 38ff.

28. Thera, Akrotiri, Xeste 3. A frescoe with a procession leading to a sacred building surmounted by horns of consecration. Period LM/LH I. Museum: NM.
C. Doumas, PAE (in press); FGK, 28 n.56.

29. Vaphio, beehive tomb. A gold ring found here has a scene on which there are dancers and a sacred tree. Period LH II. Museum: NM 1801.
Nilsson, MMR², 175; CMS, I, 253, No. 219; FGK, 30, 52, 99.

30. Vaphio, beehive tomb. A seal discovered here has a scene showing demons pouring out a libation in front of an altar. Period LH II. Museum NM 1776.
Evans, TPC, 101; Evans, PofM, IV, 453; Nilsson, MMR², 146; CMS, I, No. 264; Mylonas, MycMA, 149 No. 27; FGK, 47, 87, 89.

31. Volos, beehive tomb at the Kapakali site. A scene on a gold plaque found here shows the façade of a building used for religious, or more probably for secular purposes. Period LH II. Museum: NM 5609.
AE (1906), 224ff; Nilsson, MMR², 174.

XI
Domestic Sanctuaries in Mainland Greece

THIS CHAPTER concerns two types of sanctuaries: domestic sanctuaries, and the shrines in gateways or fortifications. The shrines discussed here are situated not only on the Greek mainland, but in the nearby islands as well. The important question of the value of this evidence, its reliability, and other problems, will be discussed at the end of this chapter, where we sum up the subject of the sanctuaries in this region.

Domestic Sanctuaries
Early and Middle Bronze Age

There are still a few domestic sanctuaries on the mainland and in the nearby islands. The most notable are the examples described below. For a discussion of the cult paraphernalia see the generally comparable finds from the temples (p. 198).

At Lithares[1] near Thebes, a rectangular room measuring 3.70 × 4.80 m, named the 'Sanctuary of the Bulls', was uncovered. The entrance to this room, which was the best of a four-room complex, was on the south side and was connected with a large paved court. The sanctuary is paved with small stones topped with fine clay. A unique find of 17 EH III clay figurines, mostly between 2.00 and 4.50 cm in height, was reported (Fig. 303). All the figurines except one were found in the middle of the room near a pile of burnt earth at a depth of between 0.80 and 0.50 m. One was unearthed at a depth of 0.70 m in the south-east corner of the room. Two groups of idols were described, differing from each other in their proportions and in the amount of attention given to detail. So far no parallels to these figurines have been found. It is suggested that they may have been votive offerings. But there is another possibility, propounded by Tzavella-Evjen, namely that the room was simply a coroplast workshop.

A house at Eutresis[2] which dates back to EH II is irregular in plan (Fig. 304), and consists of two parts. This house did not exceed 15 m in length, and at its widest it was between 6 m and 9 m. A narrow passage led in from the paved street to a room which had a stone paved floor, and a rubbish pit. In Goldman's opinion, this place was used as a small inner courtyard rather than as a room. Room II, which was a large one (its dimensions being 5.00-5.80 m × 5.00-5.30 m), was a dwelling-room. There was a hearth towards the end of one of the walls. Room III (whose dimensions were 6.50-7.70 × 5.00-5.40 m) had an exceptional feature which was not encountered in any other house in Eutresis: this was the irregular shape of one of the walls. Room III was entered from Room II through a doorway 1 m wide. This tiny passage and a small adjacent semi-circular area at the entrance to Room III were paved. An inside wall built askew across the room (on the plan in Fig. 304 it is indicated by diagonal lines) dates from a later period. As usual, there is a hearth up against one of the walls. In the centre of the room (marked A) a bench was excavated. It measures 1.40 × 0.60 m, and is 0.50 m high. It was made of small stones bound together with earth and clay. A round slab made of clay (and measuring 1.20 m in diameter and 0.027 m in thickness), with a protruding rim lay at spot B. There were traces of fire on it, and several animal bones were discovered lying on its surface. Between the bench and the round clay slab was a pit (0.50 m in diameter and 0.30 m in depth) which was filled with broken pottery — mainly small goblets. At spot C the excavations brought to light pieces of an EH bull-rhyton. It is not typical, as it has only one hole, in the back.[3] The surviving length is 0.236 m.

214

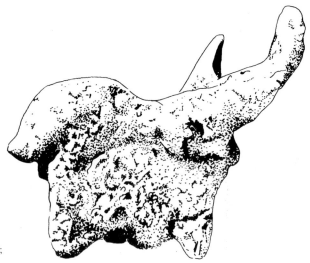

303. Lithares. A bull-figurine. AAA 5, 1972;
469 Fig. 13.

Goldman argues that if one takes into consideration the unusual amalgamation of certain features, such as the dimensions of the room, the pit dug in the floor between the bench and the clay slab, and the bull-shaped vessel (it is known that in Crete vessels of this kind were sometimes connected with religious rites), one is justified in thinking that the room was possibly used for cult purposes. This is still a matter of conjecture because no indubitable cult objects were found there, although there are certain grounds for believing that this was indeed the purpose of the room. For religious ceremonies the following objects were probably used: the round clay slab, which is similar to the three-legged portable altars of later date (e.g. at Mycenae) and bones which are most probably the remains of sacrificial victims. It is not likely that there were two hearths in the same room, and so this slab must have been used for other purposes rather than for cooking or heating. The small beakers and the rhyton must have been used for pouring out libations, and the bench may have been an altar. Anyway it is not certain if the room was used permanently or only occasionally for cult purposes.

Several rooms at Malthi have been interpreted as sanctuaries (Figs. 305, 306). We now propose to examine in detail the arguments for this supposition. Room B.64, which is referred to as a sanctuary and which comes from Neolithic or EH times, is situated in the centre of the settlement.[4] It was a rather small room, probably reached by three steps. This room opened out into the courtyard, which was reached through a doorway in one of the sides of the room. Three layers were excavated here: an LH layer at a depth of 0-0.25 m, another from MH I at a depth of 0.25-0.40 m, and an EH layer at a depth of 0.40-0.50 m. The deepest layer was directly on top of the bedrock. No walls from the earliest period were found, but the finds included EH sherds, one loom weight, one flint knife and one stone figurine of the Neolithic type, which was discovered just below the corner of a MH I wall. A layer from the MH period was indeed discovered at the height of the wall, but neither it nor the layer dating from the LH period was described in Valmin's report.

Valmin believed that this room was a sanctuary because it had a similar position and similar steps to the Sacred Repository at Knossos and also because of the Neolithic figurine found in it, which is interpreted as an image of the Fertility Goddess. According to Valmin, then, this place was a sanctuary in the Malthi I period (Neolithic) or in EH times, although the wall round it was not built until later, in the MH I period. The cult place was not abandoned. It continued to be used and a new wall was built round it in the MH II period. Valmin thought that the Neolithic or EH statuette referred to above had been lost, and that it was replaced with another one, which later on was lost in turn. Elsewhere,[5] Valmin writes that there was a sanctuary here in the LH period as well. He gives no grounds for making this statement, and we can only conclude that he bases this view on the fact that there was a cult place here in earlier times.

We must now examine the arguments that Room B.64 was a sanctuary. As an aside it should be mentioned that in EH and MH times the settlement stretched as far as Room B.69, whose function will be defined below. The fact is that apart from ordinary everyday domestic pottery

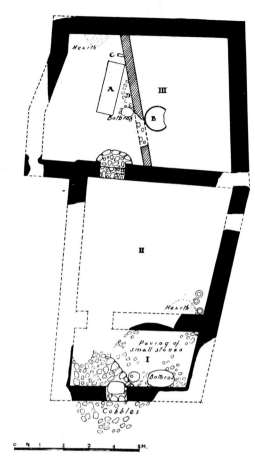

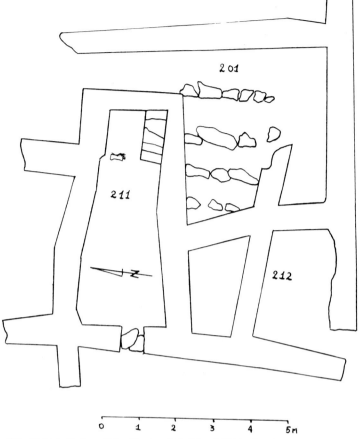

304. Eutresis. Plan of house L. H. Goldman,
Excavations at Eutresis in Boeotia (1931), Fig. 13.

305. Malthi. Shrine of Double Axes? BullLund 1936, Fig. 6.

and a single stone figurine, no other objects were found in Room B.64. Valmin submits, for example, that this room bore a similarity to the Sacred Repository at Knossos because it was small, because it was adjacent to a courtyard, and because it was reached by steps, but these are merely general comparisons. The ground here was probably no more rocky and uneven than in the other rooms. The finds from Room B.64 also invite examination. The pottery consisted of domestic ware, and the only object that could possibly have been used for cult purposes was a figurine made of green steatite. This figurine was discovered along with one Minyan sherd dating from EH II and EH III. Because of the place where it was found (below an MH I wall), and because of the context in which it was found (among potsherds dating from EH to MH), it may be conjectured that this figurine was discovered in a layer that had already been disturbed in Antiquity. It could have found its way to the spot where the MH I room was to be built later, when the site was being prepared for work to begin on the wall. Or it may have been an object of veneration that had survived from the past. The use this figurine was put to is also a matter of interest. It is only 0.047 m high, and represents a female with ample thighs. There is a hole in the upper part of the figure, obviously for hanging it up. Consequently it is rather difficult to view this as an object of worship; it is more likely that it was used as an amulet.[6]

Room B.69 was situated in the central part of the settlement.[7] The room was built with a wall, and formed two parts. According to Valmin the eastern part of the room was an open 'courtyard', measuring 5 × 2m. The ground here has a steep slope, and the eastern part of the room was 2 m lower than the western part. The western part of Room B.69 differs from the others in the carefulness of its construction. It was built of bigger blocks than the other houses. Yet the construction of the walls is not quite regular, the northern wall being somewhat tilted. A doorway links this room with the neighbouring one, B.72. The west wall is poorly preserved; it is not as strongly constructed as the other ones. Originally there was a doorway in it (probably later walled up) which led into the open. The western sector of the south wall of this room is thinner, and the stones were not set very compactly. Possibly this part of the wall

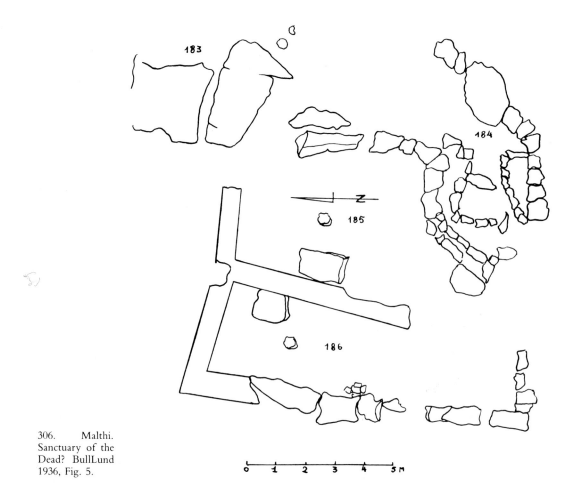

306.   Malthi.
Sanctuary of the
Dead? BullLund
1936, Fig. 5.

was added on later, and the small area B.68 was once a further extension of the courtyard of B.69. If that were so, however, the longitudinal, approximately parallel walls of B.69 (on the north and the south), that are next to B.68, were low ones.

If Valmin was right in his suggestion that the eastern part of B.69 was a separate room (or a recess), then this was the smallest room in Malthi since it measures only 1.00 m × 0.80 m. It is made of more carefully hewn blocks which are the biggest in the whole settlement. The walls have been preserved to a height of 0.80-1.20 m. The finds from this chamber were as follows. A great amount of pottery was found in the layer from the bedrock up to a height of 1 m. A few EH and MH sherds were discovered in the deepest layer. The other pottery came solely from the LH III period. None of the painted vessels found here was intact, and none of them could be reconstructed. Because they were broken, Valmin thought they were sacrificial vessels. Several unpainted vessels were found intact; one of them was large. Pieces of a big pithos were discovered right beside the south wall. Apart from the pottery, a bronze axe, weighing 984.2 gm, was also unearthed. Valmin thought it was new, and that originally it had been meant for domestic use, but that later it had become a cult or votive object. Moreover, two small stone balls were found in the recess, and two terracotta loom weights were found in the 'courtyard'. Based on this evidence Valmin thought that the 'recess' in Room B.69 had been a double axe sanctuary. He argued that this was true because the 'recess' was better constructed that the other buildings, its dimensions were small, the fragmentary painted vases used as libation vessels were discovered in it, and finally because the votive (or cult) bronze axe mentioned above was found here.[8] The room was used in LH III or more precisely in LH III B.

With the view that these two rooms, B.69 and B. 64, were sanctuaries used in the LH III period, Valmin went on to express his ideas concerning the part that these rooms played in society. Room B.69, he thought, was a sanctuary of the rulers in which they worshipped the god of war with his symbol the double axe, while Room B.64 was a sanctuary used by the conquered population which continued to venerate their own traditional cult of the fertility goddess.

Near the south gate, at Malthi, just beside the defence wall, two rooms, C.1 and C.2 (Fig. 306) were built in the MH period. Only two walls of this house have survived. They are 0.60 m thick. One of them, which runs in the east-west direction, is 8 m long, while the other one, running from north to south, is 4 m long.[9] The shorter wall has probably been preserved in its entirety, since it ends with a single large stone, probably marking the end of the wall. There are also slight traces of the presumed course of the west wall. Room C.1 probably measured about 4.00 or 4.50 sq. m and Room C.2 about 2 × 3 m, that is, about 6 sq. m. Perhaps, however, as may be conjectured from the plan of the settlement in period III-IV, the wall of Room C.2 was longer, and so the whole area of the room was bigger. There is no sign of a doorway between the two rooms. On each side of this partition wall there were traces of ash and the remains of burnt wood, and beside these remains in each room, near the partition wall, was a large flat stone. In a hollow in the rocky floor next to the wall of C.1 a child's grave (No. XXXVI) was found. It dates from MH times. In both rooms, the layer containing finds reached a depth of 0.80 m, and was explored by Valmin in strata of 0.10 m. In the layer going down to a depth of 0.30 m in both rooms, there were only LH sherds mixed with some MH sherds. At a depth of 0.30-0.60 m in Room C.1, the excavations produced fragments of kitchen pottery and tableware dating from the MH period, as well as about 100 pieces of large pithoi or roof-tiles, half of a stone axe, a flint knife, a steatite 'button', 3 loom weights, and 2 stone pestles. This layer was very firmly tramped down, and the pottery was all in small pieces. It no doubt formed the floor which was made in this way after the house had been used for some time. The remains discovered in the layer at a depth of 0.60-0.80 m consisted mainly of MH ceramics as well as EH walls, pieces of clay pithoi, a stone pestle, a large amount of animal bones and a few human bones.

In Room C.2 the layer at a depth of 0.30-0.60 m produced a large quantity of sherds dating from EH III, 150 pieces of pithoi or roof-tiles, 2 loom weights, and a stone pestle. The earth was rather firmly packed. The layer at a depth of 0.60-0.80 m produced several EH sherds and a large amount of MH sherds, as well as several fragments of pithoi, a loom weight, broken animal bones and several large human bones. In both rooms the pottery was broken into very small fragments, but the experts have succeeded in reconstructing much of it — in Valmin's opinion this ease of reconstruction shows that it was broken here on the spot. These two rooms are dated to the MH period.

It was argued that Rooms C.1 and C.2 were used as a sanctuary of the dead because of the large stones lying on the ground, which were thought to be altars of the kind often used by various population groups or various races. In the opinion of the excavator they were altars upon which sacrifices were offered up to the gods or to the heroes buried in the nearby 'grave circle' (C.3) about 2 m from House C.1.2. It is important to note, however, that these graves date from EH times — it is rather difficult to associate them with rooms C.1.2, which were built later. Valmin's views were founded on a comparison with the graves at Mycenae, and also on the assumption that there could not have been domestic hearths that lay next to each other. This idea is not very convincing, for in many rooms at Malthi, which are generally not bigger than C.1, there was a hearth next to the wall, or near the wall (e.g. B.36, B.55, B.94, A.8, A.36). It is possible that Rooms C.1 and C.2 belonged to two separate, though small, houses. All the objects found here were connected with ordinary household affairs — the kitchenware and tableware, the knife and the pestle, and the animal bones. It is possible that the human bones came here by chance, when the floor was being made as some successive owners were putting their house in order.

The proximity of the 'grave circle' cannot be used as an argument for the view that Rooms C.1 and C.2 were used as a sanctuary. In the grave area, which is marked on the plan as C.3, only three graves were found. Two of them were collective graves, and we believe they may have belonged to a large cemetery extending beyond the acropolis (as at Mycenae). When the settlement at Malthi was extended in the MH period the area already occupied by houses was ringed by defence walls. Thus these fortifications must have passed through graveyard C.3. Of course this hypothesis, which offers an explanation as to why several graves were found inside the settlement, cannot be proved at present, for no excavations have yet been carried out in the area outside the walls, near the south gate.

Finally, Room A.1 at Malthi has sometimes been regarded as a sanctuary.[10] It is situated in the centre of the acropolis, and differs from the other buildings in plan and construction. Its measurements are 13.00 × 9.60-11.00 m, and it consists of two parts which doubtless had no direct connection between them. Room A.1, which is the biggest of these rooms, stood in isolation and was said[11] to be so monumental that it surely could only have been a royal reception room, unless perhaps it was some kind of official sanctuary.[12] Its dimensions are about 8 × 6 m. Inside it a stone column base was discovered. In one of the corners, too, excavations brought to light a hearth which is worthy of special notice because of its size and its careful construction. It was apsidal in shape. The base of this hearth was a stone which lay directly on top of the bedrock, and which had split into two as a result of the heat. Around the base of this hearth was a low, oval-shaped stone wall made of rough-hewn stones. The diameter of the stone circle was 1.75 m, and the height 0.15 m. There was a layer of ash and broken bones mixed with pieces of roof-tile and lumps of clay on the hearth itself, as well as quite a distance from it, far outside the stone wall. A large number of pithoi were found near the hearth. Remains were found in all the layers, from MH II to LH III, and consisted of the principal types of pottery objects, particularly fragments of mostly domestic pots, and also of various tools such as a stone hammer, flint knives, loom weights, a whetstone, a pestle, etc.

Valmin was well aware of the difficulty of interpreting this building as a sanctuary. As far as he was concerned, he was satisfied that the discovery of the hearth, which he thought could not have been used for ordinary cooking or heating, proved the place was used for a holy purpose. Against this was the difficulty of attributing a cult function to the building in light of the fact that no cult objects were found here. And none of the objects excavated here can be interpreted as cult objects with the probable exception of the two stone objects — the axe and the hammer. On the other hand it is not unusual for the house of a chieftain to be a sanctuary as well.

New excavations at Malthi have brought to light much interesting material. During an expedition in 1952 part of a large building or group of buildings was unearthed.[13] In area 2, which was probably a courtyard, there were semi-circles of stones which had been arranged on a foundation of sherds and small stones. Both above and below them were pieces of undecorated drinking (?) vessels, pieces of charred wood, and a stone slab with a primitive hunting scene with several figures and animals. Valmin thought this area was a temenos. In the middle of Room 5, which was small, there were two stones which may have been column bases. Along one of the walls of this room, too, were a stone bench and fragments of pithoi. Pottery and a fragment of an idol of an unspecified type were found on the bench. The layer, which was 0.60 m thick, contained animal bones and sherds. About 200 fragments of pottery were discovered in this room. Half of them were kitchen-ware, and there were also 14 fragments of cups, 6 fragments of amphorae, and 3 vertical handles of other vessels. In Valmin's opinion, this room may have been used as a megaron, a kitchen or a cult place.[14] Elsewhere it is described as a small shrine.[15] There were workshops in the vicinity.

Late Bronze Age

At Akrotiri, on Thera, a house at Xeste 3 which has been dated to LM IA may, according to the excavator, be a public building or (what we suggest) a house with a sanctuary. A rather narrow entrance leads to an anteroom (Fig. 307) with a slab-covered floor and stone benches along the walls. Marinatos[16] believed it was a public building because there were very few remains of private habitation. Vessels were found only in the small room 6. Recently, finds were also reported from the small rooms unexcavated by Marinatos. A broad staircase led to the first floor. The walls were decorated with frescoes depicting what was described by Marinatos as 'pointed mountain peaks of pre-explosion Thera'. One of the peaks was depicted as a volcano. Other fragments depicted birds captured in nets against a marshy landscape. There was also a 'White Lady' head. Near the small rooms (6,7,8) there were other ones (9,10,11) which were partly excavated by Marinatos. An adjoining room is described as an adyton or a lustral basin (Figs. 191-2), the only one known outside Crete (see p. 133 for description). The big basement room (4), which was rather dark and the biggest in the house, was poor in finds. Near the south entrance is a low slab 1 m long with a shallow depression in the middle. This slab was probably an altar. A polythyron (not indicated on the plan, see Fig. 307) leads to a room with big windows (2) facing the street (Fig. 307). In the south-east corner of Room 2 a bathtub larnax was found partly excavated.

The frescoes, which had fallen down from the first floor, depicted monkeys behaving like humans: one appears to be a musician and the other seems to be about to cut off the head of a spotted sand-viper. Further on there was an elderly female figure, the Mistress Goddess,

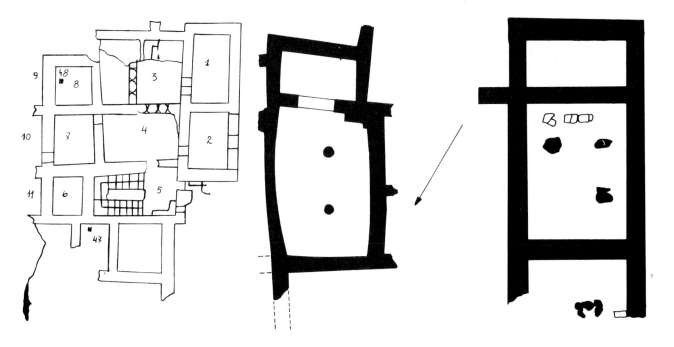

307. Thera Akrotiri. Xeste 3. S. Marinatos, Excavations at Thera VII (1976), Pl. 13.

308. Asine. Sanctuary. SympSanct, 92, Fig. 1.

309. Mouriatada. Plan of a temple? Ergon 1960, Fig. 166.

flanked by a monkey and a griffin. Nearby, on both sides, were young maidens in splendid festive attire, gathering crocuses into baskets. They were probably attendants of the goddess. This scene represents a festive celebration and a procession making its way to a sanctuary whose façade was adorned with spiral decoration and was surmounted by horns of consecration. The house is exceptionally well built, with good ashlar work. As it is not completely excavated, many points are still unsolved. But a cult significance of some kind is not improbable.

Nearly all our evidence about domestic cult places dates from the later stage of Late Bronze Age. That is the period to which we must assign the sanctuary discovered in House G13-14 (Fig. 308) at Asine.[17] The building is situated in a street in the middle of the town, in the area nearest to the bay. The cult room is a relatively large one (7 × 5 m) and two column bases were discovered inside it. The floor was of firmly tramped-down mud. No entrance was found to this building, but there may have been one on the side next to the street. Behind the shrine a small cell was found which probably could be reached only through the shrine. In one corner of the main room was a bench made of rough stone slabs, its length being 1.60 m, its width 0.50 m, and its height 0.57 m. Just beside this bench[18] were figurines and clay vessels as well as a stone axe (height 0.08 m). Part of a kernos discovered here is the most interesting find, although others included two-handled amphorae, goblets, and a kylix. A large jug found here had its base broken off. It must have been done deliberately; the base was found on the stone bench, while the neck of the vessel was discovered between two stones. Beyond doubt this must have been a libation vessel.

Of all the figurines referred to above, five were votive offerings, while only one head, 0.12 m in height, may have been part of a cult idol. Trace of white paint were found on the face, and red paint on the eyes, mouth and hair. The figure depicted by the artist is that of an elderly woman with a long chin,[19] who seems to be the Lady of Asine. The head was placed on a pole (there is an opening at the bottom of the head for fixing it). The stone axe may have been an object that was actually used — e.g. it may have been a domestic object brought here as an offering — or it may have formed part of the sacred furnishings.

Another shrine was found at Berbati (Prosymna).[20] During the MH period the dead were buried on a terrace where a house was built later, but from LH I onwards this area was used solely for domestic purposes. From the courtyard one passes into the house, which was built in LH IIIA, and which survived up to the end of LH IIIB. In one room (IX) a stone bench and a hearth were found. This was the main dwelling-room. West of it were two chambers which could have been a chapel and a repository. One of them (VIII) measured 4.70 × 1.50-2.10 m and the other (VII) measured 4.00 × 0.50 m. On a stone bench in the chapel stood an amphora dating from LH IIIA/B, a ladle with a hole in the handle, a thin, strong brick slab 0.23 m long, and four statuettes of the ordinary type, dating from LH III. In the neighbouring room there was a small pit. Near it stood a chalice and part of a figurine from LH III.

At the Lake Kopais (which probably dried up in LH III) there is a rocky island ringed round with a defence wall, with a palace at Gla (Arne). Excavations which began in 1955 came upon a marketplace, or 'agora', adjacent to the palace on the south side. According to Threpsiadis, there was a cult room, unearthed in 1962,[21] in the western row of rooms in building 'Z'. The only information published so far about this room is that it was lined with stone slabs. It is not known if any cult objects were discovered. The group of rooms discovered there can be dated to LH IIIB. At the 'agora' stone horns of consecration were also found.

On a fortified hill near Mouriatadha (Elleniko) in Messenia there was a settlement of LH III B date. A large building on the summit was uncovered and further down near a tower of the fortifications was a megaron-type construction said to be a sanctuary, with dimensions of 16.80 × 7.85 m. It was divided into three rooms. In the main room column bases were found, but no trace of a hearth (Fig. 309). The site was heavily eroded and therefore few finds survived.[22]

Shrines at the defence walls

The supposition that there were once cult places in niches of the defence walls of Mycenaean citadels arose many years ago when the citadel of Tiryns[23] was the subject of investigation. More recently, niches in Mycenae have also been suspected of having been used for similar purposes.[24] But this was no more than a supposition, for in places thought to be scenes of religious practices, no cult finds have ever been found. Now, however, the latest excavations in the lower citadel of Tiryns would seem to confirm that cult places did exist in the defence walls.[25] For it seems probable that the gateway leading to the fortress at Mycenae was under the protection of a divinity in the form of an aniconic image — this was a column (Fig. 286), one of the cult forms of sacred trees, and therefore itself a divinity. Thus the possibility that there was a sanctuary in small niches near the main entrance and near the Postern Gate at Mycenae cannot be ruled out. Its existence was connected with the cult of the divinity who guarded the entrance to the house (see above p. 143). It must be remembered that the practice of worshipping divinities in cult places near the Gate to the citadel, or in the defence walls, was very widespread in classical Greece and also in the Middle East.[26]

Cult places in the public squares and courtyards

The existence of open-air cult places in the settlements is best confirmed by the discoveries in the Sacred Area at Mycenae (see above, p. 174), and by the frescoes from Thera.[27] Nevertheless the material evidence of the existence of such places is very scarce. Aside from the two open-air cult places in the settlement on Samos (still unpublished), it is not until we come to the end of the Bronze Age at Pylos,[28] or to the period LH IIIC at Tiryns[29] that we find altars proving that divinities were worshipped in the courtyards.

General discussion

In general we have to say that studies of domestic sanctuaries, of cult places in defence walls and in public squares and courtyards are still in their infancy; this is due to the fact that little progress has been made so far on the research on towns. Suffice to say that the most important examples of temples — those in Keos, at Mycenae, Phylakopi and Tiryns — were only discovered within the last twenty years.

The most salient characteristic of this work is the paucity of evidence, which may be taken as objective proof as to the existence of a cult place. The use to which many of the places cited above were put is uncertain. At Lithares, Eutresis and Malthi traces of possible EH and MH sanctuaries are meagre, and by no means definite. Thus the point of our discussion has been mainly to make clear the foundations on which our knowledge of the cult places of those times has been based. Any doubts we have are concerned with the evidence alone. On the other hand it is likely that EH and MH cult places will be discovered at some time in the future (the temple on Keos, we must remember, was built in the MH period). What is more, it is equally certain that there were open and built cult places in the settlements at Eutresis and Malthi. But although we are convinced of this, it must be proved, if archaeology is to be strict discipline, and not just a collection of ideas based on supposition.

It was not until LM IA that clear traces of cult practices (Minoan in character, as a matter of fact) appeared on Thera. The horns of consecration and double axe stands at Akrotiri were not discovered in sacred places; their sacred context is unknown. Apart from those two categories finds, we have none that definitely confirm the existence of a sanctuary there, with the possible exception of stone kernoi. But both the fresco from Xeste 3 and the representations on the miniature fresco from the West House testify to the existence of cult buildings surmounted by horns of consecration, as well as of sacred enclosures (in the town area). Might one surmise that the entire house at Xeste 3 was used as a temple?

In mainland Greece, there is a large gap in the evidence concerning the late Bronze Age, for (except for Samos) not until the end of the Mycenaean age (that is, LH IIIB and C) do we find what are probably or definitely altars, cult niches in the defence walls, and domestic shrines. In this field, too, we are on very uncertain ground; it is therefore better to assert the probable existence of such categories of cult places, than it is to try to reconstruct the past on the basis of surviving, published evidence. Only at Asine is there a building about whose function we can be certain, and the objects discovered there — the bench inside the building, the cult idol, the figurines, the vessels, the stone axe (probably used for magic?) indicate that the domestic sanctuaries had the typical furnishings better known to us from the Mycenaean temples and Cretan sanctuaries. At this stage it would be premature to attempt to give an account of the history of the domestic sanctuaries in mainland Greece.

CATALOGUE XV
Domestic Sanctuaries

1. Asine, House G. Sacred objects and votive offerings are dated to LH IIIC1.
   O. Frödin, A. Persson, *Asine* (1938), 63, 74ff, 298, 308; Hägg, MKult, 44; Hägg, SanctSymp, 91ff.
2. Berbati, two rooms probably used for a religious purpose. LH III period.
   AA (1938), 553; BullLund (1937/8), 59ff; *Arkeologiska forskninger och fund* (1952), 32ff.
3. Eutresis. A House used in EH II may have served as a cult place but its religious purpose is uncertain.
   H. Goldman, *Excavations at Eutresis in Boetia* (1932), 17f.
4. Gla, citadel fortress. A room next to the 'agora' is referred to as a sanctuary, but no cult finds were reported there. LH III period.
   PAE (1958), 38ff; (1959), 21ff; (1960), 23ff.
5. Lithares, near Thebes. 17 clay figurines of bulls were found in a domestic sanctuary or a terracotta workshop dated to EM III.
   AD, 24 (1969), 28ff; AAA, 5 (1972), 467ff.
6. Malthi, Messenia. Different places in the settlement were interpreted as sanctuaries, but the finds do not prove it convincingly.
   N. Valmin, *Swedish Messenia Expedition* (1938), *passim*.
7. Mouriatadha, Messenia. A house in the settlement was interpreted as a sanctuary, but no cult objects were found.
   PAE (1960), 203ff.
8. Thera, Akrotiri. Xeste 3. One room, close to the lustral basin, may have served to religious purposes.
   S. Marinatos, *Excavations at Thera* (1976), VII, 26.

CATALOGUE XVI
Cult places in the public squares and in the courtyards

1. Araksos (Achaia) beside the walls of the Kalorgias fortress. Excavations revealed an altar that may have been used in the LH period.
   Ergon (1963), 186ff; AD, 18 (1963), *Chronika*, 111ff; BCH, 86 (1964), 760ff.
2. Pylos, in the courtyard of a house near the palace there is an altar dating from the LH IIIB period.
   C. Blegen, M. Rawson, *The Palace of Nestor at Pylos* (1966), I, 301ff; Hägg, MKult, 42.
3. Tiryns, in the middle of the courtyard there is a round altar which was probably used in the LH period.
   Dörpfeld, in H. Schliemann (ed.), *Tiryns* (1886), 389ff; A. Frickenhaus, *Tiryns*, I, 6f, 31ff; K. Müller, *Tiryns*, III 1, 136f, 199; AM, 30 (1905), 152; RE, 6, A:2 (1937), 1465; Yavis, Alt, 36; Hägg, MKult, 42.

XII
Conclusion

IN UNDERTAKING a study of the cult places in the Aegean we first had to define the term 'cult place'. Since no such definition could be found in the literature on the Aegean civilisation it was necessary to review these places in the Aegean, as well as comparative places elsewhere, to decide what their most important characteristics were. The conclusion was that, as in the history of religion, the definition of a cult place should take into account three elements: topography, cult practices and religious beliefs. The adaptation of this approach proved fruitful in its results. In the first place, the conception of the whole work became crystallised. Our aim was to spotlight those three characteristics with regard to every category of cult place. For the actual place of worship tells us the most about the kind of religion practised there. It illuminates many complex phenomena in the religious sphere, and reveals manifold instances of the crossing and intermingling of secular elements with elements of a religious, empirically unverifiable nature. The cult place, besides belonging to the domain of religion, was at the same time a key element in the social and economic sphere, since the priests in charge of the cult place also came to be in charge of many aspects of society. It was at the cult places that the gods of nature revealed themselves to human beings — consequently they were places of importance, since the benevolence of the gods depended on the priests' celebration of the rites and on their skill in bringing rain and averting natural catastrophes. In this sense the cult place exerted an influence — sometimes a decisive one — on the economic development of society. Some cult places, especially the very popular ones, became subordinated to the interests of the secular rulers. They were used to sanction and spread the idea of the divine right of kings. Probably in every age the struggle for power has been paralleled by attempts to bring the places of worship under secular control.

When this general framework had been decided upon, our next step was to study all the available information — the archaeological remains, the pictorial art and the Mycenaean script. We also sought information in other disciplines (such as geology, speleology, botany, and zoology), since they could lead to a better interpretation of the archaeological material.

Obviously when one studies a subject, one's understanding of it is much fuller if one reviews the research done on it. But strangely, no history of research on Aegean civilisation, or even on any of the periods of Aegean civilisation, has yet appeared. Some of the archaeologists and historians who have written on the more general topics have preceded their presentation with a brief review of past excavations or of the literature, but there is not a single publication wholly devoted to the history of Aegean studies. Our intention was to trace the history of research back to its beginnings. Another of our aims was to study the links between the history of the cult places, the great political and cultural events of the times, and religion. Of course it has not been possible to achieve all these aims fully. But at any rate an endeavour has been made to show that the beginning of an interest in this subject can be traced as far back as Antiquity. From Antiquity onwards interest in this field continued, and kept expanding, and from time to time exploration of the past in the Aegean world became intertwined with various political aims or cultural trends. The emergence of a new branch of scholarship — Aegean archaeology — towards the end of the nineteenth century did not indicate a clean break from the era of philological studies and surface investigations. On the contrary, even at the beginning of the twentieth century, archaeologists were still working mainly on problems that had first been formulated by the classical philologists. For the sake of clarity, and to make the links between ancient and modern times better understood, we have distinguished six periods of interest in the Aegean world. We have endeavoured to prove that interest in cult places (and even in pre-Greek religion) can be traced as far back as Antiquity, and also — as one realises when one follows the clues — that the very people who themselves were active in the field of religion were the ones who stimulated an objective, scientific approach to these matters. In the first half of the first millenium B.C., the Greeks used to visit the cult places, and especially the grottoes (which were supposed to date back to heroic times), for purely religious reasons. But later on — probably in Hellenistic times — their motives changes, sometimes becoming scientific and exploratory. We have a fine example of this in the history of investigations into the tomb of Zeus. Views expressed in Antiquity stimulated the interest of scholars of the early Renaissance (early fifteenth century), who made an important advance by trying to locate the tomb of Zeus on a high mountain near Candia. Investigations of this kind — attempts to locate the grave of the divine son of Kronos — went on for several centuries. Many names, such as those of Buondelmonti, Radziwiłł, and Savary, are associated with investigations of this type. The time of the Turkish occupation shows us most clearly how much the course of archaeological investigations was influenced by political events — there is a similar connection between the expansion of geographical discoveries, and economic and political expansion. It is highly probable that some of this interest in archaeology — especially the field work — had a political or military aim as well as a scientific one. With the arrival of the early nineteenth century, when part of Greece attained independence, and when the disintegration of the Ottoman Empire became a fact (and in particular the weakening of Turkish power in Crete as a result of the independence movements), there was a rich harvest of field discoveries that were the antecedents of the archaeological excavations. There was even a large crop of valuable theories and skill in field observations reached a state of near-perfection. At this time, too, we have the first cases of conclusions being drawn from 'prehistoric' (Pre-Hellenic) pottery.

Then an increased interest in ancient Greek texts caused an explosion of archaeological exploration. The best example of this is the search for the tomb of Zeus. During the last quarter of the nineteenth century the main ambition of many scholars was to relate passages in the Greek texts to given places. Explorations were set in hand which led to the discovery of pre-Hellenic cult places, especially caves and peak sanctuaries, in other words, traces of a civilisation whose existence had been at most suspected, rather than known for certain. Towards the end of the nineteenth century, too, attempts were made to discover the main outlines of Mycenaean religion, but these attempts ended in failure (Reichel).

The turning-point in archaeological research came at the beginning of the twentieth century, with the work of Evans. Despite the tremendous contribution he made his work nevertheless nowadays bears the stamp of a past era, particularly in his predilection for following up the ideas of past scholars. On the other hand, it was he who laid the foundations for our knowledge of religion and of cult places — and his work, after suitable amendments, became the basis for all further studies of religion in the Aegean. Although it is true that in the first quarter of the twentieth century some scholars, such as Dussaud, used a general approach, most scholars were interested in narrow fields of archaeological data and in particular excavation sites. The year 1927 was a watershed in the study of Aegean civilisation for in that year Nilsson published an important work which opened the way to the systematisation of Aegean religions. The historical method, that is, the attempt to demonstrate a connection between economic and social development, and ideology now came to the fore. This was also the time when archaeologists began to direct their attention to sources other than historical ones — for instance, the stalactites in the grottoes, and their place in religion. These various trends made little mark, but in 1950 there was a revival of interest in Aegean civilisation. This was due to several causes. First, an immense quantity of new discoveries were made, both of new sites and of new objects of pictorial art. Second, Aegean scripts began to be deciphered (Linear B). And third, archaeologists began to draw on non-archaeological sources (e.g. speleology). About the same time, basic work was done on the data pertaining to certain groups of sanctuaries.

A very important stage of this work was taken up with eliminating the unreliable finds, classifying the relics anew, and determining their importance. In the course of this work, we settled the question of the criteria to be used in determining whether or not a given place should be regarded as a cult place. It is our contention that sacred objects and votive offerings are the only reliable indicators of Bronze Age cult places in Greece, and perhaps even in many other lands as well. Other features, such as the topography or type of architecture, are nearly always of minor importance, although they will always play an important and relatively useful part as supplementary aids in the further classification of cult places already defined as such by the presence of cult finds. The shape of a building, its ground plan, its situation in the settlement, its place in a group of buildings or as part of a private house, are of no significance at all in distinguishing sanctuaries from secular buildings. Attempts to take features of the construction — such as the shape of a room, or the presence of a pillar, or the position of a building or room — as specially typical of sanctuaries have failed, as is demonstrated for instance in the chapter on the 'sacred crypts'. The method of construction is no guide, either. Indeed, it seems quite probable that the cult buildings or rooms were built more poorly and more carelessly than ordinary rooms or store-rooms. The furnishing of the interior (the presence of stone benches, the decoration of the walls with paintings, etc.) cannot be altogether relied on, either, to differentiate between shrines and ordinary secular rooms. Nor do the shape and constructional elements of shrine's interior seem to have been bound by hard and fast rules in the Aegean civilisation, for the simple reason that sanctuaries and temples inside the settlements were not of the greatest importance to the community. It was only later, when they rose to a place of prominence in the life of the community, that the accumulated experience of past generations crystallised in the form of canons and strict rules governing the shape of certain types of buildings and rooms. So in the Aegean world certain secular buildings such as palaces and megarons, and some rooms used for a special purpose, such as lustral basins, were built in a special shape, with the result that by examining the shape, or even by looking at the ground plan, the archaeologist can say what purpose a building or room was used for, even if no moveable objects were discovered, since by that time their shape had become typical. But the shape and internal appearance of the shrines in the private houses and palace sanctuaries had not yet become fixed. As time went on, certain rooms in the houses and palaces began to follow a fixed pattern because they were always used for the same secular purpose, but any of them could be used as a cult place, since in the settlements the cult places had no great importance attached to them.

To repeat, the cult or votive objects seem to be of fundamental importance in identifying the cult places. All other features, such as the stalactites or pools of water in the caves, or the relief or topography of the peak sanctuaries, are of minor significance. Of course single sacred objects were kept not only in the cult places but elsewhere as well. So groups of sacred and votive objects (not just single ones) have to be found in a place before it can be regarded as a holy spot. In our analysis of the material evidence, we kept to this rule — in other words, what we have done is to question the old hypotheses. We examined the finds once more, and in the end we illustrated how difficult it is to decide if crypts were sanctuaries or not. Having gone over the material evidence and weighed all the known arguments once more, we are convinced that what have generally been known as sacred crypts were often just ordinary domestic premises, some used for living in or storing things, and some whose purpose is not clear. A few of these have proved to be actual cult places. A great deal of our work, therefore, was taken up with deciding which of the possible cult places could definitely be said to be such.

A large number of places that have been termed domestic and palace sanctuaries also aroused doubt. The next step was to study the pictorial art in detail. The most important part of this attempt consisted of determining how these scenes could illuminate various problems connected with the cult places.

Another important step was the attempt we made to classify the cult places. We propose a distinction be drawn between the sacred places outside the settlements, and those inside the settlements. Into the first category, then, come the caves, the peak sanctuaries, the sacred enclosures, the spring sanctuaries, etc. Into the second category come the temples and domestic sanctuaries, the lustral basins, the spring sanctuaries and the sacred areas in the squares and courtyards, etc.

Only by studying the archaeological and iconographic evidence in greater detail can we say whether this material is sufficiently large, and sufficiently well studied, to give us insight into the nature of the cult places. Some finds are more revealing than others. Our knowledge about certain types of cult places (particularly the caves, the peak sanctuaries, and the sacred enclosures) has so far been rather limited, but by examining the actual sites and studying the relics in the museums, we have been able to answer many basic questions. Other finds, especially the domestic sanctuaries, to which we devoted more attention, have given us broader insight into some problems. Finally, there are other groups — such as the remains of sacred enclosures in the squares and courtyards — about which we know little at present. We merely know that they existed, but for more information about them we shall have to wait until some future date. The main problem in this field today is to estimate the value of the archaeological evidence and to assess to what extent it can be of use to the historian.

The representational art is important because it supplements the information that can be gained from the archaeological finds. The scenes, which vary in size and technique, contain many symbols which were fully comprehensible to the peoples of those times, but which are frequently incomprehensible to us. One question which arises is whether a scene's realism, and attention to detail, depends on whether it is sacred or secular. The answer is negative. In the whole of Aegean art, the precision with which a scene is depicted, and the presence of descriptive detail depends only on two factors: the main current followed by the art of the period (naturalism or schematicism), and, above all, the size, etc., of the object on which the scene was depicted. Both sacred and secular scenes on wall paintings or steatite rhyta (from the period MM II to LM II) are, in the nature of things, richer in detail. They provide more reliable evidence about everyday life (including some aspects of the cult places) than scenes dating from the same period but executed on tiny glyptic works where simplification and schematic treatment were necessitated by the size, shape, material and even purpose of the object, and where the artist was virtually compelled to express what he wanted to say in symbolic terms, as we can see, for example, from the many scenes on rings. In the case of glyptic art in particular, where the purpose was to depict a cult scene by symbols, objects belonging to the sphere of material culture were only indicated very sketchily since they were not important to an understanding of the scene. Thus the amount of information we can get from an iconographic source depends very much on the category the evidence belongs to. Each chapter of this book deals with a separate category of cult place, seen from three aspects: the topography of the site, the cult rituals and the religious beliefs. Although a place can be recognised as a cult site only if votive offerings or cult objects are found there, nevertheless the most salient and characteristic feature of many cult places outside the settlements was in effect the natural setting in which the rites were performed.

In the case of the sacred caves the general atmosphere was of immense significance, for the mystery of the underground chambers, the grotesque shapes, the murky depths, the sound of dropping water, the presence of stalactites and stalagmites and other rocks in the shape of human beings and animals, were certain to inspire awe. They may have given rise to a whole series of myths which were especially associated with the mysteries performed there. At the moment, however, we know very little of the details. The water in the caves was much colder than the temperature outside. For this reason, and also because it was believed to possess miraculous properties that could work cures and ease childbirth, it was held in special honour. In most of the sacred caves, these pools of water were among the most important natural cult characteristics of the grotto. It is not true, however, that the grottoes were cult places solely because of the pools. Many other caves had water, too, but were not used as cult places. The choice of a grotto as a cult place could equally well depend on other natural features, such as the presence of stalactites, or the mysterious atmosphere of the cave, or even on other extraneous factors, such as sheer chance, that is factors lying outside the range of the historian of Aegean religion.

On the whole, inside the sacred caves there was no need for any structures, so the only signs of building work are the walls around the stalactites, or the altars (although the latter were sometimes also made of single large pieces of stone hewn more or less to the right shape). These structures first appeared a long time after MM I. Most of the walls date from MM III (Psychro) or LM (Amnissos and Ida).

In some famous grottoes, such as those at Amnissos or Kamares, the finds consisted almost exclusively of pottery vessels, whereas in other caves there were numerous bronze and even gold objects, or objects made of stone. It should be noted that the distribution of these finds was due to chance, not to anything else. Most of the vessels found in the grottoes were ordinary, everyday ones, but some were richly decorated and were used for carrying offerings of agricultural produce, such as grain (e.g. at Kamares) and other plants. Votive figurines made of bronze or clay (e.g. at Psychro), representing human beings or else domestic and sometimes even wild animals, were frequent finds.

Other votive offerings, in the form of everyday objects (*in corpore* or simulacra), or weapons or tools, give us a great deal of information about many facets of life among the Minoans. These votive offerings were usually placed in the cracks and fissures of the rocks, or fixed onto the stalactites, or hung on the trees before the caves. The cult equipment (such as offering tables, etc.), as well as sacred emblems (especially gold or bronze double axes not meant for use) and horns of consecration were relatively frequent finds. No anthropomorphic cult statues, however, were found, but concretions shaped like a pillar or a human being or an animal, and occasionally surrounded by a stone wall (e.g. at Amnissos), were undoubtedly sometimes used as cult images.

It can now be proved that some grottoes attracted pilgrims from a distance, perhaps even from all over Crete (e.g. the grotto at Psychro), whereas others were only of local influence. It was only on the occasion of the few holy days that the pilgrims made their way to the cult places. They did not go there in the winter, since many of the grottoes were inaccessible then because of snow. Autumn was the time for such pilgrimages and the season for mysterious rites inaugurating the birth and death cycle of the vegetation.

The deity — or, rather, rather, the many deities — worshipped in the grottoes were chthonic divinities which, at the latest in the early Bronze Age, took on an identity separate from that of the Great Goddess. In the Neolithic period, for example, the deities in the grottoes had possibly been multi-functional, whereas as time went on each function became the domain of a separate divinity. For example, the god of war was worshipped at Arkalochori; another goddess, similar to the Greek Eileithyia, inhabited the cave at Amnissos. But the most widespread of all was the cult of the ancient Great Goddess, who had a great many different functions.

Most previous works on the origin of the sacred caves have applied the simple formula of evolutionism, and have assumed that the grottoes developed from places which were used for dwelling in to places which were used for burying the dead, and finally to cult places. Not all the grottoes passed through these three stages or functions; sometimes their development was quite different. Although many archaeologists believe that the Cretan caves were not yet used as cult places during the Neolithic period, it is possible that some of them, especially those that were difficult of access and uninhabitable, were already being used as such. It is also quite possible that in some grottoes (e.g. at Kamares or Amnissos) the earliest relics found their way there because the grottoes were visited on some special, sacred occasions. Thus it is highly probable that some caves were used as places of worship as soon as they were discovered by people. Yet right up to MM III the sacred caves were seldom visited, and played no special part in the lives of the Cretans.

As far as the peak sanctuaries are concerned, one of the elements which had an important effect on their development is their topography. With a few exceptions the sanctuaries were not big. They were, according to the experts, most probably situated in zones where fruit trees could gain a hold. On the whole, however, the vegetation was very sparse. Any trees that did exist were few in number and usually dwarfed, since the strong winds stunted their growth. Although we have little information about the shape of the peak sanctuaries it can be assumed that sometimes they were either rectangular or oval, although in the majority of cases their shape was irregular. Only the more important peak sanctuaries were surrounded by stone walls. The less important ones had their boundaries marked by stones. Some sanctuary buildings date from MM I, but others were erected not earlier than MM III. There were some complicated cult structures, with terraces and altars (Jouktas) or sacred screens. The shrines consisted of several rooms; stone benches were built along the inner walls, and the walls themselves were plastered. Like the domestic sanctuaries these holy buildings were meant to be the deity's home. They were also used for housing the objects used in the sacred rites, and, on occasion, the votive offerings, as well as aniconic images (e.g. baetyls). Probably people believed that deities lived in the shrines, although there is no evidence of anthropomorphic images having been kept there. As in many Greek temples, in Crete the sacred rites were performed outside the shrine. We know what the façades of the shrines were like from the sealstones and paintings — these façades were either in one part, or tripartite. The façade was very important, like the Egyptian Gate of Heaven, since it symbolised the power of the divinity. It was ornamented with cult symbols such as sacred horns, etc., and — the most important feature — at the very top there was an aniconic image of the divinity in the form of a stylised mountain. It is likely that the façade of the shrine was the background against which the cult rituals took place, although examination of the various sites, such as that at Pyrgos, shows that in front of the façade there was not much space for a crowd of worshippers. In front of the building, or at the sides of it, there were free-standing high wooden pillars.

Inside the temenos there were altars of various kinds: some were made of stone and some were merely ordinary fire pits. Stone tables, and instruments of various kinds, such as bronze knives, were frequently used in the ceremonies. Figurines constituted one of the most popular kinds of votive offering. They were usually made of clay, though in exceptional cases of bronze, and represented men and women in supplicating postures, or animals (mainly domestic ones), or beetles.

It is difficult to determine the names of the deities worshipped in the peak sanctuaries but we already know a great deal about their character. Undoubtedly the people believed they ruled the heavens and governed the weather and that, in particular, they could produce rain or strong gales. Another function of these deities was to ensure the welfare of the people and the animals belonging to them. In some sanctuaries the divinities were believed to have the power to make women fertile and to ease them in childbirth, and even to cure the sick. A very important point that can be deduced from the pictorial art is that the goddess on the mountain top, believed to be the ruler of the world, was in the habit of conveying her powers over mundane things to the king, a mere human, who then ruled in her name. This, at any rate, is the interpretation which can be put on a scene depicted on clay impressions of a gold ring found at Knossos where we find the goddess on the mountain top apparently handing over some of her powers to the king, who is standing in a suppliant position before her. This motif — the endowment of the king with divine power — is also to be found in early Greek literary sources and in an Israelite myth. This relationship between the king and the deity, and the patronage of the king by the god, is borne out by other sources as well. For example, it seems probable that the royal throne at Knossos is a symbol of this relationship, for the back of the throne is shaped like a mountain, reminding us of the mountain goddess who was the guardian of the anakt and the defender of the royal authority. From what has been said above it is clear that it was in the interests of both the king and the entire ruling class to foster the development of the peak sanctuaries. Valuable information about the lives and ideas of the ancient Cretans can also be gained from the many clay models of beetles. These beetles do not belong to the species *ocryctes nasicornis* (garden pests) as was generally believed, but to the species *copris hispanus L*, which, after the scarab, is the biggest scaraboid beetle. This species is bound up with the existence of sheep, on whose faeces it feeds. So where sheep are the copris beetle is to be found. Moreover, even if the copris was not regarded as a sacred animal (and we have no proof of this), it must have been regarded as a representative of the goddess who ruled over heaven and earth. In bringing to the cult places models of beetles that usually were much bigger in size than the real live beetle, the supplicants were begging the goddess to multiply their flocks of sheep.

The ceremonies in the peak sanctuaries must have taken place once or twice a year. The priests, watched by a crowd of worshippers, made sacrifices. Bonfires were probably lit and the votive offerings cast into the dying flames. This part of the rites took place to the accompaniment of music, and the goddess was worshipped with dancing as well.

In Crete some cult places were sacred enclosures situated outside the villages and towns. From the archaeological surface research, and to some extent from the pictorial art, we can reconstruct some of the details as to the location, shape (oval, rectangular or polygonal), and size of the enclosures, as well as the kind of vegetation that grew there. Sacred trees, and above all cultivated trees such as the olive and the fig, were probably of prime importance. The enclosures were surrounded by stone walls that cut them off from their surroundings. Another way of marking the boundaries was probably used too — namely, single large stones or isolated trees. The gateway leading into the sacred enclosure was a very important feature, for it symbolised the power of the goddess. Although shrines were not always needed, they were sometimes built in the more important enclosures. Usually these were small, modest buildings consisting of one or two rooms. The cult building's façade, which constituted a single whole or which was tripartite, was very important because of the cult images or sacred emblems that surmounted it. It cannot be denied that the façade was occasionally the setting of cult ceremonies. The shrine was the goddess's dwelling-place, in which her image was kept, at least from the Bronze Age onwards, although the earliest anthropomorphic images date from LM III. Of course we have no reason to doubt that earlier on the Cretans believed their goddess lived invisible in the shrine — in which case there may have been a cult image, although it was not absolutely necessary. The goddess's property, such as the objects used in the rites as well as the votive offerings, was also kept in the shrine.

An altar was another element needed in the sacred enclosure. It was made of stone and was sometimes covered with painted spirals. Pits in the ground were occasionally used as altars, or even ordinary large stones, bare rocks, or the ground itself. On other occasions the altar was simply a bonfire — the votive offerings were cast into the dying embers. The presence of the divinity was symbolised not only by cult images, but also by double axes, vertical pillars or poles, or baetyls. The objects used in the liturgy included vessels, especially rhyta, as well as shell trumpets, which were used to summon the god. Votive offerings in the form of clay vessels containing grain, as well as figurines, etc., were brought to the sacred enclosure.

In the course of the rites, which were sometimes performed in front of the façade of the shrine, the priests or priestesses would offer up the sacrifices. They would also summon the goddess by means of dances, several types of which are known to us. The divinity worshipped in the sacred enclosures was the Great Goddess, and she was worshipped in ceremonies and rites representing the birth and death cycle of the vegetation.

The cult places in the settlements can be divided into two categories: public and private. In the past years more has been published on the public cult places. Evidence suggests that sometimes these public cult places consisted of a temple or a sacred enclosure in the town or village square. The temples differed little from shrines or ordinary houses. They were small, detached buildings (e.g. at Gournia and Mallia) to which every inhabitant of the settlement had access. They were the abodes of the divinities, and often contained cult images (e.g. at Gournia and Karphi), as well as objects used in the rituals, and votive offerings. The sacred rites were no doubt held in the open space in front of the temple (e.g. at Karphi), or in a nearby agora (e.g. at Gournia). Occasionally there were sacred enclosures in the squares, too. Their most important feature was the altar, which was sometimes surmounted with horns of consecration (as at Gournia). The temples were inhabited by the goddess of the town or village, who had all the attributes of the Household Goddess.

The private sanctuaries, especially those in the palaces, call for a separate and thorough discussion. Many scholars have conjectured that in all the Cretan palaces the entire west wing was intended for ceremonial and religious or official purposes. But although the presence of ceremonial apartments is certain it is doubtful whether there were many sacred rooms here. The most important evidence comes from Knossos. Apart from the 'Temple Repository' and the sanctuary above it, the main argument for the view that the west wing of the palace was a sacred and a state place centred on the area forming the Throne Room. Two or three rooms around the Throne Room including the lustral basin were used for cult purposes. It is difficult to determine whether they were simply royal apartments surrounded by cult rooms in which the throne, its back in the form of a stylised hill, symbolised the fact that the king was under the protection of the goddess, or whether they constituted a sanctuary complex. In other palaces too, e.g. at Mallia, there is no real evidence that the western wing had cult rooms. On the other hand it is certainly true that in the western part some rooms may have been used by the royal family both for living in and for official purposes, but that in exceptional cases (e.g. in Knossos) some rooms may have been used as shrines as well.

Another widespread view is that many other rooms in the Cretan palaces were used for sacred purposes, that is, as shrines, sacred crypts, etc., but this view is doubtful. Shrines in the palaces (together with the lustral basins) are comparatively few in number, and they are modest places generally situated in the side wings, which clearly means that they were for private use. These shrines were the habitations of the Household Goddess, whose presence was sometimes (certainly in LM IIIA) indicated by cult images. Occasionally the shrines also contained the goddess's emblems (horns of consecration and double axes), as well as objects used in the rituals and votive offerings.

The shrines belonging to the private houses were quite modest. Sometimes they were situated indoors, which is only natural. On rare occasions the domestic shrine was a more or less isolated room looking onto the main courtyard. Possibly, then, in exceptional cases, when the façade of the shrine looked onto an open space, it was richly decorated and formed the background for the cult ceremonies. A study of these shrines and temples shows that only important buildings or rooms, such as palaces, megarons, or bathrooms, acquired in the course of time a definite shape, so that ultimately their use could be inferred from the shape of their ground plan. None of the other buildings, or, in particular, rooms used for sacred purposes, acquired a special shape of its own, since these rooms had no special part in the lives of the users. This is of course because the principal cult places were situated not inside the settlements but in natural spots out in the country, such as caves, or on mountain peaks, or in the middle of the woods or fields, or on the banks of streams.

The cult places on the Greek mainland constitute an exceptionally difficult problem since the number of relics is extremely small. At the present time it is easiest to draw conclusions from the sacred enclosures. In the case of other cult places, such as the caves, high places and domestic sanctuaries, one can do little more than describe the excavated sites. On the mainland, as in Crete, the sacred enclosures were situated outside the settlements. But although they were sometimes located on hilltops on the whole they have little in common with the peak sanctuaries of the Cretan type and so we use the term high places for them. Most, however, were situated on the sides of hills. Very little is known about the size of the sacred enclosures — perhaps with the exception of the one at Delphi-Marmaria. But we know rather more about the kind of vegetation that grew there. Cultivated trees, such as olives and figs, which were regarded as sacred, grew in the sacred enclosures. They were surrounded by walls of various kinds, or their boundaries were denoted by means of stones or trees. The gateway leading into the enclosure was imposing, although we can judge only from the indirect evidence provided by the gateway to the citadel at Mycenae or the façade of the Tomb of Agamemnon. Shrines were not necessarily built in the sacred enclosures, although we have evidence that sometimes they did exist. From the gold plaque found at Mycenae it can be argued that the façade of the cult building was tripartite. It can also be presumed that, as in the cult places in Crete, the façade formed the background of the sacred rites. There was probably always an altar, usually made of stone. Altars of other types were sometimes used as well — a stone used for this purpose was found at Delphi-Marmaria, for example. The most important feature of the sacred enclosure, however, was the sacred tree, which was sometimes surrounded by a wall. The shrines in the sacred enclosures were no doubt used for storing baetyls and cult images (so far no statues have been found), as well as objects used in the sacred rites and votive offerings. The gem carvings and frescoes tell us about the processions and dances forming part of the ceremonies that were held in honour of deities such as the Great Goddess. One of these deities can be identified with Posidaon, who is mentioned in the Linear B tablets from Pylos. These tablets, which are concerned with the presentation of offerings to cult places not situated in the palaces, lend support to a conclusion reached on the basis of the archaeological finds and the representational art, namely, that some of the most important cult places on the Greek mainland were situated in the countryside, that is away from the towns and villages.

Although we know the caves on the Greek mainland were used as cult places in the Bronze Age, we have little idea of how they functioned for the simple reason that the evidence is too scarce.

Rather more is known about the temples but little is known about the domestic shrines. At Keos and at Mycenae we know there were temple complexes with altars, open-air spaces and several cult buildings. It is also interesting to note the connection between the temple area and some economic activity. Shrines in the palaces are very rare. Two shrines which are in better condition (at Asine and Berbati), and which served as domestic sanctuaries represent only the final phase of the Hellenic culture on the Greek mainland.

The origin of the cult places in Greece is shrouded in mystery. Despite the imposing progress that has been made in research on the earlier periods such as the Palaeolithic, not much is known about the cult places were. But at the moment there is no need, really, to go so far back, since as yet there is no proof of cultural continuity between the Mesolithic and the neolithic periods. In early Neolithic times communities already existed whose economy was based on agriculture and stockbreeding, as well as on hunting and gathering. Although our knowledge of the religion of that era comes nearly exclusively from clay figurines, we cannot ignore the fact that religion in those days was firmly connected with nature and the divinity worshipped was the Great Goddess, who, people believed, could by her magic improve their crops, increase their flocks and herds, and bring them success in hunting. It is almost certain that the magic rites must have been performed in places consecrated to the gods. In this case we can presume the existence of sacred enclosures — a presumption that stems from the cult of trees and branches that was so much a part of the culture of the Bronze Age. Although there is no trace of these earliest cult places, there is evidence to show that other natural cult places, especially the caves, can be traced back to the Neolithic age. It is also almost certain that in the early Neolithic period the tribal organisation must have had an efficient system of authority. In Nea Nikomedeia we see that the biggest house in the whole village, which can be termed the Chieftain's House, was not only the ruler's abode, but also contained a public cult place (a temple) with several clay figurines. It is possible that the head of the tribe was the High Priest as well. It is likely that in most of the houses, especially in northern Greece, clay idols were hung at the side of the fire inside the house — in this sense it can be said that the holy place was in the vicinity of the hearth, which gave out light and warmth and where the food was cooked. Although we know a great deal about the development of primitive society in Greece, little can be said about the appearance of the holy places. Up to the end of the Early Bronze Age the sacred enclosures and the caves were probably the most important tribal cult places, as can be seen from the relics on Crete and the Greek mainland (e.g. at Marathon).

In the early Bronze Age, in Crete especially, there were already signs of economic change, reflected in the emergence of big population centres, which at the same time were centres of social and political life. These changes took place in the Bronze Age, i.e. about 2000 B.C., when a new social system was coming into being, with power concentrated in the palaces situated in the centre of the towns. Yet the traditions that had survived from primitive times were not visibly weakened by the development of palace and urban life. In the Middle Bronze Age there was a steep increase in agriculture and also in stockbreeding, which now became the basis of the economy in Crete. This was the economic and social background which was the setting for the growth of the natural cult places, and in particular between economic development and religion. Since agriculture and stockbreeding were of mounting importance in the life of Crete the Cretans naturally wanted to ensure the best possible conditions for the cultivation of their crops and the rearing of their sheep. But of course in those days scientific methods of saving crops or keeping sheep alive were unknown, so the people of Crete resorted to magic and religion. It was therefore natural that these people, solicitous for their livelihood, should commend themselves to the care of the Goddess of the heavens, the bringer of life-giving rain and strong winds. The importance of cattle and sheep rearing is documented above all by the discovery of a great many clay models of animals and also of beetles (copris hispanus L.) whose existence is completely bound up with the presence of sheep. In MM I, apart from the peak sanctuaries, the traditional cult places of the primitive communities — that is, the sacred enclosures and spring sanctuaries, and, to a lesser extent, perhaps the grottoes as well — must have been of considerable importance.

The spontaneous development of the principal cult places, and of the peak sanctuaries in particular, suffered a check in the period MM III, and the peak sanctuaries, or at any rate the most important ones, came under the control of the king. Their character changed, too: whereas previously the local peasants had worshipped there, the peak sanctuaries now attracted pilgrims from town and country alike — in other words, from the whole population. The king's patronage of the cult places was not disinterested. For as the royal power grew the myth that the king's authority was of divine origin (since it had been conveyed to him by the goddess of the peak sanctuary) was assiduously cultivated. The cult places grew in importance because the esteem in which the goddess was held bolstered the prestige and authority of the king. The first shrines were for the most part built in the peak sanctuaries in MM I. It was probably at this time that another deity began to be worshipped as well — the divine husband of the goddess. In his honour, high pillars were erected before the sanctuaries. These were essential elements in the magic rain-bringing ceremonies. This was the period when the cult finally became institutionalised. Priests took over the cult places and organised the cult ceremonies on high feast days.

At this time, i.e. in MM I, the role of the temples and sanctuaries was no doubt still very modest. Until the end of LM I the domestic sanctuaries were confined to the private houses and palaces, where the cult of the Household Goddess was practised. Although sometimes the courtyards inside the palaces and private houses, and sometimes even theatrical areas, were used for cult purposes, throughout the whole Minoan period the principal cult places were situated outside the inhabited areas, in natural sites out in the country. This was due to the strong survival of traditions coming from a pre-urban society.

The great flowering of Minoan culture was put to a sudden stop by the eruption of a volcano on the island of Santorini in LM I. This tremendous event had an influence on the development of Crete that has not been fully appreciated until now. The magnitude of its economic results are in dispute. Other effects of the eruption on Santorini were even more fundamental; these were far-reaching psychological effects, and changes in the beliefs and ways of thinking of the people. At this time, too, the faith in the power of the deities of heaven who appeared in the peak sanctuaries was severely shaken. These places were partly neglected and, as so often happened in ancient times, the people in their despair turned away from the powerless gods

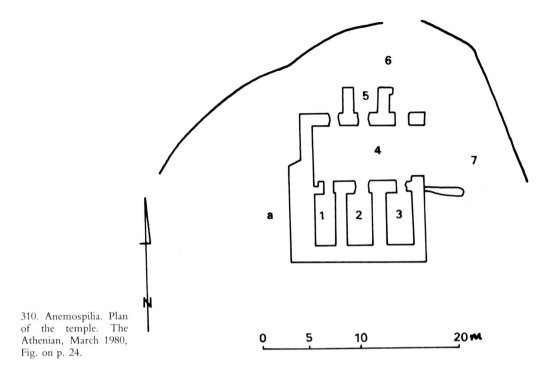

310. Anemospilia. Plan of the temple. The Athenian, March 1980, Fig. on p. 24.

and looked for help from the deities in the caves. We have evidence of this trend in the increased number of sacred caves from MM III onwards. We also know that there was a development of cults in the grottoes. This movement reached its apex in LM I. The Great Goddess, who was supposed to have taken over some of the powers of the Goddess of the Heavens, would, it was hoped, save the inhabitants of Crete from the disasters caused by volcanic eruptions and their after-effects.

The crisis which took place in Crete in LM I was of long duration. LM II finally saw the decline of the palaces, and from LM III onwards a change in social and political organisation took place, resulting in an alteration of the principles of the government. The power of the kings who ruled over various parts of Crete was seriously weakened. Yet despite the disasters that came in the wake of the volcanic eruptions and other events in LM II, even later attempts were being made to bring about a return to the old beliefs. One manifestation of this trend was the attempt to revive the cult of the deities on the mountain peaks, even if only to a minor degree. This trend was most likely due not only to the fact that the inhabitants of Crete had been in the habit of worshipping these deities, but also to the fact that the cult of the deities on the mountain peaks shored up people's belief in the divine origin of the king's power. This myth as to the divine character of the royal authority found expression in the glyptic works of art, as well as in various symbols found in the palaces such as the mountain-shaped back of the throne in the Throne Room at Knossos. But the cult on the mountain peaks never recovered its old glory. The main functions of this cult were taken over in LM III by the sacred caves, as well as the sacred enclosures and spring sanctuaries. In LM III the domestic shrines and temples retained the basic functions that they had acquired earlier.

On the Greek mainland, social, political and economic development was manifestly different from that on Crete. The first thing that strikes us is that a pre-urban system survived right up to MM III, and probably it was only in MM III that power came to be centred on the palaces. The number of palaces grew, especially in Argolid and Messenia. Although there is practically no evidence at all as to the history of the cult places in MH, it may be presumed that the principal cult places continued to be sited not in the towns and villages but in the countryside. These cult places were mainly sacred enclosures, but they may also have been grottoes. As in Crete, on the Greek mainland the cult places in the citadels, villages and towns played a minor role in the lives of the inhabitants. Apart from the domestic sanctuaries, which were separate rooms in private houses or palaces, the cult ceremonies were held round about

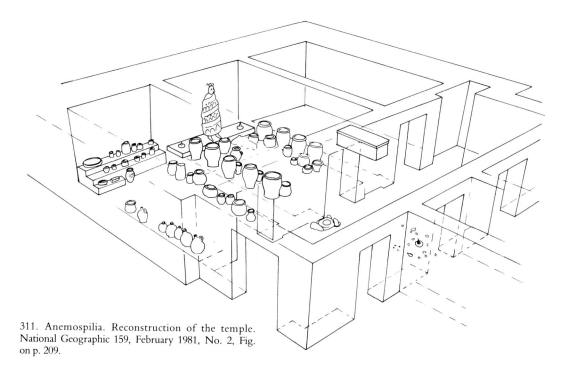

311. Anemospilia. Reconstruction of the temple.
National Geographic 159, February 1981, No. 2, Fig.
on p. 209.

the hearths which sometimes, in the palaces, were of monumental size. Temples (e.g. at Keos) had already been built in the main part of the town.

The decline of Aegean culture towards the end of the Bronze Age did not mean that there was nothing left of the past. Certainly material forms of the cult still survived in the peripheral areas of the Aegean world, e.g. at Prinias, Dreros and Lato. But of course these survivals were not widespread in the Greek period. In Greece proper it is very much harder to trace the survival of elements of the Aegean cults. In all the important Greek cult centres, on the other hand, there are survivals of Mycenaean culture. In some of these centres the remains of villages and of cult places both inside and outside the villages (e.g. at Delphi) can still be found. As a rule, however, we can speak only of the remains of Mycenaean settlements.[1] For instance, we know that a Greek cult place was set up on the site of a former LH fishing village. In the light of these facts we must carefully weigh up the frequently advanced statement that the development of the great Greek sanctuaries (from 800 B.C. onwards) stemmed from Mycenaean traditions, and from traces of Mycenaean cults that had survived till Greek times. It has been argued elsewhere that the Mycenaean tradition was not the principal factor behind the emergence and development of the Greek cult places, e.g. Olympia. It could even be argued that it was the political, social and economic factors rooted in the Greek society of the eighth century B.C., as well as the development of new forms of religion there, that formed the main basis for the development of the great Greek cult places.[2]

Addenda

Discoveries made in 1979 and 1981 at Anemospilia[1] on the border of Archanes, at the foot of Mount Jouktas are noteworthy because their interpretation has changed public opinion and resulted in controversy among scholars. Inside the temenos wall, probably in the shape of horse-shoe (Fig. 310, cf. Fig. 311) there is a small temple destroyed c. 1700 B.C., filled with important finds (Figs. 312, 313). It occupies an area of about 10 × 10 m. The shape of the temple approximates the storerooms (Fig. 314) or the typical tombs in the form of houses (Fig. 315). Although the plan of the temple at Anemospilia is different from that of the temple at Mallia (Fig. 216), it is similar in its form to the houses of square plan. We tend to believe that this new discovered temple is not of a specific form but that it imitates the shapes of dwelling-houses, what — as we have written — is a distinctive feature of the Minoan sacred building. An entrance into the temple led presumably from one side, the east one, where there was not to much space for the assembly of worshippers, for the distance between the entrance and the wall of the temenos was about 7 m here. The situation in the northern part of the temple is not very clear on the ground of the published information (Room 5). There was an entrance here into the temple through which worshippers could see a cult statue staying in Room 2. It seems that the area before the temple (6) might have been used for assemblies of worshippers, though it is not a large one, for the largest length between the temenos wall and Room 5 is about 8 m. The temple, despite its small measurements, was built in the western part

312. *(below)* Anemospilia. Pair of clay feet. The Athenian, March 1980, Fig. on p. 27.

313. Anemospilia. Cult vessel. The Athenian, March 1980, Fig. on p. 25.

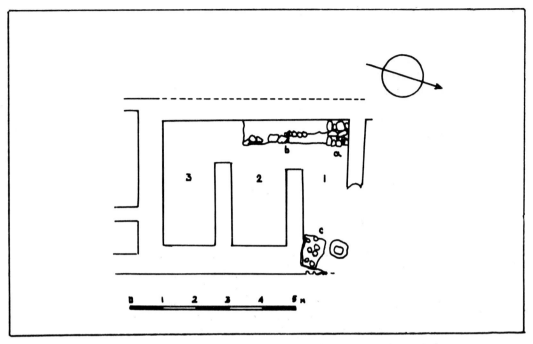

314. Gournia. Store-room at House Aa. AJA 83, (1973) 152, III. 1 (fragment).

of a very thick wall (approximately 2.50 m), which seems to indicate that outside there was either a wide platform or a second floor at least in the western part of the temple.[2] The main part of the temple, excluding Room 5, consists of a corridor and three narrow rooms (1-3). The corridor served as a place where the sacrifices were prepared, and where auxiliary altars stood. The main rooms of the temple (1-3) are narrow and oblong. In the central room (2) a cult statue was presumably situated — only remains of wood and clay feet left from it. These feet were pointed in such a way that it was possible to put a statue on them (Fig. 312). Despite of the fact that the feet were life-size the height of the statue cannot be established. Sanctity of a statue does not depend on its size, and feet do not define the height of a statue. It could be life-size, and feet do not define the height of a statue. It could be life-size or much smaller (Fig. 311). Wooden cult statues from the Minoan period have not been preserved until present time, but they are well known from the later periods in Greece. In this room there were many vessels

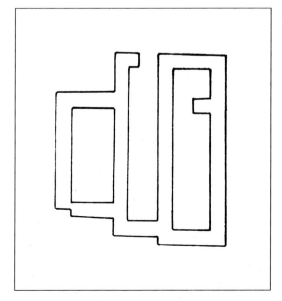

315. Archanes. A tomb. Ergon 1966, Fig. 154.

in which gifts to the goddess were stored. Near the statue there was a low rock, 20 cm high — an important cause for the origin of many cult places, for example, peak sanctuaries (see above p. 75). As E. and Y. Sakellarakis think the holy rock had great importance in the cult ritual; priests poured blood offerings to the deity. In Room 3 there was a stepped altar, on which presumably sacred symbols and vessesls with offerings stood. This altar is a prototype of stepped sacrificial structures, which in their later form were preserved in the Shrine of the Double Axes in Knossos (Fig. 184). In Room 1 a low platform was discovered. It was preserved only to a few centimetres in height, but originally it was certainly higher. On this platform a skeleton of a youth, 18 years old, and a long bronze dagger were found. E. and Y. Sakellarakis suppose that on the platform–altar the youth was killed in a ritual sacrifice. His blood has been perhaps carried over by another participant of the ritual in a bucket-vessel (Fig. 313), which was unearthed in the corridor. Interesting discovery at Anemospilia we have to add that the reconstruction of the ritual which took place in the temple requires further studies as well as a complete publication of the site.

Notes

INTRODUCTION

1. G. Karo, ARW, 7 (1904), 117ff.
2. M. P. Nilsson, *The Minoan-Mycenaean Religion* (1927), 49ff; cf. Nilsson, MMR², 53ff.
3. CPl, *passim*; cf. Gesell, *passim* and Tyree *passim*.
4. Nilsson, MMR², 53ff.
5. M. P. Nilsson, *Geschichte der griechischen Religion I²* (1955), 256ff; Mylonas, MycMA, 136ff; CPl, *passim*; Mylonas, CCent, 11ff; J. T. Hooker, *Mycenaean Greece* (1976), 191; Mylonas, MycRel 3ff.
6. FGK, 11ff.
7. CPl, 38ff, cf. Mylonas, MycRel 3ff.
8. Faure, Fonct, *passim*, and E. Platakis. *To Idaion Antron* (1965), 11ff; *idem, Spelaia kai allai karstikai morphai tes Kretes I* (1973), II (1975); Cf. the papers in DESE.
9. Cf. the early Christian basilicas.
10. R. Gansiniec, *Rocznik Orientalistyczny*, 2 (1919-24), 318.
11. C. C. McCown, *Journal of Biblical Literature*, 69 (1950), 210.
12. The program of studies in Aegean religions proposed by N. Chao, 'Perspectives on the religion of prehistoric Crete', in *Valcamonica Symposium '72. Actes du symposium international sur les religions de la préhistoire* (1975), 221ff. was already introduced in the first edition of this book, *passim*. See a review of Chao's paper by A. Tamvaki, 'Symposium international sur les religions de la préhistoire', *Anthropos*, 3 (1976), 12f.
13. In this book the sepulchral cults are studied in a very limited way.
14. 'Temenos' had only secular connotations in Mycenaean texts, but nevertheless we use that term meaning the whole saved area. For discussion of this problem see in particular H. van Effenterre, REG 80, 1967, 17ff; M. Gérard-Rousseau, *Les mentions religieuses dans les tablettes mycéniennes* (1968), 208; see also B. Bergquist, *The Archaic Greek Temenos. A Study of Structure and Function* (1967), 5; K. Latte, 'Temenos', RE, 9, Halbb (1934), 435ff; P. Stengel, *Die griechischen Kultusalterthümer³* (1920), 17f.
15. Basically, the classification follows what was proposed in CPl, 38f.

CHAPTER I

1. See e.g. Matz, Gött, 43, in connection with research on the significance of the column.
2. R. M. Cook, BSA, 50 (1955), 270; E. D. Phillips, *Antiquity*, 38 (1964), No. 151, 171ff; cf. also Evans, PofM, IV, 672ff.
3. Thucyd. I.8.1.
4. Ennius, Sacra hist. frag. 526 Baehrens ap. Lact. div. inst. 1.11 'sepulchrum eius est in Creta in oppido Cnossoy'.
5. Kyrill. Al.c. Iulia 10.342 (LXXVI 1028B Migne) cites Porphyrios (v. Pyth. 17) and writes of Pythagoras: 'eis de to Idaion kaloumenon antron katavas, eria echon melana'.
6. Nonn. Dion. 8.114ff; cf. Cook, I, 942 n.1.
7. These really may have been cult objects dating from the archaic and classical periods (which does not change the essence of the matter).
8. P. Faure in *Minoica*. Festschrif für J. Sundwall (1958), 134.
9. Cf. Faure, *op. cit.*
10. Already quoted by M. K. Radziwiłł, *Hierosolymitana peregrinatio* (1601), 242, cf. B. Rutkowski, BCH, 92 (1968), 85ff.
11. Psell. Anagogi eis ton Tantalon: 'tou de (Diou) ton epi tafo deikuousi kolonon'. Cf. Diod. 3.61, also quoted by J. Meursius, *Creta, Cyprus, Rhodus* (1675), 77ff and by Cook, I, 158 n.4.
12. Cook, *op. cit.*, 'a thousand years later Michael Psellos showed a hill or cairn above the grave of Zeus'. Cf. Nilsson, MMR², 458.
13. J. Meursius (see n.11), 71ff. For a list of travellers cf. D. Hemmerdinger Iliadou, *Studi Veneziani*, 9 (1967), 535ff; W. G. Rice, 'Early English Travellers to Greece and to the Levant' in *Essays and Studies in English and Comparative Literature* (1933) 205ff; P. Warren, KCh, 24 (1972), 65ff; E. Platakis, *Spilaia kai allai karstikai morfai tis Kritis*, I (1973), 206ff.
14. Fr. Barozzi, 'Descritione dell'isola di Creta' (written in 1577) in *Nobili Nozze Elisabetta Barozzi, Cesare Foscari* (1898), 18.
15. Chr. Buondelmonti, 'Descritione insulae Cretae', in E. Legrande, *Description des iles de l'Archipel par Christoph Buondelmonti I* (1897), 148f; cf. H. Brunsting, *Kreta en de mythologie* (1956), 15.
16. M. K. Radziwiłł (see n.10) 242; cf. B. Rutkowski (see n.10), 85ff.
17. Chr. Savary, *Lettres sur la Grèce faisant suite celles sur l'Égypte* (1788), 194.
18. P. Belon, *Les observations de plusieurs singularitez et choses memorables trouvées en Grece . . .* (1555), cited from edit. publ. 1588, 39, writes of the tomb of Zeus, but it is not clear from the text whether he himself actually visited the place.
19. Cf. B. Rutkowski (see n.10), 85ff.
20. P. Belon (see n.18), 17 and M. K. Radziwiłł (see n. 10), 21.
21. F. W. Sieber, *Reise nach der Insel Kreta im griechischen Archipelagus, im Jahre 1817* (1823), I, 510.
22. As far as this problem is concerned, it is not important whether we believe the labirythos signified a palace or a grotto, e.g. at Skotino, cf. Faure, Lab, 315ff.

238

23. Faure (see n.8), 141 n.25.
24. As well as economic some geographers believe.
25. R. Pashley, *Travels in Crete* (1837), I, 219f. 219f.
26. W. Baumlein, *Zeitschrift für die Altertumswissenschaft*, 6 (1839) 1139, 1182.
27. F. Lenorment, *Monographie de la Voie Sacrée éleusinienne de ses monuments et de ses souvenirs* I (1864), 451. Cf. also F. Andrian, *Der Höhencultus asiatischer und europäischer Völker. Eine ethnologische Studie* (1891), XXIII and R. Beer, *Heilige Höhen der alten Griechen und Römer* (1891), 29.
28. W. Baumlein, *op. cit.*, 1139.
29. An account of the history of these studies is given by P. Aström, Op. Ath, 5 (1964), 159ff; cf. Evans, TPC, 58ff. An interesting statement on this is made by E. Dodwell, *A Classical Tour through Greece, during the years 1801, 1805 and 1806*, II (1819), 239f (quoted by Aström, *op. cit.*, 160).
30. See list of references given by R. Gansiniec, *Le double-hache est-elle un symbole religieux?* (1925). Offprint from *A Tribute to Oswald Balzer*, 7ff.
31. E. Fabricius, AM, 10 (1885), 59-72, 280; F. Halbherr, MI, 2 (1888), 690-766; P. Orsi, MI, 2 (1888), 769-904.
32. F. Halbherr, MI, 2 (1888), 913-16.
33. F. Halbherr, P. Orsi, MI, 2 (1888), 905-10; D. Hogarth, BSA, 6 (1899/1900), 94-116.
34. A. Taramelli, MA, 9 (1899), 356.
35. I. Hazzidakis, *Parnassos*, 10 (1886), 339-42.
36. A. Taramelli, AJA, 5 (1901), 437-51.
37. It was not until 1921 that this site was included in the literature on the peak sanctuaries (Evans, PofM, I, 151). Faure, NRT, 138f included it among the 'rural sanctuaries' (sacred enclosures). Cf. p. 116.
38. Faure, NRT, 138 now includes these in the 'rural sanctuaries' (sacred enclosures). Cf. n. 37.
39. Pendlebury, AC, 136, assigned this site to the peak sanctuaries but it is now thought that it was a 'rural sanctuary' (Faure, NRT, 140ff).
40. Evans, TPC, 112ff.
41. W. Reichel, *Über Vorhellenische Götterkulte* (1897), *passim*. Some scholars supposed that totemism was an early form of Greek religion; cf. in particular A. B. Cook, JHS, 14 (1897), 81ff; G. Thomson, *Studies in ancient Greek Society. The Prehistoric Aegean* (1949), 18ff. and 92ff. But many others refuted this conception; cf. in particular Nilsson, MMR², 376 n.22.
42. H. Schmidt, *Berliner Philologische Wochenschrift*, 18 (1898), 942ff, in a review of the book by W. Reichel, *op. cit.* and of the paper by H. von Fritze, 'Die mykenische Goldringe und ihre Bedeutung für das Sacralwesen' in *Strena Helbigiana* (1900), 77ff; *Rheinisches Museum für Philologie*, NF, 55 (1900), 588ff; for the representations in art see FGK, *passim*.
43. Furtwängler, AG, III, 45 n.2.
44. Cf. above, n.42 and 43.
45. Evans, TPC, *passim*.
46. W. H. D. Rouse, JHS, 21 (1901), 268ff; R. Dussaud, RHR, 51 (1905), 32ff.
47. G. Karo, ARW, 7 (1904), 117ff.
48. G. Karo, *Religion des ägäischen Kreises, Bilderatlas zur Religionsgeschichte*, H. 7, IX. Leipzig 1925.
49. Nilsson, MMR², *passim*.
50. See above (n.34), 350ff.
51. Evans, PofM, I, 153ff.
52. Dussaud, CivPr, 327ff.
53. Pashley (see n.25), I, 220.
54. A. Taramelli (n. 34), 355.
55. Evans, PofM, I, 163.
56. J. Hazzidakis, BSA, 19 (1912/13), 35ff.

57. R. M. Dawkins, M. L. W. Laistner, BSA, 19 (1912/13), 1ff.
58. J. Myres, BSA, 9 (1902/3), 356ff.
59. S. Xanthoudides, *Panathenaia*, 6 (1906), September, 32; Xanthoudides, VTM, 1 and 49.
60. Evans, PofM, I, 153ff.
61. A. Evans, BSA, 6 (1899/1900), 32ff; Evans, PofM, I, 425, 441f. 463ff. (Temple Repositories); BSA, 8 (1901/2), 28ff; Evans PofM, I, 248 ('The Sanctuary of the Dove Goddess'); BSA, 10 (1903/4), 39ff. (sanctuary over the palace magazines No. 11-13, but uncertain); BSA, 8 (1901/2), 95ff; Evans, PofM, I, 576; Evans, PofM, II, 335ff ('Shrine of the Double Axes'); L. Pernier, MA 12 (1901), 33ff; 14 (1903), 405; RendLinc, 12 (1907), 286; Festos, I, 195f (sanctuary in the palace).
62. S. Xanthoudides, AE (1906), 117ff (Chamaizi, see also Chapter II. 13); R. M. Dawkins, BSA, 10 (1903/4), 217ff (Palaikastro); Gournia, 47f (see Chapters II and VII).
63. Cf. above n.61. The excavations at Knossos were important because among other things they influenced our ideas about the cult images. W. Reichel's belief (*op. cit.*, n.41) that no cult images were known in the Aegean civilisation still finds acceptance today.
64. See Chapter III.
65. H. R. Hall, *Oldest civilisation of Greece* (1901), 293-302; A. Mosso, *The Dawn of the Mediterranean Civilisation* (1910), 341ff. W. Ridgeway, *Early Age of Greece* (1901), 481ff. II (1931), 416ff; Dussaud, CivPr, 327ff; H. R. Hall, *Aegean Archaeology* (1915), 145ff; Evans, PofM, *passim*; G. Glotz, *La civilisation égéenne* (1923), 296ff.
66. Cf. remarks on the cult places in the works cited in n.65, also B. E. Williams, in Gournia, 51-3; D. Hogarth, *The Aegean Religion, Encyclopaedia of Religions and Ethics*, ed. J. Hastings, I (1908), 141ff.
67. V. L. Bogayevski, *Primitive-Communist Way of Production in Crete and Mycenae* (in Russian), *non vidi*, Leningrad 1934, see K. Majewski, *New Trends of Research in Aegean Archaeology* (in Polish) *Rocznik dziejów społeczno-gospodarczych*, 4 (1935), 18ff.
68. R. Pettazzoni, *La religione nella Grecia antica fino ad Alessandro* (1921), cited from the French translation: *La religions dans la Grèce antique des origines à Alexandre le Grand* (1953).
69. Nilsson, MMR, *passim*. Nilsson, MMR², *passim*. Nilsson, *Geschichte der griechischen Religion*, I (1940) (2nd edit., 1955).
70. Pendlebury, AC, 272-5.
71. Persson RelGr, *passim*.
72. Picard RelPreh, *passim*.
73. S. Marinatos, *Höhlenforschungen in Kreta, Mitteilungen über Höhlen und Karstforschung* (1928), 4, 2ff.
74. N. Platon, AE (1930), 160ff. For remarks on the cult places see also Evans, *Palace of Minos*, I-III. Likewise cf. C. Tsountas, *Mikinai kai mikinaikos politismos* (1893), *passim*, R. Paribeni, MA, 19 (1908), 1ff, and R. Gansiniec, 'Labrys', in RE, 23 (1924), 286ff.
75. G. E. Mylonas, K. Kouroniotes, AJA, 37 (1933), 271ff, cf. G. Karo, RE, Suppl. 7 (1935), 601 and others.
76. O. Frödin, A. Persson, *Asine* (1938), 74ff.
77. S. Marinatos, PAE (1929), 95ff; (1930), 91ff; AA (1930), 156.
78. N. Platon, IK, 96ff see also Catalogue II (especially Katphi and Maza); K. Davaras, *To Mouseion Aghiou Nikolaou* (n. date), Figs. 26ff.
79. F. Chapouthier, BCH, 53 (1929), 523f (Room XVIII); F. Chapouthier, P. Demargne, Etcret, 12

(1962), 3-5 (Room XIV); S. Marinatos, AA (1933), 297; (1935), 246ff; AD, 15 (1933/5), Parart. 54f (as a cult place suggested by S. Hood, P. Warren, G. Cadogan, BSA, 59 (1964), 78); J. Pendlebury, M. Money-Coutts, BSA, 38 (1937/8), 75ff.

80. See Chapter III.

81. CPl, 42 n.14.

82. We have already started work on the final publication of the finds from the Eileithyia cave at Amnissos, the A. Phaneromeni grotto at Avdou, the cave of Hermes at Patsos and the British School 1903 Excavations at the peak sanctuary at Petsophas.

83. On the iconography see FGK, 122ff. Some general problems were touched upon also by the present author and by R. Hägg, K. Killian, J. C. van Leuven, C. Renfrew and others (SanctSymp, *passim*). The present author hopes to publish soon an extensive study on the problems and methods of the Aegean cult places.

84. Banti, CulM, 10ff.

85. N. Platon, IK, 96ff; recently D. Levi, PP, 181 (1978), 294ff.

86. Platon, MOI, 428ff.

87. Yavis, Alt, 12ff.

88. Gesell; Tyree; Mirie. In works of a more general character many scholars have devoted their attention to the sanctuaries. We mention here only some of them: G. Glotz, CivEg, 296ff; L. A. Stella, *Pepragmena*, I, 253ff; R. Hutchinson, *Prehistoric Crete* (1962), 213ff; F. Schachermeyr, *Die minoische Kultur des alten Kreta* (1964), 158ff; N. Platon, *Crete* (1966) 182ff; S. Alexiou, *Minoikos politismos* (no date) 87ff; S. Hood, *The Minoans* (1967), 133ff; Hägg MCult 39ff; K. Branigan, *The Foundations of Palatial Crete* (1970), 92ff; P. Faure, *La vie quotidienne en Crète au temps de Minos* (1973), 184ff; Vermeule, Götterkult, 8ff, 32ff. W. Burkert, *Mycenaean Greece* (1976), 193ff. W. Burkert, *Griechische Religion der archaischen und klassischen Epoche* (1977), 55ff; J. L. Bintliff, *Natural Environment and Human Settlement in Prehistoric Greece*, I (1977), 147ff; S. Hiller, *Das minoische Kreta nach dem Ausgrabungen des letzten Jahrzehnts* (1977), 63ff and 168ff. R. Willetts, *The Civilisation of Ancient Crete* (1977), 115ff.

89. FGK, 11ff.

90. See, for example, the excavations at Tsoutsouros; and the new section of the Idaean Cave. New discoveries in the cave at Skotino were made by Davaras and Faure.

91. Faure, Fonct, 9, on the research that has been done on the caves.

92. Especially in eastern Crete, see Catalogue II.

93. See Catalogue II.

94. See Catalogue III.

95. See Chapters II, VII, IX and Addenda.

CHAPTER II

1. Platon, MOI, 432; Faure, NRT, 114f; CPl, 39.

2. See Catalogue I Nos.: 2, 4, 6, 8, 10, 11, 13a, 17, 18, 21, 23, 26, 28, 29, 30.

3. See Catalogue I Nos.: 1, 3, 5, 7, 9, 14-16, 19, 20, 22, 25, 27, 28, 31-33.

4. If indeed this cave was thoroughly explored, cf. AA (1935), 248ff.

5. See Catalogue I, Nos.: 2, 4, 6-8, 11, 12, 13, 18, 21, 22, 23, 24, 26, 30.

6. Boardman CC, 10ff. The publication of the finds from the caves is still (as is suggested in CPl, 42 n.14) one of the most important tasks awaiting scholars in the field of research on ancient religion.

7. V. Raulin, *Description physique de l'ile de Crète*, I (1869), e.g. 92 and 414.

8. Marinatos in 1928 and Platon in 1930 (cf. Chapter I).

9. Especially Lindberg, Faure and Platakis.

10. See Chapter IV.

11. A list of more important finds is published by Tyree, 216ff.

12. D. Hogarth, BSA, 6 (1899/1900), 94ff.

13. By 1950 7 sites were known, see Pendlebury AC, 102ff, see also Nilsson, MMR², 68ff, while a year later a list of 11 sites was drawn up, cf. Platon, IK, 96ff. By 1972 a list of over 30 sites was published, cf. Faure, NRT, 114ff; Faure, STSS, 174ff; CPl, 320ff. Today we know of more than 40 sites, cf. Catalogue II.

14. Especially Faure, NRT, 114ff; BSA, 72 (1977), 13ff.

15. The sites at Jouktas, Petsophas, Kophinas, Traostalos, Pyrgos and Vrysinas.

16. See Catalogue II.

17. Faure, CulS, 496 n.1.

18. See Catalogue II.

19. See Catalogue II.

20. J. Myres, BSA, 9 (1902/3), 356ff; Platon, IK, 96ff.

21. E.g. some figurines from Petsophas.

22. The building at Gazi, AE (1937), 278ff; has generally been classified as a domestic sanctuary; Faure, NRT, 145 rightly counted it as one of the 'rural sanctuaries' (sacred enclosures). The sites at Sphakia (N. Platon, PAE (1955), 296f), at Piskokephalo (Platon, IK, 124ff; PAE (1952), 631ff) and at Aski (N. Platon, KCh, 10 (1956), 419f) have until recently been classified as peak sanctuaries. But Faure, NRT, 115ff, suggested that they were 'rural sanctuaries' (sacred enclosures). At Kremasma (A. Dessenne, BCH, 73 (1949), 307ff) relics dating from post-Minoan times were discovered (S. Alexiou, KCh, 17 (1963), 405).

23. See especially PAE (1952), 621 and KCh, 6 (1952), 474.

24. See Catalogue III. Little is known about the sites at Arkokephalo. The statue of a goddess found not long ago at Sachturia (Y. Tsedakis, BSA, 62 (1967), 203ff) no doubt indicates that there was a sacred enclosure there. It is not certain whether the sites at Kostili and Skinias were sacred enclosures or domestic sanctuaries.

25. CPl, 310.

26. CPl, 56. As a town shrine (= temple): Hood, TS, 169ff.

27. See Catalogue V.

28. The other possibility is that the horns of consecration may have fallen down from an upper storey.

29. On the inverted cups of bowl see p. 44.

30. Hood, TS, 169, wrote that the building 'stood at the foot of a slope, Tourkissa, where appears to have been the site of an extensive Minoan settlement'. But Tourkissa is too distant a mountain to have had any link with Rousses. The building at Rousses was near Kephala, where stood the LM III A-B settlement. Anyway Rousses seems to be a distinctly isolated building surrounded by olive groves and cultivated fields.

31. Hood, TS, 169, believes that there was 'lack of evidence for an upper storey'. Nevertheless in our opinion the thickness of the walls of Room 1 which reaches 0.70-1.00 m, does provide such evidence. There did not need always to be stone steps, for the upper storey could be reached by a ladder or wooden staircase.

32. CPl, 52ff.

33. Evans, PofM, IV, 202ff.

34. A. Dessenne, Etcret, 11 (1959), 91ff, especially 102ff and 110ff.

35. S. Marinatos, PAE (1950 (1951)), 242-8; *idem* PAE (1951 (1952)), 258ff; *idem*, PAE (1952 (1955)), 592ff; *idem*, PAE (1955 (1959)), 309f; Mylonas, MycMA, 146, doubts whether the building with the annex was a tripartite sanctuary.
35a. Evans, PofM II, 136ff.
36. S. Marinatos, PAE (1955), 306ff; F. Schachermeyr, AA (1962), part 2, 143.
37. A. Mosso, *Memorie della Reale Accademia delle Scienze di Torino* 58 (1907), 375ff; MA 19 (1908), 151ff; L. Pernier, in *Festos*, I, 67-112.
38. Pendlebury, AC, 39.
39. In fact, all the finds testify to a dwelling-house.
40. Gesell, 212ff.
41. BCH, 50 (1926), 576; Etcret, 12 (1962), 8.
42. Evans, PofM, II, 123ff.
43. PAE (1966), 160ff.
44. Gournia, 25. It has previously been supposed that the horns of consecration came from the styloblat.
45. J. W. Graham, AJA, 61 (1957), 255ff, suggested a connection with bull-sports.
46. H. van Effenterre, *Revue Historique*, 231 (1963), 1ff.
47. See FGK, 122ff.
48. See FGK, 11ff.
49. Nilsson, MMR², 273 fig. 137 (Sphoungaras) and n.5; E. Grumach, *Kadmos*, 1 (1962), 153ff; CPl, 62.
50. One bronze axe had fifteen hieroglyphic signs: S. Marinatos, AA (1935), 248, 254; M. Pope BSA, 51 (1956), 135; Buchholz, Herk, 33. Part of a silver axe with an inscription: S. Marinatos, AA (1935), 248; M. Buphidis, AE (1953/4), 64; Pope, *op. cit.*, 134; C. W. Brice, Inscriptions in the Minoan Linear Script of Class A (1961), 24; Buchholz, Herk, 33. The gold axe is said to have been found at Arkalochori: Pope, *op. cit.*, 134; Buchholz, Herk, 33c; E. T. Vermeule, Bulletin, Museum of Fine Arts, Boston, 57, 1959, No. 307, 5-16; A. Evans, JHS, 17 (1897), 350ff; *idem* (1909), 13ff; J. Boardman, BICS, 5 (1958), 11f. There is also an inscription on a clay vessel from Chamaizi (S. Xanthoudides, AE (1906), 152 fig. 7). For example an inscription on a gold double axe discovered at Arkalochori has been read as da-ma-te (Demeter), cf. Pope, *op. cit.*, 124; Vermeule, *op. cit.*, 6ff. A considerable amount of literature has already appeared on the decipherment of the name of the goddess Asasara. But see critical remarks on this by E. Grumach, *Kadmos*, 7 (1968), 16f.
51. Stella, Pepragmena, 253ff.
52. Cf. R. F. Willetts, *Classical Quarterly*, 8 (1958), 221ff.
53. Oddysei 19.178f.
54. See Chapter I, 2.
55. Cf. Faure, Fonct, 81ff.
56. For review of finds see Hägg, MCult, 49ff.
57. It is, of course, a Biblical term, for its use see the papers cited in Chapter V n.99.
58. H. Walter, *Das Heraion von Samos* (1976), 14ff.
59. See B. Rutkowski, in *Pepragmenta III*, I, 290ff (cf. CPl, 215ff); *idem*, 'Neues über die vordorische Tempel und Kultbilder', in H. Buchholz (ed.), forthcoming.
60. See Catalogue XV.
61. See in Chapter XII. Conclusion p. 233.
62. See Chapter XII n.1.
63. A. C. Choremis, AAA, 2 (1969), 10ff.
64. I. Trepsiadis, PAE (1958), 38ff; (1959), 21ff.
65. Remains of baths have been found at other sites as well e.g. at Mycenae and Tiryns.
66. FGK, 11ff.
67. L. Stella, *La civiltà micenea nei documenti contemporanei* (1965), 251ff; cf; L. Palmer, *Mycenaeans and Minoans* (1965), 132f; Vermeule, GBA, 295f.

CHAPTER III

1. Evans, TPC, *passim*. Later Evans, TDA, 64ff

modified his views. Cf. Evans, PofM, I, 425ff cf. also B. Rutkowski, *Levi Studies*, I, 148ff and FGK, 51ff.
2. Nilsson, MMR², 236ff.
3. Ibid., 248f.
4. Platon, MOI, *passim*. Cf. Faure, NRT, 114 n.3.
5. The movable finds are also important.
6. E.g. the sanctuary at Koumasa, we included to the peak sanctuaries (see below p. 275, n.69).
7. A. Schörgendorfer, *Forschungen auf Kreta* (1942), ed. F. Matz (1951), 13ff; Platon MOI, 457; C. Long, AJA, 63 (1959), 59f. I. Pini, *Beiträge zur minoischen Gräberkunde* (1968), 30, Gesell, 212f.
8. According to A. Schörgendorfer, *op. cit.*
9. In the paper by A. Schörgendorfer, *op. cit.*, neither a photograph nor the dimensions of this idol were given.
10. K. Branigan, *The Tombs of Mesara* (1970), 166.
11. AA 22, 1907, 108; Xanthoudides, VTM, 49f; Platon, IK, 146; Platon, MOI, 457, No. 33.
12. Gesell, 252f.
13. S. Marinatos, AE (1939/41), 69ff.
14. Cf. G. Karo, AA (1930), 159 (referring to Marinatos's belief that it was a sanctuary); S. Marinatos, AE (1939/41), 76 (kitchen); Platon, MOI, 452f (sacred crypt).
15. S. Marinatos, *op. cit.*
16. A. Evans, BSA, 8 (1901/2), 109f; 9 (1902/3), 3ff; Evans, TDA, 68; Evans, PofM, I, 425ff; Platon, MOI, 440; CPl, 77; Gesell, 246, No. 54.
17. One was observed by Evans, *op. cit.*, and the other two by Graham, Palaces, 138f.
18. Evans, PofM, I, 345, fig. 249.
19. Evans, PofM, II, 386ff; Platon, MOI, 441f; Gesell, 245f.
20. The bench in the crypt is 0.34 m in height, and the bench in the upper room above is lower.
21. J. Hazzidakis, Etcret, 3 (1934), 34ff; Platon MOI, 451f.
22. Gesell, 274: 'a part of the paving'.
23. Evans, PofM, IV, 962ff; Platon, MOI, 446f.
24. M. R. Popham, *The Destruction of the Palace at Knossos* (1970), 74f, see also Gesell, 249f.
25. J. Hazzidakis, *Tylissos à l'époque minoenne* (1921), figs. 6, 12, 28, 29, 31, pł. VI; Etcret, 3 (1934), 13ff; Platon, MOI, 450f; Gesell, 273.
26. No traces of plastering are left.
27. Loom weights have also been discovered in cult rooms, e.g. at Karphi.
28. Although walls had been noticed earlier at the site at Armilides, excavations were first carried out in 1918-19. Soon a preliminary report was published; S. Xanthoudides (1922), 1ff.
29. Although they could equally well have been used for everyday purposes.
30. Platon MOI, 449f; Xanthoudides (*see above* n.28) (a sanctuary or a workshop); Nilsson MMR², 104 (no room used as a sanctuary); Gesell, 261.
31. Xanthoudides (*see above* n.28).
32. Evans, TDA, 33ff.
33. Its height is 1.80 m, width — 0.285/0.265 m.
34. Evans, TDA, 36.
35. Platon, MOI, 445.
36. Platon, MOI, 461. Excavations were carried out by A. Wace in 1920-1: BSA, 25 (1921/3), 181ff; *idem*, Mycenae (1949), 75 (Room 61); G. Mylonas, *Ancient Mycenae* (1957), 50 and 65.
37. It is not certain if rhyta were used solely for religious purposes.
38. Festos, I, 357ff; II, 393, 583.
39. L. Pernier, Festos, II, 393, was not quite sure whether this room could really be called a kitchen.
40. Platon, MOI, 454.
41. It is difficult to decide, because the walls are in a poor state of preservation.

42. BSA, 6 (1899/1900), 74ff; Evans, PofM, II, 548; Platon, MOI, 444.
43. See above n.13.
44. See also Gesell, 272f.
45. A. Evans, BSA, 8 (1901/2), 106ff; 9 (1902/3), 17ff; Evans, PofM, I, 144.
46. S. Marinatos, *Minos*, 1 (1951), 40f; J. Raison, *Kadmos*, 2 (1963), 17ff.
47. Platon, MOI, 439.
48. A. Evans, BSA, 6 (1899/1900), 32ff; Evans, TDA, 66; Evans, TPC, 12f; Evans, PofM, I, 425, 441f; II, 818f, J. M. Cook, JHS, 66 (1946), 117; Platon, MOI, 433ff.
49. The height of the foundations is not mentioned in the published report, and cannot be ascertained now.
50. In R. Hutchinson's opinion Prehistoric Crete (1962), 215, this was a layer discovered between floors dating from MM I-III. See Gesell, 233.
51. Etcret, 1 (1928), 27 ff; 12, 1962, 26ff; 63f; Platon, MOI, 450. It is reported that the only finding from the crypt was 'one Neopalatial sherd'. On the other hand we are not sure if at the time of excavations less significant sherds would have been mentioned at all.
52. F. Chapouthier, J. Charbonneaux, Etcret, 1 (1928) (see n.51).
53. Evans, PofM, II, 322.
54. P. Demargne, Etcret, 12 (see n.51).
55. See also the find from Kannia (p. 144).
56. Festos, I, 121ff; Platon, MOI, 453.
57. Platon, *op. cit.*
58. Festos, I, 170ff.
59. It has survived to a height of 0.63 m.
60. See n.58.
61. Platon, MOI, 454.
62. PofM, IV, 400ff.
63. Probably after the completion, cf. the plan in 1918, the rooms lying to the east of the crypt Room A and an entire corridor were explored.
64. One of those is 1.60 m long and 0.64 m wide.
65. The signs were first described in CPl, 87f.
66. See n.62.
67. Platon, MOI, 436.
68. See below, n.134.
69. Cf. the complex of well-constructed magazines described above. Evans dated the North Pillar Basement to MM IIIA, whereas Platon, judging by the construction, dated it to MM IIIA-LM II.
70. EEKS, 3 (1940), 489; 4 (1941), 271f; N. Platon, PAE (1951), 246ff.
71. Platon, MOI, 448f.
72. There are some doubts as to the function of the room.
73. Seager PS, 26f, Platon, MOI, 458.
74. S. Marinatos, PAE (1932), 76ff; Room 6 measured 5 × 5 m.
75. Platon, MOI, 447.
76. In old peasant houses, e.g. at Monastiriki, there are no windows at all, only slits in the walls or in the roof, and yet the interior is light enough.
77. R. Hutchinson, BSA, 49 (1954), 224, pl. 20; M. Seiradaki, BSA, 55 (1960), 28 n.60. On the other hand it is not altogether certain that the slit above the door was restored properly.
78. E.g. at Palaikastro.
79. F. Halbherr, *Memorie del Reale Instituto Lombardo*, Ser. III, 21/2 (1905), 238.
80. The figurines of two votaries are illustrated in H. Bossert, *Altkreta* (1937), 3rd ed., Figs. 311 and 312.
81. See n.79 and Evans, PofM, II, 624.
82. Banti, CulM, 18ff; Magazines 8 and 18 at Ayia Triada, Magazine 33 at Phaistos, magazines at Mallia and Tylissos.
83. Banti, CulM, 19.
84. Platon, MOI, 454f.
85. A. Evans, BSA, 9 (1902/3), 25; Evans, PofM, II, 814; Evans, PofM, III, 15ff; CPl, 94f; Gesell, 237, No. 34.
86. Cf. A. Evans, BSA, 7 (1900/1), 35; 9 (1902/3), 22ff; Evans, PofM, I, 136.
87. Platon, MOI, 435f.
88. Evans, PofM I, 265; N. Platon, KCh, 1 (1947), 506ff.
89. Evans, TDA, 64ff. Evans, PofM, II, 525ff; Platon, MOI, 437.
90. Evans, TDA, 72ff; Evans, PofM, II, 525f; Platon, MOI, 437f.
91. It is one of the smallest stands.
92. A. Evans, BSA, 9 (1902/3), 132; Evans, PofM, II, 406; Platon, MOI, 438f.
93. But Evans makes no mention of finds at all.
94. Platon, MOI, 443f.
95. C. W. Brice, *Inscriptions in the Minoan Linear Script of Class A* (1961), 23, No. V 10, wrote that not one sign can be deciphered.
96. Brice, *op. cit.*, 13 No. I S. It is just possible, however, that there may have been a domestic sanctuary on the first floor.
97. BSA, 11 (1904/5), 278f; Platon, MOI, 459.
98. Platon, 447f. See S. Marinatos, PAE (1951), 258ff; (1952), 592ff.
99. See also Gesell, 275.
100. D. Hogarth, BSA, 7 (1900/1), 130ff.
101. Under the blue layer there was another layer of plaster as well.
102. Cf. similar finds at Vathypetro.
103. Platon, MOI, 460.
104. Brice, *op. cit.*, 20 No. IV 4.
105. Seager, Ps, 15ff; Platon, MOI, 458.
106. See n.16.
107. Platon, MOI, 457f.
108. Evans, PofM, IV, 3ff; Platon MOI, 436.
109. Gesell, 240.
110. Evans, PofM, II, 380ff.
111. Platon, MOI, 441.
112. Platon, MOI, 442f, cf. Evans, PofM, II, 616ff; BSA, 9 (1902/3), 112ff.
113. The dimensions according to the plan.
114. T. Atkinson, R. Bosanquet, *et al*. Excavations at Phylakopi in Melos (1904), 17f.
115. But see Platon, MOI, 461.
116. Platon, MOI, 462.
117. R. Paribeni, MA, 14 (1905), 720ff.
118. Gesell, 219.
119. D. Hogarth, BSA, 6 (1899/1900), 70ff; Platon, MOI, 444.
120. D. Hogarth, BSA, 6 (1899/1900), 79; cf. Evans, PofM, II, 390; Platon, MOI, 442.
121. Evans, PofM, II, 392ff; Platon, MOI, 441.
122. BSA, 9 (1902/3), 293; Platon, MOI, 458.
123. BSA, 9 (1902/3), 287; Platon, MOI, 458f.
124. Nilsson, MMM², 243ff; O. Pelon, BCH, 106 (1982), 185 gives no argument in favour of his statement that the pillars in some crypts were 'induscutablement' venerated as sacred. He believes (*op. cit.*, 185 n.55) that the present author drew a totally negative conclusion as to the pillar cult. Of course, it is not true, see p. 37 above and B. Rutkowski in Levi Studies, I, 148ff; FGK, 51ff; *idem*, Der Baumkult in der Ägäis, Visible Religion, 2 (1985), forthcoming.
125. See especially Chapter V.
126. On the subject of the sigs see Nilsson, MMR², 246 with references; F. Chapouthier, 'Les écritures minoennes au Palais de Mallia', Etcret, 2 (1930), 75ff; J. Sakellarakis, Europa, 277ff; and J. Shaw, Ann N.S. 33, 1971, 109ff.

127. Graham, *Palaces*, Fig. 78.

128. Etcret, 12, 1962, Fig. 2; see also an offertory receptacle with three signs from Psychro: Boardman, CC, Fig. 29 No. 272.

129. Etcret (see n.128), Pl. XXII 1-2.

130. See the signs on sacred objects (see n.129).

131. Nilsson, MMR², 247, does not deny the importance of signs on the pillars.

132. Nilsson, MMR², 248, also thinks that these basins were used for some everyday purpose, though the exact nature of it is unknown.

133. FGK, 75ff.

134. S. Marinatos, BSA, 46 (1951), 113 ('Double axe . . . it may possibly be the more special emblem of the Knossian district'), see also FGK, 96.

135. FGK, 83.

136 S. Marinatos, AA (1929), 167, suggests that the inverted cups under which there were food remains can be compared with similar finds dating from later times, mainly Aramaic and Arabian, in Asia Minor. Upturned bowls were also discovered in the temples of Nippur and Babylon. Various extant texts tell us that the priests imprisoned demons under these cups, see H. Hilprecht, *Die Ausgrabungen der Universität von Pennsylvania in Bel-Tempel zu Nippur* (1903), 19f and R. Koldewey, *Das wieder entstehende Babylon²* (1913), 242. But even if this similarity does exist, one cannot altogether rule out the possibility that in Minoan Crete these plants (or food?) were put under the cups for some practical purpose.

137. J. Sakellarakis, PAE (1976), 136.

138. See the use of wine presses for sacral purposes in classical Greece.

139. See n.137.

140. Personal communication of C. Doumas.

CHAPTER IV

1. F. Halbherr, MI, 2 (1888), 913ff; Faure, Fonct, 136ff.

2. J. Forsdyke, BSA, 28 (1926/7), 248ff.

3. A. Petrochilou, DESE, 10 (1970), 90ff; Tyree, 63.

4. S. Marinatos, PAE (1929), 95ff; Faure, Fonct, 82ff. E. Platakis, *Kretika Protochronia*, 5 (1965), 218ff.

5. J. Hazzidakis, BSA, 19 (1912/3), 35ff.

6. S. Marinatos, AA (1934), 252ff; AA (1935), 248ff.

7. Faure, SPT, 508ff; Faure, Fonct, 162ff; Faure, Lab, 315ff.

8. C. Davaras, BCH, 93 (1969), 620ff.

9. R. M. Dawkins, M. L. Laistner, BSA, 19 (1912/3), 1ff.

10. S. Marinatos, AA (1937), 222f.

11. See Catalogue I.

12. D. Hogarth, BSA, 6 (1899/1900), 94ff cf. Boardman, CC, 3; Faure, Fonct 151ff.

13. F. Halbherr, MI, 2 (1888), 690ff; S. Marinatos, Ergon (1956), 108ff; EEPhSPA (1956/7), 239ff; KCh, 11 (1956), 409f; PAE (1956), 224f. E. Platakis, *To Idaion antron* (1965), 17ff.

14. Faure, GRCr, 98; S. Spanakis, *Periegitiki*, 60 (1963), December, 33ff; Faure, Fonct, 131ff. Although the objects found in the cave do little to suggest it was used for a religious purpose (see J. Deshayes, REG, 89 (1966), 508), the interior of the cave gives that impression.

15. S. Marinatos, PAE (1950), 250; Faure, GRCr 97; Faure in Minoica, 143; Faure, Fonct, 175f.

16. S. Marinatos, PAE (1950), 248ff.

17. N. Platon, AE (1930), 160ff.

18. J. Mellaart, *Archaeology*, 16 (1963), 3f; *idem*, Çatal-Hüyük (1967), 77ff.

19. In sanctuary E.VI.10 a large number of concretions were found, as well as fragments of stalactites from limestone grottoes (see n.18).

20. Faure, Fonct, 21.

21. See n.12.

22. See n.14 and A. Petrochilou, DESE (1965), 61ff; Tyree, 43ff.

23. See Catalogue I.

24. See n.1.

25. Faure, CulS, 195; Faure, Fonct, 140ff.

26. It is not quite certain that this cave was used for a religious purpose.

27. Cf. n.26.

28. Cf. n.26.

29. S. Marinatos, AA (1937), 222f.

30. Faure, CulS, 500f; Faure, Fonct, 176.

31. K. Lindberg, *Fragmenta balcanica musei macedonici*, 1 (1955), No. 19, 169.

32. Faure, Fonct, 85.

33. Faure, Fonct, 90ff.

34. Lindberg (n.31), 169f.

35. Faure, GRCr, 98.

36. Faure, CulS, 500f.

37. Faure, Fonct, 144ff.

38. S. Marinatos, PAE (1950), 248ff.

39. See n.29.

40. S. Marinatos, PAE (1929), 103.

41. Strabo, X 4.8.

42. See n.12.

43. See n.13.

44. S. Marinatos, PAE (1956), 224f.

45. S. Marinatos, AA (1935), 248ff.

46. A. Taramelli, AJA, 5 (1901), 437ff.

47. See n.9.

48. Faure, Fonct, 162ff.

49. See n.13.

50. See n.1.

51. Faure, GRCr, 96; Faure, Fonct, 187.

52. Faure, GRCr 96; Faure, Fonct, 187.

53. J. Younger, AAA, 9 (1976), 168.

54. See n.9.

55. Cf. especially D. Hogarth, BSA, 6 (1899/1900), 94ff.

56. Teophrastus, hist. pl. 3.3.4.

57. W. Boyd-Dawkins, 'Remains of Animals found in the Dictaen Cave in 1901', *Man*, 2 (1902), 162ff.

58. A. Taramelli, AJA, 5 (1901), 448; Faure, Fonct, 179 n.2 for a different opinion.

59. L. Mariani, MA, 6 (1895), 333ff.

60. See n.9.

61. S. Marinatos, PAE (1929), 97.

62. Faure, Fonct, 83.

63. S. Marinatos, PAE (1950), 248ff.

64. D. Hogarth (n.55), 94ff, also Boardman, CC, 3 (who drew attention to the material underneath layer IV).

65. J. Hazzidakis, BSA, 19 (1912/13), 35ff.

66. S. Marinatos, AA (1935), 248ff; PAE (1935), 212ff.

67. S. Marinatos, AA (1935), 250; Fig. 3, in the opinion of Faure, Fonct, 161 n.5, this object was simply a gold ingot.

68. S. Marinatos, Kadmos, 1 (1962), 87ff.

69. F. Halbherr, P. Orsi, MI, 2 (1888), 905ff; F. Halbherr, MI, 2 (1888), 913ff; Boardman, CC, 76ff; S. Hood, P. Warren, BSA, 61 (1966), 186f.

70. Boardman, CC, 78, fig. 34C; S. Hood, P. Warren, *op. cit.*, 186.

71. S. Marinatos, AA (1937), 222f; Tyree 253f; U. Naumann, *Subminoische und protogeometrische Bronzeplastik auf Kreta* (1976), 101. On the dating see Cl. Rolley, REG, 90 (1977), 482.

72. See Naumann, *op. cit.*, and Rolley, *op. cit.*

73. AJA, 5 (1901), 442.

74. See n.8.

75. Faure, Fonct, 162ff.
76. S. Marinatos, PAE (1956), 224f, *idem*, EEPhSPA (1956/7), 251; Faure, Fonct, 105.
77. F. Halbherr (n. 69).
78. References given by E. Platakis, *To Idaion Andron* (1965), 65ff.
79. M. Guarducci, *Inscriptiones Creticae*, I, XII, 1, also Ergon (1956), 108ff.
80. Faure, CulS, 500ff; Faure, Fonct, 177.
81. Nilsson, MMR², 57.
82. Faure, CulS, 502; Faure, Fonct, 90ff.
83. E.g. the Amnissos cave is situated 700 m from a 'villa' near Paliochora.
84. A. Taramelli, AJA, 5 (1901), 437ff.
85. See n.9.
86. S. Marinatos, PAE (1950), 248ff.
87. Faure, Fonct, 47f.
88. R. M. Dawkins, BSA, 20 (1913/14), 1ff; L. Watrous, *An Archaeological Survey of the Lasithi Plain in Crete from the Neolithic to the Late Roman Period* (1974), 254ff.
89. P. Pelagatti, KCh, 15/16 (1961/2), 100 n.2, quotes as an example some fragments of pottery in the Fitzwilliam Museum at Cambridge.
90. Tablet Kn Gg 705, which reads as follows:
    a-mi-niso e-re-u-ti-ja ME + RI AMPHORA 1
    pa-si-te-o-i ME + RI AMPHORA 1
    o-ne ME + RI AMPHORA 1
    cf. M. Gérard, SMEA 3, 1967, 31ff; M. Gérard — Rousseau, *Les mentions religieuses dans les tablettes mycéniennes* (1968), 101.
91. Oddysey, 19.188.
92. Faure, Lab, 315ff.
93. See n.90 also Stella, Pepragmena, I, 253ff.
94. E.g. the cult of Zeus in the Diktaean cave (Hesiod, Theog, 479f) as regards interpretation of the text, see Faure, Fonct, 94ff, with references and Watrous *op. cit.*, 246; on the cult of Hermes at Patsos, where a dedication to this god dating from the first century B.C. has survived, see M. Guarducci, *Inscriptiones Creticae* (II.IX.1, the cult of this god at Melidoni), 1st or 2nd century B.C. inscription to Hermes, cf. *op. cit.*, II, 302–4; the cult of the nymph Akakalis in the Leras grotto, P. Faure, KCh, 15/16 (1961/2), 195ff.
95. E.g. in the Tsoutsouros grotto.
96. R. Willetts, *Classical Quarterly*, 8 (1958), 221.
97. See n.96.
98. Judging from the large amount of weapons in the cave, it seems possible that the divinity of war was worshipped in it. Cf. S. Marinatos, PAE (1935), 212ff; AA (1935), 248ff. See also below.
99. Cf. e.g. E. O. James, *From Cave to Cathedral* (1964), 15ff; R. R. Marett, 'Cave-Worship', *The Hibbert Journal*, 38 (1939/40), 296ff emphasises that it was not the place alone that made the cave sacred, but its contents — for instance, the fact that the remains of a dead person had been laid there. Marett gives various interesting examples which illustrate the reasons for regarding a certain grotto as sacred. Cf. also the opinion of S. Marinatos, *Mitteilungen über Höhlen und Karstforschung* (1928), 98f.
100. Pendlebury, AC, 103.
101. This possibility is propounded by F. Matz, *Kreta und frühes Griechenland* (1962), 26, who cites Amnissos as an example.
102. S. Marinatos, PAE (1929), 27; Faure, Fonct 55 and 68, interprets the early remains as a burial dating from sub-Neolithic and EM period.
103. For information on the relics, see Faure, SPT, 501 n.4; he thinks the grotto was used for a holy purpose from LM I.
104. I. Papadimitriou, Ergon (1958), 15ff.
105. See n.9.
106. S. Marinatos, PAE (1930), 95 fig. 6. Cf. Ch. Mortsou, EEEPA, 3 (1972), Pls. 26ff.
107. Faure, Fonct, 55f.
108. S. Marinatos, PAE (1935), 212ff.
109. W. Boyd-Dawkins, *op. cit.*, 162ff.
110. E.g. the grottoes at Arkalochori, Psychro and Skotino. Pottery was also discovered at Skotino, Trapeza, Stravomyti, Chosto Nero and Vigla.
111. I do not know of any modern technological studies of the bronze objects found in the Arkalochori grotto; but see analogous studies by H. Coghlan, *Notes on the Prehistoric Metallurgy of Copper and Bronze in the Old World* (1951), *passim*. Cf. n.5,47.
112. Iliad 4.351ff; H. L. Lorimer, *Homer and the Monuments* (1950), 273, writes that the term 'made of bronze' must have been a purely conventional expression when referring to Iron Age swords.
113. See Chapter V.
114. S. Hood, BSA, 47 (1952), 243ff; 51 (1956), 82ff.
115. Cf. Chapter V.

CHAPTER V

1. N. Platon, AD, 17 (1961/2), *Chronika*, 287; Faure, NRT, 124.
2. See especially, R. Pashley, *Travels in Crete* (1837), I, 210ff; A. Taramelli, MA, 9 (1899), 70ff; Evans, TPC, 23f; Evans, PofM, I, 154; Platon, IK, 144; cf. on Pyrgos see especially Faure, CulS, 500f; S. Alexou, KCh, 18 (1963), 404f; Faure, NRT, 125f; description of Traostalos: C. Davaras, *Kadmos* 6 (1967), 102; the holy place at Keria (altitude 1,160 m) occupied a platform measuring 15 × 22 m (Faure, STSS, 183).
3. Y. Dewolf, F. Postel, H. van Effenterre, Etcret, 13 (1963), 9ff.
4. A. Philippson, *Das Klima Griechenlands* (1948), especially 157ff; see also N. Creuzburg, KCh, 15/16 (1961/2), 336ff.
5. A. Philippson, *op. cit.*, 136ff.
6. Especially those at Ai Lias (470 m), Ankouseliana (510 m), Choudetsi (440 m), Etia (615 m), Goulas (521 m), Koumasa (420 m), Maza (457 m), Modhi (539 m), Traostalos (515 m). The altitudes are quoted after Faure, NRT, 116ff.
7. Especially those at Jouktas (780 m), Kophinas (970 m), Plagia (819 m), Pyrgos (685 m), Vigla (714 m), Vrysinas (858 m), Xykephalo (705 m) and Zou (725 m); the altitudes are quoted from Faure (n.6), 118ff.
8. Pashley, *op. cit.*, 211ff.
9. A. Taramelli, MA, 9 (1899), 353ff, believed that the wall was in the shape of an irregular rectangle.
10. See n.13.
11. Pashley, *op. cit.*, I, 220.
12. Evans, PofM, I, 156; a different view on the dating of the walls is taken by S. Alexiou, in Pepragmena IV (1980), 14.
13. A. Karetsou, Ergon (1979), 30.
14. AD 17 1961/2, *Chronika*, 288.
15. Some scholars (e.g. Pendlebury, AC, 103), think the holy buildings (made of wood) in the peak sanctuaries already existed by MM cf. Platon, IK, 96ff. See, however, below, n.23.
16. A. Karetsou, PAE (1974), 228ff; (1975), 331ff; (1976), 408ff; Ergon (1977), 181ff; (1978), 62ff; (1979), 29f.
17. This is clear from the plan of the temenos: Ergon (1979), Fig. 71.
18. Evans, PofM, I, 157 believed it was a sanctuary building.
19. The dimensions of the bulwark: it is 4.98 m long, 1.05 m wide and 1.65 m in height (according to A. Karetsou).

20. B. Rutkowski, Acts of the International Archaeological Symposium, The Relations between Cyprus and Crete, c. 2000-500 B.C.' (1979), 226 and FGK, 24f.

21. Five pairs of fragmentary horns were found. One of them is about 0.80 m in height and 0.40 m in length (PAE (1974), 231).

21a. FGK, Fig. 10.2.

22. For a detailed study of the site see B. Rutkowski, Nature Sanctuaries in Minoan Crete: a catalogue of sites (1985), No. II.34.

23. S. Alexiou, AD, 22, 1967, Chronika, 484f; Faure, STSS, 184.

24. K. Davaras, AAA, 7 (1974), 212.

25. S. Alexiou, KCh, 17 (1963), Chronika, 404f. See also B. Rutkowski, op. cit., No. II, 39.

26. Faure, NR, 192ff; Faure, Cav, 37f: Faure, NRT, 118. An attempt was made to give an interpretation of the walls, see B. Rutkowski, op. cit., No. II, 31, Figs. 43a-c.

27. KCh, 17 (1963), 405f.

28. N. Platon, Zakros (1971), 161ff.

29. FGK, 32f.

30. Similar isolated pillars probably stood in front of the sanctuaries on the mountain peaks in other countries as well, e.g. Israel; the material was collected by Ch. Kardara, AE (1966), 149ff. See also S. Alexiou, AAA, 2 (1969), 84ff.

31. FGK, 48.

32. Platon, IK, 154ff; S. Alexiou, KCh, 13 (1959), 346ff. See especially S. Alexiou, KCh, 17 (1963), 339ff.

33. It is possible that this pillar likewise really stood in front of the building. For a discussion on the significance of these pillars, see below.

34. See FGK, 25ff.

35. The first opinions expressed about the sacred buildings date from 1878, when Schliemann published information about the gold plaque found at Mycenae. Here we shall only mention the main lines of interpretation of the iconographic sources and their relation to the sanctuaries discovered in the field. In the past half century various authors have asked whether the buildings represented on the iconographic sources were sacred or secular. H. Bulle, Orchomenos, I (1907), 77, differed from the others in his view that on the miniature fresco from Knossos, a garden scene was represented. The majority of scholars, however, have taken the view that these finds, such as the painting referred to here, and also the gold plaques found at Mycenae, represent sacred buildings. Thus various lines of interpretation can be discerned. One group is concerned with the interpretation of the façade and the connection between the façade and the rooms behind it. Probably no-one today follows W. Reichel, Über vorhellenische Götterculte (1897), 9, in thinking that the gold plaque from Mycenae depicted a throne placed on a tombstone. Many authors merely stated in general terms that this plaque depicted the façade of a sacred building (Temple), without going into details. One is struck especially by the accurate description given by H. Schliemann, Mykenae (1878), 307f. But more detailed views have been expressed as well. For instance, Evans, TPC, 191, thought an altar could be seen in the upper part of the plaque from Mycenae. This kind of interpretation was probably influenced by the representations of altars in Aegean art, and also by early nineteenth century statements on how altars were depicted in Aegean representational art (e.g. see Dodwell (1819), on the interpretation of a column at the Lion Gate at Mycenae, quoted by P. Aström, Op. Ath 5 (1964), 160). L. B. Holland, AJA, 21 (1917), 119f suggested that the golden plaque from Mycenae represented a porticoed building. Still another interpretation can be traced back to Greek tradition. In connection with the ideas put forward by Evans, TPC, 191ff, R. Zahn propounded a very original conception (see summary of his paper in AA (1901), 98f), namely, that the plaque portrayed not a tripartite building, but a building similar to a Greek temple, consisting of three parts — naos, pronaos and opisthodomos. As in the case of the Egyptian finds, he thought this scene should not be interpreted literally, but that the part on the right and the part on the left should be swung round at an angle of 90° to the main part. Many other authors believed the building represented here was supposed to be a tripartite one, e.g. Evans, TPC, 191 and 196; Dussaud, CivPr, 337; R. Paribeni, Architetture dell'Oriente Antico (1937), 390. These, however, are no more than general statements. A more detailed paper was published by K. Majewski, Studi e materiali di storia delle religioni 31 (1960), 57ff.

Another problem, that of the location of the buildings, has attracted less attention. Here I shall merely mention the chief lines of interpretation. The most generally held view is that these buildings were situated inside the palaces or citadels. But these were the views that were put forward in the early stages of archaeology. On the basis of one of these buildings Evans (PofM, II, Fig. 532) reconstructed a fragment of the façade of what was thought to be a sanctuary in the western part of the palace courtyard at Knossos. But the discovery of the rhyta at Zakro and Gypsades suggested that the painting discovered at Knossos may have depicted a building situated not in a palace at all, but elsewhere (S. Alexiou, KCh, 17 (1963), 350), or in a peak sanctuary (Ch. Kardara, AE (1966), 176f). The buildings depicted on some of the paintings and rings probably represent chapels in the sacred enclosures (see Chapter VI).

The significance of the façade was seldom discussed. In regard to the Lion Gate at Mycenae, F. Matz, Kreta, Mykene, Troja² (1956), 82. 110 and 141; Matz, Gött, 421ff thought it symbolised a cult façade — that is, he thought this was where the deity made appearances, and that dances, ceremonies and prayers took place in front of it. K. Majewski, (op. cit.) arrived at a further conclusion, namely that the scenes depicted on frescoes, on gold plaques and on some rings (e.g. on Fig. 128) showed tripartite buildings which were the background against which religious ceremonies and theatrical performances took place.

But, as we have said above, the most important iconographic sources, which were discovered recently (Fig. 94) tell us why the façade was thought sacred. Interpretation is still difficult, however, for the clay models of sanctuaries tell us nothing about the tripartite façade of the sanctuary, while the few existing remains of detached sanctuaries and temples (see Chapter VII) do not show us clearly how the tripartite façade was used in religious buildings. For recent discussion see B. Rutkowski, Nature Sanctuaries in Minoan Crete (in the press). Of course apart form this type of architecture, there must have also been sanctuaries that formed part of a building.

36. N. Platon, IK, 98ff.

37. See Chapter VII, p. 121.

38. See Chapter VI, p. 107.

39. See Chapter VII, p. 145.
40. Archaeological Museum at Iraklion, Nos. 14199 and 14200.
41. Faure, CulS, 496, n.1; Faure, Lab. 28; Faure, NRT, 119; S. Alexiou, KCh, 17 (1963), 399, 406.
42. Faure, Lab, 28.
43. J. Myres, *op. cit.*, 370, pl. XII: 34 (Inv. No. 4841).
44. E.g. Boardman, CC, No. 477.
45. Evans, PofM, I, 154ff.
46. B. Rutkowski, Levi Studies, 148ff.
47. See Chapter VI, p. 107.
48. See p. 107.
49. N. Platon, AD, 17 (1961/2), *Chronika*, 287.
50. PAE (1974), 232ff.
51. Evans, PofM, I, Fig. 461.
52. Evans, PofM, I, 151.
53. N. Platon, *op. cit.*, 288.
54. Ibid., 287f.
55. Evans, PofM, I, 154f.
56. Platon, IK, 112.
57. BSA, 9 (1902/3), pl. XIII, 66.
58. See n.49.
59. Naturally the objects found in the peak sanctuaries were mostly made of clay. On Kophinas (S. Alexiou, AD, 19 (1964), *Chronika*, pl. 514 and on Traostalos (C. Davaras, *Kadmos*, 6 (1967), 102) votive figurines of bronze were discovered, while on Kophinas — votive knives of bronze were also found AD, 17 (1961/2), *Chronika*, 288. Recently many bronze objects were found on ouktas. Our information about the number of votive offerings found is very general in character; the excavation reports often say merely that there was a large amount.
60. AD, *op. cit.*, 287. Also found in many other sanctuaries.
61. Ibid., 287. Fragments of three large figurines are exhibited in one of the show cases in the Archaeological Museum at Iraklion, No. 14104, 14105 and 14107.
62. Platon, IK, 111.
63. BSA, 9 (1902/3), Pl. XIII.56.
64. AD, 17 (1961/2), *Chronika*, 288.
65. The main sources must continue to be the finds dating from the Aegean period, although comparative studies bringing in the Mediterranean region and Greek tradition are also useful. Diverse hypotheses have been propounded — for instance, of a cult of Zeus (Faure), Artemis (Guthrie), and Aphrodite Urania (Grumach).
66. Ch. Kardara, AE (1966), 176ff.
67. R. Hampe, Pepragmena, I, 166-172; idem, 'Kult der Winde in Athen und Kreta, *Sitzungsberichte der Heidelberger Akademie der Wissenschaften, Philologisch-historische Klasse*' (1967), *passim*.
68. F. Matz, KCh, 15/16 (1961/2), 222.
69. A find shaped like a phallus was discovered at Koumasa, see Xanthudides, VTM, 50.
70. J. Myres, *op. cit.*, 370 (from Petsophas), pl. XI.22 (No. 4871).
71. Some scholars have denied that people also came to the peak sanctuaries to cure their ailments (Nilsson, MMR², 74); the discovery of votive objects prove, however, that cures were effected in some of the peak sanctuaries, see J. Myres, *op. cit.*, 356ff (Petsophas); C. Davaras, *op. cit.*, 102 (Traostalos), and our Fig. 109.
72. A. Evans, BSA, 7 (1900/1), 28; BSA, 9 (1902/3), 37; Evans, PofM, II, 808; F. Chapouthier, BCH, 58 (1928), 322; Evans, PofM, IV, 608; Nilsson, MMR², 352; Matz, Gött, 394; A. Furumark, Op. Arch, 6 (1965), 94.
73. Cf. C. Davaras, BCH, 93 (1969), 620ff.
74. Evans thought the goddess was holding the shaft of a double axe, whereas Matz, Gött, 394 took the view that she was holding a sceptre. Spears were also sometimes symbols of power, see A. Alföldi, 'Hasta — Summa Imperii. The Spear as Embodiment of Sovereignty in Rome', AJA, 63 (1959), 1ff; the royal tomb at Vaphio was also found to contain a beautiful bronze sheath that once covered the shaft of a spear, see S. Marinatos, BSA, 37 (1936/7), 187. It may also have symbolised the royal power.
75. Oddysey XIX. 178 see especially: Picard, RelPreh, 145; Evans's idea that the king was also High Priest was sometimes opposed, e.g. Mylonas MycMA, 168; cf. E. L. Bennett, KCh, 15/16 (1961/2), 327ff; A. Stella, *La civiltà micenea nei documenti contemporanei* (Rome 1964), 52 n.15. In diverse interpretation, the idea that the king was of divine origin, and that his kingship was holy, occurs again and again. See S. Marinatos, *Robinson Studies*, I, 126ff; L. Cipriani, KCh, 15/16 (1961/2), 136ff; A. Furumark, in *La regalita sacra* (1959), 369f. Explanations by means of Hurit (B. C. Dietrich, *Acta Classica*, 8 (1965), 19ff), and Egyptian (P. Walcot, SMEA, 2 (1967), 53ff) analogies do not altogether solve the problem, cf. G. Mylonas, AE (1966), 127ff; W. K. C. Guthrie, BICS, 6 (1959), 42, rightly remarks that the king was rather a representative than an embodiment of divinity.
76. Cf. R. M. Dawkins, BSA, 37 (1936/7), 48ff.
77. B. Rutkowski, Atti, II (1967), 160 Fig. 4.
78. Several examples were found on Petsophas: J. Myres, *op. cit.*, Pl. XIII.63.
79. Particularly at Piskokephalo, where more than 30 models of beetles were found, see V. Müller, *Der Polos, Die griechische Götterkrone* (1915), 12, n.5 No. 7 (interpreted as a hedgehog); R. Hutchinson, BSA, 40 (1939/40), 43 pl. 20B No. 3 (interpreted as a hedgehog); Platon, IK, 136ff; PAE (1952), 634.
80. In Quarter E at Mallia, a figurine was discovered which G. Daux, BCH, 88 (1964), 915, described as a scarab. Faure, STSS, 192 n.2 took it to be a scaraboid beetle. A pendant in the form of a beetle was discovered at Pseira, cf. Platon, IK, 139; a house at Mallia (Quarter Mu): Etcret, 26 (1980), Fig. 158.
81. Platon, PAE (1952), 636.
82. There is a beetle-shaped object on the right shoulder of a fragment (the torso) of a figurine (Archaeological Museum at Iraklion, No. 9761, unpublished). Faure, NRT, 141, mentions several clay figurines representing human beings, with models of beetles attached to them.
83. A cup with clay models of beetles attached to its upper part was found in the Royal Pottery Stores at Knossos. This cup was found along with egg-shell pottery (Evans, PofM, I, 340, Fig. 180). Beetles were represented much more often in Aegean iconographic art. For example we have the finds coming from the Monolithic Pillar Crypt at Knossos (see Chapter III), including a vessel dating from MM IA that has a beetle represented on it (Evans, PofM, IV, 74, Fig. 46 bis, a); on another vessel there is a 'water beetle' (Evans, PofM, I, 182, Fig. 132a, on p. 183); and there are also representations of beetles on part of a jug dating from MM, cf. D. Mackenzie, JHS, 26 (1906), 246.
84. From Palaikastro, in a LM IA house, cf. BSA, 60 (1965), 261; AD, 18 (1963), pl. 368c; L. H. Sackett, ILN, 27.4 (1963), 260f writes that this vessel (0.15 m in length) represents a beetle of the *oryctes nasicornis* type (which is difficult to accept), and declares that vessels of this type are found,

thought rarely, in the eastern part of Crete.

85. Platon, IK, 137, No. 10, pl. 5, Fig. 1, No. 10.

86. Platon, IK, 137, No. 8, pl. 5, Fig. 1, No. 8.

87. Platon, IK, 138, pl. 5, Fig. 1, No. 5; Platon, PAE (1952), 634 Fig. 15 (photograph) (general description; these finds are exhibited in one show case in the Archaeological Museum at Iraklion).

88. Platon, PAE (1952), 634, Fig. 15.

89. Etcret 9, Pl. 45.

90. Professor M. Mroczkowski (Zoological Institute of the Polish Academy of Sciences, Warsaw) in 1966 also discussed the problem with the present author. Clay figurines of beetles were first discovered at Petsophas in 1902, but no studies of them were carried out then. Since the excavation report was written up very quickly, J. Myres did not study the votive offerings in detail. He thought that one of these figurines represented a hedgehog, which was rather a sound idea (J. Myres, see above, n.63, pl. 13:80). He also thought that three others represented hares (ibid., pl. 13:60, 62, and 63). At a later date, too, in accordance with the body of information available at that time, the figurines of beetles were interpreted as hedgehogs (Müller, *op. cit.*, and Hutchinson, *op. cit.*). This problem took on its true colours owing to the researches of Platon, IK, 136ff who described and interpreted five figurines from Piskokephalo. He also correctly interpreted figurines found at Mallia (on Prophetis Elias) and at Petsophis (ibid., 120 and 141). Platon did not refer to any scientific bibliography, but drew on the opinon of the entomologists. On this basis, he declared that these models of beetles represented the *Phylocerea* family, and the *kantharos* genus. This conclusion was reached because of the shape of the body, which was oval and widening towards the bottom, and because of the ribbing on the dorsal part and on the body. The legs were arranged in pairs, and bent at the bottom. The head part was broad. The horn was curved. This is the feature that was thought to indicate the species, *oryctes nasicornis*. Live beetles of this kind are 0.04 m long, and their body is chestnut-coloured. Platon's views have won almost universal acceptance (e.g. see R. Hutchinson, *Prehistoric Crete* (1962), 219); A. Dessenne, BCH, 73 (1949), 309, on the other hand, argued that it was difficult to say just what the figurine found at Mallia represented, but it may have been a mole (?), or a hedgehog (?). Then P. Demargne, who in 1953 had agreed with Platon (see P. Demargne and H. G. de Santerre, *op. cit.*), now pointed out that experts in the Natural History Museum in Paris were not sure whether the model of the beetle found at Mallia belonged to the *oryctes nasicornis* species or to the *scarabaeus* type. Apart from the investigations which we carried out in 1966, Faure NRT, 141 also opposed the general view that these beetles belonged to the *oryctes nasicornis* species.

In 1969, owing to the courtesy of the British Museum in London, the author was able to study figurines discovered at Petsophas. Among these, one unpublished fragment (No. 1907. 1-19.37) was described in the museum inventory as a turtle. It seems to be a figurine of a beetle. It is made of red clay, and is unpainted (the dimensions are approximately 0.01 × 0.01 m). The part that has survived is the rear part of the animal, with legs stuck onto the sides.

The clay balls: e.g. at Petsophas, which J. Myres, *op. cit*, described as prayer balls. Balls of this kind have also been found on Cyprus. At Enkomi small clay balls with Cypro-Minoan Inscriptions were discovered (now in the Louvre). Their purpose is probably not known. Stone balls (also now in the Louvre) came from Ras Shamra, from the excavations carried out by C. Schaeffer, see B. Rutkowski, Acts of the International Arch- aeological Symposium, The Relations between Cyprus and Crete, c. 2000-500 B.C.' (1979), 226 n.27.

91. J. H. Fabre, *Souvenirs entomologiques* (cinquième serie) (1922), 109ff; see also R. Paulian, *Coleoptères scarabeides, Faune de France*, 38 (1941), 59; likewise L. Bedel, 'Fauna des Coleoptère du bassin de la Seine', IV.1, *Scarabaeidae*, 41 (*non vidi*); V. Baltasar, 'Scarabaeidae des paläarktischen Faunagebietes', Monographische Bestimmungstabelle, I.1, Best. Tab. Col. XCV. Troppau (*non vidi*).

92. *Scarabeus sacer* is encountered in the form of figurines imported from Egypt as well as local imitations. See especially J. Pendlebury, *Aegyptiaca* (1930) and Evans, ScM, 136, fig. 70; Evans, PofM, I, 199, fig. 147 (Psychro); Kenna, CrS, 36, fig. 47 (from Psychro); Evans, PofM, I, 199f, fig. 148 and Evans, PofM, IV, 439 n.2 (Platanos); S. Alexiou, ILN (6 August 1960), 226 (Lebena); R. P. Charles, BCH, 89 (1965), 10-14, fig. 1.

93. See Faure, NRT, 141. Later, this author (Faure, STSS, 192 n.2) wrote: 'Comme le scarabée égyptien il semble que ce soit un symbole solaire de regenerescence et du resurrection', and further on (p. 206): 'La corne nasale, dans la symbolique du bestiaire, passe pour l'atribut de la force et de la fécondite'.

94. According to the Linear B texts, wool is supposed to have been of fundamental significance in the Cretan economy, see K. T. Killen, BSA, 59 (1964), 1ff, but cf. D. Young, Kadmos, 4 (1965), 111ff and M. I. Finley, *Early Greece. The Bronze and Archaic Ages* (1970), 39.

95. Especially Ch. Kardara, AE (1966), 149ff.

96. This cult is described by Kardara, *op. cit.*, 149ff.

97. This conclusion can be reached on the basis of analogy with Greco-Roman times. L. Heuzey, *Le Mont Olympe et l'Acarnanie* (1860), 138f and R. Beer, *Heitige Höhen der alter Griechen und Römer* (1891), 7, n.1, write that in Antiquity, religious rites were held on the summit of Olympus twice a year, whereas at present they are held only once a year, during the rites in honour of Saint Dionysus at the spot where the chapel of Saint Elias once stood.

98. A similar custom prevailed in Greece in the first millennium B.C. Cf. Platon, IK, 151 and Gansiniec, AegRel, 383f, also J. Myres, *op. cit.* 380f; Evans, PofM, I, 158; Nilsson, MMR², 75; *idem*, JHS, 43 (1923), 144ff.

99. F. Andrian, *Der Höhencultus asiatischer und europäischer Völker. Eine ethnologische Studie* (1891), *passim* (for general remarks see p. XIII ff); see also E. Dhorme, AS, 6 (1956), 57ff likewise H. Haag (ed.), 'Höhenkult', *Bibel-Lexikon* (1956), 726f; H. L. Vincent, 'La notion biblique du Haut-Lieu', *Revue biblique*, 55 (1948), 245ff and 438ff; C. C. McCown, 'Hebrew High Places and Cult Remains', *Journal of Biblical Literature*, 69 (1950), 205ff. W. F. Albright, 'The High Place in Ancient Palestine', *Vetus Testamentum*, Suppl. 4 (1957), 242ff. The bronze model of a Canaan 'high place' found at Suza, and which has been dated to the twelfth century B.C., is now in the Louvre, No. Sb 2743 (cf. P. Amiet. *Elam* (1966), 392; B. Goldman, *The Sacred Portal* (1966), 76ff, with references). This 'high place' seems to bear little resemblance to the peak sanctuaries depicted on the Minoan rhyta.

100. Cf. drawing: Evans, PofM I, 153 fig. 122.
101. Chr. Buondelmonti, 'Descriptio insulae Cretae', *Description des iles de Archipel par Christoph Buondelmonti*, E. Legrande (ed.), I (1897), 148f.
102. Cf. Pashley, *op. cit.*, I, 213ff.
103. Some figurines are made in a style which may have belonged to the period EM III or MM I, cf. Evans, PofM, I, 151.
104. See n.6 and 7.
105. C. Buondelmonti, *op. cit.*, 148.
106. M. K. Radziwiłł, *op. cit.*
107. A sanctuary belonging to Zeus Olympios was discovered during the building of a meteorological station on Olympus (on the A. Antonios peak, which has an altitude of 2,817 m, and which is only 100 m lower than the highest peak, Mytikas). Votive stelae and other objects were found, as well as coins dating from Hellenic to Byzantine times. See D. V. Kyriazopoulou and G. Livada, AD, 22 (1967), 6ff; AR (1967/8), 12. The few archaeological remains found on the mountain peaks are described by Cook, I, 420 n.3 II, 868f. At the top of Lykaion (altitude 1,420 m) for instance, there was a temple consecrated to Zeus, where pillars stood crowned with eagles. But no remains dating back further than the Archaic period have so far been discovered, see E. Meyer, RE, 26 (1924), 2235ff, with references. Excavations on a Greek mountain sanctuary have recently been conducted by J. Pollard, 'Mystery Site on Mount Lutraki', *Greece and Rome*, 15 (1968), No. 1, 78ff. See also M. K. Langdon. 'A Sanctuary of Zeus on Mount Hymettos, *Hesperia Suppl.*, XVI (1976), 1ff, 100ff.
108. The region round Palaikastro, too, was fairly densely settled.
109. On investigations in the palace at Kato Zakro, see N. Platon, *Zakros* (1971), *passim*.
110. Xanthudides, VTM, 3f, 49f.
111. W. J. T. Peters, *Landscape in Romano-Campanian Mural Painting* (1963), e.g. pl. XXVI.104.
112. Modern research has shown that the raising of goats and sheep and the cultivation of olives were of fundamental significance in Crete, see L. G. Allbaugh, *Crete: A Case Study of an Undeveloped Area* (1953), especially 242ff. The same author writes further on: 'Agriculture in Crete has changed relatively little during the past four thousand years'. Soil worth cultivating was especially scarce in eastern Crete, and so the breeding of goats and sheep was always of prime importance there, cf. L. Chalikopoulos, *Sitia, die Osthalbinsel Kretas* (1903), 129f. This picture still obtained in the Middle Ages: F. Thiriet, *La Romanie Venitienne au Moyen Age* (1959), 322. See also R. F. Willetts, *Ancient Crete. A Social History from early Times until Roman Occupation* (1965), 38ff.
113. AD, 17 (1961/2), *Chronika*, 288.
114. Found at Petsophas, J. Myres, *op. cit.*, 370.
115. See p. 114.
116. As regards social problems, scholars have been interested mainly in the possibility of reconstructing the social and political aspects of the civilisation of Crete.
117. A bibliography was drawn up by Ch. Kardara, AE (1966), 151ff, although her interpretation is different.
118. For the general discussion of this problem, see now C. Doumas (ed.), *There and the Aegean World*, I (1978), II (1980), passim.
119. Of course, the influence of the Thera eruption on Crete must be taken as more complex.
120. Already observed by Evans and Mackenzie (see unpublished Notebook of the 1909 excavation in the Ashmolean Museum, Oxford). Abundant material dated to this period was found by A. Karetsou (e.g. Ergon, 1975, 177f; PAE, 1976, 416, Fig. 3c,d).
121. Possible LM sherds were seen by the author on the site.
122. LM I and III pottery fragments were seen by the author on the site.
123. A LM I lamp was reported by J. Myres, BSA, 9 (1902/3), 360.
124. Xanthoudides, VTM, Pl. XXXIII.

Chapter VI

1. See Chapter V.
2. W. J. T. Peters, *Landscape in Romano-Campanian Mural Painting* (1963), e.g. pl. XXVI.104.
3. For instance the sacred enclosure at Kremasma, not far from Kato Sisi, Mirabellou and situated right on the seashore, lies on somewhat elevated, rocky ground, cf. A. Dessenne, BCH, 73 (1949), 307ff; Faure, NRT, 142.
4. E.g. at Askoi or Askous, Pediados on Amygdalokephalo Hill, at an altitude of 460 m on the hillside cf. N. Platon, KCh, 10 (1956), 419f; G. Daux, BCH, 81 (1957), 617; S. Hood, AR (1956), 22; F. Schachermeyr. AA (1962), Part 2, 136; Faure, Fonct, 97 n.3; Faure, NRT, 143f Fig. 17; Katsaba,in the Lionis vineyard just below the hill summit, overlooking the River Kairatos, cf. S. Alexiou, PAE (1955), 319; G. Daux, BCH, 80 (1956), 354; F. Schachermeyr, AA (1962), Part 2, 144.
5. E.g. at Epano Zakro, at the Stous Atropolitous site, at the foot of a hill summit at an altitude of 290 m, Faure, NRT, 138f; at Kephala, on a hill with an altitude of 295 m, not far from Episkopi, Pediados, cf. Faure, NRT, 144; at Kavousi, at the Plai tu Kastrou site, at an altitude of 410 m, cf. H. Boyd, AJA, 5 (1901), 149f; Faure NRT, 142, also at Kavousi at the Pachlitsani Agriada site, at an altitude of approximately 200 m, cf. S. Alexiou, KCh, 10 (1956), 7ff; Faure, NRT, 142, at Sphakia, at the Patela site, altitude 375 m, cf. KCh, 9 (1955), 563f; BCH, 80 (1956), 359, where the building was interpreted as a dwelling house; Ergon (1954), 101f; N. Platon, PAE (1955), 296f fig. 3; F. Schachermeyer, AA (1962), Part 2, 141; Faure, CulS, 497, Faure, NRT, 140, see also the site at Arkokephalo, Viannou, on a hill there, cf. S. Hood et al., BSA, 59 (1964), 87.
6. Faure, NRT, 144.
7. P. Dikaios, *The Excavations at Vounous-Bellapais in Cyprus*, (1931-2), 118ff, pl. VII and VIII, cf. FGK, 116.
8. Peters (see n.2), pl. XXVI. Fig. 104.
9. See, e.g. H. J. W. Tillyard, 'Boundary and Mortgage Stones from Attica', BSA, 11 (1904/5), 63ff; 'ordinary landmarks of fields and gardens: a wall, a ditch, or some kind of natural boundary . . . streams, ditches, olive-trees; the trees were in some cases stamped with special marks'; a stone was placed at spots where the boundary was doubtful, or where mistakes could arise. The stone did not necessarily always have an inscription, however (p. 64).
10. See above n.9, also B. Rutkowski, *Larnaksy egejskie* (1966), 89ff.
11. At Kephala, see Faure, NRT, 144.
12. Cf. Mylonas MycMA. 141ff; see also Chapter X.

248

13. Peters (see n.2), pl. XXXIV Fig. 141, XLVI Fig. 176, XXXIII Fig. 140.

14. S. I. Dakaris, AD, 16 (1960), 1ff; idem, 'Das Taubenorakel von Dodona und das Totenorakel bei Ephyra, in Neue Ausgrabungen in Griechenland, Erstes Beiheft zur Antike Kunst (1963), 35ff.

15. Peters (see n.2), pl. XXVI.104.

16. A two-roomed building inside a semi-circular enclosure has been preserved at Askoi, cf. N. Platon, KCh, 10 (1956), 419f; Faure, NRT, 143f. At the Plai tou Kastrou site at Kavousi there was a small sanctuary, the wall 2.20 m long, cf. H. Boyd, AJA, 5 (1901), 149f; Faure, NRT, 142; at this same locality but at the Pachlitsami Agriada site, a small sanctuary measuring 4.45 × 3.50 m was discovered, cf. S. Alexiou, KCh, 10 (1956), 7ff; Faure, NRT, 142; several partly preserved rooms of a sanctuary have been found at Sphakia, cf. N. Platon, PAE (1955), 296f; Faure, NRT, 140; the remains of a building have also been seen at Epano Zakro, at the Stous Atropolitous site (Pendlebury, AC, 102); at Pankalochori the remains of a building which was probably a sanctuary were found, cf. S. Marinatos, AA (1933), 297, idem, AD, 15 (1933), Parartima, 55f; Pendlebury, AC, 256; S. Alexiou, KCh, 12 (1958), 188; Faure, NRT, 145; walls probably dating from Minoan times were observed at Arkokephalo, cf. S. Hood et al., BSA, 59 (1964), 87.

17. This conclusion can be reached owing to the discovery of clay models of what are possibly oval sanctuaries, e.g. at Archanes, at the Phyties site, cf. S. Alexiou, KCh, 4 (1950), 445ff; Marinatos-Hirmer, Kr, 103; N. Platon, KCh, 11 (1957), 338; an oval naiskos was recently discovered at Amnissos (G. Daux, BCH, 91 (1967), 777f, Fig. 2); the clay model found at a spring sanctuary at Knossos, cf. Evans, PofM, II, 128, Fig. 63, and the model found at Phaistos, cf. L. Pernier, MA, 12 (1902), 128. Fig. 55; S. Alexiou, KCh, 12 (1958), 279 n.392; Faure, NRT, 145 n.1, no doubt represent sanctuaries; see also FGK, 19f. Some scholars believed that oval shapes on sealstones represented sanctuaries, cf. V. E. G. Kenna, The Cretan Talismanic Stones in the Late Minoan Age (1969), pl. 14, but see also Chapter II, p. 17.

18. Cf. n.16 above.

19. Faure, NRT, 144.

20. Cf. n.16 above.

21. Cf. n.16 above.

22. Judging from the place where it was found, D. Levi, Ann, 23/4 (1961/2), 129ff, interpreted this model as a tomb sanctuary, cf. also FGK, 16, 18, 40, 108.

23. R. Hutchinson, BSA, 49 (1954), 215ff.

24. M. Seiradaki, BSA, 55 (1950), 28 n.60; FGK, 18 n.26.

25. See n.17 above.

26. N. Platon, KCh, 10 (1957), 336; G. Daux, BCH, 82 (1958), 788.

27. Cf. the building on the miniature fresco from Knossos see Evans, PofM, II, 597 and III, 46ff, pl. 16; for different interpretation see Ch. Kardara AE (1966), 176, Fig. 26.

28. On a seal impression from Zakro, cf. D. G. Hogarth, JHS, 22 (1902), 76f, No. 1.

29. See especially R. Paribeni, MA, 19 (1908), 1ff; Nilsson, MMR² 426ff; Rutkowski (see n.10), 126, Ch. R. Long, The Ayia Triadha Sarcophagus (1974), pl. 17ff; FGK, 10, 26, 29, 46, 48f.

30. Cf. a building at Sphakia, see n.17.

31. A model from Kamilari, cf. n.22.

32. Cf. n.28. On the function of the façade see above p. 81.

33. See the ring from Archanes: J. Sakellarakis, Archaeology, 20 (1967), 280; for the site Kadmos, 4 (1965), 177f; ILN 26.III.1966, 33; PAE (1966), 174ff; see also FGK, 26.

34. Cf. Chapter V, p. 84.

35. Evans TPC, 101ff; Nilsson MMR², 256. For the interpretation of the clay models from Piskokephalo and from Knossos see FGK, 22ff.

36. Cf. n.35 above.

37. Cf. n.35 above.

38. On the fragment of the rhyton from Knossos cf. n.35 above, and also e.g. on a sealstone from the Idaean cave, cf. R. Vallois, REA, 28 (1926), 122 and 128.

39. Cf. also the altar constructions depicted on the Ayia Triada sarcophagus, see FGK, 26.

40. Cf. n.38 above.

41. J. Sakellarakis, ILN (26 March 1966), 32 fig. 2.

42. Cf. Nilsson, MMR², 117ff and Yavis, Alt, 1ff; FGK, 42f.

43. D. Levi, Ann, 23/4 (1961/2), 12ff.

44. Cf. Nilsson, MMR², 123ff.

45. M. Möbius, dI, 48 (1933), 14f.

46. C. Boetticher, Der Baumkultus der Hellenen (1856), 437.

47. A recently discovered fragment of wall-painting that fits this scene was published by M. Cameron, in Europa, 65ff.

48. Cf. K. Elderkine, AJA, 29 (1925), 53ff.

49. C. Boetticher (see above n.46).

50. There is a palm on the top of a schematically represented hill (or mound) on, for instance, an agate sealstone from central Crete in the Ashmolean Museum in Oxford, cf. Evans, PofM, I, 275, Fig. 204d, and V. Kenna, Cretan Seals (1960), 103 No. 112; does the plant depicted on the black jasper seal found at Tragana represent a cactus or prickly pear, as claimed by S. Marinatos, PAE (1955), 253 pl. 95 Fig. 2, or a palm tree? On the palm tree motive see recently: P. Aström, The Cuirass Tomb and other finds at Dendra I (1977); 13f.

51. Cf. e.g. Glotz CivEg, 187f.

52. Cf. n.48 above.

53. On the cult statues see especially Matz, Gött, passim (contra D. Levi, PP, 14 (1959), 377ff) and FGK, 110ff.

54. Most of them were discovered in the temples and in the domestic sanctuaries, which are discussed in Chapters VIII-IX.

55. Chr. Kardara, AE (1966), 180, asserts that the object interpreted as a baetyl on a gold ring from Knossos (see n.57) is really a censer.

56. Seager, Moch 89f, Fig. 52 and Persson, RelGr, 82ff.

57. Persson, RelGr, 60ff; cf. also n.55.

58. C. Picard, REA, 32 (1930), 101, Fig. 1.

59. N. Platon, AE (1930), 168.

60. On the baetyl cult see especially M. W. de Visser, Die nicht menschengestaltigen Götter der Griechen (1903); H. V. Hermann, Omphalos (1959), 27ff; FGK, Chapter III.

61. Cf. Chapter IV.

62. Cf. n.54 above.

63. Cf. n.53 above and Chapter VII.

64. S. Marinatos, AA (1933), 198 (Pankalochori); Y. Tsedakis, BSA, 62 (1967), 203ff (Sachtouria).

65. S. Alexiou, KCh, 4 (1950), 445ff; Marinatos-Hirmer, Kr, 103; S. Alexiou, KCh, 12 (1958), 277ff.

66. Evans, TDA, 10; Nilsson, MMR², 279; Brandt,

GG, 5 and S. Alexiou, Gnomon, 39 (1967), 612.

67. Matz, Gött, 391f; Nilsson, MMR², 256.

68. D. G. Hogarth, JHS, 22 (1902), 76f; Matz, Gött, 14f; Ch. Delvoye, BCH, 70 (1946), 120ff.

69. Cf. Nilsson, MMR², 309ff; cf. N. Platon, *Mélanges Picard*, I (1949), 833ff.

70. On the analogy with those shown on the rhyton from Zakro (Fig. 94).

71. FGK, 16.

72. Evans, TPC, 170 Fig. 48; Matz, Gött, 391f; FGK, 26.

73. Cf. n.29 above.

74. E. Petersen, JdI, 24 (1909), 162f, thinks the birds sitting on the top of the pillars were cuckoos.

75. Cf. especially Chapter V.

76. E.g. on a bronze signet ring found at Knossos (cf. S. Hood, AR (1958), 19).

77. Examples of triton shells being used as cult objects and musical instruments were collected by Evans, PofM, IV, 344, and Nilsson, MMR², 153f; on the finds from the domestic sanctuaries see Chapter VII.

78. A. Evans, BSA, 7 (1900/1), 19 and 101; Evans, PofM, II, 767 and IV, 395; E. Herkenrath, AJA, 41 (1937), 411.

79. See especially Chapter VII.

80. On analogy to the domestic sanctuaries, cf. G. C. Gesell, AJA, 80 (1976), 274ff.

81. Some scholars have called her a goddess, cf. K. Elderkine, AJA, 29 (1925), 53ff; but most are agreed that she is a priestess, cf. K. Majewski, *Kreta-Hellada-Cyklady* (1963), 189, Fig. 118, or a votary, cf. Evans, TPC, 141f; Evans, PofM, IV, 211.

82. Many scholars have thought that these figures were all dancers or votaries, cf. Evans, TDA, 10; Evans, PofM, III, 68; Biesantz, KSG, 22 (awaiting the epiphany of a deity); Rodenwaldt, Fr, 13 n.2; two women dancers and two female worshippers; Matz, Gött, 10, cf. D. Levi, PP, 14 (1959), 383f; some scholars have taken the view that one of the large figures could have been a goddess, cf. S. Alexiou, KCh, 12 (1958), 231; Brandt, GG, 5.

83. F. Halbherr, MA, 13 (1903), 42f; D. Levvi, Ann, 8/9 (1925/6), 141; Evans, PofM, II, 341; Fig. 194a; Nilsson, MMR², 268; D. Levi, PP, 14 (1959), 384.

84. See above n.33 (Archanes); cf. also on a gold ring from Phaistos (Kalyvia), cf. L. Savignoni, MA, 14 (1904), 577f; Persson, RelGr, 35f; Matz, Gött, 23, cf. also seal impressions from Ayia Triada, see above n.83.

85. Cf. n.84 above.

86. Taking a different view from most scholars, Mylonas, MycMA, 141ff thinks the woman dancer is merely touching the tree.

87. Cf. V. Kenna, *Cretan Seals* (1960), 125, No. 250; Evans, PofM, I, 160 thought the woman represented a goddess; the conviction that this scene was set against a hilly background, cf. Evans, TPC, 170, was based exclusively on the fact that the artist had denoted some vegetation and some rocks (?) which Evans, TPC, 170 referred to as 'steep rocks'.

88. Cf. Nilsson, MMR², 175; Matz, Gött, 386; S. Alexiou, KCh, 17 (1963), 349.

89. Alexiou (see above n.88), 349 rightly drew attention to the fact that this scene seems on the whole to be taking place in a palce.

90. Evans, TPC, 101ff; FGK, 14, 20, 46.

91. K. Majewski, *Archeologia*, 3 (1949), 12; his interpretation is based on his use of ethnological material from places outside Greece, and on his use of ethnographical comparisons with Greece; it is also based on the assumption that relics of totemism could still be found in Greece right up to the middle of the second millennium B.C.

92. Majewski (see above n.91) is of the opinion that other dances, too, were performed in the 'sacred groves', from the iconographic evidence in Crete. These other dances were as follows: 1. a dance in which the female dancers put on demon masks, while the dance leaders were attired completely as demons; this dance was performed in connection with the baetyl cult; 2. a dance in bird masks; 3. a dance in bull masks; 4. a dance in masks representing other animals whose species is difficult to determine; 5. a dance in asses' skins; 6. an orgiastic dance which formed part of the cult mysteries, which was similar to the dances in the Dionysius cult in the Greece of later times; 7. a snake dance connected with magic and the plant growth cycle, a dance that accompanied the mysteries held in honour of the Great Goddess; 8. a dance with a goat.

93. D. G. Hogarth, JHS, 22 (1902), 76f.

94. D. Levi, Ann, 23/4 (1961/2), 139ff.

95. These figurines were often similar to those found in the peak sanctuaries, as for instance those from Piskokephalo cf. L. Mariani, MA, 6 (1895), 171; F. Forster, BSA, 8 (1901/2), 273f, Fig. 1; Platon, IK, 142ff; PAE (1952), 631ff, and from many other places, e.g. Kostili (Faure, NRT, 146); Vaveloi (Faure, NRT, 146 n.5); Kremasma (A. Dessenne, BCH, 73 (1949), 307ff; at Askoi) N. Platon, KCh, 10 (1956), 419f; at Epano Zakro, at the Stous Atropolitous site, cf. R. C. Bosanquet, BSA, 9 (1902/3), 276 (leg fragments belonging to clay figurines similar to a figurine found at Petsophas); L. Mariani, MA, 6 (1895), 183.

96. E.g. from Piskokephalo Kostili, Vaveloi, Kremasma and Epano Zakro, cf. n.95.

97. Fragments of clay figurines representing animals have been found at nearly every site, cf. n.95 above.

98. Cf. Chapter V.

99. Cf. Chapter VIII.

100. A lamp dating from LM I was found at Kostili, Ayiou Vasilou, cf. Faure, NRT, 146.

101. These were probably votive offerings cf. N. Platon, PAE (1955), 296, pl. IIIb (upper row). They were discovered at Sphakia.

102. Cf. N. Platon (see above n.101), pl. IIIb (lower row, middle).

103. As a general rule it is difficult to put a hard and fast date to the sites with sacred enclosures. But we know that a number of sites should be dated to MM (e.g. Epano Zakro). In other cases, we know that the objects found there generally come from the Minoan period (e.g. Arkokephalo) or from LM I or LM III (e.g. Pankalochori). A few sites have produced relics which date from MM I — such as the site at Keramoutsi (S. Alexiou, Ergon (1966), 153, 155).

104. See Chapter V.

CHAPTER VII

1. In this book, the 'sacred repository' is taken to mean a place where things belonging to the sanctuary or temple were stored.

2. Cf. M. Nilsson, *Greek Popular Religion* (1953), *passim*; on the function of the Greek agora, see F. Trietsch, ÖJ, 27 (1932), 64ff; W. A. McDonald, *The Political Meeting Places of the Greeks* (1943), 7ff; R. Martin, *Recherches sur l'Agora grecques* (1951), 1ff (especially on the political, commercial and

religious functions of the agora); R. E. Wycherley, *How the Greeks Built Cities* (1962), 2nd ed., 50ff; cf. A. Schott, ÖJ, 45 (1960), 68ff.

3. Gournia, 24f.
4. H. Boyd Hawes, Gournia, 25, and other scholars supposed that the horns of consecration were set on the stylobate.
5. H. Boyd Hawes (above n.3) 25: 'market-place'; cf. F. Trietsch (above n.2), 65ff and R. Martin (above n.2), 80ff.
6. T. D. Atkinson, R. C. Bosanquet *et al.*, Excavations at Phylakopi in Melos (1904), 55f.
7. R. M. Dawkins, BSA, 20 (1913/14), 1ff (only part of the square was excavated).
8. H. van Effenterre, in Pepragmena, I, 273; H. and M. van Effenterre, 'Le Centre politique. I. L'agora (1960-1966), Fouilles executées à Mallia', Etcret, 17 (1969), especially 143f.
9. H. van Effenterre, M. C. Salaün, KCh, 15/6 (1961/2), 186ff.
10. Etcret, 12 (1962), 22, 25 (1980), 131ff; FGK, 48. On Knossos see n.2.
11. See Chapter V, p. 83.
12. Etcret, 12, 20ff.
13. N. Platon, *Zakros* The Discovery of the lost Palace of Ancient Crete (1971), e.g. the plan on p. 150; see also FGK, Ch. III, passim. We admit that very few finds prove the cult use of the altars.
14. A. Evans, BSA, 6 (1899/1900), 10; 7, 1900/1, 21 Evans, PofM, II, 612f. Evans thought, too, that there had been an altar opposite the Sacred Repository in the central courtyard: BSA, 9 (1902/3), 37.
15. FGK, 79.
16. A different view was published by L. Banti, in Festos, II, 585, but cf. J. W. Graham, AJA, 61 (1957), 257, n.21; on the function of the courtyard J. W. Graham, *op. cit.*; A. Ward, *Antiquity*, 42 (1968), 117ff.
17. See Chapter VI, n.29.
18. Evans, PofM, II, 578ff.
19. Some scholars (e.g. Marinatos-Hirmer, Kr, 78, Fig. 29) were of the opinion that the theatral areas were places where the spectators could watch the cult ceremonies. One place where a box was found was interpreted by Marinatos as a chapel. According to A. Dalski, *Theatrical Performances in Crete and Mycenae in the II Mill.* B.C., (1937), 152ff (in Russian), the theatral areas were used for the performance of dances connected with the cultivation of the land, and with the work of a patriarchal society (Crete) or of a matriarchal one (Mycenae).
20. E.g. the Thera fresco: see B. Rutkowski, *Thera and the Aegean World*, ed. C. Doumas, I (1978), 662.
21. See e.g. a double axe stand found in the long Corridor at the Palace at Knossos, Evans, PofM, I, 437.
22. The idea was suggested to the author by S. Hood.
23. Evans, PofM, II, 122.
24. Evans, PofM, II, 123ff; Gesell, 250f.
25. The stone vases of LM I date found in the Spring Chamber might have been used in a religious ritual.
26. A large amount of sub-Minoan offering vessels testify also of the cult function of the Chamber.
27. N. Platon, PAE (1966), Fig. 6.
28. According to the scale on the plan.
29. The other possibility is that the horns of consecration were placed on the wall surrounding the cistern. Anyway water-supply on water-intake seem to be under divine protection.
30. N. Platon, PAE (1964), 158f.
31. Gesell, 278.
32. B. Rutkowski, *Double Axe Stands* (in the press).
33. E.g. Graham, 'The Palaces of Crete', 140. Cf. also: F. Chapouthier, R. Joly, Etcret, 2 (1936), 12ff; 12 (1962), 63.
34. Many scholars thought this figurine represented a goddess: e.g. Nilsson, MMR², 83ff and 311ff (a cult idol); Matz, Gött, 412ff; others say she was a serpent-charmer priestess: K. Majewski, *Archeologia*, 6 (1954), 24, pl. VII 68-72; D. Levi, PP, 14 (1959), 384 (a priestess robed as a goddess).
35. See Chapter III, p. 29.
35a. A. Evans, BSA, 6 (1899/1900), 35ff Evans, PofM, II, 607f; IV, 901ff; N. Platon, KCh, 5 (1951), 392ff; H. Reutsch, *Minoica*, 334ff; *idem*, *Minoica und Homer* (1961), 31ff; C. Hopkins, AJA, 67 (1963), 416ff; R. Popham, AJA, 68 (1964), 353; H. Reutsch, *Kadmos*, 3 (1965), 179ff; A. Furumark, Op. Arch, 6 (1965), 94f; Mirie, 1ff. The conception of the Throne Room as a religious hall was published very early, cf.: 'The plan of the "throne room" with its throne, bench, and tank, resembles a hall of initiation dedicated to Men Ascaenius and a Mother Goddess near Pisidia, so that likewise at Cnossus it may have been a hall of religious ceremonial' (W. J. Anderson, B. Spiers, The Architecture of Greece, 2nd Ed. (1927), 23, note.)
36. B. Rutkowski, Atti II, 160; H. Reutsch's conception, in *Minoica und Homer* (1961), 39, that 'the priestess or priestess-queen sat on the throne at Knossos only during the main part of the ceremony, when she was regarded as a goddess in human form' is difficult to accept. It is also necessary to add that so far there is no undisputable evidence indicating that there was any cult of thrones in the Aegean Bronze Age culture. As far as Greek civilisation is concerned, this problem was studied very early; e.g. R. Pashley, *Travels in Crete*, II (1837), 64ff; W. Reichel, *Über Vorhellenische Götterculte* (1897), 1ff, tried to prove that the cult of thrones was of a great importance in the Aegean Bronze Age civilisation. But this conception was discredited at the end of the nineteenth and the beginning of the twentieth century (see Chapter I, p. 4). N. Platon, KCh, 5 (1951), 385ff; came back to Reichel's theory. But Platon's whole article, as far as we can see, is based on the following three principal arguments: 1. the Throne Room at Knossos had a religious function, as a sanctuary or 'consistory', which had cult rooms nearby, 2. the religious function of thrones in Asia Minor suggests that they had a similar function in Minoan Greece, 3. examples of sacred thrones are known to us in the Greece of the first millennium B.C. Unfortunately none of the examples collected by Platon corroborates the existence of a throne cult in the Minoan civilisation. Nevertheless it is worth noting an interesting study by H. Danthine, 'L'imagerie des trones porteurs de symboles dans le Proche Orient Ancien', in *Mélanges Syriens offerts à Monsieur René Dussaud*, II (1939), 857ff, in which attention is drawn to a throne cult, which seems to be attested by a scene in which votive offerings are being placed before an empty throne. In this scene the throne (but also all the other objects found in the sanctuary, as well as the tree growing in the holy place) can be interpreted as a hypostasis of the deity. Yet in Minoan civilisation the throne was also sometimes sacred in a narrower sense of the word, that is, as an object belonging to the deity, or an object symbolising the god's authority, which on earth was wielded by the king. On the subject of the Hittite thrones see a paper by A. Archi, SMEA, 1 (1966), 76ff.

37. A triglyph motif was common in the pictorial art — e.g. on the large gold ring from Tiryns. Even if we accept that altars are depicted in the fresco in the Throne Room, this does not yet prove that the room had a religious use.

38. See also Mirié, passim, who follows, in the main, Reutsch concept (cf. n. 35a).

39. For the evidence see Etcret from volume I onwards.

40. See. S. Alexiou, Levi Studies, I, 7ff.

41. See Chapter III, p. 29.

42. A. Evans, BSA, 8 (1901/2), 28; Evans, PofM, I, 248ff; Nilsson, MMR², 86ff.

43. The idea put forward by A. Evans, BSA, 10 (190/4), 39ff, that there had been a sanctuary at one time above magazines 11-16 at Knossos is difficult to accept.

44. F. Chapouthier, P. Demargne, Etcret, 12 (1962), 3-5 and 9-13.

45. Festos, I, 195f; II, 573.

46. See. p. 133.

47. Dimensions according to the scale given under the drawing.

48. Festos, I, 195ff; II, 573ff.

49. F. Chapouthier, P. Demargne, Etcret, 12 (1962), 9.

50. Nevertheless wooden tables seldom left traces.

51. Graham, op. cit., 99ff; N. Platon, in Europa, 236ff; S. Alexiou, KCh, 24 (1972), 414ff; Gesell, 77ff; J. W. Graham, in Schachermeyr Festschrift (1977), 110ff; Mirie, 62ff.

52. S. Marinatos, Excavations at Thera, VII (1976), 26.

53. B. Rutkowski, Larnaksy egejskie (1966).

54. Festos, II, 171ff; at least three conical clay rhyta were found. It would be difficult to agree with A. D. Lacy, Greek Pottery in the Bronze Age (1967), 89ff, that the vessels generally described as rhyta, meaning vessels that 1. were shaped like an animal's head, and 2. were conical vessels like the steatite vase found at Zakro (which Lacy called 'ritual sprinklers') were used solely in the cult. Both pottery and stone vessels were used for everyday purposes as well as for religious or ceremonial ones. But the vessel found at Zakro was undoubtedly meant to be used solely in the religious rites, as is shown by the theme of the decoration. C. Seltman, in Robinson Studies, I, 12f rightly argues against the view that rhyta (in the wide sense) were used solely for religious purposes, cf. Nilsson, MMR², 145f. Lacy, op. cit., 89 and 287, illustrates this point of view by referring to the conical vessels with a hole at the bottom, which are known as 'fillers'. Until now their use has not been known for certain, but it was thought they were utensils used in the cult rites. Lacy, however, noticing their similarity to contemporary vessels, refers to them as 'conical wine filters'. Here we have an excellent example illustrating how dangerous it is to interpret objects whose function is not known, as cult utensils (cf. Introduction, p. XVI). See also n. 32 and 98.

55. A. Evans, BSA, 10 (1904/5), 2ff; Evans, TDA, 59ff; Evans, PofM, II, 380, 513f.

56. The position of the sanctuaries inside the buildings is not clear at Knossos-Gypsades (S. Hood, AR (1957), 22), nor beside the Royal Road at Knossos (S. Hood, AR (1961/2), 25ff); see AD, 17 (1961/2), Chronika, 295f.

57. L. Sackett, M. Popham, P. Warren, BSA, 60 (1965), 253.

58. The sanctuary in Block B, see R. Bosanquet, BSA, 8 (1901/2), 289 and 314 has been dated to LM IIIA1.

59. The D sanctuary, R. M. Dawkins, BSA, 10 (1903/4), 217ff; BSA, 9 (1902/3), pl. VI; BSA, 60 (1965), pl. 65; dates from LM IIIA2.

60. For dimensions see scale under drawing.

61. Three rooms Chi 101, 105 and 24 in which rhyta shaped like a bull's head were found, have also been described as a sanctuary, R. Hutchinson, BSA, 40 (1939/40), 39; R. C. Bosanquet, op. cit., 66ff; on the function of the rhyta see n.54. A temple to Zeus Dikteios occupied this site in the seventh century B.C.

62. J. Pendlebury et al., BSA, 38 (1937/8), 84ff.

63. The two sanctuaries at Knossos which are sometimes called 'sacred crypts' are discussed in Chapter III, p. 29ff; probably there were also sanctuaries at Pseira (Seager, Ps, 26f) and at Apodoulou: S. Marinatos, AA (1933), 297; AA (1934), 251; AA (1935), 246ff; E. Kirsten, in Forschungen auf Kreta 1942 (1951), 137ff; S. Hood, G. Cadogan, BSA, 59 (1964), 78.

64. N. Platon, KCh, 10 (1956), 417; 11 (1957), 330f; 13 (1959), 368f; PAE (1957), 136ff; Ergon (1957), 85ff; Ergon (1959), 134ff; Ergon (1960), 202f. The village has been dated to LM IIIA 2-LM IIIB (F. Schachermeyr, AA (1962), part 2, 162).

65. Room 5 linking 7 and 8 must also have belonged to the sanctuary.

66. S. Alexiou, PAE (1955), 311ff.

67. Were it not for the presence of tube vessels, such as hitherto had been found solely in holy places, this altar could have been interpreted as a hearth, and the whole room as a kitchen.

68. See above Chapter II, p. 134.

69. D. Levi, BdA, 44 (1959), 237fff.

70. See Chapter VIII, p. 155.

71. S. Xanthoudides, AE (1906), 117ff; K. Davaras, in Pepragmena, III, vol. I, 46ff.

72. See Chapter II, p. 13.

73. It is not impossible, however, that the cult rooms were situated on a no longer existing first floor, above Room A, see Chapter II, p. 13.

74. For instance, little of the sanctuary in Block N at Palaikastro has survived: L. Sackett, M. Popham, BSA, 60 (1965), 253.

75. Of course we are now in a position to study more closely the various particular parts belonging to the sanctuaries. We can now undoubtedly distinguish the principal central rooms, and a number of subsidiary ones, such as the repositories (Fig. 182). Some of the sanctuaries were entered through porches (see the Kamilari model, Fig. 139).

76. There is a particularly good example from A. Triada.

77. Cf. B. Rutkowski, KCh, 18 (1964), 271ff and in: Pepragmena, II, vol. I, 234f.

78. See Chapter VIII.

79. G. Daux, BCH, 81 (1957), 695ff.

80. See Chapter III.

81. See Chapter V.

82. N. Platon, AE (1930), passim, cf. the one at Apesokari, Chapter III, p. 21.

83. V. Karageorghis, RDAC, 1970, 10ff.

84. The statues date mostly from LM IIIB and C, see S. Alexiou, Kch 12 (1958), 195ff. See also the fragmentary statue found at Ai Jannis by Sachtouria (Agiou Vasiliou), in an environment, which would recall a sacred enclosure (cf. Ch. VI, p. 108). It has been dated to a period not later than LM IIIA: Y. Tsedakis, BSA 62, (1967), 203FF. Hood, TS, 162 believes in a LM I dating.

85. D. Levi, Bolletin d'Arte, 44 (1959), 245, Fig. 34a.

86. Ibid., 249, Fig. 35.

87. R. Bosanquet, BSA 8 (1901/2), 289 and 314.

88. L. Sackett, M. Popham, BSA 60, (1965), Pl 79c.

89. S. Marinatos, AA, 1935, 245ff.

90. See e.g. the LM IIIC altar at Katsaba (cf. n.66 above); a portable altar or stand comes from Karphi: BSA 38, 1937/8, Pl. 35.
91. D. Levi (n.85) Fig. 24.
92. S. Marinatos (n.89).
93. N. Platon, PAE (1957), 145ff.
94. See Chapter II. p. 13.
95. E.g. the examples from Gournia and Koumasa (Nilsson MMR², Figs. 14 and 28); the buildings were probably used as temples.
96. See e.g. a rhyton from Kannia: PAE (1957), Pl. 75c.
97. Knossos, by the Royal Road: S. Hood, AR (1961/2), 25ff.
98. For Kannia vano V see Levi (n.85), 247. Vessel shaped as a parturient woman was discovered at Kephala Chondrou: N. Platon, PAE (1957), Pl. 72a. For rhyta in general see now R. Koehl, in: SancSymp, 179ff and J. Shaw, Hesperia, 49 (1980), 216.
99. Cf. e.g. the altar from Kannia decorated with horns of consecrations: Levi (n.85) 253, Fig. 24.
100. See n.104 below.
101. Cf. Chapter III. p. 43.
102. Marinatos Hirmer, Kr, 99.
103. P. Darque, BCH, 107 (1983), 3ff.
104. On the Dove Goddess Sanctuary: A. Evans, BSA, 8 (1901/2), 28ff. See also the objects from the temple at Mallia: J. C. Poursat, BCH, 90 (1966), 526.
105. Cf. Chapter III, 44; incense-burners had a very important place in the rites. One found at Mallia, in Room XIV (Etcret, 12 (1962), 3ff) contained juniper berries (Juniperus oxycedrus L.), from which one can get oleum cadinum (that is, an aromatic oil), and also coriander seeds (Coriandrum sativum L.), which are used for various purposes, including medicine, because of their aroma, cf. J. Politis, Détermination de fruits trouvés dans un encensoir du palais Minoen de Mallia, Praktika tis Akademias Athinon, 8 (1933), 217ff.
106. A pottery pinax was found at Kannia: Levi (n. 85) 247, Fig. 19.
107. Ibid., 249.
108. S. Xanthoudides, AE 1922, 1ff.
109. Nilsson, MMR², 325ff.
110. Evans, PofM IV, 138ff.
111. Nilsson, MMR², 32f and 335ff.
112. Ibid., Fig. 14, 81.
113. Also see my remarks on this subject in Chapter IV, 52f.
114. Cf. above p. 94.
116. S. Mowinckel, General Oriental and Specific Israelite Elements in the Israelite Conception of the Sacral Kingship, in: La regalita sacra, Leiden 1959, 288ff.
116. Cf. Chapter V, p. 95.
117. For Nea Nikomedeia see Chapter VIII, p. 155. A cult place (in a hut) is also said to have been found at Cheroneia, and to have been used in initiation rites. It held eight figurines. Three figurines are also said to have been discovered in a sacrificial pit at Otzaki Magoula, cf. however, P. Ucko, Anthropomorphic Figurines of Predynastic Egypt and Neolithic Crete with Comparative Materials from the Prehistoric Near East and Mainland of Greece, London 1968.

Chapter VIII

1. E.g. W. J. Anderson, B. Spiers, The Architecture of Ancient Greece (1927), 2nd ed., 12; W. Dinsmoor, The Architecture of Ancient Greece (1950), 24f; D. S. Robertson, A Handbook of Greek and Roman Architecture (1954), 2nd ed., 16ff.
2. A. Furtwängler, Die antiken Gemmen. Geschichte der Steinschneidekunst im klassischen Altertum (1901), III, 46ff; G. Karo, ARW, 7 (1904), 117ff; Dussaud, CivPr, 326, G. Rodenwaldt, Gnomon, 5 (1929), 178f ('Bildlosigkeit des Kultus'), and others.
3. F. Matz, Kreta, Mykene, Troja (1956), 79ff.
4. Nilsson, MMR², 77.
5. G. Mylonas, Eleusis and the Eleusinian Mysteries (1961), 34ff, cf. Dinsmoor, op. cit., 24.
6. G. Karo, Pauly-Wissowa, RE Supll. 7 (1935), 601.
7. Banti, CulM, 10ff, 40 ('after MM III sanctuaries began to be independent from palaces or houses').
8. J. Caskey, Hesperia, 40 (1971), 384ff.
9. W. Taylour, Antiquity, 44 (1970), 270ff.
10. P. Faure, BCH, 93 (1969), 209 (and references). Later also Hood, TS, 169ff (Kannia as a public sanctuary).
11. P. Faure, La vie quotidienne en Crète au temps de Minos (1500 av. J.-C.), 1973, 186ff ('Les grandes sanctuaires'), Cf. also the interpretation of the palaces as tombs: H.-G. Wunderlich, The Secret of Crete (1975).
12. Hood, TS, 158ff; cf. also the studies on the temples by B. Rutkowski in Pepragmena, 3 (1973), I, 290ff; idem, CPl, 217f, 314; idem, in Wege der Forschung. Probleme der ägäischen Bronzezeit, Ed. by H.-G. Buchholz (forthcoming).
13. R. J. Rodden et al., PPS, 28 (1962), 267ff; R. J. Rodden, Balkan Studies, 5 (1964), 110ff; idem, Scientific American, 212 (1965), Part 4, 83ff; R. J. Rodden, J. M. Rodden, ILN, 11 April 1964, 564ff; 18 April 1964, 604ff; R. J. Rodden, Antiquity, 38 (1964), 294f (frog figurines); cf. J. Mellaart, The Neolithic of the Near East (1975), 249; D. Theocharis (ed.), Neolithic Greece (1973), passim and Fig. 180; F. Schachermeyr, Die Ägäische Frühzeit (1976), I, 118; H. Hauptmann, AA (1971), 375ff; S. Weinberg, 'The Stone Age in the Aegean' in The Cambridge Ancient History (1970), 3rd ed. I, 1, 578 (a cult place and a chief's house in the same time). According to J.Ch. Hourmouziadis, Ta neolithika eidolia tis Thessalias (1974), 200 n.78 there is no argument in favour of a sanctuary at Nea Nikomedeia.
14. S. Bottema, Late Quarternary Vegetation History of North-western Greece (1974), 147, see also J. Bintliff, PPS, 42 (1976), 241ff.
15. J. Evans suggested to me that some neolithic houses e.g. at Magasa, cf. R. Dawkins, BSA, 11 (1904/5), 260ff, and at a house in Knossos, layer III, J. Evans, BSA, 59 (1964), 132ff; were sanctuaries, see also F. Schachermeyr, AA (1971), 300.
16. J. Mellaart, Excavations at Hacilar, I (1970), 35f Figs. 21 and 22.
17. J. Mellaart, op. cit., n.13, 219 Fig. 136.
18. J. Mellaart, op. cit., 213, Fig. 130b.
19. G. Hourmouziadis, AAA, 2 (1969), 36ff; FGK, Fig. 5.1.
20. K. Branigan, The Foundations of Palatial Crete (1970), 40, Fig. 4; FGK, Fig. 5.4.
21. See M. Gimbutas, The Gods and Goddesses of Old Europa 7000-3500 B.C. (1974), 67ff; FGK, Fig. 6.
22. P. Warren, Myrtos (1972), 80ff; idem in Levi Studies, 137ff; AAA, 10 (1977), 196f; J. Schäfer, PZ, 52 (1977), 254, expressed doubts on the social interpretation of the architecture.
23. Hood, TS, 162f.
24. Suggested by J.-P. Poursat to the author (1979).
25. J.-C. Poursat, BCH, 90 (1966), 514ff; Hood, TS, 164f; cf. also R. Treuil, BCH, 95 (1971), 13ff; (a stone with cavities found in a wall at the entrance to the sanctuary).

26. The other possibility is that the burnt layer was created when the fire destroyed the sanctuary.

27. Gournia, 47f; Hood (see above n.12) 160ff.

28. Or in LM III: P. Russell, Temple University Aegean Symposium, 4 (1979), 28.

29. B. Rutkowski, Der Tempel von Gurnia (forthcoming).

30. Gournia, 47; Evans, PofM, IV, 143 n.6, quoting an observation by R. Seager, communicated to him, believes that the fragment of the tube stand was not found on the tripod.

31. Gournia, 47, pl. 9; Hood, TS, 161.

32. J. Tsedakis, BSA, 62 (1967), 203ff.

33. J.-P. Poursat, (see above n.24), 535; on the tubular stands: Evans, PofM, IV, 140ff; G. Cadogan, 'Clay Tubes in Minoan Religion', in Pepragmena (1973), I, 34ff; G. C. Gesell, 'The Minoan Snake Tube: A Survey and Catalogue', AJA, 80 (1976), 247ff. For the find from Komo see p. 199.

34. G. Cadogan, AR (1977/8), 76f.

35. Hood, TS, 161.

36. RendLinc, 12 (1903), 318.

37. Banti, CulM, 28ff.

38. E. S. Hirsch, Painted Decoration on the Floors of Bronze Age Structures on Crete (1977), 9f.

39. Ibid., 9.

40. G. C. Gesell, op. cit., 250.

41. Seager, Ps, 10; Hood, TS, 165ff.

42. H. W. and J. D. S. Pendlebury, 'M.B. Money Coutts', BSA, 38 (1937/8), 75f, B. Rutkowski, Der Tempel von Karfi (forthcoming).

43. From the study of the pottery it is clear that the settlement was founded in LM IIIC.

44. Main Temple Road was not indicated on the plan of the settlement published by Pendlebury.

45. From the report of the excavations it is not clear if any of the statues were found on the bench, but the unpublished sketch-plan of the temple in the excavation notebook (now in the British School of Archaeology at Athens) gives the only indication as to the finding place of the statues in Room 1.

CHAPTER IX

1. J. Caskey, Hesperia, 40 (1971), 384ff; cf. also Hesperia, 31 (1962), 263ff; 33 (1964), 314ff; 35 (1966), 363ff; AD, 17 (1961/2), Chronika, 275ff; 22 (1967), Chronika, 476f; 24 (1969), 395ff; Archaeology, 16 (1963), 284f; 17 (1964), 277ff; Mycenaean Studies: Proceedings of the Third International Colloquim for Mycenaean Studies held at 'Wingspread' 4-8 September 1961, ed. by E. L. Bennett Jr. (1964), 193f; idem, in XI International Congress of Classical Archaeology, London, 3-9 September 1978 (1978), 57 (summary); M. R. Caskey, SancSymp, 12ff. Cf. also: S. Hood, AR (1960/1), 30f; (1961/2), 19ff; (1964-5), 22f; G. Daux, BCH, 85 (1961), 837ff; 86 (1962), 845ff; 88 (1964), 821ff; 89 (1965), 849ff; R. Eisner, GRBS, 13 (1972), 123ff; Hood, TS, 168f.

2. J. L. Davies, Fortifications at Ayia Irini, Keos: Evidence for History and Relative Chronology (1977).

3. J. L. Davies, Thera and the Aegean World, II (1980), in C. Doumas (ed.), 257ff; cf. the contrary opinions of P. Warren, PPS, 33 (1967), 37ff and S. Hood, The Minoans (1971), 52, 118.

4. A figure in the middle with one hand lowered: Evans, TDA, 10; Evans, PofM, III, 68; G. Rodenwaldt, Der Fries des Megarons von Mykenai (1921), 13; E. Bielefeld, Wissenschaftliche Zeitschrift der E. Moritz Arndt Universität Greifswald, 4 (1954/5), 397; Nilsson, MMR², 279; Matz, Gött, 10; S. Alexiou, KCh, 12 (1958), 231f; D. Levi, PP, 14 (1959), 383f; Biesantz, KSG, 22; Brandt GrG, 5; S. Alexiou, Gnomon, 39 (1967), 612.

5. CMS, I, 126; FGK, Fig. 1.5.

6. J. Caskey, AD, 22 (1967), 476; M. R. Caskey, op. cit., 134, Fig. 10.

7. Found in the temple at Karphi: see Chapter VIII n.42.

8. See also C. Davaras, Kadmos, 19 (1980), 90.

9. J. Caskey, Hesperia, 33 (1964), 325f (L 82 known in Linear B as sign 131-Vinum). Bennet believes it denotes two units of wine.

10. Chr. Tsountas, Prakt (1886), 74ff; A. J. B. Wace, JHS, 71 (1951), 254ff; Lord W. Taylour, Antiquity, 43 (1969), 91ff; 44 (1970), 270ff; Mylonas, CCent, 36ff; Mylonas, MycRel, 92ff; G. Mylonas, ValSymp, 243ff; idem, Prakt (1966), 109f; (1970), 118ff; (1971), 152ff; (1972), 116ff; (1973), 99ff; (1974), 89ff; (1975), 153ff. E. French, SympSanct, 48ff.

11. FGK, pl. 12.1.

12. On the masks in the Aegean see N. Platon, Melanges d'Archeologie et d'histoire offerts à Charles Picard, RA 31/2, (1948/9), II, 841ff, cf. also the masks in the Cyrpus Bronze Age, e.g. a bull-mask from Toumba tou Skourou (E. T. Vermeule, Toumba tou Skourou: The Mound of Darkness (1974), Fig. 29).

13. Cf. the representation of the sarcophagus from Ayia Triada (Ch. Long, The Ayia Triada Sarcophagus (1974), pl. 30; Marinatos-Hirmer, Kreta, pl. XXXI) and on the larnax from Tanagra — B. Rutkowski, Levi Studies, pl. XXIV 2.

14. FGK, Chapter II.

15. G. Mylonas, Prakt (1975), 153ff.

16. G. Mylonas, CC, pl. XIIIa, XIV.

17. C. Renfrew, Antiquity, 52 (1978), 7ff; SympSanct, 64ff.

18. Ibid., 74ff.

19. See also FGK 118, pl. 14. It is also illustrated in Greek Art of the Aegean Islands (1980), ed. D. V. Bothmer, Figs. 39, 40.

20. K. Kilian, AA (1978), 449ff; (1979), 379ff; SympSanct, 49ff.

21. Cf. FGK, 118, pl. 16.

22. W. Baumlein, Pelasgischer Glaube und Homer's Verhaeltniss zu demselben, Zeitschrift für die Althertumswissenschaft, 6 (1839), 1183.

23. F. Lenorment, Monographie de la Voie Sacrée éleusinienne de ses monuments et de ses souvenirs, I (1864), 424.

24. D. Philios, PAE (1883), 50; (1884), 64 quoted also by G. Mylonas, Eleusis and the Eleusinian Mysteries (1961), 12ff.

25. A. Person, 'Der Ursprung der eleusinischen Mysterien', ARW, 21 (1922), 292ff, cf. recently Hutchinson, Prehistoric Crete (1962), 217.

26. F. Noack, Eleusis. Die baugeschichtliche Entwicklung des Heiligtums (1927), 48.

27. G. Mylonas, K. Kouroniotes, AJA, 37 (1933), 271ff, cf. K. Kouroniotes, ARW, 32 (1935), 52ff.

28. G. Mylonas, K. Kouroniotes (see above n.27), 271ff; Mylonas (see above n.24); Mylonas, MycRel, 90f. On the fortifications near Megaron B see Mylonas (see above n.24) 33. Cf. the doubts of Ålin, MFund, 112.

29. G. Karo, RE, Suppl., 7 (1935), 601 (similar views are to be found in Dinsmoor, also D. Levi, Ann 23/24 (1961/2), 129 and Hope Simpson, Gaz, 110, Bo. 383.

30. M. Nilsson, Geschichte der griechischen Religion, I (1941), 445; Nilsson, MMR², 468ff; idem, ARW, 32 (1935), 79ff. A. W. Lawrence, Greek Architecture (1957), 81, and P. Demargne, Aegean Art (1964), 218.

31. Nilsson, MMR², 468ff.

32. Mylonas (see above n.24), 33ff; Mylonas MycMA, 147.

33. Argument 2. The above discussion was already published in a Polish periodical (*Euhemer*, 8 (1964), 30ff), tending, however, to a conclusion that there was no sanctuary at all in Eleusis) in the Mycenaean period. This idea was taken up by P. Darque, BCH, 105 (1981), 593ff. But certain doubts arise: 1. Two Geometric finds (p. 599) uncovered in Room B1,0.05 m under the surface cannot be satisfactory proof to date the telesterion to the Geometric period, because over the later telesterion there was a big accumulation of earth, brought from elsewhere. The Geometric finds might be brought with the terracing works. 2. There is no safe grounds for rejecting the dating of the north section of wall X to LH IIIB-C. 3. In our opinion there is no reason to believe that there was a connection between the western section of what is called by Darque a Mycenaean palace and its eastern section, that is Mylonas Megaron B.4. A peribolos could be easily overlooked in the excavations of those days!

34. R. Vallois, *L'architecture hellénique et hellénistique à Delos* I (1944), 8ff, H. Gallet de Santerre, *Delos primitive et archaique* (1958), 127ff; Ph. Bruneau, J. Ducat, *Guide de Delos* (1966), 2nd ed., 100, Fig. 14 (an accurate plan of the building).

35. H. Gallet de Santerre, J. Trehaux, BCH, 71/2 (1947/8), 148ff.

36. C. Blegen, M. Rawson, *The Palace of Nestor at Pylos* I (1966).

37. For the types of houses see e.g. S. Sinos, *Die Vorklassischen Hausformen in der Ägäis* (1971), *passim* and I. Shear, *Mycenaean Domestic Architecture* (1968), *passim*.

38. V. Karageorghis. *Kition. Mycenaean and Phoenician Discoveries in Cyprus* (1976), 61ff.

39. See above Chapter II.

40. Karageorghis, *op. cit.*

41. I. Beyer, *Die Tempel von Dreros und Prinias A* (1976), Taf. II.

42. H. Drerup, 'Griechische Baukunst in geometrischer Zeit', ArchHom, II (1969), Pl. IIIa.

43. Drerup, *op. cit*, 14ff (Thermos) and A. E. Kalpaxis, *Früharchaische Baukunst* (1976), 28.

44. See also E. Vermeule, ArchHom, vol. III fasc. V, passim.

45. For a different opinion see B. Schweitzer, *Die geometrische Kunst Griechenlands* (1969), 232ff.

46. I. Aksit, Ancient Civilisation of Turkey (1982), Pl. 78.

47. FGK, 118.

48. This observation is supported by the studies of E. French (personal communication).

49. G. Gesell, AJA, 80 (1976), 247ff.

50. J. Shaw, Archaeological Newsletter, N.S., 137 (1976), Kommos, Fig. 1.

51. See the finds from the temple at Mallia (Fig. 221).

Chapter X

1. The grotto is situated 3 km from the village of Ninoi. Undoubtedly this cave is mentioned by Pausanias. Excavations were carried out there in 1957 and 1958 by J. Papadimitriou, but came to a cessation when he died. Papadimitriou did not carry out systematic diggings, but merely sank trial-pits in the first chamber, and also in Room 1 and 4 as one goes in at the west entrance. The rockbed was never reached, since the deepest pits went down no more than 2 m. Cf. J. Papadimitriou, Ergon (1958), 15ff; A. Petrochilou, DESE (1961), 31 (plan of the grotto); Hägg, MKult, 50.

2. The grotto lies to the north-west of the village of Lykotrypa. Excavations were carried out in 1900 by A. Skias, PAE (1900), 38ff; see also R. C. Bosanquet, JHS, 21 (1901), 350; R. Romaios, AE (1906), 89ff; Nilsson, MMR², 67f.

3. The grotto was first explored by H. Schliemann, in 1864 and later by V. Vollgraff in 1904. It was again explored meticulously by S. Benton, BSA, 35 (1934), 45ff.

4. C. Tsountas, AE (1898), 166; U. Karstedt, AE, 38 (1913), 166 (he mistakenly refers to the remains of buildings).

5. C. Tsountas, *op. cit.*, 166.

6. Hägg, MKult, 50ff, mentions three more grottoes that may have been cult places (see references there): Keratea (Attica), Klenies (not far from Corinth), and A. Sophia (Kythera). The main reason for regarding these grottoes as cult places was in one case the presence of stalactites (at A. Sophia). Cult objects which were doubtful (as at Keratea) or which were unspecified (as at Klenies) were further grounds for classifying them as such. Hägg also drew up a list of other caves which might have been used for religious purposes in LH times.

7. M. K. Langdon, 'A Sanctuary of Zeus on Mount Hymettos', *Hesperia Suppl. XVI* (1976), 100ff.

8. See Chapter V, n. 99.

9. Hope Simpson, Gaz, 20 No. 22; V. Lambrinoudakis, SanctSymp, 63.

10. J. Papadimitriou, PAE (1948), 90ff; (1949), 91ff; (1950), 197ff; BCH, 73 (1949), 361ff; V. Lambrinoudakis, PAE (1974), 94ff; (1975), 162ff; (1976), 202ff; (1977), 187ff; Ergon (1978), 37ff; (1979), 20f; (1981), 46ff; SanctSymp, 59ff.

11. J. Papadimitriou, PAE (1950), 200, Fig 10; A. Sakellariou, RA, 1 (1971), 3ff.

12. V. Lambrinoudakis, SanctSymp, 64, Fig. 10.

13. Ibid.

14. Athens, MN, No. 19180a.

15. It derives from the Papadimitriou's excavation, Athens, MN, 19177. Analogous motif: FGK, Fig. 16.

16. Did Mycenaean Meleatos, like the Cretan gods, possess the function of health giving? In fact, at Epidauros, medical implements were found. Dr. A. Deilaki informed me that in a Mycenaean tomb (unpublished), among other things two medical tools were discovered.

17. This place is sometimes referred to as a roadside temenos, or as a ruined temple (G. Karo, RE, Suppl. 6 (1935), 600; AA (1913), 116).

18. R. Demangel, *Fouilles de Delphes*, II, fasc. 5 (1926), 5ff; BCH, 82 (1957), 708ff; Mylonas MycMA, 148.

19. C. Tsountas, AE (1892), 1ff; A. Furtwängler, JdI, 33 (1918), 109ff; E. Buschor, W. V. Massow, AM, 52 (1927), 1ff; H. Waterhouse, R. Hope Simpson, BSA, 55 (1960), 74ff; K. Dimakopoulou, To Mykinaiko iero sto Amyklaio kai i IEIII periodos sti Lakonia (1982). (Probably it was a high place).

20. This cult place was situated on the summit of the hill; there may have been a Mycenaean sacred enclosure at Galataki (Korynthia), too (Hope Simpson, Gaz, 28f, No. 52).

21. None of them was found outside the area of the temenos dating from the Archaic period.

22. Mylonas, MycMA, 141ff; most scholars have thought that the woman on the left of the scene was bent over the altar (Evans, TPC, 177; Evans, PofM, I, 161f; III, 142; Nilsson, MMR², 256). But Mylonas, MycMA, 141ff, is of a different opinion.

23. These have also been interpreted as dogs' skulls (E. Herkenrath, AJA, 41 (1937), 413).

24. Evans, TPC, 182, Fig. 56.

25. Evans, TPC, 184, thought this was a sacred gateway, but C. Tsountas, RA (1900), 9, and

Nilsson, MMR², 182, thought it was a sanctuary, for the upper row can be interpreted as the square-shaped ends of beams; see also FGK, 29, 84.

26. On the Lion Gate at Mycenae see: P. Aström, OpArch, 5 (1964), 159ff.

27. But on coins dating from Roman times, which showed the temple of Aphrodite at Paphos, a courtyard is sometimes depicted in front of the cult building (C. Blinkenberg, 'Le temple de Paphos, Det. Kgl. Danske Videnskabernes Selskab'. *Historiskfilologiske Meddelelelser*, 9 (1924), part 2, 1ff, especially Fig. 2-4, Cook, II, Fig. 325).

28. If the motif here was triglyphic, it may have been meant to symbolise the building in front of which the cult scene was taking place.

29. At Amyklai, see above n.19.

30. Persson, RelGr, 40ff.

31. On a gold ring said to have been found at Mycenae (Mylonas, MycMA, 140 No. 4).

32. Mylonas, MycMA, 140; Brandt GG, 8 (goddess sitting in front of an altar). Nilsson, MMR², 179; see also FGK, 54, 84.

33. Mylonas, MycMA, 140f, No. 6.

34. Different view is taken by Nilsson, MMR², 178 (an altar).

35. FGK, 25ff.

36. FGK, Fig. 3.2.

37. It is generally thought that this place was a spring sanctuary or a holy spring (Evans, PofM, III, 137, Fig. 89; Persson, RelGr, 62ff; Nilsson, MMR², 182, 287; Mylonas MycMA, 144), Marinatos-Hirmer, Kr, 121 thought it was a building similar to the alleged sanctuary at Vathypetro (see also FGK, 14).

38. But some scholars take the view that altars, not sanctuaries, were frequently portrayed on rings, e.g. that from Thebes.

39. See above Chapter VI.

40. R. Demangel, *op. cit.*, 13.

41. Evans, TPC, 117; Evans, PofM, IV, 455.

42. The god's statue on the rock (e.g. K. A. Romaios, AE (1908), pl. 8).

43. A glass plaque from Mycenae: Evans, TPC, 117, Fig. 14; Evans, PofM, IV, 454, Fig. 379a (explains it as a sacred column).

44. Ergon (1956), 92, Fig. 92, No. 2.

45. See above n.40.

46. Of course one can also take into consideration the honour in which the olive tree was held in later times.

47. See also above Chapter V, p. 84. Some scholars think the Psi type figurines were images of the deities.

48. Evans, TPC, 190; Mylonas, MycMA, 140, No. 4.

49. R. Demangel, *op. cit.*, 13ff (Delphi-Marmaria); see also the finds at A. Vasilios (200 figurines), and Amyklai (a large number of figurines).

50. M. Gérard-Rousseau, *Les mentions religieuses dans les tablettes mycéniennes* (1968), 166ff.

51. See e.g. C. Tsountas, *Mykinai kai Mykenaios politismos* (1893), 166, pl. 5: 3; Nilsson, MMR², 181; Mylonas, MycMA, 139, No. 1. Meyer's concept, which was developed by Persson, RelGr, 57f, was based on comparisons with scenes found in Asia Minor. But his view is unacceptable, despite the fact that the women's busts have not been clearly indicated by the artist (see Nilsson, MMR², 181, n.64). The figures seem to be women because they are dressed not only in skirts but in bodices as well (as indicated by the edge of the short sleeves of the bodice; Persson, on the other hand, thought that the line interpreted by us as the edge of the bodice was in fact a bracelet).

52. Persson, *op. cit.*, without any justification for doing

so, thought the women votaries were wearing boots.

53. No-one today adheres to Reichel's idea that a throne is represented here; some scholars are inclined to interpret this construction as an altar (Evans, TPC, 189f. and others). The idea that it was a sanctuary is more convincing (C. Tsountas, *op. cit.*, 166; Persson, *op. cit.*, 56; Nilsson, MMR², 181; Mylonas, MycMA, 139).

54. C. Tsountas, RA (1900), 9 and Persson, *op. cit.*, 58, thought this figure was holding a knife. What we see at the side of this scene is not a butterfly, as Persson thought (*op. cit.*, 57), but a plant (C. Tsountas, Mykinai, *op. cit.*, 166), probably a prickly pear (A. Sakellariou, CMS, I, 102), or a tree with three branches (Mylonas, MycMA, 172, n.81).

55. C. Tsountas, RA (1900), pl. VIII 3; Evans, TPC, 184 thought this was a sacred gateway; other scholars, however, have regarded this construction as a sanctuary (e.g. Mylonas, MycMA, 140).

56. CMS, I, 142.

57. Mylonas, MycMA, 141 is opposing Evans' thoery that the man in this picture was shaking the tree.

58. C. Tsountas, AE (1889), 170; Evans, PofM, III, 140; Persson, RelGr, 36ff; Nilsson, MMR², 275; Mylonas, MycMA, 143 No. 12.

59. Persson, RelGr, 134.

60. See above Chapter VI.

61. L. Stella, *La civiltà micenea nei documenti contemporarei* (1965), 227ff.

62. See remarks by Glotz, CivEg, 183ff.

63. On the subject of changes in Mycenaean society, see: Desborough, LM, 1ff.

CHAPTER XI

1. H. Tzavella-Evjen, AAA, 5 (1972), 467ff.

2. H. Goldman, *Excavations at Eutresis in Boetia* (1932), 17f.

3. On the function of the rhyta see R. B. Koehl, SympSanct, 179ff.

4. N. Valmin, BullLund (1933/4), part 2; N. Valmin, *Swedish Messenia Expedition* (1938), 112f, cf. CPl, 289ff, also Vermeule, Götterkult, V, 37, and Mylonas MycRel, 94.

5. N. Valmin, Swedish Messenia Expedition, *op. cit.*, 180.

6. Cf. J. Ucko, *Anthropomorphic Figurines of Predynastic Egypt and Mainland of Greece* (1968), 376, 398.

7. N. Valmin, Swedish. Messenia Expedition, *op. cit.*

8. As cult object: for its recognition are G. Karo, AA (1935), 206, and H. L. Lorimer, *Homer and the Monuments* (1950), 434, and others. Against: H.-G. Buchholz, *Zur Herkunft der kretischen Doppelaxt* (1959), 11 n.35, 20 n.6, 48 No. 11, cf. also Vermeule, GBA, 348 n.4, Mylonas MycMA, 147f and Mylonas MycRel, 94.

9. N. Valmin, Swedish Messenia Expedition, *op. cit.*

10. N. Valmin, BullLund (1933/4), part 2, 16ff (plan on Fig. 6); N. Valmin, Swedish Messenia Expedition, *op. cit.*, 126ff, 238, cf. also G. Karo, AA (1935), 206.

11. N. Valmin, Swedish Messenia Expedition, *op. cit.*, 78ff.

12. Ibid, 79.

13. N. Valmin, OpAth, 1 (1953), 29ff; *idem*, AD, 16 (1960), 119ff.

14. N. Valmin, OpAth, 1 (1953).

15. N. Valmin, AD, 16 (1960), 122.

16. S. Marinatos, *Excavations at Thera*, VI (1974), 15ff; VII (1976), 22ff; Ch. Doumas, PAE (forthcoming).

17. Nilsson, MMR, XXff; Nilsson, MMR², 110ff; O. Frödin, A. Persson, *Asine* (1938), 63, 74ff, 298, 308; Hägg, MKult, 44.

18. Cf. R. Hägg, SanctSymp, 91ff on the finding place where the figurines were discovered.

19. As a god: A. Persson, *Frödin*, Persson, see n.17, *op. cit.*, 308; as a goddess: Evans, PofM, IV, 756, later A. Persson, *New Tombs at Dendra near Midea* (1942), 100f; Nilsson, MMR[2], 114, also believed that the head was male. He maintains that the white paint on the face does not necessarily indicate that a female was meant, for although female faces were coloured white in paintings, we do not know if the same convention was used in painted sculptures. He therefore concludes that this figure is perhaps meant to represent a god — probably Zeus with his thunderbolt, for in ancient Greece stone axes were sometimes believed to be symbols of a thunderbolt. Nevertheless, neither of Nilsson's arguments is very convincing, for the head definitely gives one the impression of an old woman. Cf. Mylonas, MycMA, 155, who submits that the Asine head is so like the figures found at Keos that it must be regarded as the head of a woman. On the other hand C. Laviosa, AttiCongrMic I, 87ff, argues that the Asine head may have been the head of a sphinx. *See also* Vermeule, GBA, 217.

20. U. Jantzen, AA, 1938, 553; BullLund, 1937/8, III, 59ff; A. Åkerström, *Arkeologiska forskningar och fynd, Studier utgivna ned anledning av H.M. Konnung Gustaf VI Adolfs sjuttioårsdag 11.11.1952* (1952), 32ff; A. Åkerström, in: Atti-CongrMic III, 3ff; Vermeule, GBA, 384 n.4, however, questions the general view.

21. The exploration of the palace was begun by A. de Ridder, BCH 18(1894), 271ff, cf. F. Noack, AM 19, 1894, 406ff. New excavations are being conducted by J. Trepiadis, PAE, 1958, 38f; for a plan of the citadel *see* Fig. 2 p. 41; PAE, 1959, 21ff, pl. 16 (air photograph of the citadel); 1960, 23ff, cf. Hope Simpson, *Gaz*, 116f, No. 402; HopeSimp-Dick, 239f.

22. S. Marinatos, *Prakt*, 1960, 203ff; AD 16(1960), B116; *Ergon*, 1960, 149ff, cf. also Ålin, MFund, 80; Desborough, LM, 40; Mylonas, MycMA, 146; Hope Simps-Dick, *Gaz* 168, D 201.

23. K. Müller, Tiryns, III, 53.

24. S. Chahritonidis, AM, 75 (1960), 1ff; S. Hiller, Antike Welt, 4 (1973), Part 4, 21ff. These tiny chambers were interpreted, in spite of their small dimensions, as a porter's lodge, see A. Wace, Mycenae. An Archaeological History and Guide (1949), 54, or as a watchdog place, see G. Mylonas, Ancient Mycenae (1957), 30 and 41.

25. Information by K. Kilian.

26. For the classical world see F. G. Maier, in Eranion. Festschrift für Hildebrecht Hommel, (1961), 93ff; G. Pugliese Carratelli, Studi clasici e orientali, 14, (1965), 5ff.

27. S. Marinatos, Excavations at Thera (1974), VI, Pl. 112b; B. Rutkowski in C. Doumas, Thera and the Aegean World (1978), I, 662.

28. C. Blegen, M. Rawson, The Palace of Nestor at Pylos (1966), I, 301ff.

29. K. Müller, Tiryns, III, 136f.

CHAPTER XII

1. At Perachora, see Alin, MFund, 60; Hope Simpson, Gaz 35, No. 75; it seems that the traces of LH sanctuaries are very doubtful at Tegea, Sparta, Menelaion, Brauron, Athens, Delos and other places.

2. Note. Recent studies tend to prove that the cult continuity was probably more evident, see H.-V. Herrmann, in Forschungen au ägäischen Vorgeschichte. Das Ende des mykenischen Welt, ed by Thomas (in the press).

ADDENDA

1. E. and Y. Sakellarakis, Ergon (1979), 31f; (1981), 71; National Geographic, 159, No. 2, February 1981, 205ff.

2. This problem must be left unresolved until the complete publication of results of the excavations. On the platform or nearby it, horns of consecration presumably have been discovered.

Select Bibliography

Banti, L., I Culti Minoici e Greci di Haghia Triada, Ann 3/4, 1941/3, 10ff.

Boardman, J., The Cretan Collection in Oxford, Oxford· 1961.

Boyd Hawes, H., Williams B. E., Seager, R. B., and Hall, E. H., Gournia, Vasiliki and other Prehistoric Sites on the Isthmus of Hierapetra, Crete, Philadelphia 1908.

Evans, A., The Mycenaean Tree and Pillar Cult, HS 21 (1901), 99ff.

The Tomb of the Double Axes and Associated Groups and the Pillar Room and Ritual Vessels of the 'Little Palace' at Knossos, Archaeologia 65 (1914), 1-94.

The Palace of Minos at Knossos, vols. I-IV, London 1921-1935.

Faure, P., Cavernes et Sites aux deux extremités de la Crète, BCH 86, 1962, 36-56.

Cultes de sommets et cultes de cavernes en Crète, BCH 87 (1963), 493-508.

Fonctions des cavernes crétoises, Paris 1964.

Nouvelles recherches sur les trois sortes de sanctuaires crétois, BCH 91 (1967), 114-150.

Sur trois sortes de sanctuaires crétois, BCH 93, 1969, 174-213.

Gesell, G., The Archaeological Evidence for the Minoan House Cult and its Survival in Iron Age Crete, Ann Arbor 1972.

Hägg, R., Mykenische Kultstätten im archäologischen Material, OpAth 8 (1968), 39-60.

Hägg, R., Marinatos, N. (eds.), Sanctuaries and Cults in the Aegean Bronze Age. Proceedings of the First International Symposium at the Swedish Institute of Athens, Stockholm 1981.

Hood, S., Minoan Town Shrines, in: Greece and the Eastern Mediterranean in Ancient History and Prehistory. Studies presented to Fritz Schachermeyr, ed. by K. H. Kinzl, Berlin-New York 1977, 158-172.

Karo, G., Altkretische Kulstätten, ARW 7 (1904), 117-156.

Kilian, K., Ausgrabungen in Tiryns 1978, AA 1978, 449-467; 1979, 379-411.

Levi, D., Immagini di culto minoiche, PP 14 (1959), 377-391.

Caratteri w Continuità del Culto cretese sulle Vette Montane, PP 181 (1978), 294-313 — Features and Continuity of Cretan Peak Cults, in: A. Biran (ed.), Temples and Cult Places in Biblical Times, Jerusalem 1977, 38-46.

Mylonas, G., Mycenae and the Mycenaean Age, Princeton 1966.

The Cult Centre of Mycenae, Pragmateiai tis Akademias Athinon 33, 1972.

Mycenaean Religion. Temples, altars and temenae, Pragmateiai tis Akademias Athinon 39, 1977.

Nilsson, M., The Minoan-Mycenaean Religion and its Survival in the Greek Religion, second ed., Lund 1950.

Platakis, E., To Idaion Andron, Iraklion 1965.

Spilaia kai allai karstikai morphai tis Kritis, vol. I (1973), vol. II (1975), Iraklion.

Platon, N., Peri tis en Kritis latreias ton stalaktiton, AE 1930, 160-168.

To Ieron Maza (Kalou Choriou Pediadou) kai ta minoika Iera Koryphis, KCh 5 (1951), 96-160.

Ta Minoika oikiaka Iera, KCh 8(1954), 428-483.

Kritomykinaiki Thryskeia, Thessaloniki 1970.

Renfrew, C., The Emergence of Civilisation. The Cyclades and the Aegean in the Third Millennium B.C., London 1972.

Renfrew, C., The Mycenaean Sanctuary at Phylakopi, Antiquity 52 (1978), 7-15.

Rutkowski, B., Cult Place in the Aegean World, Wrocław 1972.

Frühgriechische Kultdarstellungen, Berlin 1981.

Nature Sanctuaries in Minoan Crete: a Catalogue of Sites (in the press).

Stella, L. A., Testimonianze di santuarii cretesi in testi Cnosii in lineare B, in: Pepragmena tou 'B' Diethnous Kritologikou Synedriou, vol. I, Athens 1968, 253-262.

Taylour, W., Mycenae, 1968, Antiquity 43 (1969), 91-97.

New Light on Mycenaean Religion, Antiquity 44, 1970, 270-280.

Tyree, L., Cretan Sacred Caves: Archaeological Evidence, Ann Arbor 1975.

Van Effenterre, H., Le Palais de Mallia et la cité minoenne, vols. I and II, Rome 1980.

Vermeule, E., Götterkult, Archaeologia Homerica ed. by F. Matz and H. G. Buchholz, Göttingen 1974.

Yavis, C., Greek Altars, St. Louis 1949

Index